AMERICAN POETRY
OF THE SEVENTEENTH CENTURY

AMERICAN POETRY
OF THE SEVENTEENTH CENTURY

EDITED WITH AN INTRODUCTION,
NOTES, AND COMMENTS BY

HARRISON T. MESEROLE

THE PENNSYLVANIA STATE UNIVERSITY PRESS
University Park, Pennsylvania

Grateful acknowledgment is made to the following for permission to reprint material copyrighted or controlled by them:

From THE POEMS OF EDWARD TAYLOR, edited by Donald E. Stanford. Copyright 1960 by Yale University Press. Reprinted by permission of the publisher.

From THE POETICAL WORKS OF EDWARD TAYLOR, edited by T. H. Johnson. Copyright Rockland Editions, 1939; Princeton University Press, 1943. Reprinted by permission of Princeton University Press.

Library of Congress Cataloging in Publication Data

Seventeenth-century American poetry.

American poetry of the seventeenth century.

Previously published as: Seventeenth-century American poetry.
Bibliography: p. 517
Includes index.
1. American poetry—Colonial period, ca. 1600-1775.
I. Meserole, Harrison T.   II. Title.
PS601.S45   1985   811'.1'08   85-21701
ISBN 0-271-00419-3
ISBN 0-271-00418-5 (pbk.)

CONTENTS

MINOR WRITERS

OTHER REPRESENTATIVE WRITERS

A SELECTION OF ANONYMOUS VERSE

Introductory Note to the
Penn State Press Edition

Twenty years ago, when I began final work on this collection of America's earliest verse, the study of seventeenth-century American literature was, to borrow a phrase, a fair field needing folk, and only a few universities offered courses focused on the literature of our first century. Today, specialists must bestir themselves to keep up with the steadily increasing numbers of books and articles in the field, and it is a rare university that does not schedule an undergraduate lecture or graduate seminar on the Colonial Period.

For this reason, and because those who have used this book in teaching or have commented on its contents in reviews have been generous in their assessments of its value, it is a pleasure for me to write a brief word for this new issue and to note with satisfaction that its appearance will coincide with the publication, also by The Pennsylvania State University Press, of a new and stimulating collection of critical essays on *Puritan Poetry and Poetics*, edited by Peter White.

Editors at The Pennsylvania State University Press have kindly permitted me to correct a few printing errors that crept into the original edition and to rewrite one or two notes to take advantage of recent scholarship. Otherwise, the text and apparatus of *American Poetry in the Seventeenth Century* are those of the first edition, published under the title *Seventeenth-Century American Poetry*.

Harrison T. Meserole
August 1, 1985

INTRODUCTION

Jamestown in Virginia, New Netherland in New York and New Jersey, and the colonies at Plymouth and Massachusetts Bay had been firmly established years before Thomas Tillam arrived in the New World. But on that June day of 1638, when, standing in the bow of a ship that had weathered three thousand miles of ocean, Tillam had his first sight of American land, he was the first to frame memorable lyric lines in response to what he saw:

> Hayle holy-land wherin our holy lord
> Hath planted his most true and holy word
> Hayle happye people who have dispossest
> Your selves of friends, and meanes, to find some rest
> For your poore wearied soules, opprest of late . . .
> Posses this Country.

Composed in one of the great years of early migration, Tillam's lines spoke for all those who had left behind their homes and friends and traditions to seek the freedoms of a New Jerusalem: guided by Divine Providence, they would possess the new land and in it find their solace. Here was lyrical expression of the American credo a century and a half before there was a nation to embrace it in the crisp prose of its political documents. It is markedly significant that Tillam chose poetic form for his expression, for seldom has a people been so moved to the writing of verse as the seventeenth-century Americans.

Yet students of early America have been largely unaware of the considerable body of verse written by the men and women of our first century. Not until now has there been a full-length edition devoted entirely to poetry written in America before 1725. To be sure, some poems of the period have been included in anthologies of American literature, but too often these selections have done little to represent the range of what was written in the era, and consequently have given an imperfect view of the poetic achievement during the first century of this country's history.

There are reasons for this myopia. To begin with, time and circumstance have been unkind to the poetry of the era. In the first century of settlement most verse, and much of the prose, remained in manuscript, despite the impressive number of imprints recorded in Charles Evans' *American Bibliography*. Of the published verse, much was ephemeral. Almanac verse, for example, was sure to be discarded as each year's prognostication went out of date and was succeeded by a new one. Broadside elegies, circulated among the bereaved at funerals, reposed in family attics for a time, after which they were lost as decades, then centuries, passed. Moreover, printers issued published verse in small editions (with the notable exception of Michael Wigglesworth's *Day of Doom*), and only a very few titles earned reprinting.

In New England particularly, there were strictures against too consummate an attention to poetry. "A little recreation," asserted Cotton Mather, was a good thing, and one should not contemplate an unpoetical life. But to turn one's mind and energies wholly to the composition of verse was to prostitute one's calling, to risk opprobrium, and most important, to lose sight of the proper balance God envisioned for man on earth. The sheer quantity of verse that has come down to us proves that these strictures were not completely heeded. It is similarly clear that these strictures had their effect not only in the nature and intent of much of the surviving verse but also in the sparse numbers of poems printed in America before 1725.

Yet only in recent years have scholars begun to explore in any systematic way the *embarras de richesse* contained in these sources, and even today, there is still much we do not know about the verse of the period. This anthology, containing 246 poems, 59 published for the first time, may open the way for further study.

Considering these adverse circumstances, a considerable quantity of early verse has survived, by far the largest portion of it in manuscript, copied into commonplace books, contained in letters, or inscribed on the endpapers of treasured books of the period. The fact that so much is extant today is in part the result of Americans' reverence for the past—books, papers, records, family memorabilia and artifacts of all sorts were more often stored away in trunks than thrown out—and in part the result of dedicated antiquarian efforts of the last century, when historians and historical societies undertook to collect, preserve, and record in print the writings of our ancestors. The proceedings, transactions, and collections of these societies are mines of information and rich in sources of texts.

Poets and Their Subjects

One persistent misconception about poets of early America has been that all of them were austere Puritan ministers writing pedestrian verses about a wrathful God. Evidence proves otherwise. Certainly a great number of the verse writers were ministers, for the clergy were the best-educated of the colonists and had been trained in a literary tradition in which poetry was a measurable influence. In addition, a people who had crossed three thousand miles of unpredictable ocean for the sake of their religious convictions would naturally turn to religion as the subject of much of their verse. But it was not the only subject for early American poetry, any more than ministers were the only writers of it.

A glance at the lives of seventeenth-century poets reveals their occupational diversity. Among their number are judges, local government officials, military men, businessmen, sea captains, attorneys, adventurers, schoolmasters, physicians, travelers, and housewives—in short, men and women of all conditions of wealth and social position. The nearly indigent schoolmaster Benjamin Tompson, who frequently petitioned his community to pay—if they so pleased—his annual salary, stands poetically alongside the merchant John Saffin, one of the few to prosper economically in the same years as Tompson's struggle. Equally in contrast, though in another context, are Cotton Mather and Roger Williams. Both forceful leaders, Mather spent his lifetime trying to shore-up. the doctrinaire Puritanism against which Williams rebelled and which drove him in disgrace to Rhode Island. Both men, poles apart in conviction, felt the need for poetic expression. Still another contrast, this time in response to experience, is the one between the two travelers Richard Steere and Sarah Kemble Knight. From Steere, a merchant, we have the "tarpolin tongue" verse account of a perilous sea voyage, while Madame Knight, a schoolmistress, chooses to versify her feeling about a tavern's "Potent Rum." Their methods and attitudes are disparate, yet both chose verse as the means of expression.

It is possible to continue juxtaposing material conditions, intellectual persuasions, perceptions of experience, and so on. But there is no need for such cataloguing, for clearly no single class, occupation, state of mind, or sex held a monopoly on poetic expression. Verse writing in seventeenth-century America was the province of diverse persons compelled to compose for equally diverse reasons.

Their subjects are as varied as the authors. They chose exploration, love, Indians, the land, sea voyages, and of course religion, as poetic topics. Religion is unquestionably the most pervasive single subject, yet it cannot be dismissed as a narrow poetic obsession; the range is too great for that. If on the one hand Edward Taylor can seek knowledge of personal salvation, Benjamin Tompson is ready on the other to suggest dire implications for a prosperous colony's failure to prove its spiritual mettle before the Creator. Anne Bradstreet, falling somewhere between the two, speaks implicitly as a Christian parent raising her "eight birds" in a godly way, and offers thanks when one of her family is delivered from sickness.

Frequently reaching outside the spectrum of subjects entirely religious, early verse writers explored various aspects of the new country. The land meant many things. To Tillam it signified promise and reward for the colonists' voluntary exile from native homelands. But the hardness of colonial life made the land become a burden instead of a promise, a "wilderness-condition" to be faced. At the same time, New England settlers began to civilize this wilderness, which prior to their arrival had been a "Soil and dreary Coast" of darkness. At the end of the century, one poet spoke idealistically of the bountiful trout and salmon, the cedars and elms that had so engaged the imagination of the narrative writer of *New England's Prospect*. For him the American land was "an Eden so long hid." But there were also the Indians, dark dwellers in the garden who did not escape poetic notice. Cotton Mather speculates in verse about their history shrouded in "black oblivion." Whatever their genealogy (there was some conjecture that the Indians might have been descendants of one of the biblical Lost Tribes), the Indians assumed diabolical dimension during the brutal King Philip's War of 1675–76. Their image in verse was then "Scare-crows clad with oaken leaves . . . Like *Vulcans* anvilling *New-Englands* brains."

With early settlement principally along the coast, emigrant-laden vessels crowding harbors, and busy shipping churning the coastal waters, Americans developed a keen consciousness of things nautical, which was accordingly reflected in their poetry. In one swift-moving ballad stanza, a small fleet sails from Scituate Harbor to Boston, with details of wind direction and velocity, tide data, and precise rigging information meticulously provided. Such detail is not unusual, for another poet, describing a terrifying ocean crossing, graphically records stuffing rags into holes to prevent further shipping of water.

This is not to commend poets of early America for supplying meteorological information in their verse, or for chronicling in detail Indian insurrections, or for recording topographical measurements in rhyme. The point is rather that the seventeenth-century American had a keen eye for the new country; his awareness of the land and his experiences in it became the subjects for his verse. Frequently he linked what he saw to his religious bent. But this did not cancel his objectivity or blur his sharpness of focus.

Audiences and the Uses of Poetry

It is not really possible to speak of *a* seventeenth-century audience for verse. There were varied audiences, ranging in age from school children to septuagenarians, in occupation from farmers to college presidents, and in size from a single person to whole communities. Some poets had no audience at all, nor wished one. For forty-three years Edward Taylor, the most accomplished poet of the period, was content that God alone be the audience of the *Meditations,* which Taylor composed and reworked carefully until their final form was acceptable to him. It is doubtful that the private verses John Saffin scribbled into his Notebook were intended for an audience. The poetry of Anne Bradstreet might not have been published if her brother-in-law had not spirited it away and seen to its publication in London. These poets were not writing for audiences but for themselves and their God at the urging of their consciences.

Other poets did enjoy a critical audience even if it were small and their works not likely to see print. It was common practice to send manuscript verses to friends for comment, a practice Samuel

Sewall often reports, frequently mentioning his revisions, which he seemed constantly to be about. Sewall liked to write on the same subject in both English and Latin, refurbishing and tightening until his lines attained the epigrammatic quality he liked. Later he might be driven to still further revision, until finally he had his verses printed in little leaflets which he gave as gifts to his friends. In turn, they at times reciprocated, a fact which Sewall notes appreciatively in his diary.

Broadside elegies, too, found frequent if not large audiences, for the high mortality rate in seventeenth-century America gave opportunity for every poet and poetaster to compose elegies which, along with rings and scarves, were distributed among the bereaved family and friends as commemorative tokens. Clearly, audiences for such verses cut across economic and social lines.

Occasions other than funerals also supplied audiences for poetry. Francis Daniel Pastorius delighted in recording in verse the goings and comings of his Germantown friends, the results of his horticultural experiments, and his opinions on new books by Sir John Denham, Abraham Cowley, and John Locke. The same Edward Taylor who years later, in the seclusion of his study, wrote sequences of private meditations, had delivered on the day of his college commencement, a thirty-minute verse account of the superiority of English over other languages. At Harvard College, he spoke before President Chauncy and the Fellows, and there is no reason to suppose that Taylor was setting a precedent. Nor was he outside the tradition: such verses, composed for such an audience, on such an occasion, strained to carry the weight of intellection which freighted each line with arcane, abstruse, or pedantic allusions, not all of which were familiar even to the learned Increase Mather.

Of course, the Harvard audience was a learned one which could be addressed in verse packed with references to the classics, philosophy, metaphysics, alchemy, logic, history, and biblical lore. But the public audience outside the university was by no means uninformed. Stories from Greek and Roman mythology were widely known, enabling the poet to elicit the response he sought by the mere mention of a name or situation. Biblical allusions caused no scurrying for concordances, for the Puritan clergy were a preaching ministry who instructed church members two or three times a week in erudite sermons delivered not only at regular meetings but also

on every sort of public occasion. And there was wide familiarity
with such works of general learning as Peter Heylyn's *Cosmographie*
(1652). Thus, readers of almanac verse, many of them farmers,
tradesmen, artisans, and merchants, were comfortable with lines
in which Phoebe and Phoebus sported according to the season, or
in which the intricacies of the zodiac were punned upon unremit-
tingly, or in which mention of the name Regiomontanus could call
forth in readers a complete recollection of a dramatic moment in
history. Indeed, almanac verse probably reached consistently a
broader audience than any other type of seventeenth-century Amer-
ican verse.

Single works, too, enjoyed a high degree of popularity. The
phenomenon of Michael Wigglesworth's *Day of Doom* made it
America's first best-seller, with the proportion of copies sold to popu-
lation so high that American publishers have yet to equal the record.
"God's Controversy With New England," by the same author, and
Benjamin Tompson's "New-England's Crisis," were also widely read.
Nor can one forget that an English audience welcomed works by
American writers. A slightly altered version of the Tompson poem,
entitled "New England's Tears," was printed in London the same
year the "Crisis" appeared in Boston. London audiences were de-
lighted with Anne Bradstreet's verse in *The Tenth Muse Lately
Sprung up in America*. The reception was so warm that twenty-five
years after their publication Milton's nephew remarked, "the mem-
ory of [these] poems . . . is not yet wholly extinct."

Readers of history were also an audience for verse; it was rare
that the history of an early colony did not contain poems, fragments
of verse, or portions of longer poetic works. George Alsop's *A Char-
acter of the Province of Maryland* was spiced with poetic shots at
Cromwell, mock complaints in verse about babbling servant girls,
and the ubiquitous acrostic. Captain Edward Johnson moved
easily from prose narrative into stanzas of verse whenever he felt
the moment appropriate, and two other writers of histories, Nathan-
iel Morton and Cotton Mather, frequently inserted long and short
poems throughout the texts of their works. Many of the verses
Mather includes in his *Magnalia* are not of his authorship, and
only one in *New Englands Memoriall* can be safely attributed to
Morton. Not that Mather or Morton was claiming authorship for what

he had not written; rather, both freely used any verses they felt best memorialized situations or persons.

Still another seventeenth-century American audience—though probably not without parental or ministerial direction—were the children. "Milk for Babes" exemplified the Puritan doctrine of instruction tempered with entertainment. Although frequently wrenched verse, the *Bay Psalm Book* was standard fare for children who remembered their catechism better if it were rhymed and rhythmic. At least so their elders thought, pre-eminent among whom were the group of illustrious divines whose verse rendering of the psalms demonstrates all the expected failings of committee poetry. The *Bay Psalm Book* was not the only verse to reach a young audience, however, for Michael Wigglesworth's *Day of Doom* was also assigned to children for its mnemonic quality and soundness of doctrine.

Mnemonics, of course, was one use of poetry for the seventeenth-century American. Another, as noted, was commemoration of lives or events in eulogistic verses embedded in histories and elsewhere. But there were many other uses of poetry. Frequently it expressed romantic love, as in John Saffin's tender lyrics to his Martha and in Anne Bradstreet's to her husband Simon. The voice of gratitude is often heard, as in Anne Bradstreet's poem of thanks that she and her children are delivered from illness, or Madame Knight's lines describing how the bright moonlight helped her to find a nocturnal way across the Connecticut River. Other private observations were similarly turned into poetry, as when John Saffin views man "eagerly grasping what creates his pain."

Nor were poets reluctant to write public poems to express their views on the state of the society. "New-England's Crisis" is Benjamin Tompson's interpretative account of the Indian wars visited upon a corrupt colony. Sewall's "Superanuated Squier, wigg'd and powder'd with pretense" was directed at John Saffin in connection with Saffin's attempt to bring Adam, a Negro, back into slavery. John Cotton of Queen's Creek illuminated Bacon's Rebellion in the most famous poem to come out of Virginia during the century. And many a ballad, anonymous or by known writers, exclaimed against Indian atrocities, recorded difficulties with plantings or harvests, or deplored periwiggery. In short, seventeenth-century poets used poetry as it has always been used—to tell stories, to celebrate, to mourn, to praise, commemorate, describe, instruct, and to express both sacred and profane love.

The Aesthetic View

"Aesthetic" has been a word too rarely used in connection with early American poets, particularly the Puritan poets and their art. Yet it can be applied to both without equivocation. Our frequent failure to understand this is linked to persistent misunderstanding of the Puritan himself as a religious fanatic, who repressed his sensual appetites with eyes glued to heaven and whose every breath was a prayer that God had chosen him to dwell there eternally. That such a creature could harbor an aesthetic sensibility seemed improbable, if not grotesque.

But this sketch of the New England Puritan is no more than a caricature, one that has been effectively demolished in the course of the twentieth century. It seems hardly necessary to be reminded once again that the Puritan was a man fond of his world—of beer and wine, of household amenities, of fashionable clothing in rich color, of music. A social man who enjoyed the company of his friends, he went about his business very much in the world and with delight in his natural environs.

Nor is the assertion in recent decades that the Puritan was human after all, a mere attempt to make him palatable in this century, for while some aspects of his life require explanation, the Puritan needs no apologia to shape him for contemporary taste. To know about John Winthrop's appreciation of "good beer and venison pasty," Sewall's enjoyment of pleasant summer rides into the country, delicious strawberries, a well-roasted pheasant, or his concern about the shipment of a clavier for his wife, is to know that these were not persons rejecting the world. A glance at merchants' shipping lists of colored cloth and good lace affirms again the Puritan enjoyment of fine things. One need only remark the graceful lines of silver pitchers and candlesticks bearing the mark of John Hull, Boston silversmith, to recognize that the Puritan was a man of aesthetic sensibilities.

The key to Puritan aesthetics lies in their idea of proportion and utility. The notion of art for art's sake would have horrified them, if they had understood it. In their view nothing produced by man was for its own sake, but ultimately for God's. A successful business venture by a man who felt God had intended him to be a merchant could only contribute to the greater glory of the Almighty, provided the merchant were not so hedonistic as to gloat over his triumph, forget the Providential hand in the affair, and become acquisitive to the dangerous point of greed. Similarly, a well-appointed home whose furnishings were appreciated by the owners ought to uplift the spirit and evoke gratitude for God's gifts. It was only when the furnishings themselves became a source of overweening pride that their owners deserved rebuke. Thus the same Judge Sewall who so enjoyed things of the world spoke approvingly of a fire that burned a prideful woman's laces, bringing her to recognition of her error.

At the same time, the Puritans had no sympathy for the monastic, cloistered life, which they felt to be another violation of proportion. God had given this world for use, and refusal of that gift was a perversion of His will. In one of the few poems of the period whose central theme is aesthetic attitude, Richard Steere capsules the Puritan view:

> But for a man to know the highest joys
> This World affords, and yet without offence;
> To Live therein, and as a Master use them,
> In all Respects, and yet without abuse . . .
> This Man subjects to one, Commands the other,
> Owns God his Master, makes the World his Slave.

Owning God his master, the Puritan sought in his life a balance of degree and order that was acceptable to God. Accordingly, the overriding religious structure of Puritan life set for art a disciplined framework in which sensuous overindulgence and aesthetic aridity were equally deplorable. At either extreme the individual perverts God's intention, on the one hand by drowning the intellect in a sensate world without check on the animal nature, and on the other by denying the world as a gift sent by God for use. In each instance he undermines his humanity.

The Puritan aesthetic operated in poetry as in other areas of life. Paramount was its ultimate usefulness in glorifying God. As Edward Taylor writes,

> Nature doth better work than Art: yet thine
> Out vie both works of nature and of Art.

God's creation, nature, was but one perceivable aspect of Him, which a man, even if of the elect, could trace only imperfectly in art, itself a mirror held up to nature. By co-ordinating Roger Williams' poetic statement that "Truth is a Native, naked Beauty," and John Saffin's "And Native Beauty doth most clearly Shine / When its own Ornaments makes it Divine," we can better understand that the poet's task was to describe as best he could the godly truth insofar as it was perceivable by him in nature. And though the poem, since it was written by man, was several removes from formal perfection (from a theological standpoint, not one of literary criticism), it still had a significant place in man's life. As Cotton Mather says, denying that poetry is a "morisce-dancing with bells," and thereby trivial: "I cannot wish you a soul that shall be wholly unpoetical."

The need for balance and proportion is continually reiterated. Nicholas Noyes warns in verse against what he sees as current poetic excess:

> By over-praising of the Dead
> Nor they, nor we are Bettered.
> Poetick Raptures Scandalize,
> And pass with most for learned Lies . . .
> Such high Flights seem Design'd to raise
> The *Poets,* not the *Person's* praise.

What Noyes is obviously concerned about is excessive pride in poets who have lost sight of moral purpose, and instead become enraptured by verbal fireworks. In a society whose aesthetic sensibility was so focused on moderation and temperance, a self-indulgent poet could only be regarded as sunk deep into gravest error, far from the "Native Beauty" of truth.

Literary Influences, and Poetic Variety

Two opposing—and equally inaccurate—views of seventeenth-century American poets have been that they either were rustics whose rural naïveté is reflected in their embarrassingly simple verse, or that, lacking imagination, they could but imitate at several removes a few English verses learned before their emigration or from their elders at New England firesides. These myths are gradually being dispelled, or at least properly clarified. Investigations of English school curriculums, of early American library holdings, of shipping lists of books sent to the colonies, as well as increasing documentation of direct influences discovered in literary works, have led in recent years to a general reassessment of the cultural ambience of early America.

In the center of the literary background of seventeenth-century American poetry stands the Bible, particularly the books of the Old Testament. No other influence is so pervasive, no other source wells so regularly to the surface, no other text is so often quoted verbatim or paraphrased or echoed. But this is not to argue that the Bible stands alone. The classical poets, historians, and rhetoricians, studied at Cambridge and at Harvard by every undergraduate, are often heard: Ovid, Cicero, Seneca, Virgil, Juvenal, Horace, Tacitus, Livy; and, with somewhat less frequency: Hesiod, Xenophon, Homer, Demosthenes, and Theocritus.

Seventeenth-century Americans were familiar, too, with Renaissance and early English writers of prose and poetry. John Danforth admired Campion and Bacon; Anne Bradstreet memorialized Sidney and acknowledged herself student to Du Bartas; Steere, Cotton Mather, and John James owned copies of or quoted from the works of Sidney, William Drummond, and Michael Drayton. Francis Daniel Pastorius, perhaps the most industrious reader among early American poets, wrote verses on the flyleaves of works by Sir John Denham, Cowley, Locke, and Samuel Daniel. And though direct allusions to Shakespeare do not occur often in early American poetry, there are echoes enough—and other suggestions enough—to make clear that Shakespeare was well known.

At Harvard the sons of Puritan ministers were as ebullient as modern undergraduates—and much attracted by the luscious verse in *Witts Recreations Augmented, with Ingenious Conceits for the Wittie, and Merrie Medecines for the Melancholie* (1641). Elnathan Chauncy and Seaborn Cotton copied Herrick's "Gather Ye Rosebuds" and "A Willow Garland Thou Didst Send" into their commonplace books, along with Joseph Beaumont's "Psyche: or Loves Mysteries," numerous of John Cleveland's amorous bits, and portions of Spenser's *Shepheardes Calender* and *Epithalamium*.

For other early Americans the English metaphysical poets, principally Herbert and Quarles, were strongly influential. Their impact is apparent in Edward Taylor's work; their poetry was part of the school curriculum where Taylor spent his boyhood. Francis Quarles was the one English poet who seems to have exerted the most pervasive influence on early American verse writers. His *Emblems* and verse paraphrase of the Song of Songs, *Sions Sonnets,* were popular among nonconformists, both for their acceptable doctrine and for their imagery. Suspicious as the Puritans were of excessive sensuousness, they found in Quarles a poet who did not yield to overindulgence in sensuous images. Thus it is not surprising to find that all early libraries of which we have record, including Harvard's, had copies of his work. John Josselyn reports that he delivered some of Quarles's verse paraphrases of the Psalms to the committee of ministers charged with the task of creating the Bay Psalm Book, and though the Fathers of the Bay Colony themselves finally did most of the work of versification, a few of the versions in the 1640 volume argue for attribution to the author of *Sions Sonnets.* While Quarles's influence was widely acknowledged among early New England poets, only rarely is their work blatantly derivative of him. Indeed no three poets are more dissimilar in style from Quarles than Taylor, Wigglesworth, or Bradstreet; and yet all three owe a debt to him.

Herbert and Quarles, however, are only a part of the Baroque movement pervasive in Europe in the seventeenth century and felt in American verse of the same period. The Baroque might be broadly characterized by startling conceits, hyperbole, dramatic contrasts, and tightly packed language pushing words to the very limits of their meanings. This is apparent in Edward Johnson's work. Taylor can certainly be considered part of the movement. It is revealed as well in Puritan poems of wit, the anagrams and acrostics.

For while some poets and literary movements had a demonstrable influence on seventeenth-century American verse, our early writers were general heirs to a vast historical legacy of poetic forms and types.

Aside from the many formal elegies, lyrics, hymns, and ballad stanzas, seventeenth-century Americans had a great fondness for exercising their poetic wit, particularly in the anagram, the acrostic, and the epigram. The first two, formally structured on a person's name, demanded that the writer use the letters of the name to form words which revealed something of the person's character. In the acrostic the first letter of each line, or the last, read downward, spelled the name of the subject of the poem. It was for the poet to compose cogently within the formal stricture of the name, using as many relevant words formed from the subject's name as he could.

The anagram differed somewhat from the acrostic, for rather than offering a downward reading of the subject's name, the poem derived its major theme from a motto or epigram the author formed from the letters of the name and used as an epigraph. Thus, a denigratory anagram concerning the Quaker Claudius Gilbert, was entitled, "Tis Braul I Cudgel." This sort of poetry was obviously facilitated by uninhibited seventeenth-century orthography, but it would be a mistake to think it mere verbal virtuosity. It had as its basis the Puritan belief that nothing in this world, including nomenclature, was haphazard. God had somehow intended that a person's name, if carefully examined, could reveal aspects of his character. To a people constantly engaged in self-examination, all latent indications of God's attitude toward an individual assumed high importance. The result is the spate of seventeenth-century acrostics and anagrams. And admittedly strained though they can be, they must at their wittiest invite admiration.

Puritan wit ranged over a broad spectrum, from the quintessential verbal niceness of the acrostic and anagram (or, on occasion, a combination of the two); to the pun, which through the sixteenth and seventeenth centuries was accepted literary usage; through satire; and finally to the broad humor of almanac verses, in which lads and lasses were as likely to roll in the hay as sit primly at meeting. Here were Puritans at their least "puritannical"—not turning from the world, but looking critically at their society in hope of effecting reform. They did not, of course, condone haystack dalliance, but they were realistic enough about nature to have their joke at it.

And they could joke as well in the lugubrious mode of the mockepic. Early Americans developed a tough strain of irony that enabled them to exploit poetically the disparity between things as they ought to be and as they actually were. Thus Benjamin Tompson's chuckle as he versifies efforts of women to fortify Boston Neck with mud barricades is clearly ironic. His mode is, appropriately, the mock-epic.

Tompson, like other early poets, developed his craft by patient practice during hours unoccupied by his classroom responsibilities. Yet despite the literary influences and established poetic forms whose impact on early American writers is apparent, there were poets who composed without literary self-consciousness and who learned their craft more from intuition than from imitation. The ebullient and indefatigable Philip Walker, who recorded in 456 quatrains the ambush by Indians of "Captain Perse and his coragios Company" on March 26, 1676, and whose orthography even by seventeenth-century standards reaches sometimes beyond the limits of the language, employed no models, depended upon no established form of verse or tactic of rhetoric, and echoed no standard image. His narrative is strikingly dramatic, recording the brutalities of hand-to-hand combat in grim, taut lines framed from personal observation.

Sometimes forms from popular culture edged themselves into established literary currents. The ballad, long sung and hawked about the London streets, had become by the seventeenth century a familiar form in print. Its enduring popularity ensured its place in literature. And while the simple ballad stanza might be the very form executed by the self-schooled typesetter writing his first halting lines about *Sol* in springtime, it could be put to loftier uses in Michael Wigglesworth's *Day of Doom,* a poem indisputably epic in scope.

For whatever forms seventeenth-century verse writers appropriated for their use, they did possess an epic view, as Edward Taylor demonstrates in *Gods Determinations,* or as Edward Johnson proves in his *Wonder-Working Providence.* Theirs was a sense of godly relevance as they confronted the world. Their awareness of history-in-process was keen; their belief that this was their divinely appointed moment in time and space was unshakable. For them it was imperative that what happened daily be recorded in prose and in verse. They may not have used all the devices, trappings, and tactics of the conventional epic, but their world-view moved them to find their own forms in which to embody the spirit of God's chosen people.

TEXTUAL AND ORGANIZATIONAL NOTE

Texts for this edition have been drawn from manuscript sources, early printings, and wherever possible, modern scholarly editions. Roughly half the verse included has not been printed since the seventeenth century; 59 poems are printed here for the first time.

The principal textual problems in compiling this collection have been those of locating complete original texts and of establishing reliable texts through use of the earliest printed versions rather than reprints. Unlike other volumes in this series, there are few textual notes because, with rare exceptions—notably Wigglesworth's *Day of Doom*, Taylor's *Preparatory Meditations*, and Anne Bradstreet's poems—only one complete text is extant for each poem. Numerous modernized printings and reprintings in the welter of earnestly prepared nineteenth-century American local histories, and in similar early anthologies, have been examined and rejected, unless a poem exists today solely in such a text.

In each copy text, original spelling, capitalization, punctuation, and usage have been retained, except that punctuation has been added when necessary to avoid ambiguity. The distinction between roman and italic type used in early printed texts has also been retained. Seventeenth-century manuscript shorthand has been expanded as it would have been in contemporary print; the modern "s" has been substituted for the earlier long form, ampersand regularized to "and" except in the construction "&c.", and lower-case "ff" expressed as F when "ff" was intended as capital letter. U and V have been regularized, *u* for the vowel, *v* for the consonant; and *i* and *j* employed as in modern usage. Stanzaic structure and original indentation have been retained, and to facilitate modern reading the initial letter of each line of verse has been capitalized. No attempt has been made to reproduce black-letter or bold-face type, ornamental initials, or varied sizes of majuscules.

Annotation has been kept to a minimum. Standard seventeenth-century usages, such as *then* for *than*, *vild* for *vile*, *least* for *lest*, *there* for *their*, have not been glossed unless ambiguous in context. Foreign language words and phrases have been translated and sources supplied. Lines and phrases of Latin both in texts and in marginalia are left untranslated when the English text within the poem actually provides the translation. Allusions to persons, events, and places have been explained when such data are not obvious or readily obtained from one of the standard dictionaries, encyclopedias, histories, or concordances.

This anthology is organized into four parts. The first contains a substantial and representative selection from the works of Edward Taylor, Anne Bradstreet, and Michael Wigglesworth—the three poets of early America who in the quality of their art and in the range and quantity of their extant verse stand forward clearly as Major Writers. In the second part are selections from the writings of fourteen poets who, though assiduous and competent in their art, in some significant aspect fall short of the level reached by Taylor, Bradstreet, and Wigglesworth. Urian Oakes, for example, probably the most accomplished Puritan elegist, is known as a poet to us today by a single extant poem—the memorable *Elegie upon . . . Thomas Shepard*. Benjamin Tompson, successful in *New Englands Crisis*, composed an equal body of undistinguished verse. Richard Steere, controlled and effective in "Sea Storm nigh the Coast" and "A Poem upon the Caelestial Embassy," was unable to sustain his art throughout "Earth Felicities, Heavens Allowances." These fourteen, then, are the Minor Writers.

The third part contains a group of writers and verse selected to represent the more than 200 other writers and their more than 1,500 poems of which we have record in America before 1725. The fourth part contains anonymous verse chosen, like the group in part three, to represent the very large body of such verse written in the period.

Because of its special character, the *Bay Psalm Book* has been represented in a separate section.

Within parts one, two, and three, the organization is chronological, by birth date of the poet; in part four, by established or probable date of composition of the verse.

Quality and significance of the poetry have been the principal guides for selection throughout this anthology. In parts three and four particularly, however, the range and number of selections are an attempt to reflect the phenomenal outpouring of verse that marked this era in which the first American poetry was composed. It is not too much to argue, I think, that a reading through parts three and four of this collection can add dimension to our view not only of seventeenth-century American literature but also of that portion of the society whose lively interest in the writing of verse moved them so often and so voluminously to its composition.

ACKNOWLEDGMENTS

Texts for this edition have been drawn from early published books and pamphlets contained in the microcard reprints of Charles Evans' *American Bibliography*, the indispensable source for study of all aspects of early American literature, and from manuscript sources and printed books and pamphlets consulted in the libraries and societies listed below. It is a pleasant duty to record my thanks to the curators and librarians of these institutions for their advice and assistance, for supplying photocopies of materials in their collections, and for permission to publish the texts in the following pages: American Antiquarian Society, Connecticut Historical Society, Historical Society of Pennsylvania, Massachusetts Historical Society, New York Historical Society, Rhode Island Historical Society, Boston Athenaeum, Boston Public Library, British Museum, Brown University Libraries, Harvard University Libraries, Henry E. Huntington Library, Library of Congress, Libraries of the University of Pennsylvania, The Pennsylvania State University Libraries, and the Yale University Library.

To Professor Harold S. Jantz of Johns Hopkins University I am deeply indebted for his assistance and encouragement as this edition took shape, and for his generosity in permitting me access to his library and collection of early Americana. Professor J. A. Leo Lemay of the University of California at Los Angeles provided leads to several key texts. Professor Robert W. Frank, Jr. of The Pennsylvania State University assisted in translation of some Latin passages and epigraphs.

Research for this edition was assisted by a grant from the Central Fund for Research of The Pennsylvania State University.

To my students, Miss Cecilia Halbert, Mrs. Marjorie McCune, Dr. Alyce E. Sands, and Miss Astrid von Mühlenfels, I owe particular thanks for their work in several aspects of seventeenth-century American literature, which contributed materially to this collection.

Miss Priscilla Letterman prepared the final typescript from the original manuscript draft. And my wife assisted in all phases of the work, particularly with transcription of texts from original sources and collation of textual versions.

Harrison T. Meserole

The Pennsylvania State University
October 1967

Major Writers

ANNE BRADSTREET

(c. 1612–1672)

At mid-seventeenth century there appeared in London a volume of poems grandiloquently titled *The Tenth Muse Lately Sprung up in America*. Its subtitle advertised the book as containing *Severall Poems, compiled with great variety of Wit and Learning, full of delight*. Yet at that time its author had no knowledge that her work was in print, for Mistress Anne Bradstreet, the "Tenth Muse," was busy in North Andover, Massachusetts, as wife and mother of several children. Unknown to her, Reverend John Woodbridge, her brother-in-law, had carried her work to London and had seen it through the press and into a warm London acceptance. No one then —not her appreciative public, nor John Woodbridge, nor Anne Bradstreet herself—could know that virtually none of the poems on which her reputation now rests were included in that 1650 edition. The lyrical and meditative verses, whose variety of "wit" and ability to evoke "delight" are today praised, had not yet been written. They would appear twenty-eight years later in Boston, together with revised and corrected poems from *The Tenth Muse*, under the title *Several Poems*. By then Anne Bradstreet was six years in her grave.

America's first woman poet of distinction was born Anne Dudley in 1612, in Northampton, England. Her father, Thomas Dudley, who was to occupy a prominent position in the public life of the Massachusetts Bay Colony, was at that time financial officer in the household of the Earl of Lincoln. Known in later years as a stern and austere man, Dudley nonetheless offered his daughter educational opportunity uncommon for the time. Anne, who called her father "a magazine of history," acknowledged him as her "guide" and "instructor." It was doubtless through his encouragement that she read, probably having had access to the library of the Earl of Lincoln. Her era was intellectually a lively one to grow up in, for the excitement of Elizabethan England lingered on. It is evident from her earlier poems that Anne Dudley must have known Shakespeare's work, and it is possible that she had also read the recently translated Cervantes. Her knowledge of Sylvester's translation of the French poet Du Bartas is well documented, and the influence of Raleigh's *History of the World* on some of her work can be similarly demonstrated.

Anne's education was not only a bookish one, however, for the Earl's household attracted a distinguished company, including men from Cambridge whose non-conformist religious convictions plunged them into a religious controversy unequalled in intensity since the seventeenth century. We may be sure that the young Anne was witness to much lively discussion and debate.

In 1628 at the age of sixteen Anne Dudley married Simon Bradstreet, a young man nine years her senior and, like her father, a member of the Earl of Lincoln's household. Bradstreet had taken bachelor's and master's degrees at Emmanuel College, the most outspokenly non-conformist of the Cambridge colleges. Just two years later he took his young wife to America where he, like his father-in-law, was to be active in public affairs. Along with Thomas Dudley the young couple traveled with the Winthrop party aboard the *Arbella*, the flagship on which the first prominent emigrants sailed. When they reached America after a three-month voyage, the Bradstreets lived for brief periods in Salem, Boston, Cambridge, and Ipswich, before settling permanently sometime between 1638 and 1644 on a farm at North Andover, Massachusetts, near the Merrimac River. It was here that Anne Bradstreet was to raise her eight children, and to share the excitement of her husband's life as he became judge, legislator, royal councilor, and ultimately governor of the colony.

Anne Bradstreet's initial response to America is not altogether a matter of conjecture, for in her little book of "Contemplations," written at the request of her son Simon, she says she "found a new world and new manners, at which [her] heart rose," but that she "submitted to it and joined to the church at Boston." Certainly it could not have been an easy transition from a comfortable gentlewoman's life in England to that of mistress of a wilderness farm where Indian attack was imminent. Further, Anne Bradstreet was not a strong woman, and for years was subject to fits of sickness, fevers, fainting, and lameness. Still more troubling was her failure during the first years in Massachusetts to have children. To the Puritan who believed every aspect of his life was governed by God, this apparent barrenness could only be interpreted as a reflection of personal unworthiness.

But Anne Bradstreet had her consolations. She recalls in her jottings the solace she found in prayer and in reading Scripture. And though her conscience was at times troubled, as those of all good Puritans were, her faith deepened as years passed. Then, in answer to her prayers, came her children, eight of them. Of her four sons, two graduated from Harvard, one to become a minister and the other a physician. A third served as colonel in the militia, and of the four, two represented North Andover in the General Court, the Massachusetts legislative body. Mistress Bradstreet was survived by all but one of her children, each of whom married and had a large family of his own. The kind of mother she was can be inferred not only from the filial tribute paid her, but also from one of her "Contemplations," in which she says, "Diverse children have their different natures; some are like flesh which nothing but salt will keep from putrefaction; some again like tender fruits that are best preserved with sugar: those parents are wise that can fit their nurture according to their Nature." That Anne Bradstreet could see the wisdom of flexible adaptability doubtless made her not only a better mother, but also enabled her to adjust to life in the wilderness.

She had yet another consolation for the hard New England life, her husband Simon. Their marriage was a supremely happy one which became the subject of some of her finest lyrics. Simon Bradstreet's absences from home pained her sorely but were, because of his position, often necessary. Probably the most difficult of their separations occurred in 1661–62, when Bradstreet and John Norton traveled to England to plead the colony's case at the Restoration Court of Charles II. Despite disturbing rumors of detention and imprisonment in the Tower of London, both men returned to New England to resume places as heads of their families and leaders in the colony.

The family life that Anne Bradstreet found so congenial a subject for her poems was in New England regarded as an ordinance of God. While marriage was no sacrament, it was a godly duty. And though connubial bliss may have been suspect, a proper amount of love between husband and wife was expected. This ought not to be excessive love that would draw a person's attention away from God and toward the transient things of this world, but rather a tender, affectionate regard for one's mate. Children, too, were His gifts and, though just as inherently sinful as their parents, they were deserving of parental affection and love tempered with proper chastisement. Parents held the responsibility for the spiritual lives of their children, and a group that had risked their own lives on hazardous sea voyages and had accepted the physical hardship of New England was not a group to take lightly the spiritual development of children biologically charged to them by their Creator. In the poetry of Anne Bradstreet it is this tone of sincere piety, tenderness, and sense of responsibility that one hears most often.

It is remarkable that Anne Bradstreet wrote any poetry at all. At a time and place where literacy alone was unusual for a woman, this New England mistress with her talent for verse was unique. Since her duties as wife and mother took precedence over all else, her poetry had to be written at odd moments of the day, or perhaps late at night when sleeping children made no demands upon her. The long hours required at devotional services on two days of the week, coupled with her physical frailty, did not allow her time and ease for writing. Further, there must have been pressure from her neighbors to lay down the pen that made her somewhat of an anomaly in the community, for she wrote, "I am obnoxious to each carping tongue / Who says my hand a needle better fits." It is more likely that Anne Bradstreet plied the needle for long hours before finding free minutes to write her poems.

But she did write a quantity of poetry, both considerable in bulk and good in quality. Her earlier work, written in admitted imitation of her acknowledged master, Du Bartas, was a group of quaternians on the Four Elements, Constitutions, Ages of Man, and Seasons. She finished three of the "Four Monarchies," but did not complete the poem. For when her manuscript was destroyed in a 1666 fire that burned the Bradstreet home to the ground, she did not attempt a reconstruction of the fourth monarchy. It was just as well that she did not, for Anne Bradstreet's early works are "literary," often stiff and bookish, and frankly derivative. Though it is easy to censure her from a critical perspective of three centuries, it is well to recall that Du Bartas, after whose manner she wrote, enjoyed an immense popularity in England, not the least of his admirers being Milton and Dryden.

Still, Anne Bradstreet is now appreciated for the personal poems in which her feelings and the qualities of her New England life shine through. The poignance with which she views the charred ruins of her house evokes a more valuable poetic insight than the fourth monarchy that fell victim to the conflagration. Otherwise, Anne Bradstreet deals with several subjects in varied forms and tones, ranging from tongue-in-cheek irony in "The Author to her Book," through illness whose pain is assuaged by prayer, to the love she bears her husband when she writes, "If ever a man were loved by wife, then thee." As a mother she speaks of her "eight birds hatcht in one nest," then sustains the figure to record their upbringing. And she was also able to write in elegiac strains when those near to her, notably her father and her grandchildren, died.

We know relatively little of Anne Bradstreet from official records or diaries. No headstone marks her grave, nor is there an extant portrait of her. But the portrait revealed in her poetry says more about her perceptions and responses than could any official record. Viewed in its full range her work must be adjudged uneven, but at her best Anne Bradstreet achieved a level of artistic merit that led Cotton Mather to say of her poetry: "it afforded a grateful Entertainment unto the Ingenious, and a Monument for her Memory beyond the Stateliest *Marbles*."

The Prologue[1]

1

To sing of Wars, of Captains, and of Kings,
Of Cities founded, Common-wealths begun,
For my mean pen are too superiour things:
Or how they all, or each their dates have run
Let Poets and Historians set these forth,
My obscure Lines shall not so dim their worth.

[1] To *The Tenth Muse* . . . (London, 1650), repr. with corrections in *Several Poems* . . . (Boston, 1678).

2

But when my wondring eyes and envious heart
Great *Bartas*[2] sugar'd lines, do but read o're
Fool I do grudg the Muses did not part
'Twixt him and me that overfluent store;
A *Bartas* can, do what a *Bartas* will
But simple I according to my skill.

3

From school-boyes tongue no rhet'rick we expect
Nor yet a sweet Consort from broken strings,
Nor perfect beauty, where's a main defect:
My foolish, broken, blemish'd Muse so sings
And this to mend, alas, no Art is able,
'Cause nature, made it so irreparable.

4

Nor can I, like that fluent sweet tongu'd Greek[3]
Who lisp'd at first, in future times speak plain
By Art he gladly found what he did seek
A full requital of his, striving pain
Art can do much, but this maxime's most sure
A weak or wounded brain admits no cure.

5

I am obnoxious to each carping tongue
Who says my hand a needle better fits,
A Poets pen all scorn I should thus wrong,
For such despite they cast on Female wits:
If what I do prove well, it won't advance,
They'l say it's stoln, or else it was by chance.

[2] Guillaume du Bartas (1544–90), French poet translated into English by Joshua Sylvester in 1605–7.

[3] Demosthenes (385?–322 B.C.), Athenian orator who, to cure his speech defect, tried to outshout the sound of the sea while rehearsing his speeches.

6

But sure the Antique Greeks were far more mild
Else of our Sexe, why feigned they those Nine[4]
And poesy made, *Calliope's* own Child;
So 'mongst the rest they placed the Arts Divine,
But this weak knot, they will full soon untie,
The Greeks did nought, but play the fools and lye.

7

Let Greeks be Greeks, and women what they are
Men have precedency and still excell,
It is but vain unjustly to wage warre;
Men can do best, and women know it well
Preheminence in all and each is yours;
Yet grant some small acknowledgement of ours.

8

And oh ye high flown quills that soar the Skies,
And ever with your prey still catch your praise,
If e'er you daigne these lowly lines your eyes
Give Thyme or Parsley wreath, I ask no bayes,[5]
This mean and unrefined ure[6] of mine
Will make you glistring gold, but more to shine.

The Author to her Book

Thou ill-form'd offspring of my feeble brain,
Who after birth did'st by my side remain,
Till snatcht from thence by friends, less wise then true
Who thee abroad, expos'd to publick view,[1]

[4] The nine Muses, goddesses who presided over song, poetry, and the arts and sciences.
[5] laurels.
[6] ore.
[1] Reference to the fact that the first edition of her poems, *The Tenth Muse* (1650), was published in London without her knowledge by John Woodbridge, or possibly John Rogers. Anne Bradstreet's corrections and revisions were incorporated in the second edition, *Several Poems . . .* , published in Boston in 1678, six years after her death.

Made thee in raggs, halting to th' press to trudg,   5
Where errors were not lessened (all may judg)
At thy return my blushing was not small,
My rambling brat (in print) should mother call,
I cast thee by as one unfit for light,
Thy Visage was so irksome in my sight;   10
Yet being mine own, at length affection would
Thy blemishes amend, if so I could:
I wash'd thy face, but more defects I saw,
And rubbing off a spot, still made a flaw.
I stretcht thy joynts to make thee even feet,   15
Yet still thou run'st more hobling then is meet;
In better dress to trim thee was my mind,
But nought save home-spun Cloth, i'th' house I find
In this array, 'mongst Vulgars mayst thou roam
In Criticks hands, beware thou dost not come;   20
And take thy way where yet thou art not known,
If for thy Father askt, say, thou hadst none:
And for thy Mother, she alas is poor,
Which caus'd her thus to send thee out of door.

Contemplations

[1]

Some time now past in the Autumnal Tide,
When *Phœbus* wanted but one hour to bed,
The trees all richly clad, yet void of pride,
Where gilded o're by his rich golden head.
Their leaves and fruits seem'd painted, but was true
Of green, of red, of yellow, mixed hew,
Rapt were my sences at this delectable view.

2

I wist not what to wish, yet sure thought I,
If so much excellence abide below;
How excellent is he that dwells on high?
Whose power and beauty by his works we know.
Sure he is goodness, wisdome, glory, light,
That hath this under world so richly dight:
More Heaven then Earth was here, no winter and no night.

3

Then on a stately Oak I cast mine Eye,
Whose ruffling top the Clouds seem'd to aspire;
How long since thou wast in thine Infancy?
Thy strength, and stature, more thy years admire,
Hath hundred winters past since thou wast born?
Or thousand since thou brakest thy shell of horn,
If so, all these as nought, Eternity doth scorn.

4

Then higher on the glistering Sun I gaz'd,
Whose beams was shaded by the leavie Tree,
The more I look'd, the more I grew amaz'd,
And softly said, what glory's like to thee?
Soul of this world, this Universes Eye,
No wonder, some made thee a Deity:
Had I not better known, (alas) the same had I.

5

Thou as a Bridegroom from thy Chamber rushes,
And as a strong man, joyes to run a race,
The morn doth usher thee, with smiles and blushes,
The Earth reflects her glances in thy face.
Birds, insects, Animals with Vegative,
Thy heart from death and dulness doth revive:
And in the darksome womb of fruitful nature dive.

6

Thy swift Annual, and diurnal Course,
Thy daily streight, and yearly oblique path;
Thy pleasing fervor, and thy scorching force,
All mortals here the feeling knowledg hath.
Thy presence makes it day, thy absence night,
Quaternal Seasons caused by thy might:
Hail Creature, full of sweetness, beauty and delight.

7

Art thou so full of glory, that no Eye
Hath strength, thy shining Rayes once to behold?
And is thy splendid Throne erect so high?
As to approach it, can no earthly mould.
How full of glory then must thy Creator be?
Who gave this bright light luster unto thee:
Admir'd, ador'd for ever, be that Majesty.

8

Silent alone, where none or saw, or heard,
In pathless paths I lead my wandring feet,
My humble Eyes to lofty Skyes I rear'd
To sing some Song, my mazed Muse thought meet.
My great Creator I would magnifie,
That nature had, thus decked liberally:
But Ah, and Ah, again, my imbecility!

9

I heard the merry grashopper then sing,
The black clad Cricket, bear a second part,
They kept one tune, and plaid on the same string,
Seeming to glory in their little Art.
Shall Creatures abject, thus their voices raise?
And in their kind resound their makers praise:
Whilst I as mute, can warble forth no higher layes.

10

When present times look back to Ages past,
And men in being fancy those are dead,
It makes things gone perpetually to last,
And calls back moneths and years that long since fled.
It makes a man more aged in conceit,
Then was *Methuselah*, or's grand-sire great:
While of their persons and their acts his mind doth treat.

11

Sometimes in *Eden* fair, he seems to be,
Sees glorious *Adam* there made Lord of all,
Fancyes the Apple, dangle on the Tree,
That turn'd his Sovereign to a naked thral.
Who like a miscreant's driven from that place,
To get his bread with pain, and sweat of face:
A penalty impos'd on his backsliding Race.

12

Here sits our Grandame in retired place,
And in her lap, her bloody *Cain* new born,
The weeping Imp oft looks her in the face,
Bewails his unknown hap, and fate forlorn;
His Mother sighs, to think of Paradise,
And how she lost her bliss, to be more wise,
Believing him that was, and is, Father of lyes.

13

Here *Cain* and *Abel* come to sacrifice,
Fruits of the Earth, and Fatlings each do bring,
On *Abels* gift the fire descends from Skies,
But no such sign on false *Cain's* offering;
With sullen hateful looks he goes his wayes.
Hath thousand thoughts to end his brothers dayes,
Upon whose blood his future good he hopes to raise.

14

There *Abel* keeps his sheep, no ill he thinks,
His brother comes, then acts his fratricide,
The Virgin Earth, of blood her first draught drinks
But since that time she often hath been cloy'd;
The wretch with gastly face and dreadful mind,
Thinks each he sees will serve him in his kind,
Though none on Earth but kindred near then could he find.

15

Who fancyes not his looks now at the Barr,
His face like death, his heart with horror fraught,
Nor Male-factor ever felt like warr,
When deep dispair, with wish of life hath sought,
Branded with guilt, and crusht with treble woes,
A Vagabond to Land of *Nod*[1] he goes.
A City builds, that wals might him secure from foes.

16

Who thinks not oft upon the Fathers ages.
Their long descent, how nephews sons they saw,
The starry observations of those Sages,
And how their precepts to their sons were law,
How Adam sigh'd to see his Progeny,
Cloath'd all in his black sinfull Livery,
Who neither guilt, nor yet the punishment could fly.

17

Our Life compare we with their length of dayes
Who to the tenth of theirs doth now arrive?
And though thus short, we shorten many wayes,
Living so little while we are alive;
In eating, drinking, sleeping, vain delight
So unawares comes on perpetual night,
And puts all pleasures vain unto eternal flight.

18

When I behold the heavens as in their prime,
And then the earth (though old) stil clad in green,
The stones and trees, insensible of time,
Nor age nor wrinkle on their front are seen;
If winter come, and greeness then do fade,
A Spring returns, and they more youthfull made;
But Man grows old, lies down, remains where once he's laid.

[1] The unknown land east of Eden to which Cain was banished after slaying Abel.

20 [19]

By birth more noble then those creatures all,
Yet seems by nature and by custome curs'd,
No sooner born, but grief and care makes fall
That state obliterate he had at first:
Nor youth, nor strength, nor wisdom spring again
Nor habitations long their names retain,
But in oblivion to the final day remain.

20

Shall I then praise the heavens, the trees, the earth
Because their beauty and their strength last longer
Shall I wish there, or never to had birth,
Because they're bigger, and their bodyes stronger?
Nay, they shall darken, perish, fade and dye,
And when unmade, so ever shall they lye,
But man was made for endless immortality.

21

Under the cooling shadow of a stately Elm
Close sate I by a goodly Rivers side,
Where gliding streams the Rocks did overwhelm;
A lonely place, with pleasures dignifi'd.
I once that lov'd the shady woods so well,
Now thought the rivers did the trees excel,
And if the sun would ever shine, there would I dwell.

22

While on the stealing stream I fixt mine eye,
Which to the long'd for Ocean held its course,
I markt, nor crooks, nor rubs that there did lye
Could hinder ought,[2] but still augment its force:
O happy Flood, quoth I, that holds thy race
Till thou arrive at thy beloved place,
Nor is it rocks or shoals that can obstruct thy pace.

[2] aught: anything.

23

Nor is't enough, that thou alone may'st slide,
But hundred brooks in thy cleer waves do meet,
So hand in hand along with thee they glide
To *Thetis* house,[3] where all imbrace and greet:
Thou Emblem true, of what I count the best,
O could I lead my Rivolets to rest,
So may we press to that vast mansion, ever blest.

24

Ye Fish which in this liquid Region 'bide,
That for each season, have your habitation,
Now salt, now fresh where you think best to glide
To unknown coasts to give a visitation,
In Lakes and ponds, you leave your numerous fry,
So nature taught, and yet you know not why,
You watry folk that know not your felicity.

25

Look how the wantons frisk to tast the air,
Then to the colder bottome streight they dive,
Eftsoon to *Neptun's* glassie Hall repair
To see what trade they great ones there do drive,
Who forrage o're the spacious sea-green field,
And take the trembling prey before it yield,
Whose armour is their scales, their spreading fins their shield.

26

While musing thus with contemplation fed,
And thousand fancies buzzing in my brain,
The sweet-tongu'd Philomel[4] percht ore my head,
And chanted forth a most melodious strain
Which rapt me so with wonder and delight,
I judg'd my hearing better then my sight,
And wisht me wings with her a while to take my flight.

[3] the sea.
[4] the nightingale.

28 [27]

O merry Bird (said I) that fears no snares,
That neither toyles nor hoards up in thy barn,
Feels no sad thoughts, nor cruciating cares
To gain more good, or shun what might thee harm
Thy cloaths ne're wear, thy meat is every where,
Thy bed a bough, thy drink the water cleer,
Reminds not what is past, nor whats to come dost fear.

28

The dawning morn with songs thou dost prevent,[5]
Sets hundred notes unto thy feathered crew,
So each one tunes his pretty instrument,
And warbling out the old, begin anew,
And thus they pass their youth in summer season,
Then follow thee into a better Region,
Where winter's never felt by that sweet airy legion.

29

Man at the best a creature frail and vain,
In knowledg ignorant, in strength but weak,
Subject to sorrows, losses, sickness, pain,
Each storm his state, his mind, his body break,
From some of these he never finds cessation,
But day or night, within, without, vexation,
Troubles from foes, from friends, from dearest, near'st Relation.

30

And yet this sinfull creature, frail and vain,
This lump of wretchedness, of sin and sorrow,
This weather-beaten vessel wrackt with pain,
Joyes not in hope of an eternal morrow;
Nor all his losses, crosses and vexation,
In weight, in frequency and long duration
Can make him deeply groan for that divine Translation.

[5] precede.

31

The Mariner that on smooth waves doth glide,
Sings merrily, and steers his Barque with ease,
As if he had command of wind and tide,
And now become great Master of the seas;
But suddenly a storm spoiles all the sport,
And makes him long for a more quiet port,
Which 'gainst all adverse winds may serve for fort.

32

So he that saileth in this world of pleasure,
Feeding on sweets, that never bit of th' sowre,
That's full of friends, of honour and of treasure,
Fond fool, he takes this earth ev'n for heav'ns bower.
But sad affliction comes and makes him see
Here's neither honour, wealth, nor safety;
Only above is found all with security.

33

O Time the fatal wrack of mortal things,
That draws oblivions curtains over kings,
Their sumptuous monuments, men know them not,
Their names without a Record are forgot,
Their parts, their ports, their pomp's all laid in th' dust
Nor wit nor gold, nor buildings scape times rust;
But he whose name is grav'd in the white stone[6]
Shall last and shine when all of these are gone.

[As Weary Pilgrim, now at Rest]

As weary pilgrim, now at rest,
  Hugs with delight his silent nest
His wasted limbes, now lye full soft
  That myrie steps, have troden oft

[6] Rev ii 17: "To him that overcometh will I give to eat of the hidden manna, and will give him a white stone, and in the stone a new name written, which no man knoweth saving he that receiveth it."

Blesses himself, to think upon   5
  His dangers past, and travailes done,
The burning sun no more shall heat
  Nor stormy raines, on him shall beat.
The bryars and thornes no more shall scratch
  Nor hungry wolves at him shall catch   10
He erring pathes no more shall tread
  Nor wild fruits eate, in stead of bread,
For waters cold he doth not long
  For thirst no more shall parch his tongue
No rugged stones his feet shall gaule   15
  Nor stumps nor rocks cause him to fall
All cares and feares, he bids farwell
  And meanes in safity now to dwell.
A pilgrim I, on earth perplext
  With sinns with cares and sorrows vext   20
By age and paines brought to decay
  And my Clay house mouldring away
Oh how I long to be at rest
  And soare on high among the blest.
This body shall in silence sleep   25
  Mine eyes no more shall ever weep
No fainting fits shall me assaile
  Nor grinding paines my body fraile
With cares and fears ne'r cumbred be
  Nor losses know, nor sorrowes see   30
What tho my flesh shall there consume
  It is the bed Christ did perfume
And when a few yeares shall be gone
  This mortall shall be cloth'd upon
A Corrupt Carcasse downe it lyes   35
  A glorious body it shall rise
In weaknes and dishonour sowne
  In power 'tis rais'd by Christ alone
Then soule and body shall unite
  And of their maker have the sight   40
Such lasting joyes shall there behold
  As eare ne'r heard nor tongue e'er told
Lord make me ready for that day
  Then Come deare bridgrome Come away.

Aug: 31, [16]69

The Flesh and the Spirit[1]

In secret place where once I stood
Close by the Banks of *Lacrim*[2] flood
I heard two sisters reason on
Things that are past, and things to come;
One flesh was call'd, who had her eye 5
On worldly wealth and vanity;
The other Spirit, who did rear
Her thoughts unto a higher sphere:
Sister, quoth Flesh, what liv'st thou on
Nothing but Meditation? 10
Doth Contemplation feed thee so
Regardlesly to let earth goe?
Can Speculation satisfy
Notion without Reality?
Dost dream of things beyond the Moon 15
And dost thou hope to dwell there soon?
Hast treasures there laid up in store
That all in th' world thou count'st but poor?
Art fancy sick, or turn'd a Sot
To catch at shadowes which are not? 20
Come, come, Ile shew unto thy sence,
Industry hath its recompence.
What canst desire, but thou maist see
True substance in variety?
Doth honour like? acquire the same, 25
As some to their immortal fame:
And trophyes to thy name erect
Which wearing time shall ne're deject.
For riches dost thou long full sore?
Behold enough of precious store. 30
Earth hath more silver, pearls and gold,
Then eyes can see, or hands can hold.
Affect's thou pleasure? take thy fill,
Earth hath enough of what you will.
Then let not goe, what thou maist find, 35
For things unknown, only in mind.

[1] Cf. Romans vii for the Pauline theme: strife between flesh and spirit.
[2] lachrym, thus, river of tears.

Spir. Be still thou unregenerate part,
Disturb no more my setled heart,
For I have vow'd (and so will doe)
Thee as a foe, still to pursue.   40
And combate with thee will and must,
Untill I see thee laid in th' dust.
Sisters we are, ye[a] twins we be,
Yet deadly feud 'twixt thee and me;
For from one father are we not,   45
Thou by old Adam wast begot,
But my arise is from above,
Whence my dear father I do love.
Thou speakst me fair, but hatst me sore,
Thy flatt'ring shews Ile trust no more.   50
How oft thy slave, hast thou me made,
When I believ'd, what thou hast said,
And never had more cause of woe
Then when I did what thou bad'st doe.
Ile stop mine ears at these thy charms,   55
And count them for my deadly harms.
Thy sinfull pleasures I doe hate,
Thy riches are to me no bait,
Thine honours doe, nor will I love;
For my ambition lyes above.   60
My greatest honour it shall be
When I am victor over thee,
And triumph shall, with laurel head,
When thou my Captive shalt be led,
How I do live, thou need'st not scoff,   65
For I have meat thou know'st not off;[3]
The hidden Manna I doe eat,
The word of life it is my meat.
My thoughts do yield me more content
Then can thy hours in pleasure spent.   70
Nor are they shadows which I catch,
Nor fancies vain at which I snatch,
But reach at things that are so high,
Beyond thy dull Capacity;
Eternal substance I do see,   75
With which inriched I would be:
Mine Eye doth pierce the heavens, and see

[3] of.

What is Invisible to thee.
My garments are not silk nor gold,
Nor such like trash which Earth doth hold,⁣   80
But Royal Robes I shall have on,
More glorious then the glistring Sun;
My Crown not Diamonds, Pearls, and gold,
But such as Angels heads infold.
The City⁴ where I hope to dwell,⁣   85
There's none on Earth can parallel;
The stately Walls both high and strong,
Are made of pretious *Jasper* stone;
The Gates of Pearl, both rich and clear,
And Angels are for Porters there;⁣   90
The Streets thereof transparent gold,
Such as no Eye did e're behold,
A Chrystal River there doth run,
Which doth proceed from the Lambs Throne:
Of Life, there are the waters sure,⁣   95
Which shall remain for ever pure,
Nor Sun, nor Moon, they have no need,
For glory doth from God proceed:
No Candle there, nor yet Torch light,
For there shall be no darksome night.⁣   100
From sickness and infirmity,
For evermore they shall be free,
Nor withering age shall e're come there,
But beauty shall be bright and clear;
This City pure is not for thee,⁣   105
For things unclean there shall not be:
If I of Heaven may have my fill,
Take thou the world, and all that will.

⁴ Rev xxi 10: "And he carried me away in the spirit to a great and high mountain, and showed me that great city, the holy Jerusalem, descending out of heaven from God." The poet's description of the city in the ensuing lines follows closely the description in Revelation xxi and xxii.

The Four Seasons of the Year

Spring

Another four I've left yet to bring on,[1]
Of four times four the last *Quaternion*,
The Winter, Summer, Autumn and the Spring,
In season all these Seasons I shall bring:
Sweet Spring like man in his Minority,   5
At present claim'd, and had priority.
With smiling face and garments somewhat green,
She trim'd her locks, which late had frosted been,
Nor hot nor cold, she spake, but with a breath,
Fit to revive, the nummed earth from death.   10
Three months (quoth she) are 'lotted to my share
March, April, May of all the rest most fair.
Tenth of the first, *Sol* into *Aries* enters,
And bids defiance to all tedious winters,
Crosseth the Line,[2] and equals night and day,   15
(Stil adds to th' last til after pleasant *May*)
And now makes glad the darkned northern wights
Who for some months have seen but starry lights.
Now goes the Plow-man to his merry toyle,
He might unloose his winter locked soyl: 20
The Seeds-man too, doth lavish out his grain,
In hope the more he casts, the more to gain:
The Gardner now superfluous branches lops,
And poles erects for his young clambring hops.
Now digs then sowes his herbs, his flowers and roots   25
And carefully manures his trees of fruits.
The *Pleiades their influence*[3] now give,
And all that seem'd as dead afresh doth live.
The croaking frogs, whom nipping winter kil'd
Like birds now chirp, and hop about the field,   30
The Nightingale, the black bird and the Thrush
Now tune their layes, on sprayes of every bush.

[1] In *The Tenth Muse* this poem was preceded by poems on "The Four Elements," "The Four Humours," and "The Four Ages of Man."

[2] Tropic of Cancer.

[3] The Pleiades rise in the spring sky and are thus a sign for seed sowing; they set in the fall sky and are then a sign for harvest.

The wanton frisking Kid, and soft-fleec'd Lambs
Do jump and play before their feeding Dams,
The tender tops of budding grass they crop,   35
They joy in what they have, but more in hope:
For though the frost hath lost his binding power,
Yet many a fleece of snow and stormy shower
Doth darken *Sol's* bright eye, makes us remember
The pinching North-west wind of cold *December*.   40
My second moneth is *April*, green and fair,
Of longer dayes, and a more temperate Air:
The Sun in *Taurus* keeps his residence,
And with his warmer beams glanceth from thence.
This is the month whose fruitful showrs produces   45
All set and sown for all delights and uses:
The Pear, the Plum, and Apple-tree now flourish
The grass grows long the hungry beast to nourish.
The Primrose pale, and azure violet
Among the virduous[4] grass hath nature set,   50
That when the Sun on's Love (the earth) doth shine,
These might as lace set out her garment fine.
The fearfull bird his little house now builds
In trees and walls, in Cities and in fields.
The outside strong, the inside warm and neat;   55
A natural Artificer compleat:
The clocking hen her chirping chickins leads
With wings and beak defends them from the gleads.[5]
My next and last is fruitfull pleasant *May*,
Wherein the earth is clad in rich aray,   60
The Sun now enters loving *Gemini*,
And heats us with the glances of his eye,
Our thicker rayment makes us lay aside
Lest by his fervor we be torrifi'd.
All flowers the Sun now with his beams discloses,   65
Except the double pinks and matchless Roses.
Now swarms the busy, witty, honey-Bee,
Whose praise deserves a page from more then me
The cleanly Huswifes Dary's now in th' prime,
Her shelves and firkins[6] fill'd for winter time.   70
The meads with Cowslips, Honey-suckles dight,

[4] green-growing.
[5] the European kite.
[6] small casks for butter, lard, etc.

One hangs his head, the other stands upright:
But both rejoyce at th' heavens clear smiling face,
More at her showers, which water them a space.
For fruits my Season yields the early Cherry,   75
The hasty Peas, and wholsome cool Strawberry.
More solid fruits require a longer time,
Each Season hath his fruit, so hath each Clime:
Each man his own peculiar excellence,
But none in all that hath preheminence.   80
Sweet fragrant Spring, with thy short pittance fly
Let some describe thee better then can I.
Yet above all this priviledg is thine,
Thy dayes still lengthen without least decline.

Summer

When *Spring* had done, the *Summer* did begin,   85
With melted tauny face, and garments thin,
Resembling Fire, Choler, and Middle age,
As *Spring* did Air, Blood, Youth in's equipage.
Wiping the sweat from of[f] her face that ran,
With hair all wet she puffing thus began;   90
Bright *June, July* and *August* hot are mine,
In'th first *Sol* doth in crabbed *Cancer* shine.
His progress to the North now's fully done,
Then retrograde must be my burning Sun,
Who to his southward Tropick[7] still is bent,   95
Yet doth his parching heat but more augment
Though he decline, because his flames so fair,
Have throughly dry'd the earth, and heat the air.
Like as an Oven that long time hath been heat,
Whose vehemency at length doth grow so great,   100
That if you do withdraw her burning store,
Tis for a time as fervent as before.
Now go those frolick Swains, the Shepherd Lads
To wash the thick cloth'd flocks with pipes full glad
In the cool streams they labour with delight   105
Rubbing their dirty coats till they look white:
Whose fleece when finely spun and deeply dy'd
With Robes thereof Kings have been dignifi'd.
Blest rustick Swains, your pleasant quiet life,

[7] Tropic of Capricorn.

Hath envy bred in Kings that were at strife, 110
Careless of worldly wealth you sing and pipe,
Whilst they'r imbroyl'd in wars and troubles rife:
Which made great *Bajazet* cry out in's woes,
Oh happy shepherd which hath not to lose.
Orthobulus, nor yet *Sebastia* great, 115
But whist'leth to thy flock in cold and heat.[8]
Viewing the Sun by day, the Moon by night
Endimions, Dianaes dear delight,
Upon the grass resting your healthy limbs,
By purling Brooks looking how fishes swims. 120
If pride within your lowly Cells ere haunt,
Of him that was Shepherd then King go vaunt.
This moneth the Roses are distil'd in glasses,
Whose fragrant smel all made perfumes surpasses
The Cherry, Gooseberry are now in th' prime, 125
And for all sorts of Pease, this is the time.
July my next, the hott'st in all the year,
The sun through *Leo* now takes his Career,
Whose flaming breath doth melt us from afar,
Increased by the star Canicular. 130
This month from *Julius Caesar* took its name,
By Romans celebrated to his fame.
Now go the Mowers to their flashing toyle,
The Meadowes of their riches to dispoyle,
With weary strokes, they take all in their way, 135
Bearing the burning heat of the long day.
The forks and Rakes do follow them amain,
Which makes the aged fields look young again.
The groaning Carts do bear away this prize.
To Stacks and Barns where it for Fodder lyes. 140
My next and last is *August* fiery hot
(For much, the *Southward* Sun abateth not)

[8] "When *Tamerlane* had taken *Sebastia,* hee put all the men to the sword, and bringing the women and children into the fields without the citie, there over-ran them with his horsemen, excepting some few which were reserved for prisoners. As also that *Baiazet* there lost his eldest sonne *Erthogruel* (of some called *Orthobules*) whose death with the losse of the citie so much grieved him (as is reported) that marching with his great armie against *Tamerlane,* and by the way hearing a country shepheard merrily reposing himself with his homely pipe . . . break forth in these words: O happie shepheard, which haddest neither *Orthobules* nor *Sebastia* to loose. . . ." Richard Knolles, *The Generall Historie of the Turkes* (London, 1610), p. 216. Bajazet I became Sultan of the Turks in 1389, and died in 1403.

The Moneth he keeps with *Virgo* for a space,
The dryed Earth is parched with his face.
August of great *Augustus* took its name, 145
Romes second Emperour of lasting fame,
With sickles now the bending Reapers goe
The russling tress of *terra* down to mowe;
And bundles up in sheaves, the weighty wheat,
Which after Manchet[9] makes for Kings to eat: 150
The Barly, Rye and Pease should first had place,
Although their bread have not so white a face.
The Carter leads all home with whistling voyce,
He plow'd with pain, but reaping doth rejoyce;
His sweat, his toyle, his careful wakeful nights, 155
His fruitful Crop abundantly requites.
Now's ripe the Pear, Pear-plumb, and Apricock,
The prince of plumbs, whose stone's as hard as Rock
The Summer seems but short, the Autumn hasts
To shake his fruits, of most delicious tasts 160
Like good old Age, whose younger juicy Roots
Hath still ascended, to bear goodly fruits.
Until his head be gray, and strength be gone.
Yet then appears the worthy deeds he'th done:
To feed his boughs exhausted hath his sap, 165
Then drops his fruits into the eaters lap.

Autumn

Of *Autumn* moneths *September* is the prime,
Now day and night are equal in each Clime,
The twelfth of this *Sol* riseth in the Line,
And doth in poizing *Libra* this month shine. 170
The vintage now is ripe, the grapes are prest,
Whose lively liquor oft is curs'd and blest:
For nought so good, but it may be abused,
But its a precious juice when well its used.
The raisins now in clusters dryed be, 175
The Orange, Lemon dangle on the tree:
The Pomegranate, the Fig are ripe also,
And Apples now their yellow sides do show.
Of Almonds, Quinces, Wardens,[10] and of Peach,

9 superior white bread.
10 medium-size winter pear, used chiefly for cooking.

The season's now at hand of all and each.   180
Sure at this time, time first of all began,
And in this moneth was made apostate Man:
For then in *Eden* was not only seen,
Boughs full of leaves, or fruits unripe or green,
Or withered stocks, which were all dry and dead,   185
But trees with goodly fruits replenished;
Which shews nor Summer, Winter, nor the Spring
Our Grand-Sire was of Paradice made King:
Nor could that temp'rate Clime such difference make,
If scited[11] as the most Judicious take.   190
October is my next, we hear in this
The Northern winter-blasts begin to hiss.
In *Scorpio* resideth now the Sun,
And his declining heat is almost done.
The fruitless Trees all withered now do stand,   195
Whose sapless yellow leavs, by winds are fan'd,
Which notes when youth and strength have past their prime
Decrepit age must also have its time.
The Sap doth slily creep towards the Earth
There rests, until the Sun give it a birth.   200
So doth old Age still tend unto his grave,
Where also he his winter time must have;
But when the Sun of righteousness draws nigh,
His dead old stock, shall mount again on high.
November is my last, for Time doth haste,   205
We now of winters sharpness 'gins to tast.
This moneth the Sun's in *Sagitarius*,
So farre remote, his glances warm not us.
Almost at shortest is the shorten'd day,
The *Northern* pole beholdeth not one ray.   210
Now *Greenland, Groanland,*[12] *Finland, Lapland,* see
No Sun, to lighten their obscurity:
Poor wretches that in total darkness lye,
With minds more dark then is the dark'ned Sky.
Beaf, Brawn, and Pork are now in great request,   215
And solid meats our stomacks can digest.
This time warm cloaths, full diet, and good fires,
Our pinched flesh, and hungry mawes requires:
Old, cold, dry Age and Earth *Autumn* resembles,

[11] cited.
[12] Grönland (Danish).

And Melancholy which most of all dissembles.   220
I must be short, and shorts, the short'ned day,
What winter hath to tell, now let him say.

Winter

Cold, moist, young flegmy[13] winter now doth lye
In swadling Clouts, like new born Infancy
Bound up with frosts, and furr'd with hail and snows,   225
And like an Infant, still it taller grows;
December is my first, and now the Sun
To th' Southward *Tropick*, his swift race doth run:
This moneth he's hous'd in horned *Capricorn*,
From thence he 'gins to length the shortned morn,   230
Through *Christendome* with great Feastivity,
Now's held, (but ghest)[14] for blest Nativity.
Cold frozen *January* next comes in,
Chilling the blood and shrinking up the skin;
In *Aquarius* now keeps the long wisht Sun,   235
And Northward his unwearied Course doth run:
The day much longer then it was before,
The cold not lessened, but augmented more.
Now Toes and Ears, and Fingers often freeze,
And Travellers their noses sometimes leese.[15]   240
Moist snowie *February* is my last,
I care not how the winter time doth haste.
In *Pisces* now the golden Sun doth shine,
And Northward still approaches to the Line,
The Rivers 'gin to ope, the snows to melt,   245
And some warm glances from his face are felt;
Which is increased by the lengthen'd day,
Until by's heat, he drive all cold away,
And thus the year in Circle runneth round:
Where first it did begin, in th' and its found.   250
My Subjects bare, my Brain is bad,
Or better Lines you should have had:
The first fell in so nat'rally,
I knew not how to pass it by;
The last, though bad I could not mend,   255

13 cold and moist.
14 guest.
15 lose.

Accept therefore of what is pen'd,
And all the faults that you shall spy
Shall at your feet for pardon cry.

The Vanity of all worldly things

As he said vanity,[1] so vain say I,
Oh! vanity, O vain all under Sky;
Where is the man can say, lo I have found
On brittle Earth a Consolation sound?
What is't in honour to be set on high?   5
No, they like Beasts and Sons of men shall dye:
And whil'st they live, how oft doth turn their fate,
He's now a captive, that was King of late.
What is't in wealth, great Treasures to obtain?
No, that's but labour, anxious care and pain,   10
He heaps up riches, and he heaps up sorrow,
It's his to day, but who's his heir to morrow?
What then? Content in pleasures canst thou find,
More vain then all, that's but to grasp the wind.
The sensual senses for a time they please,   15
Mean while the conscience rage, who shall appease?
What is't in beauty? No that's but a snare,
They're foul enough to day, that once were fair.
What is't in flowring youth, or manly age?
The first is prone to vice, the last to rage.   20
Where is it then, in wisdom, learning arts?
Sure if on earth, it must be in those parts:
Yet these the wisest man of men did find
But vanity, vexation of mind.
And he that knowes the most, doth still bemoan   25
He knows not all that here is to be known.
What is it then, to doe as *Stoicks* tell,
Nor laugh, nor weep, let things go ill or well.
Such Stoicks are but Stocks[2] such teaching vain,
While man is man, he shall have ease or pain.   30
If not in honour, beauty, age nor treasure,

[1] Eccles i 1–2: "The words of the Preacher, the son of David, king in Jerusalem. Vanity of vanities, saith the Preacher, vanity of vanities; all is vanity."
[2] dull, stupid, or lifeless persons. Cf. Shakespeare, *Taming of the Shrew*, I i 31: "Let's be no stoics nor no stocks, I pray."

Nor yet in learning, wisdome, youth nor pleasure,
Where shall I climb, sound, seek search or find
That *Summum Bonum* which may stay my mind?
There is a path, no vultures eye hath seen,   35
Where Lion fierce, nor lions whelps have been,
Which leads unto that living Crystal Fount,
Who drinks thereof, the world doth nought account
The depth and sea have said tis not in me,
With pearl and gold, it shall not valued be.   40
For Saphire, Onix, Topaz who would change:
Its hid from eyes of men, they count it strange.
Death and destruction the same hath heard,
But where and what it is, from heaven's declar'd,
It brings to honour, which shall ne're decay,   45
It stores with wealth which time can't wear away.
It yieldeth pleasures far beyond conceit,
And truly beautifies without deceit,
Nor strength, nor wisdome nor fresh youth shall fade
Nor death shall see, but are immortal made.   50
This pearl of price, this tree of life, this spring
Who is possessed of, shall reign a King.
Nor change of state, nor cares shall ever see,
But wear his crown unto eternity:
This satiates the Soul, this stayes the mind,   55
And all the rest, but Vanity we find.

In memory of my dear grand-child Elizabeth
Bradstreet, who deceased August, 1665.[1]
being a year and half old

1

Farewel dear babe, my hearts too much content,
Farewel sweet babe, the pleasure of mine eye,
Farewel fair flower that for a space was lent,
Then ta'en away unto Eternity.
Blest babe why should I once bewail thy fate,
Or sigh the dayes so soon were terminate;
Sith thou art setled in an Everlasting state.

[1] Elizabeth, the eldest child of Anne Bradstreet's son Samuel.

2

By nature Trees do rot when they are grown.
And Plumbs and Apples throughly ripe do fall,
And Corn and grass are in their season mown,
And time brings down what is both strong and tall.
But plants new set to be eradicate,
And buds new blown, to have so short a date,
Is by his hand alone that guides nature and fate.

To My Dear and Loving Husband

If ever two were one, then surely we.
If ever man were lov'd by wife, then thee;
If ever wife was happy in a man,
Compare with me ye women if you can.
I prize thy love more then whole Mines of gold,
Or all the riches that the East doth hold.
My love is such that Rivers cannot quench,
Nor ought[1] but love from thee, give recompence.
Thy love is such I can no way repay,
The heavens reward thee manifold I pray.
Then while we live, in love lets so persever,
That when we live no more, we may live ever.

A Letter to Her Husband, Absent upon Publick Employment

My head, my heart, mine Eyes, my life, nay more,
My joy, my Magazine of earthly store,
If two be one, as surely thou and I,
How stayest thou there, whilst I at *Ipswich* lye?
So many steps, head from the heart to sever   5
If but a neck, soon should we be together:
I like the earth this season, mourn in black,
My Sun is gone so far in's Zodiack,
Whom whilst I 'joy'd, nor storms, nor frosts I felt,
His warmth such frigid colds did cause to melt.   10

[1] aught.

My chilled limbs now nummed lye forlorn;
Return, return sweet *Sol* from *Capricorn;*[1]
In this dead time, alas, what can I more
Then view those fruits which through thy heat I bore?
Which sweet contentment yield me for a space,   15
True living Pictures of their Fathers face.
O strange effect! now thou art *Southward* gone,
I weary grow, the tedious day so long;
But when thou *Northward* to me shalt return,
I wish my Sun may never set, but burn   20
Within the Cancer[2] of my glowing breast,
The welcome house of him my dearest guest.
Where ever, ever stay, and go not thence,
Till natures sad decree shall call thee hence;
Flesh of thy flesh, bone of thy bone,   25
I here, thou there, yet both but one.

Another [*Letter to her Husband, Absent upon Publick Employment*]

As loving Hind that (Hartless) wants her Deer,
Scuds through the woods and Fern with harkning ear,
Perplext, in every bush and nook doth pry,
Her dearest Deer, might answer ear or eye;
So doth my anxious soul, which now doth miss,   5
A dearer Dear (far dearer Heart) then this.
Still wait with doubts, and hopes, and failing eye,
His voice to hear, or person to discry.
Or as the pensive Dove doth all alone
(On withered bough) most uncouthly bemoan   10
The absence of her Love, and loving Mate,
Whose loss hath made her so unfortunate:
Ev'n thus doe I, with many a deep sad groan
Bewail my turtle true, who now is gone,
His presence and his safe return, still wooes,   15
With thousand dolefull sighs and mournfull Cooes.
Or as the loving Mullet, that true Fish,
Her fellow lost, nor joy nor life do wish,

[1] i.e. winter. The sun enters the zodiacal sign Capricorn about December 21.
[2] i.e. summer. The sun enters the zodiacal sign Cancer about June 21.

But lanches[1] on that shore, there for to dye,
Where she her captive husband doth espy.   20
Mine being gone, I lead a joyless life,
I have a loving phere,[2] yet seem no wife:
But worst of all, to him can't steer my course,
I here, he there, alas, both kept by force:
Return my Dear, my joy, my only Love,   25
Unto thy Hinde, thy Mullet and thy Dove,
Who neither joyes in pasture, house, nor streams,
The substance gone, O me, these are but dreams.
Together at one Tree, oh let us brouze,[3]
And like two Turtles roost within one house,   30
And like the Mullets in one River glide,
Let's still remain but one, till death divide.

> *Thy loving Love and Dearest Dear,*
> *At home, abroad, and every where.*

On my dear Grand-child Simon Bradstreet[1] Who dyed on 16. Novemb. 1669. being but a moneth and one day old

No sooner come, but gone, and fal'n asleep,
Acquaintance short, yet parting caus'd us weep,
Three flours,[2] two scarcely blown, the last i'th' bud,
Cropt by th' Almighties hand; yet is he good,
With dreadful awe before him let's be mute,
Such was his will, but why, let's not dispute,
With humble hearts and mouths put in the dust,
Let's say he's merciful as well as just.
He will return, and make up all our losses,
And smile again, after our bitter crosses.
Go pretty babe, go rest with Sisters twain
Among the blest in endless joyes remain.

[1] launches: leaps.
[2] var. of *fere:* companion, spouse, consort.
[3] browse.
[1] Fourth child of Anne Bradstreet's eldest son, Samuel.
[2] Elizabeth, Anne, and Simon, Samuel Bradstreet's children.

Here followes some verses upon the burning of our
House, July 10th, 1666. Copyed out of a
loose Paper

In silent night when rest I took,
For sorrow neer I did not look,
I waken'd was with thundring nois
And Piteous shreiks of dreadfull voice.
That fearfull sound of fire and fire,   5
Let no man know is my Desire.

I, starting up, the light did spye,
And to my God my heart did cry
To strengthen me in my Distresse
And not to leave me succourlesse.   10
Then coming out beheld a space,
The flame consume my dwelling place.

And, when I could no longer look,
I blest his Name that gave and took,
That layd my goods now in the dust: 15
Yea so it was, and so 'twas just.
It was his own: it was not mine;
Far be it that I should repine.

He might of All justly bereft,
But yet sufficient for us left.   20
When by the Ruines oft I past,
My sorrowing eyes aside did cast,
And here and there the places spye
Where oft I sate, and long did lye.

Here stood that Trunk, and there that chest;   25
There lay that store I counted best:
My pleasant things in ashes lye,
And them behold no more shall I.
Under thy roof no guest shall sitt,
Nor at thy Table eat a bitt.   30

No pleasant tale shall 'ere be told,
Nor things recounted done of old.
No Candle 'ere shall shine in Thee,
Nor bridegroom's voice ere heard shall bee.
In silence ever shalt thou lye;   35
Adeiu, Adeiu; All's vanity.

Then streight I 'gin my heart to chide,
And did thy wealth on earth abide?
Didst fix thy hope on mouldring dust,
The arm of flesh didst make thy trust?   40
Raise up thy thoughts above the skye
That dunghill mists away may flie.

Thou hast an house on high erect,
Fram'd by that mighty Architect,
With glory richly furnished,   45
Stands permanent though this bee fled.
It's purchased, and paid for too
By him who hath enough to doe.

A Prise so vast as is unknown,
Yet, by his Gift, is made thine own.   50
Ther's wealth enough, I need no more;
Farewell my Pelf, farewell my Store.
The world no longer let me Love,
My hope and Treasure lyes Above.

MICHAEL WIGGLESWORTH

(1631–1705)

No copy of the original edition of Michael Wigglesworth's *Day of Doom* survives today. Within one year of its publication in 1662 all eighteen hundred copies of the dramatic account of Judgment Day had been sold and were literally being read to pieces. No single poem—indeed no other work of literature—so captured the popular imagination of Puritan America as did *The Day of Doom*. The sale of the first edition alone meant there was in circulation one copy of the poem for each thirty-five New Englanders, a figure all the more impressive when one recalls that just 20 per cent of the population were officially church members. Immediately after that first edition sale, *The Day of Doom* was reissued in both America and England, and was for over one hundred years to have a popular influence second only to the Bible and the Shorter Catechism. It was, in fact, assigned for memorization along with the Catechism, and a century after its first publication New England grandmothers and grand-fathers were able still to recite *The Day of Doom* from memory.

The author of this doctrinaire, Calvinistic epic was, according to Cotton Mather, "a feeble, little shadow of a man." Certainly, as far as we know, the Reverend Michael Wigglesworth exhibited no youthful inclinations toward literary art. Born in Yorkshire, England, in 1631, the son of a successful non-conformist businessman, Michael emigrated with his parents to New England in 1638 when he was seven years old. Only after a stormy seven-week sea voyage did the Wigglesworths and fellow Yorkshire voyagers of the same religious persuasion reach Charlestown, Massachusetts, where the family remained for seven weeks before moving to their new home at Quinnipiac, renamed New Haven by the English settlers.

It may have been a home in a spiritual sense, but New Haven was physically little more than a wilderness. The plot of ground assigned to the newcomers had on it no shelter, and Michael Wigglesworth recalled in writing that the family spent their first year in a cellar partly underground, where heavy rain broke in at least once. In the following year his father built a house and assumed duties as a planter, pasturing his animals in the common meadow and cultivating the twenty-two acres allotted him.

Yet Michael Wigglesworth's father was no rude farmer, content to see his son grow up unlettered. Like virtually all New England Puritans, he placed a high value on education. For if an individual were to be able to worship God in the best way, then he must know God's will. And that will was revealed in Scripture, which could only be read and interpreted properly by those who knew how, those who had been educated. This is not to say, of course, that all the simple, unschooled creatures of God were damned by Him from their lack of formal education. Not so. But the Puritans believed that from the time of man's Fall, he was depraved, ruined. This was man's fault entirely, and it was only through God's great mercy, His gift of grace to man, that some humans would be saved to have eternal life. Meanwhile, man must make do on earth as best he could, and since his faculties for understanding were impaired, he needed education to apprehend the will of God. There were "dark places" in the Scripture that no amount of well-meaning, earnest faith could help explain. One needed education for that. And for education Goodman Edward Wigglesworth sent his son Michael to school.

For the next two years the boy studied nothing but Latin, which was then considered a necessity for the educated man needing a first-hand familiarity with the classical writers. Under the tutelage of Ezekiel Cheever, who later became the famous master at the Boston Latin School, Michael Wigglesworth learned quickly. Doubtless he would have continued his education uninterrupted had it not been for a crippling injury which left his father "lame," weak and suffering from vertigo, and unable to carry on the farm work alone. By now there was another mouth to feed, that of Michael's sister, and the boy was withdrawn from school to work in the fields at home.

It soon became clear that Michael Wigglesworth had no talent for farm work, and though he was by his own admission not eager to return to a school whose lessons he had long ago forgotten, the boy submitted to his father's wishes that he resume his studies in preparation for entrance into Harvard. It was at considerable sacrifice that the still-invalid husbandman of modest income saw his son through three preparatory years, and then through the college.

His sacrifice was not in vain. Michael Wigglesworth completed the three-year Harvard program to graduate first in his class. In a curriculum that emphasized logic, rhetoric, Greek, Hebrew, ethics, and metaphysics, young Wigglesworth intended ultimately to prepare for a career as a physician. However, he recounts how at Harvard he felt the experience of God's saving grace working within him, and how he began submitting to God's will rather than to his own. This individual experience of God's grace was central to Puritan theology, for only with grace could one be saved; otherwise he was eternally damned, no matter what the conduct of his life. The Puritan individual's knowledge of his salvation followed a pattern: first he must feel his depravity, his utter unworthiness before God, and despair of high spiritual attainment. Thus humiliated, the sinner would begin to feel God stirring his heart, and only after long prayer and self-examination would he come to a knowledge of Christ having redeemed him, justified him in God. Then he would know that God had chosen him as one of the saints, not through mystical union (for Puritans were not mystics) nor through a tabulation of good works counted against sinful ones, but rather through a soul-searching self-examination accompanied by prayer and supplication. With this awareness Michael Wigglesworth decided to become a minister.

When he had received his bachelor's degree Wigglesworth was called as pastor to Salem, Cambridge, and Hartford, but he decided instead to remain at Harvard as a tutor to undergraduates at a salary of two pounds annually, while studying for his master's degree in a program leaving him free to pursue his studies as he wished. Wigglesworth took his tutorial duties seriously; he felt a responsibility not only for the academic welfare of his charges but also for their spiritual development. That they occasionally displayed the animal spirits typical of youth dismayed him, and at one point we find Wigglesworth upbraiding himself in his diary for turning his attention during a church service from God to his students. It was a mental digression he found unpardonable. During his graduate school years, also, Wigglesworth records the struggles of his own backsliding soul. Though he had felt God's grace working within him, that was no reason as a Puritan to relax his spiritual vigil. To do so would be to commit the grievous sin of pride. It was at this time that Wigglesworth began to suffer from the poor health that was to plague him until the last twenty years of his life, and to impair his ability to carry out fully his ministerial duties.

When Wigglesworth achieved his master's degree in 1656, he accepted a call as minister from Malden, Massachusetts, and then wed Mary Reyner, the first of his three wives. Malden was not a large community and, perhaps because it was rural, had not easily found a minister. There had been a history of factional strife resulting in the departure of one too-liberal divine, and though Wigglesworth protested that his poor health might keep him from his duties, the church at Malden pressed him to accept the call. When he had been there just three years, his wife died, leaving him one daughter. He did not marry again for twenty years; then Martha Mudge, his housekeeper, became his second wife and subsequently the mother of six of his children. Ten months after her death in 1690 Wigglesworth married Sybil Sparhawk Avery, a physician's widow with three children, who was to bear him one son. One argument in Wigglesworth's proposal to her was that, as a physician's widow, she could be helpful to him, another physician.

For as his years at Malden passed, Wigglesworth had become more physician than regular minister. His precarious health had made it necessary that the church engage additional ministerial colleagues to assist him. For a community to have two divines, one as minister and one as teacher, was not unusual at that time, but in Malden Wigglesworth was seldom able to bear an equal share of duties.

As minister and physician, Wigglesworth exerted no small influence, yet his power in the pulpit and at the bedside never matched the effect of his *Day of Doom*. What he set out to do in his verses, subtitled *A Poetical Description of the Great and Last Judgment*, was to present in easily memorized lines the chief tenets of New England Puritanism. In this he succeeded. He set his poem on a Judgment Day come suddenly to an unsuspecting and carnal world. In ballad lines of seven feet, "fourteeners," Wigglesworth depicts the righteous sheep assembled at God's right hand, with the sinning goats herded at the left. The virtuous sheep are listed according to kind, and then there is a cataloguing of the sinners, from hypocrites to procrastinators to Sabbath-breakers to those God simply chose not to save. Divine rewards and punishments are meted out, and the trial finally ends after two hundred and twenty-four stanzas of rhythmic and at times powerful narrative.

Perhaps no poem in American literature has been so maligned as *The Day of Doom*. It has been repeatedly denounced as inexorably stern doggerel by those who would have it be what it is not. In order to understand what Wigglesworth was about, it is worth while to glance at one sentence from his college oration entitled "The Praise of Eloquence," which he probably delivered at Harvard in 1650. Discussing the uses of written and spoken eloquence, Wigglesworth argues that it "doth not only revive the things known but secretly convey life into the hearers' understanding rousing it out of its former slumber, quickening it beyond its natural vigor, elevating it above its ordinary conception." This was what Wigglesworth intended his verse to do, to stir his readers to a heightened emotional awareness of what they already knew intellectually. Certainly he was not offering them new or startling doctrine, for the awful Day of Reckoning was traditional throughout Christianity, and the particularly Puritan doctrinal coloration of Wigglesworth's poem was familiar to those who read the poem in book form or from the broadsides on which it was also printed. Wigglesworth's eloquence is directed at "the apprehension of the meanest." He speaks in plain style to an audience on whom subtle literary and historical allusion might be lost, an audience ill-equipped to appreciate intricate syntax and sophisticated diction. That he could often rise to dramatic levels in *The Day of Doom* is all to his credit. And it must be said that, whatever its shortcomings, Wigglesworth's *Day of Doom* succeeds on its own terms.

While *The Day of Doom* is Wigglesworth's best-known work, his poem *God's Controversy With New England* is also significant. Just as he intended to communicate to his readers the imperative need to stand in awe of God's reckoning, so he wished to remind them that they were softening from their earlier vigilance and that God's patience with them was wearing thin. Written on the occasion of a drought in 1662, *God's Controversy* depicted New England "planted, prospered, declining, threatned, punished." Since the Puritans believed that all historical events, no matter how small, were deliberate acts of God, it was not unusual that the drought be interpreted as divine warning to the backsliding churches of the Bay. The feeling that some of the early zeal was disappearing in New England had early become a major theme, expounded both from pulpit and press. Thus Wigglesworth was arguing in verse a belief prevalent in New England—that prosperity was taking its spiritual toll, and that God was accordingly displeased.

In addition to *The Day of Doom* and *God's Controversy*, Wigglesworth wrote a large number of miscellaneous poems in several verse forms. The intention of his "Meat out of the Eater; or, Meditations concerning the necessity, end, and usefulness of afflictions unto God's children, all tending to prepare them for and comfort them under the Cross" is self-explanatory. With death striking fast and often, and to no apparent purpose (though any good Puritan would concede divine purpose operating), the Puritans found comfort in a literature that suggested a meaning and use for their suffering. First published in 1669, "Meat out of the Eater" went through four editions in ten years.

Considering the range of Wigglesworth's poetry, one sees not only quantity but variety. There is narration and description as well as the lyrical and dramatic, in tones ranging from didactic to hortatory. Wigglesworth was capable of varied patterns of meter and rhyme, and he spoke forcefully while deliberately employing images comprehensible to his audience. His was, of course, a voice of New England Puritanism, an uncompromising and urgent voice. But it was a poetic voice as well, and one that ranks Michael Wigglesworth among the major seventeenth-century American writers of verse.

God's Controversy with New-England

Written in the time of the great drought Anno 1662
By a lover of New-England's Prosperity

Isaiah, 5. 4.—What could have been done more to my vineyard, that I have not done in it? wherefore, when I looked that it should bring forth grapes, brought it forth wilde grapes?

The Authors request unto the Reader

Good christian Reader judge me not
    As too censorious,
For pointing at those faults of thine
    Which are notorious.

For if those faults be none of thine 5
   I do not thee accuse:
But if they be, to hear thy faults
   Why shouldest thou refuse.

I blame not thee to spare my self:
   But first at home begin, 10
And judge my self, before that I
   Reproove anothers sin.
Nor is it I that thee reproove
   Let God himself be heard
Whose awfull providence's voice 15
   No man may disregard.

Quod Deus omnipotens regali voce minatur,
Quod tibi proclamant uno simul ore prophetæ
Quodq' ego cum lachrymis testor de numinis irâ,
Tu leve comentū ne ducas, Lector Amice.[1] 20

New-England planted, prospered, declining, threatned, punished

Beyond the great Atlantick flood
   There is a region vast,
A country where no English foot
   In former ages past:
A waste and howling wilderness, 25
   Where none inhabited
But hellish fiends, and brutish men
   That Devils worshiped.

This region was in darkness plac't
   Far off from heavens light, 30
Amidst the shaddows of grim death
   And of eternal night.
For there the Sun of righteousness
   Had never made to shine
The light of his sweet countenance, 35
   And grace which is divine:

[1] "What God omnipotent tells with a ruler's voice,
What the prophets proclaim unto you with one mouth,
And what I with many tears testify to in wrath,
You may not consider lightly, Dear Reader."

Until the time drew nigh wherein
  The glorious Lord of hostes
Was pleasd to lead his armies forth
  Into those forrein coastes.   40
At whose approach the darkness sad
  Soon vanished away,
And all the shaddows of the night
  Were turnd to lightsome day.

The stubborn he in pieces brake,   45
  Like vessels made of clay:
And those that sought his peoples hurt
  He turned to decay.
Those curst Amalekites,[2] that first
  Lift up their hand on high   50
To fight against Gods Israel,
  Were ruin'd fearfully.

Thy terrours on the Heathen folk,
  O Great Jehovah, fell:
The fame of thy great acts, o Lord,   55
  Did all the nations quell.
Some hid themselves for fear of thee
  In forrests wide and great:
Some to thy people croutching came,
  For favour to entreat.   60

Some were desirous to be taught
  The knowledge of thy wayes,
And being taught, did soon accord
  Therein to spend their dayes.
Thus were the fierce and barbarous   65
  Brought to civility,
And those that liv'd like beasts (or worse)
  To live religiously.

O happiest of dayes wherein
  The blind received sight,
And those that had no eyes before   70
  Were made to see the light!
The wilderness hereat rejoyc't,
  The woods for joy did sing,

[2] a marauding Bedouin tribe settled about Kadesh who, according to Gen xxxvi 12, were descended from Esau; i.e. any marauders.

The vallys and the little hills   75
    Thy praises ecchoing.

Here was the hiding place, which thou,
    Jehovah, didst provide
For thy redeemed ones, and where
    Thou didst thy jewels hide   80
In per'lous times, and saddest dayes
    Of sack-cloth and of blood,
When th' overflowing scourge did pass
    Through Europe, like a flood.

While almost all the world beside   85
    Lay weltring in their gore:
We, only we, enjoyd such peace
    As none enjoyd before.
No forrein foeman did us fray,
    Nor threat'ned us with warrs: 90
We had no enemyes at home,
    Nor no domestick jarrs.

The Lord had made (such was his grace)
    For us a Covenant
Both with the men, and with the beasts,   95
    That in this desert haunt:
So that through places wilde and waste
    A single man, disarm'd,
Might journey many hundred miles,
    And not at all be harm'd.   100

Amidst the solitary woods
    Poor travellers might sleep
As free from danger as at home,
    Though no man watch did keep.
Thus were we priviledg'd with peace,   105
    Beyond what others were.
Truth, Mercy, Peace, with Righteousness,
    Took up their dwelling here.

Our Governour[3] was of our selves,
    And all his Bretheren,   110
For wisdom and true piety,
    Select, and chosen men.

[3] John Endecott, installed May 23, 1655, and re-elected annually until 1665.

Who, Ruling in the fear of God,
   The righteous cause maintained,
And all injurious violence,   115
   And wickedness, restrained.

Our temp'rall blessings did abound:
   But spirituall good things
Much more abounded, to the praise
   Of that great King of Kings.   120
Gods throne was here set up; here was
   His tabernacle pight:[4]
This was the place, and these the folk
   In whom he took delight.

Our morning starrs shone all day long: 125
   Their beams gave forth such light,
As did the noon-day sun abash,
   And 's glory dazle quite.
Our day continued many yeers,
   And had no night at all: 130
Yea many thought the light would last,
   And be perpetuall.

Such, o New-England, was thy first,
   Such was thy best estate:
But, Loe! a strange and suddain change   135
   My courage did amate.[5]
The brightest of our morning starrs
   Did wholly disappeare:
And those that tarried behind
   With sack-cloth covered were.   140

Moreover, I beheld and saw
   Our welkin overkest,
And dismal clouds for sun-shine late
   O'respread from east to west.
The air became tempestuous;   145
   The wilderness gan quake:
And from above with awfull voice
   Th' Almighty thundring spake.

Are these the men that erst at my command
Forsook their ancient seats and native soile,   150

[4] archaic form of "pitch," as in "pitch a tent": i.e. established.
[5] dishearten, daunt.

To follow me into a desart land,
Contemning all the travell[6] and the toile,
Whose love was such to purest ordinances
As made them set at nought their fair inheritances?

Are these the men that prized libertee   155
To walk with God according to their light,
To be as good as he would have them bee,
To serve and worship him with all their might,
Before the pleasures which a fruitfull field,
And country flowing-full of all good things, could yield?   160

Are these the folk whom from the brittish Iles,
Through the stern billows of the watry main,
I safely led so many thousand miles,
As if their journey had been through a plain?
Whom having from all enemies protected,   165
And through so many deaths and dangers well directed,

I brought and planted on the western shore,
Where nought but bruits and salvage[7] wights did swarm
(Untaught, untrain'd, untam'd by vertue's lore)
That sought their blood, yet could not do them harm?   170
My fury's flaile them thresht, my fatall broom
Did sweep them hence, to make my people Elbow-room.

Are these the men whose gates with peace I crown'd,
To whom for bulwarks I salvation gave,
Whilst all things else with rattling tumults sound,   175
And mortall frayes send thousands to the grave?
Whilest their own brethren bloody hands embrewed[8]
In brothers blood, and Fields with carcases bestrewed?

Is this the people blest with bounteous store,
By land and sea full richly clad and fed,   180
Whom plenty's self stands waiting still before,
And powreth out their cups well tempered?
For whose dear sake an howling wildernes
I lately turned into a fruitfull paradeis?

Are these the people in whose hemisphere   185
Such bright-beam'd, glist'ring, sun-like starrs I placed,
As by their influence did all things cheere,

6 travail.
7 savage.
8 obs. form of imbrued: stained, defiled.

As by their light blind ignorance defaced,
As errours into lurking holes did fray,
As turn'd the late dark night into a lightsome day? 190

Are these the folk to whom I milked out
And sweetnes stream'd from consolations brest;
Whose soules I fed and strengthened throughout
With finest spirituall food most finely drest?
On whom I rained living bread from Heaven, 195
Withouten Errour's bane, or Superstition's leaven?

With whom I made a Covenant of peace,
And unto whom I did most firmly plight
My faithfulness, If whilst I live I cease
To be their Guide, their God, their full delight; 200
Since them with cords of love to me I drew,
Enwrapping in my grace such as should then ensew.⁹

Are these the men, that now mine eyes behold,
Concerning whom I thought, and whilome spake,
First Heaven shall pass away together scrold,¹⁰ 205
Ere they my lawes and righteous wayes forsake,
Or that they slack to runn their heavenly race?
Are these the same? or are some others come in place?

If these be they, how is it that I find
In stead of holiness Carnality, 210
In stead of heavenly frames an Earthly mind,
For burning zeal luke-warm Indifferency,
For flaming Love, key-cold Dead-heartedness,
For temperance (in meat, and drinke, and cloaths) excess?

Whence cometh it, that Pride, and Luxurie 215
Debate, Deceit, Contention and Strife,
False-dealing, Covetousness, Hypocrisie
(With such like Crimes) amongst them are so rife,
That one of them doth over-reach another?
And that an honest man can hardly trust his Brother? 220

How is it, that Security, and Sloth,
Amongst the best are Common to be found?
That grosser sinns, in stead of Graces growth,

⁹ ensue.
¹⁰ sense: the Heavens shall roll up like a scroll.

Amongst the many more and more abound?
I hate dissembling shews of Holiness.   225
Or practise as you talk, or never more profess.

Judge not, vain world, that all are hypocrites
That do profess more holiness then thou:
All foster not dissembling, guilefull sprites,
Nor love their lusts, though very many do.   230
Some sin through want of care and constant watch,
Some with the sick converse, till they the sickness catch.

Some, that maintain a reall root of grace,
Are overgrown with many noysome weeds,
Whose heart, that those no longer may take place,   235
The benefit of due correction needs.
And such as these however gone astray
I shall by stripes reduce into a better way.

Moreover some there be that still retain
Their ancient vigour and sincerity;   240
Whom both their own, and others sins, constrain
To sigh, and mourn, and weep, and wail, and cry:
And for their sakes I have forborn to powre
My wrath upon Revolters to this present houre.

To praying Saints I always have respect,   245
And tender love, and pittifull regard:
Nor will I now in any wise neglect
Their love and faithfull service to reward;
Although I deal with others for their folly,
And turn their mirth to tears that have been too too jolly.   250

For thinke not, O Backsliders, in your heart,
That I shall still your evill manners beare:
Your sinns me press as sheaves do load a cart,
And therefore I will plague you for this geare
Except you seriously, and soon, repent,   255
Ile not delay your pain and heavy punishment.

And who be those themselves that yonder shew?
The seed of such as name my dreadfull Name!
On whom whilere compassions skirt I threw
Whilest in their blood they were, to hide their shame!   260
Whom my preventing love did neer me take!
Whom for mine own I mark't, lest they should me forsake!

I look't that such as these to vertue's Lore
(Though none but they) would have Enclin'd their ear:
That they at least mine image should have bore,   265
And sanctify'd my name with awfull fear.
Let pagan's Bratts pursue their lusts, whose meed
Is Death: For christians children are an holy seed.

But hear O Heavens! Let Earth amazed stand;
Ye Mountaines melt, and Hills come flowing down: 270
Let horror seize upon both Sea and Land;
Let Natures self be cast into a stown.
I children nourisht, nurtur'd and upheld:
But they against a tender Father have rebell'd.

What could have been by me performed more?   275
Or wherein fell I short of your desire?
Had you but askt, I would have op't my store,
And given what lawfull wishes could require.
For all this bounteous cost I lookt to see
Heaven-reaching-hearts, and thoughts, Meekness, Humility.   280

But lo, a sensuall Heart all void of grace,
An Iron neck, a proud presumptuous Hand;
A self-conceited, stiff, stout, stubborn Race,
That fears no threats, submitts to no command:
Self-will'd, perverse, such as can beare no yoke;   285
A Generation even ripe for vengeance stroke.

Such were that Carnall Brood of Israelites
That Josua and the Elders did ensue,
Who growing like the cursed Cananites[11]
Upon themselves my heavy judgements drew.   290
Such also was that fleshy Generation,
Whom I o'rewhelmed by waters deadly inundation.

They darker light, and lesser meanes misused;
They had not such Examples them to warn:
You clearer Rules, and Precepts, have abused,   295
And dreadfull monuments of others harm.
My gospels glorious light you do not prize:
My Gospels endless, boundless grace you clean despize.

[11] When Noah divided the earth among his sons Ham, Shem, and Japheth, Palestine was allotted to Shem. Canaan, Ham's son, nevertheless took possession of it despite the objections of his father and his children who cursed him, saying, "Thou art cursed, and cursed wilt thou remain before all the sons of Noah."

My painfull messengers you disrespect,
Who toile and sweat and sweale[12] themselves away,   300
Yet nought at all with you can take effect,
Who hurrie headlong to your own decay.
In vain the Founder melts, and taketh pains:
Bellows and Lead's consum'd, but still your dross remains.

What should I do with such a stiff-neckt race?   305
How shall I ease me of such Foes as they?
What shall befall despizers of my Grace?
I'le surely beare their candle-stick away,
And Lamps put out. Their glorious noon-day light
I'le quickly turn into a dark Egyptian night.   310

Oft have I charg'd you by my Ministers
To gird your selves with sack cloth, and repent.
Oft have I warnd you by my Messengers;
That so you might my wrathfull ire prevent:
But who among you hath this warning taken?   315
Who hath his Crooked wayes, and wicked works forsaken?

Yea many grow to more and more excess;
More light and loose, more Carnall and prophane.
The sins of Sodom, Pride, and Wantonness,
Among the multitude spring up amain.   320
Are these the fruits of pious Education,
To run with greater speed and Courage to Damnation?

If here and there some two, or three, shall steere
A wiser course, then their Companions do,
You make a mock of such; and scoff, and jeere   325
Becaus they will not be so bad as you.
Such is the Generation that succeeds
The men, whose eyes have seen my great and awfull deeds.

Now therefore hearken and encline your ear,
In judgement I will henceforth with you plead;   330
And if by that you will not learn to fear,
But still go on a sensuall life to lead:
I'le strike at once an All-Consuming stroke;
Nor cries nor tears shall then my fierce intent revoke.

Thus ceast his Dreadful-threatning voice   335
    The High and lofty-One.
The Heavens stood still Appal'd thereat;

[12] waste, or melt (as does a candle).

The Earth beneath did groane.
Soon after I beheld and saw
  A mortall dart come flying: 340
I lookt again, and quickly saw
  Some fainting, others dying.

The Heavens more began to lowre,
  The welkin Blacker grew:
And all things seemed to forebode   345
  Sad changes to ensew.
From that day forward hath the Lord
  Apparently contended
With us in Anger, and in Wrath:
  But we have not amended.   350

Our healthfull dayes are at an end,
  And sicknesses come on
From yeer to yeer, becaus our hearts
  Away from God are gone.
New-England, where for many yeers   355
  You scarcely heard a cough,
And where Physicians had no work,
  Now finds them work enough.

Now colds and coughs; Rhewms, and sore-throats,
  Do more and more abound: 360
Now Agues sore and Feavers strong
  In every place are found.
How many houses have we seen
  Last Autumn, and this spring,
Wherein the healthful were too few   365
  To help the languishing.

One wave another followeth,
  And one disease begins
Before another cease, becaus
  We turn not from our sins.   370
We stopp our ear against reproof,
  And hearken not to God:
God stops his ear against our prayer,
  And takes not off his rod.

Our fruitful seasons have been turnd   375
  Of late to barrenness,
Sometimes through great and parching drought,
  Sometimes through rain's excess.

Yea now the pastures and corn fields
   For want of rain do languish: 380
The cattell mourn, and hearts of men
   Are fill'd with fear and anguish.

The clouds are often gathered,
   As if we should have rain:
But for our great unworthiness   385
   Are scattered again.
We pray and fast, and make fair shewes,
   As if we meant to turn:
But whilest we turn not, God goes on
   Our fields and fruits to burn.   390

And burnt are all things in such sort,
   That nothing now appears,
But what may wound our hearts with grief,
   And draw foorth floods of teares.
All things a famine do presage   395
   In that extremity,
As if both men, and also beasts,
   Should soon be done to dy.

This O New-England hast thou got
   By riot, and excess: 400
This hast thou brought upon thy self
   By pride and wantonness.
Thus must thy worldlyness be whipt.
   They, that too much do crave,
Provoke the Lord to take away   405
   Such blessings as they have.

We have been also threatened
   With worser things then these:
And God can bring them on us still,
   To morrow if he please.   410
For if his mercy be abus'd,
   Which holpe us at our need
And mov'd his heart to pitty us,
   We shall be plagu'd indeed.

Beware, O sinful Land, beware;   415
   And do not think it strange
That sorer judgements are at hand,
   Unless thou quickly change.

Or God, or thou, must quickly change;
  Or else thou art undon: 420
Wrath cannot cease, if sin remain,
  Where judgement is begun.

Ah dear New-England! dearest land to me;
Which unto God hast hitherto been dear,
And mayst be still more dear than formerlie,   425
If to his voice thou wilt incline thine ear.

Consider wel and wisely what the rod,
Wherewith thou art from yeer to yeer chastized,
Instructeth thee. Repent, and turn to God,
Who wil not have his nurture be despized.   430

Thou still hast in thee many praying saints,
Of great account, and precious with the Lord,
Who dayly powre out unto him their plaints,
And strive to please him both in deed and word.

Cheer on, sweet souls, my heart is with you all,   435
And shall be with you, maugre sathan's might:
And whereso'ere this body be a Thrall,[13]
Still in New-England shall be my delight.

A Prayer unto Christ the Judge of the World[1]

O Dearest Dread, most glorious King,
I'le of thy justest Judgments sing:
Do thou my head and heart inspire,
To Sing aright, as I desire.
Thee, thee alone I'le invocate,   5
For I do much abominate
To call the Muses to mine aid:
Which is th' Unchristian use, and trade
Of some that Christians would be thought,
And yet they worship worse then nought.   10
Oh! what a deal of Blasphemy,
And Heathenish Impiety,
In Christian Poets may be found,
Where Heathen gods with praise are Crown'd,
They make Jehovah to stand by,   15

[13] servant.
[1] prefatory poem to *The Day of Doom*.

Till Juno, Venus, Mercury,
With frowning Mars, *and thundering* Jove
Rule Earth below, and Heaven above.
But I have learnt to pray to none,
Save unto God in Christ alone.   20
Nor will I laud, no, not in jest,
That which I know God doth detest.
I reckon it a damning evil
To give Gods Praises to the Devil.
Thou, Christ, art he to whom I pray,   25
Thy Glory fain I would display.
Oh! guide me by thy sacred Sprite
So to indite, and so to write,
That I thine holy Name may praise,
And teach the Sons of men thy wayes.   30

The Day of Doom

1

*The Security
of the World
before Christ's
coming to
Judgment.
Luk.* 12: 19

Still was the night, Serene and Bright,
    when all Men sleeping lay;
Calm was the season, and carnal reason
    thought so 'twould last for ay.
Soul, take thine ease, let sorrow cease,
    much good thou hast in store:
This was their Song, their Cups among,
    the Evening before.

2

Mat. 25: 5

Wallowing in all kind of sin,
    vile wretches lay secure:[1]
The best of men had scarcely then
    their Lamps kept in good ure.[2]
Virgins unwise, who through disguise
    amongst the best were number'd,
Had clos'd their eyes; yea, and the wise
    through sloth and frailty slumber'd.

[1] careless.
[2] condition.

3

Mat. 24: 37, 38

Like as of old, when Men grow bold
   Gods threatnings to contemn,
Who stopt their Ear, and would not hear,
   when Mercy warned them:
But took their course, without remorse,
   til God began to powre
Destruction the World upon
   in a tempestuous showre.

4

They put away the evil day,
   and drown'd their care and fears,
Till drown'd were they, and swept away
   by vengeance unawares:

I *Thes.* 5: 3

So at the last, whilst Men sleep fast
   in their security,
Surpriz'd they are in such a snare
   as cometh suddenly.

5

*The Suddenness,
Majesty, and
Terror of
Christ's
appearing.*
Mat. 25: 6
II *Pet.* 3: 10

For at midnight brake forth a Light,
   which turn'd the night to day,
And speedily an hideous cry
   did all the world dismay.
Sinners awake, their hearts do ake,
   trembling their loynes surprizeth;
Amaz'd with fear, by what they hear,
   each one of them ariseth.

6

Mat. 24: 29, 30

They rush from Beds with giddy heads,
   and to their windows run,
Viewing this light, which shines more bright
   then doth the Noon-day Sun.
Straightway appears (they see't with tears)
   the Son of God most dread;

Who with his Train comes on amain
To Judge both Quick and Dead.

7

Before his face the Heav'ns gave place,
    and Skies are rent asunder,
With mighty voice, and hideous noise,
    more terrible than Thunder.
His brightness damps heav'ns glorious lamps
    and makes them hide their heads,
As if afraid and quite dismay'd,
    they quit their wonted steads.

II Pet. 3: 10

8

Ye sons of men that durst contemn
    the Threatnings of Gods Word,
How cheer you now? your hearts, I trow,
    are thrill'd as with a sword.
Now Atheist blind, whose brutish mind
    a God could never see,
Dost thou perceive, dost now believe,
    that Christ thy Judge shall be?

9

Stout Courages, (whose hardiness
    could Death and Hell out-face)
Are you as bold now you behold
    your Judge draw near apace?
They cry, no, no: Alas! and wo!
    our Courage all is gone:
Our hardiness (fool hardiness)
    hath us undone, undone.

10

No heart so bold, but now grows cold
    and almost dead with fear:
No eye so dry, but now can cry,
    and pour out many a tear.

Rev. 6: 16

Earths Potentates and pow'rful States,
    Captains and Men of Might,
Are quite abasht, their courage dasht
    at this most dreadful sight.

11

Mean men lament, great men do rent
    their Robes, and tear their hair:
Mat. 24: 30   They do not spare their flesh to tear
    through horrible despair.
All Kindreds wail: all hearts do fail:
    horror the world doth fill
With weeping eyes, and loud out-cries,
    yet knows not how to kill.

12

Rev. 6: 15, 16   Some hide themselves in Caves and Delves,
    in places under ground:
Some rashly leap into the Deep,
    to scape by being drown'd:
Some to the Rocks (O sensless blocks!)
    and woody Mountains run,
That there they might this fearful sight,
    and dreaded Presence shun.

13

In vain do they to Mountains say,
    Fall on us, and us hide
From Judges ire, more hot than fire,
    for who may it abide?
No hiding place can from his Face,
    sinners at all conceal,
Whose flaming Eyes hid things doth 'spy,
    and darkest things reveal.

14

Mat. 25: 31   The Judge draws nigh, exhalted high
    upon a lofty Throne,
Amidst the throng of Angels strong,

lo, Israel's Holy One!
The excellence of whose presence
 and awful Majesty,
Amazeth Nature, and every Creature,
 doth more than terrify.

15

Rev. 6: 14

The Mountains smoak, the Hills are shook,
 the Earth is rent and torn,
As if she should be clean dissolv'd,
 or from the Center born.
The Sea doth roar, forsakes the shore,
 and Shrinks away for fear;
The wild Beasts flee into the Sea,
 so soon as he draws near.

16

Whose Glory bright, whose wondrous might,
 whose Power Imperial,
So far surpass whatever was
 in Realms Terrestrial;
That tongues of men (nor Angels pen)
 cannot the same express,
And therefore I must pass it by,
 lest speaking should transgress.

17

I *Thes.* 4: 16
*Resurrection
of the Dead.*
John 5: 28, 29

Before his Throne a Trump is blown,
 Proclaiming th' Day of Doom:
Forthwith he cries, *Ye Dead arise,
 and unto Judgment come.*
No sooner said, but 'tis obey'd;
 Sepulchers open'd are:
Dead Bodies all rise at his call,
 and's mighty power declare.

18

Both Sea and Land, at his Command,
　　their Dead at once surrender:
The Fire and Air constrained are
　　also their dead to tender.
The mighty word of this great Lord
　　links Body and Soul together
Both of the Just, and the unjust,
　　to part no more for ever.

19

The living
Changed.

The same translates, from Mortal states
　　to Immortality,
All that survive, and be alive,
　　i' th' twinkling of an eye:

Luk. 20: 36
I *Cor.* 15: 52

That so they may abide for ay
　　to endles weal or woe;
Both the Renate[3] and Reprobate
　　are made to dy no more.

20

All brought
to Judgment.
Mat. 24: 31

His winged Hosts file through all Coasts,
　　together gathering
Both good and bad, both quick and dead,
　　and all to Judgment bring.
Out of their holes those creeping Moles,
　　that hid themselves for fear,
By force they take, and quickly make
　　before the Judge appear.

21

II *Cor.* 5: 10
The Sheep
Separated from
the Goats.
Mat. 25: 32

Thus every one before the Throne
　　of Christ the Judge is brought,
Both righteous and impious
　　that good or ill had wrought.
A separation, and diff'ring station
　　by Christ appointed is
(To sinners sad) 'twixt good and bad,
　　'twixt Heirs of woe and bliss.

[3] reborn spiritually, regenerate.

22

Who are
Christ's Sheep.
Mat. 5: 10, 11

At Christ's right hand the Sheep do stand,
 his holy Martyrs, who
For his dear Name suffering shame,
 calamity and woe,
Like Champions stood, and with their Blood
 their testimony sealed;
Whose innocence without offence,
 to Christ their Judge appealed.

23

Heb. 12: 5, 6, 7

Next unto whom there find a room
 all Christ's afflicted ones,
Who being chastised, neither despised
 nor sank amidst their groans:
Who by the Rod were turn'd to God,
 and loved him the more,
Not murmuring nor quarrelling
 when they were chast'ned sore.

24

Luke 7: 41, 47

Moreover, such as loved much,
 that had not such a tryal,
As might constrain to so great pain,
 and such deep self-denyal:
Yet ready were the Cross to bear,
 when Christ them call'd thereto,
And did rejoyce to hear his voice,
 they're counted Sheep also.

25

Joh. 21: 15
Mat. 19: 14
Joh. 3: 3

Christ's Flock of Lambs there also stands,
 whose Faith was weak, yet true;
All sound Believers (Gospel receivers)
 whose Grace was small, but grew:
And them among an Infant throng
 of Babes, for whom Christ dy'd;
Whom for his own, by wayes unknown
 to men, he sanctify'd.

26

Rev. 6: 11
Phil. 3: 21

All stand before their Saviour
    in long white Robes yclad,
Their countenance full of pleasance,
    appearing wondrous glad.
O glorious sight! Behold how bright
    dust heaps are made to shine,
Conformed so their Lord unto,
    whose Glory is Divine.

27

*The Goats
described or
the several
sorts of
Reprobates
on the left
hand.*
Mat. 24: 51

At Christ's left hand the Goats do stand,
    all whining hypocrites,
Who for self-ends did seem Christ's friends,
    but foster'd guileful sprites;
Who Sheep resembled, but they dissembled
    (their hearts were not sincere);
Who once did throng Christ's Lambs among,
    but now must not come near.

28

Luk. 11: 24, 26
Heb. 6: 4, 5, 6
Heb. 10: 29

Apostates and Run-awayes,
    such as have Christ forsaken,
Of whom the Devil, with seven more evil,
    hath fresh possession taken:
Sinners in grain, reserv'd to pain
    and torments most severe:
Because 'gainst light they sinn'd with spight,
    are also placed there.

29

Luk. 12: 47
Prov. 1: 24, 26
Joh. 3: 19

There also stand a num'rous band,
    that no Profession made
Of Godliness, nor to redress
    their wayes at all essay'd:
Who better knew, but (sinful Crew)
    Gospel and Law despised;
Who all Christ's knocks withstood like blocks
    and would not be advised.

30

Moreover, there with them appear
　　a number, numberless

Gal. 3: 10
I *Cor.* 6: 9
Rev. 21: 8

Of great and small, vile wretches all,
　　that did Gods Law transgress:
Idolaters, false worshippers,
　　Prophaners of Gods Name,
Who not at all thereon did call,
　　or took in vain the same.

31

Blasphemers lewd, and Swearers shrewd,
　　Scoffers at Purity,

Exod. 20: 7 *and* 8

That hated God, contemn'd his Rod,
　　and lov'd Security;
Sabbath-polluters, Saints persecutors,
　　Presumptuous men and proud,

II *Thes.* 1: 6, 8, 9

Who never lov'd those that reprov'd;
　　all stand amongst this Crowd.

32

Heb. 13: 4
I *Cor.* 6: 10

Adulterers and Whoremongers
　　were there, with all unchast:
There Covetous, and Ravenous,
　　that Riches got too fast:
Who us'd vile ways themselves to raise
　　t' Estates and worldly wealth,
Oppression by, or Knavery,
　　by force, or fraud, or stealth.

33

Moreover, there together were
　　Children flagitious,[4]

Zach. 5: 3, 4
Gal. 5: 19,
20, 21

And Parents who did them undo
　　by Nurture vicious.
False-witness-bearers, and self-forswearers,

[4] grossly wicked.

Murd'rers, and Men of blood,
Witches, Inchanters, and Ale-house-haunters,
beyond account there stood.

34

Their place there find all Heathen blind,
    that Natures light abused,
Rom. 2: 13   Although they had no tydings glad,
    of Gospel-grace refused.
There stands all Nations and Generations
    of *Adam's* Progeny,
Whom Christ redeem'd not, who Christ esteem'd not,
    through Infidelity.

35

Act. 4: 12   Who no Peace-maker, no Undertaker,[5]
    to shrow'd them from Gods ire,
Ever obtain'd; they must be pained
    with everlasting fire.
These num'rous bands, wringing their hands,
    and weeping, all stand there,
Filled with anguish, whose hearts do languish
    through self-tormenting fear.

36

Fast by them stand at Christ's left hand
    the Lion fierce and fell,
The Dragon bold, that Serpent old,
    that hurried Souls to Hell.
I *Cor.* 6: 3   There also stand, under command,
    Legions of Sprights[6] unclean,
And hellish Fiends, that are no friends
    to God, nor unto Men.

[5] helper.
[6] spirits.

37

Jude 6

With dismal chains, and strongest reins,
    like Prisoners of Hell,
They're held in place before Christ's face,
    till He their Doom shall tell.
These void of tears, but fill'd with fears,
    and dreadful expectation
Of endless pains, and scalding flames,
    stand waiting for Damnation.

38

*The Saints
cleared and
justified.*

All silence keep, both Goats and Sheep,
    before the Judge's Throne;
With mild aspect to his Elect
    then spake the Holy One:
My Sheep draw near, your Sentence hear,
    which is to you no dread,
Who clearly now discern, and know
    your sins are pardoned.

39

II *Cor.* 5: 10
Eccles. 3: 17
Joh. 3: 18

'Twas meet that ye should judged be,
    that so the world may spy
No cause of grudge, when as I Judge
    and deal impartially.
Know therefore all, both great and small,
    the ground and reason why
These Men do stand at my right hand,
    and look so chearfully.

40

Joh. 17: 6
Eph. 1: 4

These Men be those my Father chose
    before the worlds foundation,
And to me gave, that I should save
    from Death and Condemnation.
For whose dear sake I flesh did take,
    was of a Woman born,
And did inure my self t' indure,
    unjust reproach and scorn.

41

For them it was that I did pass
    through sorrows many [a] one:
That I drank up that bitter Cup,
    which made me sigh and groan.
The Cross his pain I did sustain;
    yea more, my Fathers ire
I underwent, my Blood I spent
    to save them from Hell fire.

Rev. 1: 5

42

Thus I esteem'd, thus I redeem'd
    all these from every Nation,
That they may be (as now you see)
    a chosen Generation.
What if ere-while they were as vile,
    as bad as any be,
And yet from all their guilt and thrall
    at once I set them free?

Eph. 2: 1, 3

43

My grace to one is wrong to none:
    none can Election claim,
Amongst all those their souls that lose,
    none can Rejection blame.
He that may chuse, or else refuse,
    all men to save or spill,
May this Man chuse, and that refuse,
    redeeming whom he will.

Mat. 20: 13, 15
Rom. 9: 20, 21

44

But as for those whom I have chose
    Salvations heirs to be,
I underwent their punishment,
    and therefore set them free;
I bore their grief, and their relief
    by suffering procur'd,
That they of bliss and happiness
    might firmly be assur'd.

Isa. 53: 4,
5, 11

45

Acts 13: 48
Jam. 2: 18
Heb. 12: 7
Mat. 19: 29

And this my grace they did imbrace,
    believing on my Name;
Which Faith was true, the fruits do shew
    proceeding from the same:
Their Penitence, their Patience,
    their Love and Self-denial
In suffering losses, and bearing Crosses,
    when put upon the tryal.

46

I *Joh.* 3: 3
Mat. 25: 39, 40

Their sin forsaking, their chearful taking
    my yoke, their Charity
Unto the Saints in all their wants,
    and in them unto me,
These things do clear, and make appear
    their Faith to be unfaigned,
And that a part in my desert
    and purchase they have gained.

47

Isa. 53: 11, 12
Rom. 8: 16, 17,
33, 34
John 3: 18

Their debts are paid, their peace is made,
    their sins remitted are;
Therefore at once I do pronounce,
    and openly declare;
That Heav'n is theirs, that they be Heirs
    of Life and of Salvation!
Nor ever shall they come at all
    to Death or to Damnation.

48

Luk. 22: 29, 30
Mat. 19: 28

Come, Blessed Ones, and sit on Thrones,
    Judging the World with me:
Come, and possess your happiness,
    and bought felicitie.
Henceforth no fears, no care, no tears,
    no sin shall you annoy,
Nor any thing that grief doth bring:
    Eternal Rest enjoy.

49

Mat. 25: 34
They are
placed on
Thrones to
joyn with
Christ in
judging the
wicked.

Yóu bore the Cross, you suffered loss
    of all for my Names sake:
Receive the Crown that's now your own;
    come, and a Kingdom take.
Thus spake the Judge; the wicked grudge,
    and grind their teeth in vain;
They see with groans these plac't on Thrones
    which addeth to their pain:

50

That those whom they did wrong and slay,
    must now their judgment see!
Such whom they slighted, and once despighted,
    must now their Judges be!
Thus 'tis decreed, such is their meed,

I *Cor.* 6: 2

    and guerdon glorious!
With Christ they sit, Judging is fit
    to plague the Impious.

51

The wicked
brought to the
Bar.
Rom. 2: 3, 6, 11

The wicked are brought to the Bar,
    like guilty Malefactors,
That oftentimes of bloody Crimes
    and Treasons have been Actors.
Of wicked Men, none are so mean
    as there to be neglected:
Nor none so high in dignity,
    as there to be respected.

52

Rev. 6: 15, 16
Isa. 30: 33

The glorious Judge will priviledge
    nor Emperour, nor King:
But every one that hath mis-done
    doth into Judgment bring.
And every one that hath mis-done,
    the Judge impartially
Condemneth to eternal wo,
    and endless misery.

53

Thus one and all, thus great and small,
    the Rich as well as Poor,
And those of place as the most base,
    do stand the Judge before.
They are arraign'd, and there detain'd,
    before Christ's Judgment-seat
With trembling fear, their Doom to hear,
    and feel his angers heat.

54

Eccles. 11: 9 *and*
12: 14

There Christ demands at all their hands
    a strict and strait account
Of all things done under the Sun,
    whose number far surmount
Man's wit and thought: yet all are brought
    unto this solemn Tryal;
And each offence with evidence,
    so that there's no denial.

55

There's no excuse for their abuses,
    since their own Consciences
More proof give in of each Man's sin,
    than thousand Witnesses,
Though formerly this faculty
    had grosly been abused,
Men could it stifle, or with it trifle,
    when as it them accused.

56

Now it comes in, and every sin
    unto Mens charge doth lay:
It judgeth them, and doth condemn,
    though all the world say nay.
It so stingeth and tortureth,
    it worketh such distress,
That each Man's self against himself,
    is forced to confess.

57

*Secret sins
and works of
darkness
brought to
light.*
Psal. 139: 2,
4, 12
Rom. 2: 16

It's vain, moreover, for Men to cover
    the least iniquity:
The Judge hath seen, and privy been
    to all their villany.
He unto light, and open sight
    the works of darkness brings:
He doth unfold both new and old,
    both known and hidden things.

58

Eccles. 12: 14

All filthy facts, and secret acts,
    however closly done,
And long conceal'd, are there reveal'd
    before the mid-day Sun.
Deeds of the night shunning the light,
    which darkest corners sought,
To fearful blame, and endless shame,
    are there most justly brought.

59

Mat. 12: 36
Rom. 7: 7

And as all facts and grosser acts,
    so every word and thought,
Erroneous notion, and lustful motion,
    are unto judgment brought,
No sin so small and trivial
    but hither it must come:
Nor so long past, but now at last
    it must receive a doom.

60

*An account
demanded of
all their
actions.*
Joh. 5: 40 *and*
3: 19
Mat. 25: 19, 27

At this sad season, Christ asks a Reason
    (with just Austerity)
Of Grace refused, of light abus'd
    so oft, so wilfully:
Of Talents lent by them mis-spent,
    and on their Lust bestown;
Which if improv'd, as it behov'd,
    Heav'n might have been their own!

61

Of times neglected, of means rejected,
   of God's long-suffering,
Rom. 2: 4, 5   And Patience, to Penitence
   that sought hard hearts to bring.
Why Cords of love did nothing move
   to shame or to remorse?
Why warnings grave, and counsels, have
   nought chang'd their sinful course?

62

Why chastenings, and evil things,
   why judgments so severe
Isa. 1: 5   Prevailed not with them a jot,
   nor wrought an awful fear?
Jer. 2: 20   Why Promises of Holiness,
   and new Obedience,
They oft did make, but always brake
   the same, to God's offence?

63

Why still Hell-ward, without regard,
John 3: 19, 20   they boldly ventured,
Prov. 8: 36   And chose Damnation before Salvation,
Luk. 12: 20, 21   when it was offered?
Why sinful pleasures, and earthly treasures,
   like fools, they prized more
Than heav'nly wealth, Eternal health,
   and all Christ's Royal store?

64

Luke 13: 34   Why, when he stood off'ring his Blood
Joh. 5: 40 *and*   to wash them from their sin,
15: 22   They would embrace no saving Grace,
   but liv'd and dy'd therein?
Such aggravations, where no evasions,
   no false pretences hold,
Exaggerate and cumulate
   guilt more than can be told.

65

They multiply and magnify
   mens gross iniquities,
They draw down wrath (as Scripture saith)
   out of Gods treasuries.
Thus all their ways Christ open lays
   to men and Angels view,
And, as they were, makes them appear
   in their own proper hew.

66

Rom. 3: 10, 12

Thus he doth find of all Mankind,
   that stand at his left hand,
No Mothers Son, but hath mis-done,
   and broken God's Command.
All have transgrest, even the best,
   and merited God's wrath
Unto their own perdition,
   and everlasting scath.[7]

67

Rom. 6: 23

Earths dwellers all, both great and small,
   have wrought iniquity,
And suffer must, for it is just,
   Eternal misery.
Amongst the many there come not any,
   before the Judge's face,
That able are themselves to clear,
   of all this cursed race.

68

Nevertheless, they all express,
   Christ granting liberty,
What for their way they have to say,
   how they have liv'd, and why.

*Hypocrites plead
for themselves.*

They all draw near, and seek to clear
   themselves by making pleas.

[7] harm, punishment.

There Hypocrites, false-hearted wights,
do make such pleas as these:

69

Lord, in thy Name, and by the same,
we Devils dispossest,

Mat. 7: 21, 22,
23

We rais'd the dead, and ministred
succour to the distrest.
Our painful teaching, and pow'rful preaching
by thine own wondrous might,
Did throughly win to God from sin
many a wretched wight.

70

*The judge
replyeth.
Joh.* 6: 70
I *Cor.* 9: 27

All this, quoth he, may granted be,
and your case little better'd,
Who still remain under a chain,
and many irons fetter'd.
You that the dead have quickened,
and rescu'd from the grave,
Your selves were dead, yet never ned,[8]
a Christ your Souls to save.

71

Rom. 2: 19, 21,
22, 23

You that could preach, and others teach
what way to life doth lead;
Why were you slack to find that track,
and in that way to tread?
How could you bear to see or hear
of others freed at last,
From Satan's pawes whilst in his jawes
your selves were held more fast?

72

Joh. 9: 41

Who though you knew Repentance true,
and Faith in my great Name,
The only mean to quit you clean,
from punishment and blame,

[8] needed.

74

Rev. 2: 21, 22

Yet took no pain true Faith to gain,
    such as might not deceive,
Nor would repent, with true intent,
    your evil deeds to leave.

73

His Masters will how to fulfill
    the servant that well knew,
Luk. 12: 47 Yet left undone his duty known,
Mat. 11: 21, 22,   more plagues to him are due.
24 You against light perverted right;
    wherefore it shall be now
For *Sidon* and for *Sodoms* Land
    more easie than for you.

74

Another plea But we have in thy presence been,
of hypocrites.   say some, and eaten there.
Luk. 13: 26 Did we not eat thy Flesh for meat,
    and feed on heavenly Cheer?
Whereon who feed shall never need,
    as thou thy self dost say,
Nor shall they dy eternally,
    but live with Christ for ay.

75

We may alledge, thou gav'st a pledge
    of thy dear love to us
In Wine and Bread, which figured
    thy Grace bestowed thus.
Of strengthning Seals, of sweetest Meals,
    have we so oft partaken;
And shall we be cast off by thee,
    and utterly forsaken?

76

Is Answered. To whom the Lord thus in a word
Luk. 13: 27   returns a short reply,
Mat. 22: 12 I never knew any of you
    that wrought iniquity.

You say y'have been my Presence in:
 but friends, how came you there
With Raiment vile that did defile
 and quite disgrace my Cheer?

77

Durst you draw near without due fear
 unto my holy Table?
Durst you prophane, and render vain
 so far as you were able,
Those Mysteries? which whoso prize
 and carefully improve
Shall saved be undoubtedly,
 and nothing shall them move.

78

How durst you venture, bold guests, to enter
 in such a sordid hew,
I *Cor.* 11: 27, 29 Amongst my guests, unto those Feasts
 that were not made for you?
How durst you eat for spiritual meat
 your bane, and drink damnation,
Whilst by your guile you rendred vile
 so rare and great Salvation?

79

Your fancies fed on heav'nly Bread,
 your hearts fed on some Lust:
Mat. 6: 21, 24
Rom. 1: 25 You lov'd the Creature more than th' Creator,
 your Souls clave to the dust.
And think you by Hypocrisie,
 and cloaked Wickedness,
To enter in, laden with sin,
 to lasting happiness?

80

I *Cor.* 11: 27, 29 This your excuse shews your abuse
 of things ordain'd for good;
And doth declare you guilty are
 of my dear Flesh and Blood.

Wherefore those Seals and precious Meals
    you put so much upon
As things divine, they seal and sign
    you to Perdition.

81

Then forth issue another Crew
    (those being silenced)

*Another sort of
hypocrites make
their pleas.*

Who drawing nigh to the most High
    adventure thus to plead:
We sinners were, say they, it's clear,
    deserving Condemnation:
But did not we rely on thee,
    O Christ, for whole Salvation?

82

We did believe and oft receive
    thy gracious promises:

Act. 8: 13
Isa. 58: 2, 3
Heb. 6: 4, 5

We took great care to get a share
    in endless happiness.
We pray'd and wept, we Fast-dayes kept,
    lewd ways we did eschew:
We joyful were thy Word to hear;
    we form'd our lives anew.

83

We thought our sin had pard'ned been;
    that our Estate was good,
Our debts all paid, our peace well made,
    our Souls wash'd with thy Blood.

II *Pet.* 2: 20

Lord, why dost thou reject us now,
    who have not thee rejected,
Nor utterly true sanctity
    and holy life neglected.

84

*The Judge
uncaseth them.*

The Judge incensed at their pretenced
    self-va[u]nting Piety,
With such a look as trembling strook
    into them, made reply;

John 2: 24, 25   O impudent, inpenitent,
        and guileful generation!
    Think you that I cannot descry
        your hearts abomination?

85

You nor receiv'd, nor yet believ'd
    my Promises of Grace;

Joh. 6: 64   Nor were you wise enough to prize
        my reconciled Face:

Psal. 50: 16   But did presume that to assume
Mat. 15: 26   which was not yours to take,
And challenged the Childrens bread,
    yet would not sin forsake.

86

Rev. 3: 17   Being too bold you laid fast hold,
        where int'rest you had none,
Your selves deceiving by your believing,
    all which you might have known,

Mat. 13: 20   You ran away, but ran astray,
        with Gospel-promises,
And perished; being still dead
    in sins and trespasses.

87

How oft did I Hypocrisie
    and Hearts deceit unmask

Mat. 6: 2, 4,
24   Before your sight, giving you light
Jer. 8: 5, 6,   to know a Christians task?
7, 8   But you held fast unto the last
    your own Conceits so vain;
No warning could prevail, you would
    your own Deceits retain.

88

As for your care to get a share
    in bliss; the fear of Hell,

Psal. 78: 34, 35,   And of a part in endless smart,
36, 37   did thereunto compell.

Your holiness and ways redress,
    such as it was, did spring
From no true love to things above,
    but from some other thing.

89

Zach. 7: 5, 6
Isa. 58: 3, 4
I *Sam.* 15: 13, 21
Isa. 1: 11, 15

You pray'd and wept, you Fast-days kept;
    but did you this to me?
No, but for sin, you sought to win,
    the greater libertie.
For all your vaunts, you had vile haunts,
    for which your Consciences
Did you alarm, whose voice to charm
    you us'd these practices.

90

Mat. 6: 2, 5
John 5: 44

Your Penitence, your diligence
    to Read, to Pray, to Hear,
Were but to drown'd the clamorous sound
    of Conscience in your ear.
If light you lov'd, vain glory mov'd
    your selves therewith to store,
That seeming wise, men might you prize,
    and honour you the more.

91

Zach. 7: 15, 16
Hos. 10: 1

Thus from your selves unto your selves,
    your duties all do tend:
And as self-love the wheels doth move,
    so in self-love they end.
Thus Christ detects their vain projects,
    and close Impiety,
And plainly shews that all their shows
    were but Hypocrisy.

92

Civil honest
mens pleas.
Luk. 18: 11

Then were brought nigh a Company
   of Civil honest Men,
That lov'd true dealing, and hated stealing,
   ne'r wrong'd their Bretheren;
Who pleaded thus, Thou knowest us
   that we were blameless livers;
No Whoremongers, no Murderers,
   no quarrellers nor strivers.

93

Idolaters, Adulterers,
   Church-robbers we were none,
Nor false-dealers, no couzeners,[9]
   but paid each man his own.
Our way was fair, our dealing square,
   we were no wastful spenders,
No lewd toss-pots, no drunken sots,
   no scandalous offenders.

94

We hated vice, and set great price,
   by vertuous conversation:
And by the same we got a name,
   and no small commendation.
I *Sam.* 15: 22 God's Laws express that righteousness,
   is that which he doth prize;
And to obey, as he doth say,
   is more than sacrifice.

95

Thus to obey, hath been our way;
   let our good deeds, we pray,
Find some regard and some reward
   with thee, O Lord, this day.
Eccles. 7: 20 And whereas we transgressors be,
   of *Adam's* Race were none,

[9] cozeners: cheaters, defrauders.

No not the best, but have confest
themselves to have mis-done.

96

Then answered unto their dread,
   the Judge: True Piety
God doth desire and eke require
   no less than honesty.
Justice demands at all your hands
   perfect Obedience:
If but in part you have come short,
   that is a just offence.

97

On Earth below, where men did ow[e]
   a thousand pounds and more,
Could twenty pence it recompence?
   could that have clear'd the score?
Think you to buy felicity
   with part of what's due debt?
Or for desert of one small part,
   the whole should off be set?

98

And yet that part, whose great desert
   you think to reach so far
For your excuse, doth you accuse,
   and will your boasting mar.
However fair, however square,
   your way and work hath been,
Before mens eyes, yet God espies
   iniquity therein.

99

God looks upon th' affection
   and temper of the heart;
Not only on the action,
   and the external part.

Whatever end vain men pretend,
   God knows the verity;
And by the end which they intend
   their words and deeds doth try.

100

Heb. 11: 6

Without true Faith, the Scripture saith
   God cannot take delight
In any deed, that doth proceed
   from any sinful wight.

I *Cor.* 13: 1,
2, 3

And without love all actions prove
   but barren empty things.
Dead works they be, and vanitie,
   the which vexation brings.

101

Nor from true faith, which quencheth wrath,
   hath your obedience flown:
Nor from true love, which wont to move
   Believers hath it grown.
Your argument shews your intent,
   in all that you have done:
You thought to scale Heav'ns lofty Wall
   by Ladders of your own.

102

Rom. 10: 3

Your blinded spirit, hoping to merit
   by your own Righteousness,
Needed no Saviour, but your behaviour,
   and blameless carriages;
You trusted to what you could do,
   and in no need you stood:
Your haughty pride laid me aside,
   and trampled on my Blood.

103

All men have gone astray, and done,
   that which Gods Laws condemn:

Rom. 9: 31, 32
Mat. 11: 23, 24
and 12: 41
But my Purchase and offered Grace
    all men did not contemn.
The *Ninevites,* and *Sodomites,*
    had no such sin as this:
Yet as if all your sins were small,
    you say, All did amiss.

104

Mat. 6: 5
Again you thought and mainly sought
    a name with men t' acquire;
Pride bare the Bell,[10] that made you swell,
    and your own selves admire.
Mean fruit it is, and vile, I wiss,[11]
    that springs from such a root:
Vertue divine and genuine
    wonts not from pride to shoot.

105

Such deeds as your are worse than poor:
    they are but sins guilt[12] over
Prov. 26: 23
Mat. 23: 27
With silver dross, whose glistering gloss
    can them no longer cover.
The best of them would you condemn,
    and ruine you alone,
Although you were from faults so clear,
    that other you had none.

106

Prov. 15: 8
Rom. 3: 20
Your Gold is brass, your silver dross,
    your righteousness is sin:
And think you by such honesty
    eternal life to win?
You much mistake, if for its sake
    you dream of acceptation;
Whereas the same deserveth shame,
    and meriteth Damnation.

[10] took first place, led.
[11] know.
[12] gilt.

107

A wond'rous Crowd then 'gan aloud,
  thus for themselves to say,
We did intend, Lord to amend,
  and to reform our way:
Our true intent was to repent,
  and make our peace with thee;
But sudden death stopping our breath,
  left us no libertie.

108

Short was our time, for in his prime
  our youthful flow'r was cropt:
We dy'd in youth, before full growth,
  so was our purpose stopt.
Let our good will to turn from ill,
  and sin to have forsaken,
Accepted be, O Lord, by thee,
  and in good part be taken.

109

To whom the Judge: where you alledge
  the shortness of the space,
That from your birth you liv'd on earth,
  to compass saving Grace:
It was Free grace that any space
  was given you at all
To turn from evil, defie the Devil,
  and upon God to call.

110

One day, one week, wherein to seek
  God's face with all your hearts,
A favour was that far did pass
  the best of your deserts.
You had a season, what was your reason
  such precious hours to waste?

What could you find, what could you mind
    that was of greater haste?

111

Could you find time for vain pastime,
    for loose licentious mirth?

Eccles. 11: 9
Luk. 14: 18,
19, 20

For fruitless toyes, and fading joyes
    that perish in the birth?
Had you good leasure for carnal Pleasure,
    in dayes of health and youth?
And yet no space to seek God's face,
    and turn to him in truth?

112

Amos 6: 3 *to* 6

In younger years, beyond your fears,
    what if you were surprised?

Eph. 5: 16
Luk. 19: 42

You put away the evil day,
    and of long life devised.
You oft were told, and might behold,
    that Death no Age doth spare;
Why then did you your time foreslow,[13]
    and slight your Souls welfare?

113

Had your intent been to repent,
    and had you it desir'd,

Luk. 13: 24, 25
etc.
Phil. 2: 12

There would have been endeavours seen,
    before your time expir'd.
God makes no treasure, nor hath he pleasure,
    in idle purposes:
Such fair pretences are foul offences,
    and cloaks for wickedness.

114

Then were brought in, and charg'd with sin,
    another Company,

[13] lose by sloth.

*Some plead
Examples of
their betters.*
Mat. 18: 7

Who by Petition obtain'd permission,
    to make Apology:
They argued, We were misled,
    as is well known to thee,
By their Example, that had more ample
    abilities than we:

115

John 7: 48

Such as profest they did detest,
    and hate each wicked way:
Whose seeming grace whilst we did trace,
    our Souls were led astray.
When men of Parts, Learning and Arts,
    Professing Piety,
Did thus and thus, it seem'd to us
    we might take liberty.

116

*Who are told
that Examples
are no Rules.*
Psal. 19: 8, 11
Exo. 23: 2
Psal. 50: 17, 18

The Judge replies, I gave you eyes,
    and light to see your way,
Which had you lov'd, and well improv'd
    you had not gone astray.
My Word was pure, the Rule was sure,
    why did you it forsake,
Or thereon trample, and mens example
    your Directory make?

117

This you well knew, that God is true
    and that most men are liars,

II *Tim.* 3: 5

In word professing holiness,
    in deed thereof deniers.
O simple fools! that having rules
    your lives to regulate,
Would the[m] refuse, and rather chuse
    vile men to imitate.

118

*They urge that
they were mis-
led by godly
mens Examples.
But all their
shifts turn
to their great-
er shame.*
II *Cor.* 11: 1

But Lord, say they, we went astray,
    and did more wickedlie,
By means of those whom thou hast chose
    Salvation heirs to be.
To whom the Judge: What you alledge,
    doth nothing help the case;
But makes appear how vile you were,
    and rend'reth you more base.

119

You understood that what was good,
    was to be followed,
And that you ought that which was naught
    to have relinquished.

Phil. 4: 8

Contrariwayes, it was your guise,
    only to imitate
Good mens defects, and their neglects
    that were regenerate.

120

But to express their holiness,
    or imitate their grace,

Psal. 32: 5
II *Chron.* 32: 26
Mat. 26: 75
Prov. 1: 24, 25

You little car'd, nor once prepar'd
    your hearts to seek my face.
They did repent, and truly rent
    their hearts for all known sin:
You did offend, but not amend,
    to follow them therein.

121

*Some plead
the Scriptures
darkness.
And difference
amongst Inter-
preters.*
II *Pet.* 3: 16

We had thy Word, say some, O Lord,
    but wiser men than we
Could never yet interpret it,
    but always disagree.
How could we fools be led by Rules,
    so far beyond our ken,

Which to explain did so much pain,
and puzzle wisest men?

122

They are
confuted.
Pro. 14: 6
Isa. 35: 8
Hos. 8: 12

Was all my word abstruse and hard?
    the Judge then answered:
It did contain much truth so plain,
    you might have run and read,
But what was hard you never car'd
    to know nor studied,
And things that were most plain and clear
    you never practised.

123

Mat. 11: 25

The Mystery of Pietie
    God unto Babes reveals:
When to the wise he it denies,
    and from the world conceals.

Prov. 2: 3, 4, 5

If to fulfil Gods holy will
    had seemed good to you,
You would have sought light as you ought,
    and done the good you knew.

124

Others the
fear of
Persecution.
Acts 28: 22

Then came in view another Crew,
    and 'gan to make their pleas.
Amongst the rest, some of the best
    had such poor shifts as these:
Thou know'st right well, who all canst tell
    we liv'd amongst thy foes,
Who the Renate did sorely hate,
    and goodness much oppose.

125

John 12: 42, 43

We holiness du[r]st not profess,
    fearing to be forlorn
Of all our friends, and for amends
    to be the wickeds scorn.

We knew their anger would much endanger
   our lives, and our estates:
Therefore for fear we durst appear
   no better than our mates.

126

They are
answered.
Luk. 12: 4, 5
Isa. 51: 12, 13

To whom the Lord returns this word:
   O wonderful deceits!
To cast off aw[e] of Gods strict Law,
   and fear mens wrath and threats.
To fear hell-fire and Gods fierce ire
   less than the rage of men,
As if Gods wrath, could do less scath
   than wrath of bretheren.

127

To use such strife, a temporal life,
   to rescue and secure,
And be so blind as not to mind
   that life that will endure:
This was your case, who carnal peace
   more than true joyes did savour;
Who fed on dust, clave to your lust,
   and spurned at my favour.

128

Luk. 9: 23, 24, 25
[*and*] 16: 25

To please your kin, mens love to win,
   to flow in worldly wealth,
To save your skin, these things have bin
   more than Eternal health.
You had your choice, wherein rejoyce,
   it was your portion,
For which you chose your Souls t' expose
   unto perdition.

129

Luk. 9: 26
Prov. 8: 36
John 3: 19, 20

Who did not hate friends, life, and state,
   with all things else for me,
And all forsake, and's Cross up-take,
   shall never happy be.

Well worthy they to dye for ay,
  who death then life had rather:
Death is their due, that so value
  the friendship of my Father.

130

*Others plead
for Pardon
both from Gods
mercy and
justice.
Psal. 78: 38*

Others Argue, and not a few,
  is not God gracious?
His Equity and Clemency
  are they not marvellous?
Thus we believ'd; are we deceiv'd?
  cannot his mercy great,
(As hath been told to us of old)
  asswage his angers heat?

131

II *Kings* 14: 26

How can it be that God should see
  his Creatures endless pain,
Or hear the groans and rueful moans,
  and still his wrath retain?
Can it agree with Equitie?
  can mercy have the heart
To recompence few years offence
  with Everlasting smart?

132

Can God delight in such a sight
  as sinners misery?
Or what great good can this our blood
  bring unto the most High?

Psal. 30: 9
Mic. 7: 18

Oh, thou that dost thy Glory most
  in pard'ning sin display!
Lord, might it please thee to release,
  and pardon us this day?

133

Unto thy Name more glorious fame
  would not such mercy bring?
Would not it raise thine endless praise,
  more than our suffering?

With that they cease, holding their peace,
    but cease not still to weep;
Grief ministers a flood of tears,
    in which their words do steep.

134

But all too late, grief's out of date,
    when life is at an end.
The glorious King thus answering,
    all to his voice attend:

They answered.

God gracious is, quoth he, like his
    no mercy can be found;

Mercy that now shines forth in the vessels of Mercy.
Mic. 7: 18
Rom. 9: 23

His Equity and Clemency
    to sinners do abound.

135

As may appear by those that here
    are plac'd at my right hand;
Whose stripes I bore, and clear'd the score,
    that they might quitted stand.
For surely none, but God alone,
    whose Grace transcends mens thought,
For such as those that were his foes
    like wonders would have wrought.

136

Did also long wait upon such as abused it.
Rom. 2: 4
Hos. 11: 4

And none but he such lenitee
    and patience would have shown
To you so long, who did him wrong,
    and pull'd his judgments down.
How long a space (O stiff neck'd race)
    did patience you afford?
How oft did love you gently move,
    to turn unto the Lord?

137

Luk. 13: 34
The day of Grace now past.

With Cords of love God often strove
    your stubborn hearts to tame:
Nevertheless your wickedness,
    did still resist the same.

If now at last Mercy be past
  from you for evermore,
And Justice come in Mercies room,
  yet grudge you not therefore.

138

If into wrath God turned hath
  his long long suffering,

Luk. 19: 42, 43
Jude 4

And now for love you vengeance prove,[14]
  it is an equal thing.
Your waxing worse, hath stopt the course
  of wonted Clemency:
Mercy refus'd, and Grace misus'd,
  call for severity.

139

Rom. 2: 5, 6
Isa. 1: 24
Amos 2: 13
Gen. 18: 25

It's now high time that ev'ry Crime
  be brought to punishment:
Wrath long contain'd, and oft restrain'd,
  at last must have a vent:
Justice severe cannot forbear
  to plague sin any longer,
But must inflict with hand most strict
  mischief upon the wronger.

140

Mat. 25: 3,
11, 12
Prov. 1: 28,
29, 30

In vain do they for Mercy pray,
  the season being past,
Who had no care to get a share
  therein, while time did last.
The man whose ear refus'd to hear
  the voice of Wisdoms cry, ·
Earn'd this reward, that none regard
  him in his misery.

[14] experience.

141

Isa. 5: 18, 19
Gen. 2: 17
Rom. 2: 8, 9

It doth agree with equity,
   and with Gods holy Law,
That those should dye eternally
   that death upon them draw.
The Soul that sins damnation wins,
   for so the Law ordains;
Which Law is just, and therefore must
   such suffer endless pain[s].

142

Rom. 6: 23
II *Thess.* 1: 8, 9

Eternal smart is the desert,
   ev'n of the least offence;
Then wonder not if I allot
   to you this Recompence:
But wonder more, that since so sore
   and lasting plagues are due
To every sin, you liv'd therein,
   who well the danger knew.

143

Ezek. 33: 11
Exod. 34: 7
and 14: 17
Rom. 9: 22

God hath no joy to crush or 'stroy,
   and ruine wretched wights,
But to display the glorious Ray
   of Justice he delights.
To manifest he doth detest,
   and throughly hate all sin,
By plaguing it as is most fit,
   this shall him glory win.

144

*Some pretend
they were shut
out from
Heaven by
God's Decree.
Rom.* 9: 18, 19

Then at the Bar arraigned are
   an impudenter sort,
Who to evade the guilt that's laid
   upon them, thus retort;
How could we cease thus to transgress?
   how could we Hell avoid,
Whom Gods Decree shut out from thee,
   and sign'd to be destroy'd?

145

Whom God ordains to endless pains,
  by Law unalterable,
Repentence true, Obedience new,
  to save such are unable:

Heb. [1]2: 17
Rom. 11: 7, 8

Sorrow for sin, no good can win,
  to such as are rejected;
Ne[15] can they grieve, nor yet believe,
  that never were elected.

146

Of Man's fall'n Race, who can true Grace,
  or Holiness obtain?
Who can convert or change his heart,
  if God withhold the same?
Had we apply'd our selves, and try'd
  as much as who did most
God's love to gain, our busie pain
  and labour had been lost.

147

Their pleas
taken off.
Luk. 13: 27
II *Pet.* 1: 9, 10
compared with
Mat. 19: 6

Christ readily makes this Reply,
  I damn you not because
You are rejected, or not elected,
  but you have broke my Laws:
It is but vain your wits to strain,
  the end and means to sever:
Men fondly seek to part or break
  what God hath link'd together.

148

Acts 3: 19
and 16: 31
I *Sam.* 2: 15
John 3: 19
John 5: 40
II *Thes.* 2: 11,
12

Whom God will save, such he will have,
  the means of life to use:
Whom he'll pass by, shall chuse to dy,
  and ways of life refuse.
He that fore-sees, and fore-decrees,
  in wisdom order'd has,

[15] Nor.

94

That man's free-will electing ill,
shall bring his will to pass.

149

Ezek. 33: 11,
12, 13
Luk. 13: 34
Prov. 8: 33, 36

High God's Decree, as it is free,
so doth it none compel
Against their will to good or ill,
it forceth none to Hell.
They have their wish whose Souls perish
with Torments in Hell-fire,
Who rather chose their Souls to lose,
than leave a loose desire.

150

Gen. 2: 17
Mat. 25: 41, 42
Ezek. 18: 20

God did ordain sinners to pain
and I to Hell send none,
But such as swerv'd, and have deserv'd
destruction as their own.
His pleasure is, that none from bliss
and endless happiness
Be barr'd, but such as wrong'd him much
by wilful wickedness.

151

You, sinful Crew, no other knew
but you might be elect;

II *Pet.* 1: 10
Acts 13: 46
Luk. 13: 24

Why did you then your selves condemn?
why did you me reject?
Where was your strife to gain that life
which lasteth evermore?
You never knock'd, yet say God lock'd
against you Heav'ns door.

152

Mat. 7: 7, 8

'Twas no vain task to knock, to ask,
whilst life continued.
Whoever sought heav'n as he ought,
and seeking perished?

Gal. 5: 22, 23

> The lowly meek who truly seek
>   for Christ, and for Salvation,
> There's no Decree whereby such be
>   ordain'd to Condemnation.

153

> You argue then: But abject men,
>   whom God resolves to spill,
> Cannot repent, nor their hearts rent;
>   ne can they change their will.
> Not for his *Can* is any man
>   adjudged unto Hell:

John 3: 19

> But for his *Will* to do what's ill,
>   and nilling[16] to do well.

154

> I often stood tend'ring my Blood
>   to wash away your guilt:
> And eke my Spright[17] to frame you right,
>   lest your Souls should be split.

John 5: 40

> But you vile Race, rejected Grace,
>   when Grace was freely proffer'd:
> No changed heart, no heav'nly part
>   would you, when it was offer'd.

155

> Who wilfully the Remedy,
>   and means of life contemned,
> Cause have the same themselves to blame,

John 15: 22, 24
Heb. 2: 3
Isa. 66: 3, 4

>   if now they be condemned.
> You have your selves, you and none else,
>   your selves have done to dy.
> You chose the way to your decay,
>   and perisht wilfully.

[16] not willing.
[17] spirit.

156

These words appall and daunt them all;
    dismai'd, and all amort,[18]
Like stocks they stand at Christ's left-hand,
    and dare no more retort.
Then were brought near with trembling fear,
    a number numberless
Of blind Heathen, and brutish men,
    that did Gods Laws transgress.

157

*Heathen men
plead want of
the written
Word.*

Whose wicked ways Christ open layes,
    and makes their sins appear,
They making pleas their case to ease,
    if not themselves to clear.
Thy written Word (say they) good Lord,
    we never did enjoy:
We nor refus'd, nor it abus'd;
    Oh, do not us destroy!

158

Mat. 11: 22
Luk. 12: 48

You ne'r abus'd, nor yet refus'd
    my written Word, you plead,
That's true (quoth he) therefore shall ye
    the less be punished.
You shall not smart for any part
    of other mens offence,
But for your own transgression
    receive due recompence.

159

I *Cor.* 1: 21
*And insuffi-
ciency of the
Light of
Nature.*

But we were blind, say they, in mind,
    too dim was Natures Light,
Our only guide, as hath been try'd
    to bring us to the sight
Of our estate degenerate
    and curst by *Adam's* Fall;

[18] lifeless, dejected.

How we were born and lay forlorn
in bondage and in thrall.

160

We did not know a Christ till now,
nor how faln man be saved,
Else would we not, right well we wot,[19]
have so our selves behaved.

Mat. 11: 21
We should have mourn'd, we should have turn'd
from sin at thy Reproof,
And been more wise through thy advice,
for our own Souls behoof.

161

But Natures Light shin'd not so bright
to teach us the right way:
We might have lov'd it, and well improv'd,
and yet have gone astray.

*They are
answered.*
The Judge most High makes this Reply,
you ignorance pretend,
Dimness of sight, and want of light
your course Heav'nward to bend.

162

Gen. 1: 27
Eccles. 7: 29
Hos. 13: 9
How came your mind to be so blind?
I once you knowledge gave,
Clearness of sight, and judgment right;
who did the same deprave?
If to your cost you have it lost,
and quite defac'd the same;
Your own desert hath caus'd the Smart,
you ought not me to blame.

163

Mat. 11: 25
compared with
20 *and* 15
Your selves into a pit of woe,
your own transgression led:
If I to none my Grace had shown,
who had been injured?

[19] know.

If to a few, and not to you,
   I shew'd a way of life,
My Grace so free, you clearly see,
   gives you no ground of strife.

164

'Tis vain to tell, you wot full well,
   if you in time had known
Your Misery and Remedy,
   your actions had it shown.

Rom. 1: 20,
21, 22

You, sinful Crew, have not been true
   unto the Light of Nature,
Nor done the good you understood,
   nor owned your Creator.

165

He that the Light, because 'tis Light,
   hath used to despize,

Rom. 2: 12, 15
and 1: 32
Mat. 12: 41

Would not the Light shining more bright,
   be likely for to prize.
If you had lov'd, and well improv'd
   your knowledge and dim sight,
Herein your pain had not been vain,
   your plagues had been more light.

166

*Reprobate Infants
plead for them-
selves.
Rev.* 20: 12, 15
*compared with
Rom.* 5: 12, 14
and 9: 11, 13

Then to the Bar, all they drew near
   who dy'd in Infancy,
And never had or good or bad
   effected pers'nally,
But from the womb unto the tomb
   were straightway carried,
(Or at the last e're they transgrest)
   who thus began to plead:

167

Ezek. 18: 2

If for our own transgression,
   or disobedience,
We here did stand at thy left-hand
   just were the Recompence:

But *Adam's* guilt our souls hath split,
   his fault is charg'd on us;
And that alone hath overthrown,
   and utterly undone us.

168

Not we, but he, ate of the tree
   whose fruit was interdicted:
Yet on us all of his sad Fall,
   the punishment's inflicted.
How could we sin that had not been,
   or how is his sin our,
Without consent, which to prevent,
   we never had a pow'r?

169

O great Creator, why was our Nature
   depraved and forlorn?
Why so defil'd, and made so vild
   whilst we were yet unborn?
If it be just, and needs we must
   transgressors reck'ned be,
Psal. 51: 5   Thy Mercy, Lord, to us afford,
   which sinners hath set free.

170

Behold we see *Adam* set free,
   and sav'd from his trespass,
Whose sinful Fall hath split us all,
   and brought us to this pass.
Canst thou deny us once to try,
   or Grace to us to tender,
When he finds grace before thy face,
   that was the chief offender?

171

Their Argument
taken off.
Ezek. 18: 20
Rom. 5: 12, 19

Then answered the Judge most dread,
   God doth such doom forbid,
That men should dye eternally
   for what they never did.

But what you call old *Adam's* Fall,
    and only his Trespass,
You call amiss to call it his,
    both his and yours it was.

172

He was design'd of all Mankind
    to be a publick Head,
A common Root, whence all should shoot,
    and stood in all their stead.
I *Cor.* 15: 48, 49   He stood and fell, did ill or well,
    not for himself alone,
But for you all, who now his Fall,
    and trespass would disown.

173

If he had stood, then all his brood
    had been established
In Gods true love, never to move,
    nor once awry to tread:
Then all his Race, my Father's Grace,
    should have enjoy'd for ever,
And wicked Sprights by subtile sleights
    could them have harmed never.

174

Would you have griev'd to have receiv'd
    through *Adam* so much good,
As had been your for evermore,
    if he at first had stood?
Would you have said, we ne'r obey'd,
    nor did thy Laws regard;
It ill befits with benefits,
    us, Lord, so to reward?

175

Since then to share in his welfare,
    you could have been content,
You may with reason share in his treason,
    and in the punishment.

Rom. 5: 12
Psa. 51: 5
Gen. 5: 3

Hence you were born in state forlorn,
    with Natures so depraved:
Death was your due, because that you
    had thus your selves behaved.

176

Mat. 23: 30, 31

You think if we had been as he,
    whom God did so betrust,
We to our cost would ne're have lost
    all for a paltry Lust.
Had you been made in *Adam's* stead,
    you would like things have wrought,
And so into the self-same wo,
    your selves and yours have brought.

177

Rom. 9: 15, 18
The free gift.
Rom. 5: 15

I may deny you once to try,
    or Grace to you to tender,
Though he finds Grace before my face,
    who was the chief offender:
Else should my Grace cease to be Grace;
    for it should not be free,
If to release whom I should please,
    I have no libertee.

178

If upon one what's due to none
    I frankly shall bestow,
And on the rest shall not think best,
    compassions skirts to throw,
Whom injure I? will you envy,
    and grudge at others weal?
Or me accuse, who do refuse
    your selves to help and heal?

179

Mat. 20: 15

Am I alone of what's my own,
    no Master or no Lord?
Or if I am, how can you claim
    what I to some afford?

Will you demand Grace at my hand,
    and challenge what is mine?
Will you teach me whom to set free,
    and thus my Grace confine?

180

Psa. 58: 3
Ro. 6: 23
Gal. 3: 10
Rom. 8: 29, 30
and 11: 7
Rev. 21: 27
Luk. 12: 48

You sinners are, and such a share
    as sinners may expect,
Such you shall have; for I do save
    none but mine own Elect.
Yet to compare your sin with their,
    who liv'd a longer time,
I do confess yours is much less,
    though every sin's a crime.

181

Mat. 11: 22
*The wicked all
convinced and
put to silence.*
Ro. 3: 19
Mat. 22: 12

A crime it is, therefore in bliss
    you may not hope to dwell;
But unto you I shall allow
    the easiest room in Hell.
The glorious King thus answering,
    they cease, and plead no longer:
Their Consciences must needs confess
    his Reasons are the stronger.

182

*Behold the
formidable
estate of all
the ungodly,
as they stand
hopeless and
helpless before
an impartial
Judge, expect-
ing their
final sentence.*
Rev. 6: 16, 17

Thus all mens Pleas the Judge with ease
    doth answer and confute,
Until that all, both great and small,
    are silenced and mute.
Vain hopes are cropt, all mouths are stopt,
    sinners have nought to say,
But that 'tis just, and equal most
    they should be damn'd for ay.

183

Now what remains, but that to pains
    and everlasting smart,
Christ should condemn the Sons of men,
    which is their just desert;

Oh, rueful plights of sinful wights!
  Oh wretches all forlorn!
'T had happy been they ne're had seen
  the Sun, or not been born.

184

Yea, now it would be good they could
  themselves annihilate,
And cease to be, themselves to free
  from such a fearful state.
Oh happy Dogs, and Swine, and Frogs:
  yea Serpents generation,
Who do not fear this doom to hear,
  and sentence of Damnation!

185

Psa. 139: 2, 3, 4   This is their state so desperate:
Eccl. 12: 14   their sins are fully known;
Their vanities and villanies
  before the world are shown.
As they are gross and impious,
  so are their numbers more
Than motes i' th' Air, or then their hair,
  or sands upon the shore.

186

Divine Justice offended is
  and Satisfaction claimeth:
God's wrathful ire kindled like fire,
  against them fiercely flameth.
Their Judge severe doth quite cashier
Mat. 25: 45   and all their Pleas off take,
That never a man, or dare, or can
  a further Answer make.

187

Mat. 22: 12   Their mouths are shut, each man is put
Rom. 2: 5, 6   to silence and to shame:
Luk. 19: 42   Nor have they ought within their thought,
  Christ's Justice for to blame.

The Judge is just, and plague them must,
   nor will he mercy shew
(For Mercies day is past away)
   to any of this Crew.

188

Mat. 28: 18
Psal. 139: 7

The Judge is strong, doers of wrong
   cannot his power withstand:
None can by flight run out of sight,
   nor scape out of his hand.
Sad is their state: for Advocate
   to plead their Cause there's none:
None to prevent their punishment,
   or misery bemone.

189

O dismal day! wither shall they
   for help and succour flee?
To God above, with hopes to move
   their greatest Enemee:

Isa. 33: 14
Psal. 11: 6
Numb. 23: 19

His wrath is great, whose burning heat
   no floods of tears can slake:
His word stands fast, that they be cast
   into the burning Lake.

190

To Christ their Judge, he doth adjudge
   them to the Pit of Sorrow;

Matt. 25: 41

Nor will he hear, or cry, or tear,
   nor respite them one morrow.

Matt. 25: 10,
11, 12

To Heav'n alas, they cannot pass,
   it is against them shut;
To enter there (O heavy cheer)
   they out of hopes are put.

191

Luk. 12: 20
Psal. 49: 7, 17

Unto their Treasures, or to their Pleasures,
   all these have them forsaken:

Had they full Coffers to make large offers,
   their Gold would not be taken
Unto the place where whilome[20] was
Deut. 32: 2   their Birth and Education?
Lo! Christ begins for their great sins
   to fire the Earths Foundation:

192

II *Pet.* 3: 10   And by and by the flaming Sky
   shall drop like molten Lead
About their ears, t' increase their fears,
   and aggravate their dread.
To Angels good that ever stood
   in their integrity,
Should they betake themselves, and make
   their suit incessantly?

193

Mat. 13: 41, 42   They neither skill,[21] nor do they will
   to work them any ease:
They will not mourn to see them burn,
   nor beg for their release.
To wicked men, their bretheren
   in sin and wickedness,
Should they make mone? their case is one,
Rev. 20: 13, 15   they're in the same distress.

194

Ah, cold comfort, and mean support
   from such like Comforters!
Ah, little joy of Company,
   and fellow-sufferers!
Luk. 16: 28   Such shall increase their hearts disease,
   and add unto their woe,
Because that they brought to decay
   themselves and many moe.[22]

[20] at some earlier time.
[21] know how to.
[22] more.

195

Unto the Saints with sad complaints
   should they themselves apply?

Rev. 21: 4

They're not dejected, nor ought affected
   with all their misery.
Friends stand aloof, and make no proof
   what Prayers or Tears can do:

Psal. 58: 10

Your godly friends are now more friends
   to Christ than unto you.

196

Where tender love mens hearts did move
   unto a sympathy,
And bearing part of others smart
   in their anxiety;

I Cor. 6: 2

Now such compassion is out of fashion,
   and wholly laid aside:
No Friends so near, but Saints to hear
   their Sentence can abide.

197

One natural Brother beholds another
   in this astonied[23] fit,

Compare
Prov. 1: 26 *with*
I Joh. 3: 2 *and*
II Cor. 5: 16

Yet sorrows not thereat a jot,
   nor pitties him a whit.
The godly wife conceives no grief,
   nor can she shed a tear
For the sad state of her dear Mate,
   when she his doom doth hear.

198

He that was erst a Husband pierc't
   with sense of Wives distress,
Whose tender heart did bear a part
   of all her grievances,
Shall mourn no more as heretofore
   because of her ill plight

[23] astonished, dismayed.

Although he see her now to be
a damn'd forsaken wight.

199

The tender Mother will own no other
of all her numerous brood,
But such as stand at Christ's right hand
acquitted through his Blood.

Luk. 16: 25

The pious Father had now much rather
his graceless Son should ly
In Hell with Devils, for all his evils
burning eternally,

200

Then God most high should injury,

Psal. 58: 10

    by sparing him sustain;
And doth rejoyce to hear Christ's voice
    adjudging him to pain;
Who having all, both great and small,
    convinc'd and silenced,
Did then proceed their Doom to read,
    and thus it uttered:

201

The Judge
pronounceth
the Sentence
of condem-
nation.
Mat. 25: 41

Ye sinful wights, and cursed sprights,
    that work Iniquity,
Depart together from me for ever
    to endless Misery;
Your portion take in yonder Lake,
    where Fire and Brimstone flameth:
Suffer the smart, which your desert
    as it's due wages claimeth.

202

Oh piercing words more sharp than swords!

The terrour
of it.

    what, to depart from *Thee,*
Whose face before for evermore
    the best of Pleasures be!

What? to depart (unto our smart)
    from thee *Eternally:*
To be for aye banish'd away,
    with *Devils* company!

203

What? to be sent to *Punishment,*
    and flames of *Burning Fire,*
To be surrounded, and eke confounded
    with Gods *Revengful ire.*
What? to abide, not for a tide
    these Torments, but for *Ever:*
To be released, or to be eased,
    not after years, but *Never.*

204

Oh, *fearful Doom!* now there's no room
    for hope or help at all:
Sentence is past which aye shall last,
    Christ will not it recall.
There might you hear them rent and tear
    the Air with their out-cries:
The hideous noise of their sad voice
    ascendeth to the Skies.

205

Luk. 13: 28

They wring their hands, their caitiff-hands
    and gnash their teeth for terrour;
They cry, they roar for anguish sore,
    and gnaw their tongues for horrour.
But get away without delay,
    Christ pitties not your cry:
Depart to Hell, there may you yell,

Prov. 1: 26
    and roar Eternally.

206

*It is put in
Execution.*

That word, *Depart,* maugre their heart,
    drives every wicked one,

With mighty pow'r, the self-same hour,
   far from the Judge's Throne.

Mat. 25: 46

Away they're chaste[24] by the strong blast
   of his Death-threatning mouth:
They flee full fast, as if in haste,
   although they be full loath.

207

As chaff that's dry, and dust doth fly
   before the Northern wind:
Right so are they chased away,
   and can no Refuge find.
They hasten to the Pit of Wo,

Matt. 13: 41, 42

   guarded by Angels stout;
Who to fulfil Christ's holy will,
   attend this wicked Rout.

208

HELL.
Mat. 25: 30
Mark 9: 43
Isa. 30: 33
Rev. 21: 8

Whom having brought, as they are taught,
   unto the brink of Hell,
(That dismal place far from Christ's face,
   where Death and Darkness dwell:
Where Gods fierce Ire kindleth the fire,
   and vengeance feeds the flame
With piles of Wood, and Brimstone Flood,
   that none can quench the same,)

209

Wicked Men
and Devils
cast into it
for ever.
Mat. 22: 13 *and*
25: 46

With Iron bands they bind their hands,
   and cursed feet together,
And cast them all, both great and small,
   into that Lake for ever.
Where day and night, without respite,
   they wail, and cry, and howl
For tort'ring pain, which they sustain
   in Body and in Soul.

24 chased.

210

Rev. 14: 10, 11

For day and night, in their despight,
   their torments smoak ascendeth.
Their pain and grief have no relief,
   their anguish never endeth.
There must they ly, and never dy,
   though dying every day:
There must they dying ever ly,
   and not consume away.

211

Dy fain they would, if dy they could,
   but Death will not be had:
God's direful wrath their bodies hath
   for ev'r Immortal made.
They live to ly in misery,
   and bear eternal wo;
And live they must whilst God is just,
   that he may plague them so.

212

The unsuffer-
able torments
of the damned.
Luk. 16: 24
Jude 7

But who can tell the plagues of Hell,
   and torments exquisite?
Who can relate their dismal state,
   and terrours infinite?
Who fare the best, and feel the least,
   yet feel that punishment
Whereby to nought they should be brought,
   if God did not prevent.

213

The least degree of miserie
   there felt's incomparable,
The lightest pain they there sustain
   more than intolerable.

Isa. 33: 14
Mark 9: 43, 44

But God's great pow'r from hour to hour
   upholds them in the fire,
That they shall not consume a jot,
   nor by it's force expire.

214

But ah, the wo they undergo
  (they more than all besides)
Who has the light, and knew the right,

Luk. 12: 47
  yet would not it abide.
The sev'n-fold smart, which to their part,
  and portion doth fall,
Who Christ his Grace would not imbrace,
  nor hearken to his call.

215

The *Amorites*[25] and *Sodomites*

Mat. 11: 24
  although their plagues be sore,
Yet find some ease, compar'd to these,
  who feel a great deal more.
Almighty God, whose Iron Rod,
  to smite them never lins,[26]
Doth most declare his Justice rare
  in plaguing these mens sins.

216

Luk. 16: 23, 25
Luk. 13: 28
The pain of loss their Souls doth toss,
  and wond'rously distress,
To think what they have cast away
  by wilful wickedness.
We might have been redeem'd from sin,
  think they, and liv'd above,
Being possest of Heav'nly rest,
  and joying in God's love.

217

Luk. 13: 34
But wo, wo, wo our Souls unto!
  we would not happy be;
And therefore bear Gods Vengeance here
  to all Eternitee.
Experience and woful sense
  must be our painful teachers

25 Gen xv 16: like the Sodomites, an iniquitous people.
26 ceases.

Who n'ould[27] believe, nor credit give,
unto our faithful Preachers.

218

Mark 9: 44
Rom. 2: 15

Thus shall they ly, and wail, and cry,
 tormented, and tormenting
Their galled hearts with pois'ned darts
 but now too late repenting.
There let them dwell i' th' Flames of Hel
 there leave we them to burn,
And back agen unto the men
 whom Christ acquits, return.

219

*The Saints
rejoyce to see
Judgment execu-
ted upon the
wicked World.
Ps.* 58: 10
Rev. 19: 1, 2, 3

The Saints behold with courage bold,
 and thankful wonderment,
To see all those that were their foes
 thus sent to punishment:
Then do they sing unto their King
 a Song of endless Praise:
They praise his Name, and do proclaim
 that just are all his ways.

220

*They ascend
with Christ
into Heaven
triumphing.
Mat.* 25: 46
I *Joh.* 3: 2
I *Cor.* 13: 12

Thus with great joy and melody
 to Heav'n they all ascend,
Him there to praise with sweetest layes,
 and Hymns that never end,
Where with long Rest they shall be blest,
 and nought shall them annoy:
Where they shall see as seen they be,
 and whom they love enjoy.

221

*Their Eternal
happiness and
incomparable
Glory there.*

O glorious Place! where face to face
 Jehovah may be seen,
By such as were sinners whilere
 and no dark vail between.

[27] would not.

Where the Sun shine, and light Divine,
  of Gods bright Countenance,
Doth rest upon them every one.
  with sweetest influence.

222

O blessed state of the Renate!
  O wondrous Happiness,
To which they're brought, beyond what thought
  can reach, or words express!
Rev. 21: 4   Griefs water-course, and sorrows sourse,
  are turn'd to joyful streams,
Their old distress and heaviness
  are vanished like dreams.

223

For God above in arms of love
  doth dearly them embrace,
Psal. 16: 11   And fills their sprights with such delights,
  and pleasures in his grace;
As shall not fail, nor yet grow stale
  through frequency of use:
Nor do they fear Gods favour there,
  to forfeit by abuse.

224

Heb. 12: 23   For there the Saints are perfect Saints,
  and holy ones indeed,
From all the sin that dwelt within
  their mortal bodies freed:
Made Kings and Priests to God through Christs
Rev. 1: 6 *and*   dear loves transcendency,
22: 5   There to remain, and there to reign
  with him Eternally.

FINIS.

A Song of Emptiness To Fill up the Empty Pages Following

Vanity of Vanities

Vain, frail, short liv'd, and miserable Man,
Learn what thou art when thine estate is best:
A restless Wave o'th' troubled Ocean,
A Dream, a lifeless Picture finely drest:

A Wind, a Flower, a Vapour, and a Bubble,   5
A Wheel that stands not still, a trembling Reed,
A rolling Stone, dry Dust, light Chaff, and Stubble,
A Shadow of Something, but nought indeed.

Learn what deceitful Toyes, and empty things,
This World, and all its best Enjoyments bee: 10
Out of the Earth no true Contentment springs,
But all things here are vexing Vanitee.

For what is *Beauty*, but a fading Flower?
Or what is *Pleasure*, but the Devils bait,
Whereby he catcheth whom he would devour,   15
And multitudes of Souls doth ruinate?

And what are *Friends* but mortal men, as we?
Whom Death from us may quickly separate;
Or else their hearts may quite estranged be,
And all their love be turned into hate.   20

And what are *Riches* to be doted on?
Uncertain, fickle, and ensnaring things;
They draw Mens Souls into Perdition,
And when most needed, take them to their wings.

Ah foolish Man! that sets his heart upon   25
Such empty Shadows, such wild Fowl as these,
That being gotten will be quickly gone,
And whilst they stay increase but his disease.

As in a Dropsie, drinking draughts begets,
The more he drinks, the more he still requires: 30
So in this world whoso affection sets,
His Wealths encrease encreaseth his desires.

O happy Man, whose portion is above,
Where Floods, where Flames, where Foes cannot bereave him,
Most wretched man, that fixed hath his love   35
Upon this World, that surely will deceive him!

For, what is *Honour?* What is *Sov'raignty,*
Whereto mens hearts so restlesly aspire?
Whom have they Crowned with Felicity?
When did they ever satisfie desire?   40

The Ear of Man with hearing is not fill'd:
To see new sights still coveteth the Eye:
The craving Stomack though it may be still'd,
Yet craves again without a new supply.

All Earthly things, man's Cravings answer not,   45
Whose little heart would all the World contain,
(If all the World should fall to one man's Lot)
And notwithstanding empty still remain,

The *Eastern Conquerour* was said to weep,
When he the *Indian* Ocean did view,   50
To see his Conquest bounded by the Deep,
And no more Worlds remaining to subdue.

Who would that man in his Enjoyments bless,
Or envy him, or covet his estate,
Whose gettings do augment his greediness,   55
And make his wishes more intemperate?

Such is the wonted and the common guise
Of those on Earth that bear the greatest Sway:
If with a few the case be otherwise
They seek a Kingdom that abides for ay.   60

Moreover they, of all the Sons of men,
That Rule, and are in Highest Places set,
Are most inclin'd to scorn their Bretheren
And God himself (without great grace) forget.

For as the Sun doth blind the gazer's eyes,   65
That for a time they nought discern aright:
So Honour doth befool and blind the Wise,
And their own Lustre 'reaves them of their sight.

Great are the Dangers, manifold their Cares;
Thro' which, whilst others Sleep, they scarcely Nap:　　　70
And yet are oft surprised unawares,
And fall unweeting[1] into Envies Trap!

The mean Mechanick finds his kindly rest,
All void of fear Sleepeth the Country-Clown,
When greatest Princes often are distrest,　　　75
And cannot Sleep upon their Beds of Down.

Could *Strength* or *Valour* men Immortalize,
Could *Wealth* or *Honour* keep them from decay,
There were some cause the same to Idolize,
And give the lye to that which I do say.　　　80

But neither can such things themselves endure
Without the hazard of a Change one hour,
Nor such as trust in them can they secure
From dismal dayes, or Deaths prevailing pow'r.

If *Beauty* could the beautiful defend　　　85
From Death's dominion than fair *Absalom*
Had not been brought to such a shameful end:
But fair and foul unto the Grave must come.

If *Wealth* or *Scepters* could Immortal make,
Then wealthy *Croesus*, wherefore art thou dead?　　　90
If *Warlike-force*, which makes the World to quake,
Then why is *Julius Caesar* perished?

Where are the *Scipio's* Thunder-bolts of War?
Renowned *Pompey*, *Caesars* Enemie?
Stout *Hannibal*, *Romes* Terror known so far?　　　95
Great *Alexander*, what's become of thee?

If *Gifts* and *Bribes* Death's favour might but win,
If *Power*, if force, or *Threatnings* might it fray,
All these, and more, had still surviving been:
But all are gone, for Death will have no Nay.　　　100

Such is this World with all her Pomp and Glory,
Such are the men whom worldly eyes admire:
Cut down by Time, and now become a Story,
That we might after better things aspire.

[1] unknowing.

Go boast thy self of what thy heart enjoyes,   105
Vain Man! triumph in all thy worldly Bliss:
Thy best enjoyments are but Trash and Toyes:
Delight thy self in that which worthless is.

Omnia praetereunt praeter amare Deum.[2]

[2] "All things pass save love of God."

EDWARD TAYLOR
(c. 1642–1729)

The poetry of Edward Taylor lay unnoticed for more than two hundred years in a rough leather manuscript book containing some four hundred quarto pages in a difficult handwriting. Taylor, for undetermined reasons, had virtually willed himself into poetic anonymity for two centuries by requesting that his heirs not publish his poetry. They honored his wishes, and it was not until 1937 that his manuscript book was discovered in the Yale University Library. Publication of a generous selection from that manuscript two years later established the Puritan minister as the foremost Colonial poet of America. Since the 1939 publication of *The Poetical Works of Edward Taylor* the Puritan poet's stature has grown, and the body of criticism and biographical information about him is now substantial.

Edward Taylor was born about 1642 in Sketchley, England, near Leicestershire. The incompleteness of official town or family birth records possibly reflects the turmoil of the English Civil War period when Taylor was born. The son of a farmer, he grew up and was educated by a non-conformist schoolmaster during years that saw the rise of Oliver Cromwell, the defeat of Royalist armies, the execution of Charles I, and the establishment of the Holy Commonwealth. Taylor may have attended Cambridge, though once again there are no official records to document his university attendance. As a young man he became a schoolmaster, but the fall of the Puritan Commonwealth, and the Restoration of Charles II to the throne of England in 1660, signaled the end of Taylor's career as a teacher. His inability as a conscientious Puritan to comply with the Act of Uniformity—requiring an annual acceptance of the Anglican sacrament of communion—cost Taylor his position. In the spring of 1668 he sailed for America, never again to return to England. Taylor was then twenty-six years old.

Arriving at Boston in midsummer with letters of introduction to the intellectually prominent Increase Mather, Edward Taylor was welcomed as a house guest by Mather, then by John Hull, Boston's wealthy goldsmith and merchant, and by President Chauncy of Harvard, who admitted him to the Class of 1671. Taylor's matriculation with advanced standing attests to his considerable education while in England. His record at Harvard was sufficiently impressive that he was one of four chosen to declaim on Commencement Day before the President and Fellows of the college. Taylor's declamation, which lauded the virtues of English over Hebrew and the classical languages in relentless couplets of rhyming iambic pentameter, serves more to reveal his poetic inclinations than his poetic achievements at that time.

Although as he neared graduation Taylor seriously considered remaining at Harvard for further study, he accepted a call for the ministry at Westfield, Massachusetts, a sparsely settled community one hundred miles southwest of Boston across the Connecticut River. In 1671 it took Taylor eight days on horseback to reach the settlement where he spent the remaining fifty-eight years of his life, and where he wrote the poetry for which he is remembered.

But Taylor did not immediately begin his poetic career. Indeed, he was not soon able to gather his church, nor was he soon ordained, for the bloodiest of the Indian Wars, King Philip's War, began in 1675 and seriously threatened Westfield. There was, as it happened, no major attack on that community. But there were skirmishes, and the need for effective fortification and watchfulness was constant. As the most prominent citizen in a community of farmers, Taylor was doubtless looked to, for leadership, during the crisis. Of course, there was much more required of him than paramilitary leadership. For his own subsistence it was necessary that Taylor maintain livestock and cultivate crops. Further, he was both minister and teacher at a time when larger communities had two men to fill these positions, which meant that Taylor was obliged to visit all members of the community regularly for spiritual counseling, as well as to prepare one or two lengthy sermons each week. Nor was he only a spiritual physician, for medical treatment was the province of the New England minister in a frontier community. The seriousness with which Edward Taylor viewed his responsibility is evidenced by some eight medical treatises found in his library, including one on surgery and one on pharmacology. He himself compiled in his lifetime a book on medicinal herbs and cordials.

Taylor had still other duties. Though he had gone to Westfield as a bachelor, three years later he married Elizabeth Fitch, daughter of a Connecticut clergyman, who in their fifteen years of marriage before her death bore Taylor eight children. In those times of high mortality, Taylor saw five of his children die, their deaths prompting the poignant "On Wedlock and Death of Children." After the death of his first wife he married Ruth Wyllys, a descendant of two Connecticut governors, who bore him six additional children and raised the three surviving children of Taylor's first marriage. As head of a large family, Taylor was responsible for the material and spiritual welfare of several persons.

Yet in conscience he could not as a minister neglect the intellectual life, no matter what the demands of time upon him. It was expected that he would, as all New England Puritan ministers did, spend several hours daily in his study. Here again, the contents of Taylor's library reflect his concern for the life of the mind. His 220 books and tracts, many laboriously copied out by hand, represented in that time and place a large library of considerable value. Most of the books, published in Europe, had to be shipped at great expense. In all of Taylor's library there was just one volume of poetry, that of New England's Mistress Anne Bradstreet.

It was not until the end of King Philip's War in 1682 that Taylor "gathered" his church in a ceremony where those about to be members gave witness to their experience of God's saving grace. Taylor himself was then ordained by the imposition of hands. It was in that year also that he wrote the first of the *Preparatory Meditations,* poems which he continued to write at the rate of one every two months for the next forty-three years. It is on the *Preparatory Meditations* that Taylor's poetic reputation chiefly rests.

It is significant that this group of poems is titled *Preparatory Meditations,* for they were written in preparation for the Lord's Supper, which the Puritans recognized, along with baptism, as representing God's covenant of Grace. God had promised, or covenanted with man, that through His gift of grace some men would be given eternal life. They were the elect, the saints. By obvious implication, however, others would be damned, and the course of one's life was that of continual self-examination to determine the state of one's soul. No amount of good behavior could bring about salvation, for God had predetermined who would be saved and who damned, though naturally it was assumed that God's elect would lead exemplary lives. The Lord's Supper was not to be anticipated without preparation, without consideration of man's unworthiness, his depravity in contrast to the goodness of God, and with the wonderful possibility of living an eternal life with Him through the gift of His grace. These are the themes of Edward Taylor's *Preparatory Meditations,* themes that recur constantly, though stated in a variety of images.

Taylor's poetic images derive from a number of sources, first among which is the Bible, especially the Song of Songs. The figure of Christ as bridegroom to his bride, the church, captured the seventeenth-century poetic imagination, including Taylor's. Poetic use of biblical figures was strengthened by typology, the theory that persons, places, and events in the Old Testament prefigured those in the New Testament. Jonah's three days in the whale's stomach, for example, were thought to be a prophecy of Christ's three-day entombment after His crucifixion. Such type-antetype correspondence is discernible throughout Taylor's meditations.

Typology was one way of seeing order in God's spiritual and material world. And the Puritan rage for order ran high. Whatever occurred, no matter how trivial it might seem at the time, was to the Puritan divinely and purposively ordered, and thus could not be ignored. There is, then, the tendency toward allegory in some of Taylor's work, and the images in which the allegory is stated are frequently of the low and menial. Thus the spider waiting to ensnare insects is symbolically Satan awaiting an unwary sinner, the fly.

Taylor's use of images from everyday, readily observable activities such as farming and weaving can be traced to his boyhood and the rural life at Westfield, where, as he wrote, "little save Rusticity is." But if diction in some of his most forceful poems is not poetic, one recognizes, nonetheless, frequent echoes from the English metaphysical poets of a generation earlier. Although Taylor owned only one volume of poetry, there is evidence that he had read the works of George Herbert and Francis Quarles as a schoolboy in Leicestershire. Probably he had read others of that tradition called metaphysical, though this is not to say that Taylor was a copyist. Nothing could be further from the truth. He was, however, heir to a meditative tradition in early seventeenth-century English poetry, a tradition whose fullness had passed in England when Taylor sat writing his verses in Westfield.

The *Preparatory Meditations* are not Taylor's only significant poems. He wrote several occasional miscellaneous verses, always with a religious theme proper to New England Puritanism, yet stated in images that reveal his keen eye for detail. His well-documented interest in natural science is apparent, for example, as he traces the movements of his satanic spider in "Upon a Spider Catching a Fly." His best-known single work is the lengthy and formidably titled *Gods Determinations touching his Elect: and the Elects Combat in their Conversion and coming up to God in Christ together with the Comfortable Effects thereof,* known more simply as *Gods Determinations.* The divine drama of good opposing evil is conceived of in military terms, and the dialogue form in which the poem is shaped can be traced back to medieval debate literature, which Taylor may have known from morality plays seen in Coventry as a boy, or from other poets such as Milton or Spenser. There is the probability, too, that *Gods Determinations,* which shows the Puritan concept of God's grace in operation, was influenced by Taylor's fellow-New England divine, Michael Wigglesworth, author of *The Day of Doom.* Though *Gods Determinations* is of uneven quality, there are sections in it equal to Taylor's best.

And at his best, Taylor ranks foremost among early American poets. Indeed, Taylor achieved a level of poetic art which remained unequaled in America until the beginning of the nineteenth century.

Meditation 1. 1

What Love is this of thine, that Cannot bee
    In thine Infinity, O Lord, Confinde,
Unless it in thy very Person see,
    Infinity and Finity Conjoyn'd?
    What! hath thy Godhead, as not satisfi'de,   5
    Marri'de our Manhood, making it its Bride?

Oh, Matchless Love! Filling Heaven to the brim!
    O're running it: all running o're beside
This World! Nay, Overflowing Hell, wherein
    For thine Elect, there rose a mighty Tide!   10
    That there our Veans might through thy Person bleed,
    To quench those flames, that else would on us feed.

Oh! that thy love might overflow my Heart!
    To fire the same with Love: for Love I would.
But oh! my streight'ned Breast! my Lifeless Sparke!   15
    My Fireless Flame! What Chilly Love, and Cold?
    In measure small! In Manner Chilly! See!
    Lord, blow the coal: Thy Love Enflame in mee.

Meditation 1. 8. Joh. 6. 51. I am the Living Bread

I kening[1] through Astronomy Divine
    The Worlds bright Battlement, wherein I spy
A Golden Path my Pensill cannot line
    From that bright Throne unto my Threshold ly.
    And while my puzzled thoughts about it pore   5
    I finde the Bread of Life in't at my doore.

When that this Bird of Paradise put in
    This Wicker Cage (my Corps) to tweedle praise
Had peckt the Fruite forbid: and so did fling
    Away its Food; and lost its golden dayes,   10
    It fell into Celestiall Famine sore,
    And never could attain a morsell more.

Alas! alas! Poore Bird, what wilt thou doe?
    This Creatures field no food for Souls e're gave:
And if thou knock at Angells dores, they show   15
    An Empty Barrell: they no soul bread have.
    Alas! Poore Bird, the Worlds White Loafe is done,
    And cannot yield thee here the smallest Crumb.

In this sad state, Gods Tender Bowells[2] run
    Out streams of Grace: And he to end all strife,   20
The Purest Wheate in Heaven, his deare-dear Son
    Grinds, and kneads up into this Bread of Life:
    Which Bread of Life from Heaven down came and stands
    Disht in thy Table up by Angells Hands.

Did God mould up this Bread in Heaven, and bake,   25
    Which from his Table came, and to thine goeth?

[1] discovering.
[2] in seventeenth-century usage, the seat of pity and tenderness.

Doth he bespeake thee thus: This Soule Bread take;
    Come, Eate thy fill of this, thy Gods White Loafe?
    Its Food too fine for Angells; yet come, take
    And Eate thy fill! Its Heavens Sugar Cake.   30

What Grace is this knead in this Loafe? This thing
    Souls are but petty things it to admire.
Yee Angells, help: This fill would to the brim
    Heav'ns whelm'd-down[3] Chrystall meele Bowle, yea and
                                  higher.
    This Bread of Life dropt in thy mouth doth Cry: 35
    Eate, Eate me, Soul, and thou shalt never dy.

Meditation 1. 29. Joh. 20. 17. My Father, and your Father,
to my God, and your God

My shattred Phancy stole away from mee,
    (Wits run a Wooling[1] over Edens Parke)
And in Gods Garden saw a golden Tree,
    Whose Heart was All Divine, and gold its barke:
    Whose glorious limbs and fruitfull branches strong   5
    With Saints, and Angells bright are richly hung.

Thou! thou! my Deare-Deare Lord, art this rich Tree:
    The Tree of Life within Gods Paradise.
I am a Withred Twig, dri'de, fit to bee
    A Chat[2] Cast in thy fire, writh[3] off by Vice.   10
    Yet if thy Milkwhite Gracious Hand will take mee,
    And grafft mee in this golden stock, thou'lt make mee.

Thou'lt make me then its Fruite and Branch to spring.
    And though a nipping Eastwinde blow, and all
Hells Nymps[4] with spite their Dog's sticks thereat ding[5]   15
    To Dash the Grafft off, and its fruit to fall,
    Yet I shall stand thy Grafft, and Fruits that are
    Fruits of the Tree of Life thy Grafft shall beare.

[3] inverted.
[1] wool-gathering.
[2] piece of kindling.
[3] wrenched.
[4] imps.
[5] strike, batter.

I being grafft in thee, there up do stand
    In us Relations all that mutuall are.   20
I am thy Patient, Pupill, Servant, and
    Thy Sister, Mother, Doove, Spouse, Son, and Heire:
    Thou art my Priest, Physician, Prophet, King,
    Lord, Brother, Bridegroom, Father, Ev'rything.

I being grafft in thee am graffted here   25
    Into thy Family and kindred Claim
To all in Heaven: God, Saints, and Angells there.
    I thy Relations my Relations name.
    Thy Father's mine, thy God my God, and I
    With Saints and Angells draw Affinity.   30

My Lord, what is it that thou dost bestow?
    The Praise on this account fills up and throngs
Eternity brimfull, doth overflow
    The Heavens vast with rich Angelick Songs.
    How should I blush? how Tremble at this thing,   35
    Not having yet my gamut,[6] learn'd to sing.

But, Lord, as burnish't Sun Beams forth out fly,
    Let Angell-Shine forth in my Life out flame,
That I may grace thy gracefull Family,
    And not to thy Relations be a Shame.   40
    Make mee thy Grafft, be thou my Golden Stock:
    Thy Glory then I'le make my fruits and Crop.

Meditation 1. 32. 1 Cor. 3. 22. Whether Paul or Apollos, or Cephas

Thy Grace, Dear Lord's my golden Wrack, I finde
    Screwing my Phancy into ragged Rhimes,
Tuning thy Praises in my feeble minde
    Untill I come to strike them on my Chimes.
    Were I an Angell bright, and borrow could   5
    King Davids Harp, I would them play on gold.

But plung'd I am, my minde is puzzled,
    When I would spin my Phancy thus unspun,

    [6] musical scale containing all the notes used in medieval music.

In finest Twine of Praise I'm muzzled.
  My tazzled[1] Thoughts twirld into Snick-Snarls[2] run.   10
Thy Grace, my Lord, is such a glorious thing,
  It doth Confound me when I would it sing.

Eternall Love an Object mean did smite
  Which by the Prince of Darkness was beguilde,
That from this Love it ran and sweld with spite   15
  And in the way with filth was all defilde
  Yet must be reconcild, cleansd, and begrac'te
  Or from the fruits of Gods first Love displac'te.

Then Grace, my Lord, wrought in thy Heart a vent,
  Thy Soft Soft hand to this hard worke did goe,   20
And to the Milke White Throne of Justice went
  And entred bond that Grace might overflow.
  Hence did thy Person to my Nature ty
  And bleed through humane Veans to satisfy.

Oh! Grace, Grace, Grace! this Wealthy Grace doth lay   25
  Her Golden Channells from thy Fathers throne,
Into our Earthen Pitchers to Convay
  Heavens Aqua Vitae to us for our own.
  O! let thy Golden Gutters run into
  My Cup this Liquour till it overflow.   30

Thine Ordinances,[3] Graces Wine-fats[4] where
  Thy Spirits Walkes, and Graces runs doe ly
And Angells waiting stand with holy Cheere
  From Graces Conduite Head, with all Supply.
  These Vessells full of Grace are, and the Bowls   35
  In which their Taps do run, are pretious Souls.

Thou to the Cups dost say (that Catch this Wine,)
  This Liquour, Golden Pipes, and Wine-fats plain,
Whether Paul, Apollos, Cephas,[5] all are thine.
  Oh Golden Word! Lord speake it ore again.   40
  Lord speake it home to me, say these are mine.
  My Bells shall then thy Praises bravely chime.

[1] tangled, fuzzy.
[2] tangles.
[3] sacraments, particularly of Communion and Baptism.
[4] wine vats.
[5] Jesus' nickname for St. Peter.

Meditation 1. 39. 1 Joh. 2. 1. If any man sin, we have an Advocate

My Sin! my Sin, My God, these Cursed Dregs,
    Green, Yellow, Blew streakt Poyson hellish, ranck,
Bubs[1] hatcht in natures nest on Serpents Eggs,
    Yelp, Cherp and Cry; they set my Soule a Cramp.
    I frown, Chide, strik and fight them, mourn and Cry   5
    To Conquour them, but cannot them destroy.

I cannot kill nor Coop them up: my Curb
    'S less than a Snaffle in their mouth: my Rains
They as a twine thrid,[2] snap: by hell they're spurd:
    And load my Soule with swagging loads of pains.   10
    Black Imps, young Divells, snap, bite, drag to bring
    And pick mee headlong hells dread Whirle Poole in.

Lord, hold thy hand: for handle mee thou may'st
    In Wrath: but, oh, a twinckling Ray of hope
Methinks I spie thou graciously display'st.   15
    There is an Advocate: a doore is ope.
    Sin's poyson swell my heart would till it burst,
    Did not a hope hence creep in't thus, and nurse't.

Joy, joy, Gods Son's the Sinners Advocate
    Doth plead the Sinner guiltless, and a Saint.   20
But yet Atturnies pleas spring from the State
    The Case is in: if bad its bad in plaint.
    My Papers do contain no pleas that do
    Secure mee from, but knock me down to, woe.

I have no plea mine Advocate to give: 25
    What now? He'l anvill Arguments greate Store
Out of his Flesh and Blood to make thee live.
    O Deare bought Arguments: Good pleas therefore.
    Nails made of heavenly Steel, more Choice than gold
    Drove home, Well Clencht, eternally will hold.   30

Oh! Dear bought Plea, Deare Lord, what buy't so deare?
    What with thy blood purchase thy plea for me?

[1] pustules.
[2] thread.

Take Argument out of thy Grave t'appeare
 And plead my Case with, me from Guilt to free.
 These maule both Sins, and Divells, and amaze   35
 Both Saints, and Angells; Wreath their mouths with praise.

What shall I doe, my Lord? what do, that I
 May have thee plead my Case? I fee thee will
With Faith, Repentance, and obediently
 Thy Service gainst Satanick Sins fulfill.
 I'l fight thy fields while Live I do, although
 I should be hackt in pieces by thy foe.

Make me thy Friend, Lord, be my Surety: I
 Will be thy Client, be my Advocate:
My Sins make thine, thy Pleas make mine hereby.   45
 Thou wilt mee save, I will thee Celebrate.
 Thou'lt kill my Sins that cut my heart within:
 And my rough Feet shall thy smooth praises sing.

*Meditation 2. 1. Col. 2. 17. Which are Shaddows of things
 to come and the body is Christs*

Oh Leaden heeld.[1] Lord, give, forgive I pray.
 Infire my Heart: it bedded is in Snow.
I Chide myselfe seing myselfe decay.
 In heate and Zeale to thee, I frozen grow.
 File my dull Spirits: make them sharp and bright: 5
 Them firbush[2] for thyselfe, and thy delight.

My Stains are such, and sinke so deep, that all
 The Excellency in Created Shells
Too low, and little is to make it fall
 Out of my leather Coate wherein it dwells.   10
 This Excellence is but a Shade to that
 Which is enough to make my Stains go back.

The glory of the world slickt up in types[3]
 In all Choise things chosen to typify,

---

[1] sense: heavily weighed down with sin (leaden heels).
[2] furbish, polish.
[3] analogy, especially in reference to the Old Testament, in which a person, object, or event prefigured some person or thing yet to come; also loosely, symbol.

His glory upon whom the worke doth light,   15
    To thine's a Shaddow, or a butterfly.
How glorious then, my Lord, art thou to mee
    Seing to cleanse me, 's worke alone for thee.

The glory of all Types doth meet in thee.
    Thy glory doth their glory quite excell: 20
More than the Sun excells in its bright glee
    A nat, an Earewig, Weevill, Snaile, or Shell.
    Wonders in Crowds start up; your eyes may strut
    Viewing his Excellence, and's bleeding cut.

Oh! that I had but halfe an eye to view   25
    This excellence of thine, undazled: so
Therewith to give my heart a touch anew
    Untill I quicknd am, and made to glow.
    All is too little for thee: but alass
    Most of my little all hath other pass.   30

Then Pardon, Lord, my fault: and let thy beams
    Of Holiness pierce through this Heart of mine.
Ope to thy Blood a passage through my veans.
    Let thy pure blood my impure blood refine.
    Then with new blood and spirits I will dub   35
    My tunes upon thy Excellency good.

Meditation 2. 2. Coll. 1. 15. The First Born of Every Creature

Oh! Golden Rose! Oh. Glittering Lilly White
    Spic'd o're With heavens File[1] divine, till Rayes
Fly forth whose Shine doth Wrack the strongest Sight
    That Wonders Eye is tent of, while't doth gaze
    On thee. Whose Swaddle Bonde's Eternity.   5
    And Sparkling Cradle is Rich Deity.

First Born of e'ry Being: hence a Son
    Begot o' th' First: Gods onely Son begot.
Hence Deity all ore. Gods nature run
    Into a Filiall Mould: Eternall knot.   10

[1] polish.

A Father then, and Son: persons distinct.
Though them Sabellians[2] contrar'ly inckt.

This mall of Steel falls hard upon those foes
    Of truth, who make the Holy Trinity
Into One Person: Arrians[3] too and those   15
    Socinians[4] calld, who do Christs Deity
    Bark out against. But Will they, nill they, they
    Shall finde this Mall to split their brains away.

Come shine, Deare Lord, out in my heart indeed
    First Born; in truth before thee there was none   20
First Born, as man, born of a Virgin's seed:
    Before or after thee such up ne'er sprung.
    Hence Heir of all things lockt in natures Chest:
    And in thy Fathers too: extreamly best.

Thou Object of Gods boundless brightest Love,   25
    Invested with all sparkling rayes of Light
Distill thou down, what hony falls above
    Bedew the Angells Copses, fill our Sight
    And hearts therewith within thy Father's joy.
    These are but Shreads under thy bench that ly.   30

Oh! that my Soul was all enamored
    With this First Born enough: a Lump of Love
Son of Eternall Father, Chambered
    Once in a Virgins Womb, dropt from above.
    All Humane royalty hereby Divin'de.   35
    The First Born's Antitype: in whom they're shrin'de.

Make mee thy Babe, and him my Elder Brother.
    A Right, Lord grant me in his Birth Right high.
His Grace, my Treasure make above all other:
    His Life my Sampler: My Life his joy.   40
    I'le hang my love then on his heart, and sing
    New Psalms on Davids Harpe to thee and him.

[2] followers of Sabellius (third century) who believed that the Father, Son, and Holy Ghost were merely different modes of a single divine being.

[3] followers of Arius (fourth century) who denied that Christ was of the same substance with God.

[4] members of a sect founded by two sixteenth-century Italian theologians, Laelius and Faustus Socinus, who denied the divinity of Christ.

Meditation 2. 3. Rom. 5. 14. Who is the Figure
of Him that was to come

Like to the Marigold, I blushing close
    My golden blossoms when thy sun goes down:
Moist'ning my leaves with Dewy Sighs, half frose
    By the nocturnall Cold, that hoares my Crown.
      Mine Apples ashes are in apple shells,[1]   5
      And dirty too: strange and bewitching spells!

When, Lord, mine Eye doth spie thy Grace to beame
    Thy Mediatoriall glory in the shine,
Out spouted so from Adams typick streame,
    And Emblemiz'd in Noahs pollisht shrine: 10
      Thine theirs outshines so far it makes their glory
      In brightest Colours, seem a smoaky story.

But when mine Eye full of these beams doth cast
    Its rayes upon my dusty essence thin,
Impregnate with a Sparke Divine defac'de,   15
    All candi[e]d o're with Leprosie of Sin,
      Such Influences on my Spirits light,
      Which them as bitter gall, or Cold ice smite.

My brissled sins hence do so horrid peare,
    None but thyselfe, (and thou deck't up must bee   20
In thy Transcendent glory sparkling cleare)
    A Mediator unto God for mee.
      So high they rise, Faith scarce can toss a Sight
      Over their head upon thyselfe to light.

Is't possible such glory, Lord, ere should   25
    Center its Love on me, Sins Dunghill else?
My Case up take? make it its own? Who would
    Wash with his blood my blots out? Crown his shelfe
    Or Dress his golden Cupboard with such ware?
    This makes my pale facde Hope almost despare.   30

Yet let My Titimouses Quill suck in
    Thy Graces milk Pails some small drop: or Cart

[1] Apples of Sodom (Dead Sea Fruit) look fair on the tree but turn to smoke and ashes when picked.

A Bit or Splinter of some Ray, the wing
    Of Grace's sun sprindg'd[2] out, into my heart:
To build there Wonders Chappell where thy Praise   35
Shall be the Psalms sung forth in gracious layes.

Meditation 2. 4. Gal. 4. 24. Which things are an Allegorie

My Gracious Lord, I would thee glory doe:
    But finde my Garden over grown with weeds:
My Soile is sandy; brambles o're it grow;
    My Stock is stunted; branch no good Fruits breeds.
My Garden weed: Fatten my Soile, and prune   5
My Stock, and make it with thy glory bloome.

O Glorious One, the gloriou'st thought I thincke
    Of thee falls black as Inck upon thy Glory.
The brightest Saints that rose, do Star like, pinck.[1]
    Nay, Abrams Shine to thee's an Allegory,   10
Or fleeting Sparke in th' Smoke, to typify
Thee, and thy Glorious Selfe in mystery.

Should all the Sparks in heaven, the Stars there dance
    A Galliard,[2] Round about the Sun, and stay
His Servants (while on Easter morn his prance   15
    Is o're, which old wives prate of) O brave Play.
Thy glorious Saints thus boss[3] thee round, which stand
Holding thy glorious Types out in their hand.

But can I thinck this Glory greate, its head
    Thrust in a pitchy cloude, should strangled ly   20
Or tucking up its beams should go to bed
    Within the Grave, darke me to glorify?
This Mighty thought my hearts too streight for, though
I hold it by the hand, and let not goe.

Then, my Blesst Lord, let not the Bondmaids type[4]   25
    Take place in mee. But thy blesst Promisd Seed.

2 sprinkled, spread.
1 twinkle.
2 a lively dance, usually in triple time.
3 ornament.
4 Gal iv 22–24: "For it is written, that Abraham had two sons, the one by a bondmaid, the other by a free woman. But he who was of the bondwoman was born after the flesh; but he of the free woman was by promise. Which things are an allegory. . . ."

Distill thy Spirit through thy royall Pipe
    Into my Soule, and so my Spirits feed,
    Then them, and me still into praises right
    Into thy Cup where I to swim delight.   30

Though I desire so much, I can't o're doe.
    All that my Can contains, to nothing comes
When summed up, it onely Cyphers grows
    Unless thou set thy Figures to my Sums.
    Lord set thy Figure 'fore them, greate, or small.   35
    To make them something, and I'l give thee all.

Meditation 2. 56. Joh. 15. 24. Had I not done amongst
them the works, that none other man hath done, etc.

Should I with silver tooles delve through the Hill
    Of Cordilera[1] for rich thoughts, that I
My Lord, might weave with an angelick skill
    A Damask Web of Velvet Verse, thereby
    To deck thy Works up, all my Web would run   5
    To rags, and jags:[2] so snick-snarld[3] to the thrum.[4]

Thine are so rich: within, without refin'd:
    No worke like thine. No Fruits so sweete that grow
On th' trees of righteousness of Angell kinde,
    And Saints, whose limbs reev'd[5] with them bow down low.   10
    Should I search ore the Nutmeg Gardens shine,
    Its fruits in flourish are but skegs[6] to thine.

The Clove, when in its White-green'd blossoms shoots,
    Some Call the pleasentst s[c]ent the World doth show,
None Eye e're saw, nor nose e're smelt such Fruits,   15
    My Lord, as thine, Thou Tree of Life in'ts blow.
    Thou Rose of Sharon, Vallies Lilly true,
    Thy Fruits most sweet and glorious ever grew.

[1] various portions of Central, South, and North American mountain ranges, particularly those in which mining for precious metals was carried on.
[2] tatters, shreds.
[3] tangled.
[4] the fringelike row of warp threads on the weaver's loom when the web has been cut free.
[5] intertwined.
[6] wild plums.

Thou art a Tree of Perfect nature trim,
    Whose golden lining is of perfect Grace,   20
Perfum'de with Deity unto the brim,
    Whose fruits, of the perfection, grow, of Grace.
Thy Buds, thy Blossoms, and thy fruits adorne
Thyselfe and Works, more shining than the morn.

Art, natures Ape, hath many brave things done: 25
    As th' Pyramids, the Lake of Meris vast,[7]
The Pensile Orchards built in Babylon,[8]
    Psammitich's Labyrinth,[9] (arts Cramping task)
Archimedes his Engins[10] made for war,
    Romes Golden House,[11] Titus his Theater.[12]   30

The Clock of Strasburgh,[13] Dresdens Table-sight,[14]
    Regiamonts Fly of Steele about that flew,[15]
Turrian's Wooden Sparrows in a flight,[16]
    And th' Artificiall man Aquinas slew,[17]

[7] Lake Moeris, an artificial lake in Middle Egypt opposite the ancient site of Arsinoë.

[8] the Hanging Gardens of Semiramis at Babylon, one of the Seven Wonders of the World.

[9] Herodotus ascribes the building of the labyrinth to one of the three kings of Egypt named Psammetichus, who reigned between 664 and 525 B.C.

[10] Archimedes devised for Hiero II, King of Syracuse, engines of war that struck fear into the Romans and protracted the siege of Syracuse by three years (214–212 B.C.).

[11] Nero's famous palace, erected during the rebuilding of Rome after the great fire of A.D. 64.

[12] the Coliseum at Rome, completed by Titus Vespasianus (A.D. 40–81).

[13] a clock built by the mathematician Conrad Dasypodius in 1574.

[14] In *Electorale Saxonicum* . . . (Dresden, 1683), Tobias Beuteln describes, in Latin and German, the collection of marvelous tableware, fashioned from precious metals and jewels, kept in special repositories of the royal residence in Saxony.

[15] Johann Müller (Regiomontanus) (1436–76), German astronomer and mathematician, constructed a mechanical eagle which greeted Emperor Maximilian I upon his entry into Nurnberg.

[16] One of the automata, made by Janellus Turrianus of Cremona, with which the Emperor Charles V amused himself after his abdication from the throne. (See, e.g. Sir David Brewster, *Letters on Natural Magic, Addressed to Sir Walter Scott, Bart.* [London, 1832], pp. 266–67; also, Leslie Daiken, *Children's Toys Throughout the Ages* [New York, 1953], p. 19.) Taylor may have read of Turrian's sparrows in William Turner, *Compleat History of the Most Remarkable Providences, Both of Judgment and Mercy Which Have Happened in This Present Age . . . To Which is Added Whatever is Curious in the Works of Nature and Art* (London, 1697).

[17] Robert R. Hodges ("Edward Taylor's 'Artificiall Man'," *AL,* XXXI [1959],

Mark Scaliota's Lock and Key and Chain   35
Drawn by a Flea, in our Queen Betties reign.[18]

Might but my pen in natures Inventory
    Its progress make, 't might make such things to jump,
All which are but Inventions Vents or glory:
        Wits Wantonings, and Fancies frollicks plump: 40
        Within whose maws lies buried Times, and Treasures,
        Embalmed up in thick dawbd sinfull pleasures.

Nature doth better work than Art, yet thine
    Out vie both works of nature and of Art.
Natures Perfection and the perfect shine   45
    Of Grace attend thy deed in ev'ry part.
        A Thought, a Word, and Worke of thine, will kill
        Sin, Satan, and the Curse: and Law fulfill.

Thou art the Tree of Life in Paradise,
    Whose lively branches are with Clusters hung   50
Of Lovely fruits, and Flowers more sweet than spice.
        Bende down to us, and doe out shine the sun.
        Delightfull unto God, doe man rejoyce
        The pleasent'st fruits in all Gods Paradise.

Lord, feed mine eyes then with thy Doings rare,   55
    And fat my heart with these ripe fruites thou bear'st;
Adorn my Life well with thy works; make faire
        My Person with apparrell thou prepar'st.
        My Boughs shall loaded bee with fruits that spring
        Up from thy Works, while to thy praise I sing.

76–77) notes that this is the talking head constructed by Albertus Magnus, teacher of Thomas Aquinas. Aquinas destroyed the head.

[18] "1579.—'This year Marke Scaliot, Blackesmith, Citizen of London, for triall of his workemanship, made one hanging locke of Iron, steele & brasse of eleven severall peeces, & a pipe key, all cleane, which wated but one graine of gold. He also at the same time made a chaine of gold of forty three linkes, to which chaine the locke & key being fastned & put about a fleas necke, shee drew the same with ease. All which locke & key, chaine & flea, wayed but one grain and a halfe: a thing most incredible, but that I myselfe haue seen it.'" *An Abridgement of the English Chronicle by Mr. John Stow* (London, 1611), p. 228.

Meditation 2. 150. Cant. 7. 3. Thy two breasts are
like two young Roes that are twins

My Blessed Lord, how doth thy Beautious Spouse
    In Stately Stature rise in Comliness?
With her two breasts like two little Roes that browse
    Among the lillies in their Shining dress
    Like stately milke pailes ever full and flow   5
    With spirituall milke to make her babes to grow.

Celestiall Nectar Wealthier far than Wine
    Wrought in the Spirits brew house and up tund
Within these Vessells which are trust up fine
    Likend to two pritty neate twin Roes than run'd   10
    Most pleasently by their dams sides like Cades[1]
    And suckle with their milk Christs Spirituall Babes.

Lord put these nibbles then my mouth into
    And suckle me therewith I humbly pray,
Then with this milk thy Spirituall Babe I'st grow,   15
    And these two milke pails shall themselves display
    Like to these pritty twins in pairs round neate
    And shall sing forth thy praise over this meate.

Gods Determinations:
The Preface

    Infinity, when all things it beheld
In Nothing, and of Nothing all did build,
Upon what Base was fixt the Lath, wherein
He turn'd this Globe, and riggalld[1] it so trim?
Who blew the Bellows of his Furnace Vast?   5
Or held the Mould wherein the world was Cast?
Who laid its Corner Stone? Or whose Command?
Where stand the Pillars upon which it stands?
Who Lac'de and Fillitted the earth so fine,
With Rivers like green Ribbons Smaragdine?   10
Who made the Sea's its Selvedge,[2] and it locks

[1] pets.
[1] made ringed marks on.
[2] border.

Like a Quilt Ball within a Silver Box?
Who Spread its Canopy? Or Curtains Spun?
Who in this Bowling Alley bowld the Sun?
Who made it always when it rises set: 15
To go at once both down, and up to get?
Who th' Curtain rods made for this Tapistry?
Who hung the twinckling Lanthorns in the Sky?
Who? who did this? or who is he? Why, know
It's Onely Might Almighty this did doe.   20
His hand hath made this noble worke which Stands
His Glorious Handywork not made by hands.
Who spake all things from nothing; and with ease
Can speake all things to nothing, if he please.
Whose Little finger at his pleasure Can   25
Out mete ten thousand worlds with halfe a Span:
Whose Might Almighty can by half a looks
Root up the rocks and rock the hills by th' roots.
Can take this mighty World up in his hande,
And shake it like a Squitchen[3] or a Wand.   30
Whose single Frown will make the Heavens shake
Like as an aspen leafe the Winde makes quake.
Oh! what a might is this! Whose single frown
Doth shake the world as it would shake it down?
Which All from Nothing fet,[4] from Nothing, All: 35
Hath All on Nothing set, lets Nothing fall.
Gave All to nothing Man indeed, whereby
Through nothing man all might him Glorify.
In Nothing is imbosst the brightest Gem
More pretious than all pretiousness in them.   40
But Nothing man did throw down all by sin:
And darkened that lightsom Gem in him,
      That now his Brightest Diamond is grown
      Darker by far than any Coalpit Stone.

The Frowardness of the Elect in the Work of Conversion

      Those upon whom Almighty doth intend
His all Eternall Glory to expend,
Lulld in the lap of sinfull Nature snugg,

[3] switch, a slip of branch cut for grafting.
[4] fetched.

Like Pearls in Puddles cover'd ore with mudd:
Whom, if you search, perhaps some few you'l finde,   5
That to notorious Sins were ne're inclinde:
Some shunning some, some most, some greate, some small;
Some this, that, or the other, some none at all.
But all, or almost all, you'st easly finde,
To all, or almost all Defects inclinde: 10
To Revell with the Rabble rout who say,
'Let's hiss this Piety out of our Day.'
And those whose frame is made of finer twine
Stand further off from Grace than Wash from Wine.
Those who suck Grace from th' breast, are nigh as rare   15
As Black Swans that in milkwhite Rivers are.
Grace therefore calls them all, and sweetly wooes.
Some won come in, the rest as yet refuse,
And run away: Mercy persues apace,
Then some Cast down their arms, Cry Quarter, Grace!   20
Some Chased out of breath, drop down with feare,
Perceiving the persuer drawing neer.
The rest persude, divide into two rancks,
And this way one, and that the other prancks.[1]

Then in comes Justice with her forces by her,   25
And doth persue as hot as sparkling fire.
The right wing then begins to fly away:
But in the streights strong Baracadoes[2] lay.
They're therefore forc'd to face about, and have
Their spirits Quel'd, and therefore Quarter Crave.   30
These Captivde thus: Justice persues the Game
With all her troops to take the other train.
Which being Chast in a Peninsula
And followd close, they finde no other way
To make escape, but t' rally round about: 35
Which if it faile them that they get not out,
They're forct into the Infernall Gulfe alive,
Or hackt in pieces are, or took Captive.
But spying Mercy stand with Justice, they
Cast down their Weapons, and for Quarter pray.   40
Their lives are therefore spar'de, yet they are ta'ne
As th' other band: and prisoners must remain.

[1] capers arrogantly.
[2] barricades.

And so they must now Justice's Captives bee
On Mercies Quarrell: Mercy sets not free.
    Their former Captain is their Deadly foe,   45
    And now, poor souls, they know not what to do.

The Joy of Church Fellowship rightly attended

In Heaven soaring up, I dropt an Eare
    On Earth: and oh! sweet Melody!
And listening, found it was the Saints who were
    Encoacht for Heaven that sang for Joy.
    For in Christs Coach they sweetly sing,   5
    As they to Glory ride therein.

Oh! joyous hearts! Enfir'de with holy Flame!
    Is speech thus tasseled with praise?
Will not your inward fire of Joy contain,
    That it in open flames doth blaze?   10
    For in Christs Coach Saints sweetly sing,
    As they to Glory ride therein.

And if a string do slip by Chance, they soon
    Do screw it up again: whereby
They set it in a more melodious Tune   15
    And a Diviner Harmony.
    For in Christs Coach they sweetly sing,
    As they to Glory ride therein.

In all their Acts, publick, and private, nay,
    And secret too, they praise impart.   20
But in their Acts Divine, and Worship, they
    With Hymns do offer up their Heart.
    Thus in Christs Coach they sweetly sing,
    As they to Glory ride therein.

Some few not in; and some whose Time and Place   25
    Block up this Coaches way, do goe
As Travellers afoot: and so do trace
    The Road that gives them right thereto;
    While in this Coach these sweetly sing,
    As they to Glory ride therein.   30

Upon a Spider Catching a Fly

Thou sorrow, venom Elfe:
  Is this thy play,
To spin a web out of thyselfe
  To Catch a Fly?
    For why?   5

I saw a pettish wasp
  Fall foule therein:
Whom yet thy whorle pins[1] did not [clasp]
  Lest he should fling
    His sting.   10

But as afraid, remote
  Didst stand hereat,
And with thy little fingers stroke
  And gently tap
    His back.   15

Thus gently him didst treate
  Lest he should pet,
And in a froppish,[2] [w]aspish heate
  Should greatly fret
    Thy net.   20

Whereas the silly Fly,
  Caught by its leg,
Thou by the throate took'st hastily,
  And 'hinde the head
    Bite Dead.   25

This goes to pot, that not
  Nature doth call.
Strive not above what strength hath got,
  Lest in the brawle
    Thou fall.   30

This Frey seems thus to us:
  Hells Spider gets

[1] spinning mechanism.
[2] fretful.

His intrails spun to whip Cords thus,
    And wove to nets,
        And sets.   35

To tangle Adams race
    In's stratagems
To their Destructions, Spoil'd, made base
    By venom things,
        Damn'd Sins.   40

But mighty, Gracious Lord,
    Communicate
Thy Grace to breake the Cord; afford
    Us Glorys Gate
        And State.   45

We'l Nightingaile sing like,
    When pearcht on high
In Glories Cage, thy glory, bright:
    [And] thankfully,
        For joy.   50

Huswifery

Make me, O Lord, thy Spin[n]ing Wheele compleate;
    Thy Holy Worde my Distaff make for mee.
Make mine Affections thy Swift Flyers neate,
    And make my Soule thy holy Spoole to bee.
    My Conversation make to be thy Reele,   5
    And reele the yarn thereon spun of thy Wheele.

Make me thy Loome then, knit therein this Twine:
    And make thy Holy Spirit, Lord, winde quills:
Then weave the Web thyselfe. The yarn is fine.
    Thine Ordinances make my Fulling Mills.[1]   10
    Then dy the same in Heavenly Colours Choice,
    All pinkt[2] with Varnish't Flowers of Paradise.

Then cloath therewith mine Understanding, Will,
    Affections, Judgment, Conscience, Memory;

[1] mill in which cloth is beaten and cleaned with fuller's earth.
[2] adorned.

My Words and Actions, that their shine may fill   15
   My wayes with glory and thee glorify.
   Then mine apparell shall display before yee
   That I am Cloathd in Holy robes for glory.

The Ebb and Flow

When first thou on me, Lord, wrought'st thy Sweet Print,[1]
   My heart was made thy tinder box.
   My 'ffections were thy tinder in't:
     Where fell thy Sparkes by drops.
Those holy Sparks of Heavenly Fire that came   5
Did ever catch and often out would flame.

But now my Heart is made thy Censar trim,
   Full of the golden Altars fire,
   To offer up Sweet Incense in
     Unto thyselfe intire: 10
I finde my tinder scarce thy sparks can feel
That drop out from thy Holy flint and Steel.

Hence doubts out bud for feare thy fire in mee
   'S a mocking Ignis Fatuus,
   Or lest thine Altars fire out bee,   15
     It's hid in ashes thus.
Yet when the bellows of thy Spirit blow
Away mine ashes, then thy fire doth glow.

[1] image.

Minor Writers

EDWARD JOHNSON

(1598–1672)

In 1660, Ferdinando Gorges, Esq., grandson of the knight whose name he bore, published a protest. He said that the section called *Sion's Saviour in New England,* printed as Part III of a book he had written, was not of his authorship at all. Indeed it was not, as Judge Samuel Sewall and other Fathers of the Massachusetts Bay well knew. To them it was "a Thing familliarly known" that the real author of *The Wonder-Working Providence of Sions Saviour in New England* was Captain Edward Johnson of Woburn, Massachusetts, a leading citizen of the Bay. Sewall and his friends may likewise have known that the publication mix-up occurred because Johnson's book, first appearing in 1653 under a rather prosaic title, did not sell, and that to rid himself of the surplus copies the printer had simply bound them into Gorges' volume as "Part III."

Edward Johnson, who referred to himself obliquely as a "Kentish Soldier," was born in 1598, in Canterbury, England. Like the poet Anne Bradstreet, he traveled to America with the Winthrop party in 1630, probably aboard the flagship *Arbella.* His designation on town records as "Mr." indicates that he was of significant status, for lesser persons would have been termed "Goodman," if not merely by their names alone. Johnson did not remain in America at that time, for records show him back in England from 1631 to 1636. Quite probably he had returned to settle his estate, which was considerable, before returning to the Bay with his family. He had married about 1618 and now had five sons and two daughters. His listing on the ship's registry as a "joiner," whose sons were "carpenters," was most likely a ruse to deceive royal officials who could have caused difficulties for the non-conformist emigrant.

Once settled in America, Johnson became active in community affairs. He lived first at Charlestown, which petitioned the Massachusetts General Court for permission to expand northward in creation of a new town, finally called Woburn. Johnson recounts in his history the process of building the town, establishing its government and its church. Not only did he help in its founding, but he represented it in the General Court and served on every military committee of the colony. In 1659 he was made surveyor general of arms and munitions in the colony, and later acted as surveyor and helped in the codification of laws.

The writing of *The Wonder-Working Providence* was probably done over a three-year period, from 1649 to 1651, with most of the work done in 1650. It has been called the first major history of the founding of New England to be published before Cotton Mather's *Magnalia*. Certainly its bombastic title is significant, for it bespeaks the Puritan conviction that God's providence was specially shown to the New Englanders, and that it was a providence working "wonders." The Puritans did not believe in miracles, but they did feel that God worked his will through nature, sometimes extraordinarily so. The safe delivery of a shipload of pilgrims across such an expanse of stormy ocean seemed to them ample evidence of His special providence. Should He further prevent their massacre at the hands of Indians, or save their lives during an outbreak of typhus, or keep their houses safe when that of a non-church member was struck by lightning, then these benefices could only be looked upon as the providential intervention of God. Like all New England Puritans, Edward Johnson saw God's hand in all colonial events, no matter how small, and he wrote them down accordingly with much zeal. Further, with Satan lurking about this wilderness, the building of the Holy Commonwealth took on some qualities of military battles where forces of good contend with those of evil. The struggle is reflected in Johnson's imagery.

His poems are interspersed throughout his history, and just before offering his second of many, Johnson asks the reader to "let no man be offended at the Authors rude Verse, penned of purpose to keepe in memory the Names of such worthies as Christ made strong for himselfe, in this unwonted works of his." Thus it is Johnson's recognition of poetry as a means of fixing things into permanence that motivates his verse writing. But his use of the phrase "keepe in memory" may have another significance, for many of Johnson's verses are written in the "fourteener" ballad rhythm so easy to memorize (Michael Wigglesworth's mnemonic *Day of Doom* appears in stanzas of "fourteeners"). In any case, his meter, alliteration, and frequent rhymes give his verses a fast pace characteristic of the entire *Wonder-Working Providence.*

Johnson's verses at their worst lack taste, balance, and sense of proportion. They jog and bounce unmercifully. But at his best the "Kentish Soldier" is capable of sustaining imagery well, and of exploring with effectiveness the subtle possibilities of language.

The Reverend Mr. Higgingson,[1] *first Pastor of the Church of Christ at* Salem *in* New England

What Golden gaine made Higginson *remove,*
　　From fertill Soyle to Wildernesse of Rocks;
'Twas Christs rich Pearle stir'd up thee toile to love,
　　For him to feed in Wildernesse his flocks.
First Teacher, he here sheepe and Lambs together,
　　First crownd shall be, hee in the Heavens of all,
Christs Pastors here, but yet Christ folke had rather,
　　Him here retaine, blest he whom Christ hath call'd.

Mr. Eliot[1] *Pastor of the Church of Christ at* Roxbury, *in* New England, *much honoured for his labours in the Lord*

Great is thy worke in Wildernesse, Oh man,
　　Young Eliot *neere twenty yeares thou hast,*
In Westerne world with miccle[2] toile thy span
　　Spent well-neere out, and now thy gray hayrs gracest,
Are by thy Land-Lord Christ, who makes use of thee　　5
　　To feede his flock, and heathen people teach
In their own Language, God and Christ to see;
　　A Saviour their blind hearts could not reach,
Poore naked Children come to learne Gods Mind
　　Before thy face with reverend regard;　　10

[1] Rev. Francis Higginson (M.A. Cantab. 1613), at Salem "Elected and Ordained" July 20, 1629, was the author of *New Englands Plantation* (1630).

[1] John Eliot (1604–90) began missionary work among the Indians in 1646, brought a group of "praying Indians" into the Natick, Mass., church in 1660, and translated the Bible into their language in 1661–63.

[2] mickle: much.

Blesse God for thee may these poore heathen blind,
That from thy mouth Christs Gospell sweete have heard.
Eliot, *thy name is, through the wild woods spread,*
In Indians *mouths frequent's thy fame, for why?*
In sundry shapes the Devills made them dread;   15
And now the Lord makes them their Wigwams *fly.*
Rejoyce in this, nay rather joy that thou,
Amongst Christs Souldiers hast thy name sure set,
Although small gaine on Earth accrew to you,
*Yet Christ to Crowne will thee to Heaven soone fet.*³ 20

Yee shall not misse of a few lines in remembrance of Thomas Hooker¹

Come, Hooker, *come forth of thy native soile:*
Christ, I will run, sayes Hooker, *thou hast set*
My feet at large, here spend thy last dayes toile;
Thy Rhetorick shall peoples affections whet.
Thy Golden Tongue, and Pen Christ caus'd to be   5
The blazing of his golden truths profound,
Thou sorry worme its Christ wrought this in thee;
What Christ hath wrought must needs be very sound.
Then looke one² Hookers workes, they follow him
To Grave, this worthy resteth there a while: 10
Die shall he not that hath Christs warrier bin;
Much lesse Christs Truth, cleer'd by his peoples toile.
Thou Angell bright, by Christ for light now made,
Throughout the World as seasoning salt to be,
Although in dust thy body mouldering fade;   15
Thy Head's in Heaven, and hath a crown for thee.

³ fetch.
¹ Thomas Hooker (1586–1647), one of the founders of Connecticut, and author of *A Survey of the Summe of Church-Discipline* (1648).
² on.

Among these Troopes of Christs Souldiers, came . . .
Mr. Roger Harlackenden[1]

Harlackenden, *among these men of note Christ hath thee seated:*
  In warlike way Christ thee aray, with zeal, and love well heated.
As generall belov'd of all, Christ Souldiers honour thee:
  In thy young yeares, courage appeares, and kinde benignity.
Short are thy days, spent to his praise, whose Church work thou must aid,
  His work shall bide, silver tride, but thine by death is staid.

Mr. Thomas Shepheard[1] . . . *hee a man of*
a thousand

No hungr[y] Hawke poore Patridge to devoure
  More eager is, then Prelates Nimrod power
Thomas to hunt, my Shephard sweet pursue
  To seas brinke, but Christ saves his soule for you;
Sending thee Shepheard, safe through Seas awaie,   5
  To feede his flock unto thy ending day.
Where sheepe seek wolves, thy bosome lambs would catch;
  But night and day thou ceasest not to watch.
And warne with teares thy flock of cheaters vile,
  Who in sheepes cloathing would the weak beguile,   10
With dropping dewes from thy lips Christ hath made
  Thy hearers eyes oft water springing blade.
With pierced hearts they cry aloud and say,
  Shew us sweet Shepheard our salvations way,
Thy lovely speech such ravishment doth bring;   15
  Christ gives thee power to heale as well as sting.
Thou gates sets ope for Christ thy King to enter,
  In hearts of many spirits joy to center,
But mourne my Muse, hang downe thy head with woe,
  With teares, sighs, sobs lament thy Shepheard so.   20
(Why?) hee's in Heaven, but I one[2] Earth am left:
  More Earthly, 'cause of him I am bereft.
Oh Christ, why dost thou Shepheard take away,
  In erring times when sheepe most apt to stray.

1 Roger Harlackenden (1611–38), friend of Thomas Shepard.
1 Thomas Shepard I (1605–49).
2 on.

Onely the reverend grave and godly
Mr. Buckly[1] remaines

Riches and honours Buckley *layes aside*
 To please his Christ, for whom he now doth war,
Why Buckly *thou hast Riches that will bide,*
 And honours that exceeds Earths honour far.
Thy bodies worne, and dayes in Desert spent   5
 To feede a few of Christs poore scattered sheepe,
Like Christ's bright body, thy poore body rent;
 With Saints and Angells company shall keepe.
Thy Tongue, and Pen doth to the World declare:
 Christs covenant with his flock shall firmly stand,   10
When Heavens and Earth by him dissolved are;
 Then who can hold from this his worke at hand?
Two Bucklies[2] *more Christ by his grace hath taken,*
 And sent abroad to mannage his great wars.
It's Buklies *joy that Christ his sons new making,*   15
 Hath placest in's churches for to shine as Stars.

[Oh King of Saints, how great's thy work, say we]

1. Oh King of Saints, how great's thy work, say we,
 Done and to do, poor Captives to redeem!
Mountaines of mercy makes this work to be
  Glorious, that grace by which thy works are seen.
   Oh Jesu, thou a Saviour unto thine,
    Not works but grace makes us this mercy find.

2. Of sinners cheife, no better men they be,
 Thou by thy work hast made thy work to do:
Thy Captaines strength weak dust appears in thee,
  While thou art brought such wondrous works unto.
   Then Christ doth all, Aye all is done for his
    Redeemed ones, his onely work it is.

[1] Peter Bulkeley I (1583–1659), Pastor at Concord, Mass., and author of *The Gospel Covenant, or the Covenant of Grace Opened* (1646), alluded to in lines 9–10 above.
[2] Edward and John Bulkeley, two of Peter's twelve sons.

3. Doth Christ build Churches? who can them deface?
    He purchast them, none can his right deny:
Not all the world, ten thousand worlds, his grace
        Caus'd him once them at greater price to buy.
            Nor marvell then if Kings and Kingdomes he
                Destroy'd, when they do cause his folke to flee.

4. Christ is come down possession for to take
    Of his deer purchase; who can hinder him?
Not all the Armies earthly men can make:
        Millions of spirits, although Divels grim:
            Can *Pope* or *Turke* with all their mortall power,
                Stay Christ from his inheritance one hour?

5. All Nations band your selves together now,
    You shall fall down as dust from bellows blown:
How easie can our King your power bow?
        Though higher you in mens accompt were grown.
            As drop in bucket shall those waters be,
                Whereon that Whore[1] doth set in high degree.

6. Christs wrath is kindled, who can stand before
    His anger, that so long hath been provoked?
In moment perish shall all him before,
        Who touch'd Mount *Sinai,* and it soundly smoaked.
            New-England Churches you are Christs, you say,
                So sure are all that walk in Christs way.

7. No such need fear fury of men or Divels,
    Why, Christ among you takes his dayly walk:
He made you gold, you keeps from rusting evils,
        And hid you here from strife of tongues proud talke.
            Amongst his he for their defence doth bide,
                They need no more that have Christ on their side

8. Man be not proud of this thy exaltation:
    For thou wast dung and dogs filth, when Christ wrought
In thee his work, and set thee in this station
        To stand, from him thy strength is dayly brought,
            Yet in him thou shalt go triumphant on:
                Not thou but Christ triumphs his foes upon.

9. You people whom he by the hand did lead
    From *Egypt* land through Seas with watry wall:

1 the Pope, or the Roman Church *in toto.*

Apply your selves his Scriptures for to read:
  In reading do for eyes enlightned call,
    And you shall see Christ once being come is now
      Again at hand your stubborn hearts to bow.

10. Though scattered you, Earths Kingdoms are throughout,
  In bondage brought, cheife by those make some show
Of Jewish rights, they Christ with you cast out;
  Christ will their Cords for you in sunder hew.
    Through unbeliefe you were to bondage brought:
      Believe that Christ for you great work hath wrought.

11. He will your heart not member circumcise:
  Oh search and see, this is your Jesus sure,
Refuse him not, would God you were so wise:
  None but this King can ought[2] your hope procure.
    Once doting on an Earthly Kingdom you
      Mist[3] of your Christ; be sure be wiser now.

12. The day's at hand he will you wiser make
  To know Earths Kingdoms are too scant and base
For such a price, as Christ paid for your sake:
  Kings you shall be, but in a higher place;
    Yet for your freedom Nations great shall fall,
      That without fear of foes, him serve you shall.

13. You are the men that Christ will cause subdue
  Those Turkish Troops, that joyned *Jews* have been:
His *Gentile* Churches cast down *Babels* crue:[4]
  Then you that brood of *Mahumetts* shall win,
    Destroy his seed 'mongst *Persians, Turkes* and *Moores,*
      And for poor Christians ope the Prison doors.

14. Your Nation prov'd too scant for his possession,
  Whose pretious blood was made a price for sin:
And Nations all who were in like transgression;
  Some of the whole Christ to his Crown will win,
    And now makes way for this his work indeed,
      That through the world his Kingdom may proceed.

15. Now Nations all I pray you look about,
  Christ comes you neer, his power I pray embrace:

[2] aught.
[3] Missed.
[4] crew.

In's word him seek; he's found without all doubt:
 He doth beseech with teares, Oh seek his face:
  Yet time there is, the Battel's but begun;
   Christ, call thy folke that they to thee may run.

16. Place them in thy strong Armies newly gather'd,
 Thy Churches Lord increase and fill withall:
Those blessed ones are given thee by thy Father,
 The wickeds Rod off from their backs recall.
  Breake off their yokes, that they with freedom may
  Tell of thy workes, and praise thee every day.

17. Lord Christ, go on with thy great wonders working[,]
 Down headlong cast all Antichristian power:
Unmaske those men that lye in corners lurking,
 Whose damned doctrines dayly seates advance.
  For why, thy Folke for this are dayly longing,
  That Nations may come in thy Churches thronging.

18. What greater joy can come thy Saints among,
 Then to behold their Christ exalted high?
Thy Spirits joy with ravishment stirs strong
 Thy Folke, while they thy Kingdomes glory eye.
  Angels rejoyce because their waiting is
  In Saints assembly, where thy name they bliss.[5]

19. Thy workes are not in *Israels* Land confined,
 From East to West thy wondrous works are known:
To Nations all thou hast thy grace assigned,
 Thy spirits breathings through the World are blown.
  All Languages and tongues do tell thy praise,
  Dead hear thy voyce, them thou dost living raise.

20. Oh blessed dayes of Son of Man now seen,
 You that have long'd so sore them to behold,
March forth in's might, and stoutly stand between
 The mighties sword, and Christs dear flock infold.
  Unda[u]nted close and clash with them; for why?
  'Gainst Christ they are, and he with thee stands by.

21. No Captive thou, nor Death can on thee seize,
 Fight, stand, and live in Christ thou dayly dost:

[5] bless.

He long ago did lead as Captives these,
   And ever lives to save thee where thou goest.
   His Father still, and Spirit shall with thee
      Abide, and crowne thy Head with lasting glee.

Good News from New-England[1]

Of the reasons moving this people to transplant themselves and Families to those remote parts

The great *Jehova's* working word effecting wondrously,
   This earths vast globe, those parts unknown, to civill
          people by.
Columbus or *Alkmerricus* by providence direction,
   Found out this Western world with store of mettels cleer
          extraction.
The Spanish project working well, tooke sudden such impression   5
   In minds of many *Europe* held, who fell to like progression.
It's strange to see the Spanish fleete so many should provoke,
   In *English* searching for like prize, they are vanisht into
          smoake.
Yet these undaunted hearts stir'd up a Colony to plant,
   Hight Nova Anglia, for which they gain'd a patten grant.   10
Now all ancient seild and read in lands new population,
   No parallell like this (I deeme) you'l finde in any Nation.
These people now begin with care to vese[2] and plot, each man
   That heares of this new Colony, with diligence doth scan.
Such motives as he hath in Eye, one he desires land,   15
   Quoth he I see here landed men in reputation stand.
Hundreds and thousands I have not to purchase, but I will
   Through seas much wood-land to atchieve, and medow ground
          my fill.
Up starts another from a sad and serious contemplation,
   How he a Gentleman might be, good man is his vexation.   20
House implements being turn'd to coyne, his Cloath of fashion
          new,

[1] Harold S. Jantz argues persuasively that *Good News* is by Edward Johnson (see *The First Century of New England Verse* [New York, 1962], pp. 27–29). A review of its style, content, and point of view leads the present editor to concur, even though no conclusive evidence of Johnson's authorship has come to light.
[2] worry.

To ship he hyes, much welcome Sir, for none his person knew.
New rais'd from sleepe, another cries, my earnings are but small,
I'le venter to this new-found world, and make amends for all.
In hast halfe breathlesse running, comes a man with longing sore   25
For novelties of new-found lands, the seas he would leap o're.
His kindreds letters looking in, ha ha here's newes indeed,
From Brothers, Sisters, Uncles, Aunts, I'le ship my selfe with
speed.
These but the straglers now remaines the chiefest troopes to eye,
Truth 'tis, their standard of resort was Christianity.   30
Couragious Captaines leading on, their coynes and lands 'way
throwing,
Made many Souldiers follow fast, their bands in number
growing.
When *England* by *Elizabeth* began a Reformation,
It was a joyful day to all, the godly of that Nation.
Proh Dolor,[3] it did not goe on with joyfull acclamation,   35
But hirarchy and lordly throne of Prelacy invading,
The government of Christs deare flocke, then godlinesse
was fading.
Some men impute it to the pride of Bishops, others say,
The loosenesse of the Laity did carry most away.
But sure it is that godlinesse, and purities deriding,   40
Mov'd many godly ones to seek, a place of new abiding.
Proud Bishops skil'd in policie of machivilian learning,
Fore-saw their pomp would fall to ground by Scripture cleer
discerning.
New fangled fetches[4] were devis'd for soone intrapping those
Who to the people faithfully truth wholly did disclose.   45
While things thus craftly were contriv'd, Preachers to prisons
packe,
The Bishops Courts were fill'd with worke, and consciences
on racke.
Come sirrah quoth the Commissary, you will no Surplice weare,
Nor yet proclaime our Sunday sports, a Puritan I feare
You are, and shall no more preach forth to people stir to reare   50
Against my Lords grace, I know well, your preaching doth
him scare.
And to another: as for you, your faction is so much,
Whole townes run from their Parish Church to heare your word,
are such

[3] *pro dolor:* unhappily.
[4] tricks.

158

As for to overthrow my Lord, and his commanding power,
   If I live in this Diocesse, you shall not stand one houre.   55
In midst of all these wofull stirs grave godly men sit musing,
   How they their talents might improve, to honour God in using.
Nine hundred leagues of roaring seas dishearten feeble parts,
   Till cruell handling hasten on, and God doth strengthen hearts.
Come quoth the husband, my deare wife, canst thou the seas
                                    endure,   60
   With all our young and tender babes, let's put our faith in ure.[5]
With watry eyes the wife replies, what remedie remaines,
   Forsaking all for Christ his sake, will prove the greatest gaines.
From in-land parts poore Christians packe to Sea-ports ships
                                  to enter,
   A wonderment, in streets they passe, dividing their strange
                                  venter.   65
What meane these mad men soone sayes one, witlesse to run away,
   From *English* beere, to water, where no boone companions stay.
But tis the Surplice scares them hence, the Tippet[6] and the
                                  Crosse,
   Nay more they feare, my Lords grace here, will bring againe the
                                  masse.
Yea further I have heard of late our Puritans much wonder,   70
   Because our Metropolitan[7] intends to bring them under.
Thus passe the people to their ships, some grieve they should goe
                                  free,
   But make them sweare, and search them bare, taking what
                                coyne they see.
Now Satan seeing God had crost, his minde in making way,
   For's people and his Pastors too, in wildernesse to stay,   75
Fearing Christs Kingdom would encrease, and his to ground be
                                  falling,
   Stirs up fresh instruments like sheepe that wolfishly were haling.
Proud errour brochers, these croud in for liberty pretending,
   The overthrow of *Romish* trash, their words against it bending.
Quoth one here none but Scholler may in pulpit be a Preacher,   80
   I'le ship my selfe, for sure I am, full gifted for a Teacher.
Up starts another from a crowd, of women, her admiring,
   An able tongue in Scripture learn'd, to preach forsooth desiring,

[5] use.
[6] a cape of black cloth which clergy who are not university men are permitted to wear on their surplices in place of an academic hood.
[7] supervising bishop.

With revelations strange, yet true, as Scripture them accounting,
    Another comes to ship himselfe, in knowledge all surmounting.   85
'Gainst Magistrates another cries, none such on earth should stand,
    I'le venture o're the broadest Seas for freedome from their hand.
Thus diversly dispos'd doe people pack up and away,
    To populate new Collonies, where none but Heathen stay.

Of the Transportation of people and goods to the Mattachusets bay, and other adjacent Collonies

When as this people thus resolv'd the Ocean Sea to venter,   90
    As was their errant, so they did addresse the ships to enter.
Ship-owners seeing like it was their gain might holpen bee
    And Undertakers[1] with like hope, to hire ships were free.
Close Cabbins being now prepar'd with bread, biefe, beere and
                     fish,
    The passengers prepare themselves that they may have their
                     wish.   95
With little goods, but many words, aboord comes one, and sayes,
    I long to see my feet on shore, where cloudy pillar stayes,
As high as clouds he darts his words, but it is earth he wants:
    For having passed the fishing banks, soon smels the gay ground
                     plants
In long boat with a scouring pace comes gentle-like attended,   100
    New fashion'd by the Taylor's hand, one for his parts
                     commended.
Master at last quoth he, I'm not with labour much inured,
    Yet for to countenance good folk this toyl's to be endured.
Hee's loath to say, that men of parts to govern towns are wanting,
    And therefore he will through the seas, 'mongst others to be
                     planting.   105
His Cabin is too strait, his fare too mean for his degree,
    Now good Sir be content a while, on shore you'l be more free.
Eftsoones comes clambring up the ropes one in his mind revived,
    That hee's no servant, quoth he, this was very well contrived,
Now I may goe where I can close with people and with Preacher,   110
    But its great wages makes his close, for there he needs no
                     teacher.
Brief dancing on the decks doth walk another boasting sore
    Of godly kindred, and he longs to be with them on shore.

---

[1] managers, contractors.

These and the like may England spare, but oh it's sad to say,
    That privatly for publick work thy Worthies went away.   115
Sage, sober, grave and godly men, together counsell seeking
    At [t]h'hand of God, they fast and pray for their approved
                      liking:
And will not stirre one foot, but by his word and will directing,
    So on the seas most happily they found his hand directing.
Now large Revennewes hinder not, hoopt up in hogsheads they   120
    Transport both lands and houses too, nine hundred leagues
                      away.
Oh wee'l away, now say the poore, our Benefactors going,
    That fild our children's mouths with bread, look yonder are they
                      rowing.
O woe is me another cries, my Minister, its hee,
    As sure as may be, yonder he from Pursevant[2] doth flee.   125
With trickling tears scarce uttering speech, another sobbing sayes,
    If our poore preacher shipped be, hee'l ne're live halfe the way,
But one poore friend, another cries, my secret heart to plain,
    And he and his are shipped, now I'le after him amain.
'Mongst these doth Satan get a fraught, Angels of light they
                    seeming,   130
    Were entertain'd among the rest, as holy Saints them deeming.
Hardly beset on every side, Gods people thus attended,
    To troublous seas betake themselves, yet by their God
                    befriended.
In straits to get their goods aboord, their wives and children
                    small,
    Hard to attaine a cleering thought, cleerly dismist of all.   135
But God and godly friends, whom they find in their hard-ships
                    free,
    To send and lend them help in all, their great calamity.
The boysterous waves begin to hoyse their brittle barques on hye,
    When suddenly the billowes breake, and dash their ships awry.
Unwonted to such wondrous workes the little babes complaine   140
    For harbour in their Mothers armes, whom sicknesse doth
                    constraine
To sit as helplesse, yea, for help of others they doe cry,
    But all sea-sicke for present, all do others help deny.
Each corner's fill'd with goods and folke, the ships large womb
                    could bear,
    That hot diseases breed among this crowd, no roome to spare   145

[2] pursuer; an officer of the law.

For any weake ones, nor for those, whose fruit was ripe for light,
　On soundlesse depths their babes are borne 'mongst waves
　　　　　　　　　　　　above ships hight.
Both aged, weake, and tender ones the seas now tumbling tosse,
　Till they I forc'd to harbour turn'd, with stormy windes being
　　　　　　　　　　　　crost.
In western *Anglia,* and the Isle *Hibernia* they bide　　　　　150
　With longing for *Jehova's* help, who only windes doth guide.
As loft to lose the last long sight of their deare native soile,
　Both back and forth the winds them drive, with mickle³
　　　　　　　　　　　　restlesse toyle.
But being once in Ocean large, where depths the earth wide sever,
　Returne no more, though winds them crosse, to end their
　　　　　　　　　　　　course indere.　155
In unknown depths, and pathlesse Seas, there nights and days
　　　　　　　　　　　　they spend,
　'Mongst stormy winds and mountain waves long time no land
　　　　　　　　　　　　they kend.
At ships mast doth Christs Pastors preach, while waves like
　　　　　　　　　　　　Prelates proud,
　Would fling them from their pulpits place as not by them
　　　　　　　　　　　　allow'd.
The swelling surges raging come to stop their mouths with fome,　160
　For publishing of every truth that by God's word is known.
But Christ as once, so now he sayes peace ye waves, and be still,
　For all their height they fall downe flat, obey they must his will.
And now the Seas like medowes greene, whose ground and grasse
　　　　　　　　　　　　even are,
　Doth gently lead their ships as sheep from place to place afar.　165
Who would not wait on such a God, that heaven, earth, seas
　　　　　　　　　　　　commands,
　To serve his folke, then serve him folke, conducted by his hand.
For forty, fifty, sixty dayes and nights they safely swim,
　Preparing oft for fight, at sight of ships that pirats been.
Long looke'd for land at length the eye, unknown, yet owne
　　　　　　　　　　　　they will,　170
　To plant therein new Collonies, wide wildernesse to fill.

³ much.

Of the arrivall of our English Nation at the Mattachusets Bay, &c

With hearts revived in conceit, new land and trees they eye,
　Senting the Caedars and sweet ferne from heats reflection drye,
Much like the bird from dolsome Romes inclos'd in cage of wyre,
　Set forth in fragrant fields doth skip in hope of her desire. 175
So leap the hearts of these mixt men by streights o're seas inured,
　To following hard-ships wildernesse, doth force to be endured.
In clipping armes of out-strecht Capes, there ships now gliding
　　　　　　　　　　　　　　　　　　　　　　enter,
　In bay where many little Isles do stand in waters Center.
Where Sea-calves with their hairy heads gaze 'bove the waters
　　　　　　　　　　　　　　　　　　　　brim, 180
　Wondring to see such uncouth sights their sporting place to
　　　　　　　　　　　　　　　　　　　　swim.
The seas vast length makes welcome shores unto this wandring
　　　　　　　　　　　　　　　　　　　　race,
　Who now found footing freely for, Christs Church his resting
　　　　　　　　　　　　　　　　　　　　place.
This people landing, soonly shewd diversity of minds,
　As various heads, so actions did declare their divers kinds. 185
Now patience, *John*, give eare awhile unto a briefe digression,
　The better shalt thou understand the following progression.
Diversity of censure have past on this people, why
　Most judge the whole by lesser part, and parts run much awry.
By parts the giver, nor to part, and thou a part shalt see, 190
　To be partakers with the truth in hearts simplicity.
Yet further let me mind thee more from Satans sullin fits,
　Great rancour doth against them rise, enlarg'd by divers wits.
Yea male-contents none well content but discontentedly,
　They breath out ill, being crost in will to all lamentingly. 195
But now let's on my honest *John*, to land this people came,
　'Mongst trees and men that naked been, whom labour did not
　　　　　　　　　　　　　　　　　　　　tame.
Small entrance did they make therein, for why diseases stay,
　Their long unwonted legs to walke, in wildernesse the way.
In booths and huts lamenting lye, both men and women eake, 200
　Some breathing out their latest breath, and others faintly speak,
Unto their friends for succour soone that strength they might
　　　　　　　　　　　　　　　　　　　　recover,
　Which once attain'd, they search the land, tracing the Countrey
　　　　　　　　　　　　　　　　　　　　over.

To raising Townes and Churches new, in wildernesse they wander,
    First *Plymouth,* and then *Salem* next, were placed far asunder.   205
Charles river where they nextly land, a Towne like name they
                                                  built
    Poore Cottages them populate, with winters wet soone split.
Brave *Boston* such beginning had, *Dorchester* so began,
    Roxbury rose as mean as they, *Cambridge* forth from them ran.
Lin likewise built, when *Watertowne* first houses up did reare,   210
    Then large-limb'd *Ipswich* brought to eye 'mongst woods and
                                          waters cleer.
Hartford, New-haven, scituate, *Sandwich* and *Dover* all,
    In wildernesse 'mongst people wilde, there Scituations fall.
Newbery, Weymouth, Hingham, Hull, have their first nomination,
    Rude Island Providence brought forth by banished their station.   215
Springfield, Hamlton, Concord, eke *Deddam* and *Rowly,* wee
    New peopled in this Western world, where lands lye wast and
                                          free.
Salisbury, Sudbury, both began, to bore the Land, and plant,
    Braintre, Glocester, Exeter, plac'd where the wilde beasts haunt.
Wooborn, Wickham, Redding built, with little silver mettle,   220
    Andover, Haverhill, Berri's-banks, their habitations settle.
Southampton, Martins-vineyard, and some new nam'd Towns
                                          beside,
    All by this brood of travellers, were peopled far and wide.
With what they had stor'd up for time of scarcity, they live,
    Till tubs were empty, and the Land, could them small succour
                                         give.   225
God ne're denyes them fresh supplyes, with joy oft ships they eye,
    That bring in bread and meate for food when in those straights
                                         they cry.
Till labour blesse the earths encrease, and food each Towne doth
                                         fill,
    The land being sowne with man and beast, great store retaining
                                         still.

A *briefe description of the Land, Beasts, Birds,*
Trees, and Fruits

Unlevel'd lies this land new found with hills and vallies low,   230
With many mixtures of such mold where fruits do firtile grow.
Well watered with the pleasant springs that from the hills arise,
The waters run with warbling tunes, with stones that in them lies.
To welcome weary travellers, resting unneath the shade,

Of lofty banks, where lowly boughs, for them fresh harbour
made.   235
The lesser Rivelets rent themselves into a wider way,
Where scouring torrents furious fall, through rocks their streames
doe stray.

Spring

At end of *March* begins the Spring, by *Sols* new elivation,
Stealing away the earths white robe, dropping with sweats
vexation.
The Codfish, Holybut, and Basse, do sport the rivers in,   240
And Allewifes with their crowding sholes, in every creek do swim.
Leaving their spawn in ponds to thrive 'mongst Pikes devouring
jawes,
That swallow Trowts, Tench, Roach and Breme into their greedy
mawes.
Pirch, Shad, and Eeles, there plenty fill the panyard and the pan,
Smelts, Lobsters, Crab-fish, pranes and shrimps, with cockles,
mussels clams.   245
Plenty of oysters overgrow the flowed lands so thick,
That thousand loads to lime are turn'd, to lay fast stone and brick.
The Cormorants with greedy gut full fast the fishes follow,
And Eagles with their piercing sight look through the waters
shallow.
Ducks, Hens, and Pheasants often row upon the waters brim,   250
With plenty of their fellow fowles to welcome in the spring.
Devouring fires burning black the earths old rusty hew,
Like torch-bearers in gloomy night, their flames with wind sore
flew.
Like Phoenix rare, from ashes old, of grasse, doth grasse arise,
The earth casts off her mourning coate, gay clad like bride to
eyes.   255
With herbs and divers precious plants for physicks operation,
Diversity of fragrant flowers for scenes recreation.

Sommer

Bespread with Roses Sommer 'gins take place with hasty speed,
Whose parching heate Strawberries coole doth moderation breed.
Ayre darkening sholes of pigeons picke their berries sweet
and good,   260
The lovely cherries birds entice to feast themselves in woods.
The Turkies, Partridge, Heath-hens and their young ones tracing
passe,

The woods and medowes, Achorns eat, and hoppers in the
grasse.
Like *Virgils* knat musketo flies with buzzy humming dare
Assault the stoutest with long trunke, both blood and blisters
reare.   265
When little lineaments the Sun, or winde doth feeble make
Yea cooling dewes their swarms allay, and strength of stinging
slake.
The little hum-birds sucking sweet, from flowers draw their food,
Humilities in summer-time only find livelihood.

Autumne

Good wholsome and delightfull food, variety and store,   270
The Husband-man rejoycing keeps, with fruit the earths wombe
boare.
Peas plenty, Barley, Oats and Wheat, Rye richly stocking stands,
Such store the plough-man late hath found, that they feed
forreign lands.
Cucumbers, mellons, apples, peares, and plums do flourish faire,
Yea what delight and profit would, they still are adding there.   275
Sixe sorts of Oakes the land affords, Walnuts doe differ so,
That divers shapes their fruit retains, and food that in them
grow.
Roots are not wanting, wild and tame, in gardens they encrease,
Ground nuts, ground beans, not gathered till, warmth doth the
earth release.
Grapes wanting vintage, common grow, fit for the travellers hand,   280
With food from berries multitude, that grow throughout the
land.

Winter

Sharpe, sudden, yet with lightsome looks doth winters cold come
in,
With thicke, large Coat doth cloath the earth, both soft,
smooth, white and trim.
The large tempestuous surges are bound in with frozen band,
Where ship did anker, men doe walke, and carts as on the land.   285
The Geese flye prating night and day, to tell the approaching
season,
Brought downe by gun shot from their flight unto the Indians
geson.[1]
The tumbling beares intrapped are, 'mongst houses sudden enter,
O'rethrowe by eager hunters, who pursue them in this venter.

[1] geason: rarely.

The tripping Deer with length of leaps, do burst through frozen
snow,   290
    Hunters pursue with bracket shooes, at length they weary grow.
Then down the dogs them sudden draw, expos'd to hunters
pleasure,
    Their flesh well welcome, and their skins, are chiefe of Indian
treasure.
Whole kennels of devouring wolves both Deer and Swine destroy,
    Yet scar'd by weakest children, they them the lesse annoy.   295
The Suns bright presence most dayes doth cheere man and beast
with joy,
    With hope of pleasant springs approach to free from colds
annoy.
With mineralls the earth is fraught, though Alcumists are wanting,
    Which makes the current mettle priz'd 'mongst Merchants daily
scanting.

Of their building, planting, and giving out of LANDS

Delightfull to the eye did lye the woods and medowes greene,   300
    The paths untrod by man and beast, both smooth and clenly
seene.
Most men unlanded till this time, for large lands Eage[r] sue,
    Had not restraint knockt of their hands, too big their fermes
had grew.
Give eare I pray unto the praise set on a new Plantation,
    First for the medow sirs says one, I have found such a station.   305
Where grasse doth grow as high as I, round stalkes and very
thicke,
    No hassocks but a bottom plain, Carts cannot therein stick.
Salt hay and fresh there thousands are of acres I do deeme,
    A gallant harbour there's for ships the best that yet is seene.
Boates may come up unto our doors, the Creeks convenient lye,   310
    Fish plenty taken in them are, plains plowable hard by.
No bush nor roots to hinder them, yet stately timber is,
    In every swamp, yea uplands too, most clobberd[1] trees I wis.
Clay there for bricke and tile, pot-earth with ease, and store,
    Some men suppose black lead is there, silver and copper o're.   315
Carry but guns, and wild fowle will be brought unto our dishes,
    Venison and Moose you there may catch according to your
wishes.

[1] clapboard.

All creatures thrive exceeding well, Goats, Swine, and sheep for
                 meat,
   Horse, Cows, and Calves encrease as well, ther's store of
                 English wheat.
Five, seven, or nine old Planters doe take up their station first,   320
   Whose property is not to share unto themselves the worst.
Their Cottages like Crows nests built, new commers goods attain,
   For mens accommodation sake, they truck their seats for gaine.
Come buy my house, here may you have, much medow at your
                 dore,
   'T will dearer be if you stay till, the landed be planted o're.   325
See you that garden-plot inclos'd, Pumkins there hundreds are,
   Parsnips and Roots, with Cabiges, grow in great plenty there.
Lay out an hundred pound or two, you shall have such a seat,
   When you have planted but one crop, you cannot want for
                 meate.
This praise doth make the purchaser his gold and silver throw,   330
   Into his hand for house and land that yet he did not know.
Unseen, and yet so sudden bought, when once the sale was ended,
   His purchase makes him misse of more, with gifts he's not
                 befriended.
One he hath friends to praise his parts, his lot shall larger be,
   For usefull men are highly priz'd, such shall sell two or three.   335
Sure such mistaken, towns have been, for many have made prize,
   Get all they can, sell often, than, and thus old Planters rise.
They build to sell, and sell to build, where they find towns are
                 planting,
   Till men no more the Sea passe o're, and Customers are wanting.
Then those that boast their townes were full for company are
                 longing,   340
   Who lately fear'd land would fall short, when men to them
                 came thronging.
Insatiate minds for medow, and best land they could attain,
   Hath caused Townes, land lay by lot, I wish it were not vaine.

[To populate this howling desart Land]

To populate this howling desart Land,
   The only worke is of *Jehovah's* hand.   345
Contemn no weakest meanes in hand of him:
   See here his worke by meanes that weakest been.

In thrice five yeares a Common-wealth compleat,
    For peace, for war, for actions small and great.
Five hundred Lawes for peoples plaine direction,   350
    Englands addition as naturall Connection,
Prest to oppose haters of peace; with guide
    Of Officers, three Regiments abide.
In *Middlesex* seven Ensigns are displaid,
    There disciplin'd by Major *Sedgwick's* aide.   355
In Suffolk nine, by Major *Gibbons* led,
    Essex and *Norfolk* in one are marshalled,
By *Denison,* their Major in the field,
    Their Generall a yearly choise doth yield.
Eight times a yeare each band instructed is,   360
    And once to meet in one they may not misse.
Both Horse and Foot, force, forts and castles are,
    Prepar'd in peace for peace, yet fit for War.
To awe bruit men, Justice impartially,
    Hath hitherto with pale suspitious eye,   365
Disperst the crimes common in many Lands,
    Disgrace for vice, honour for vertue stands.
Now notice take, this is the grand complaint,
    That *English* here from priviledg'd restraint,
Have: why I pray, you'l priviledg confound,   370
    If common they with lawrell all not crown'd.
For trades, commerce, Merchants, Sea-affaires,
    Great freedoms had, large gaines their losse repaires.
Monopolies is by their lawes forbid,
    Unlesse invention rare from others hid.   375
All handy-crafts have choise of worke at will,
    And ordered are, lest working praise they spill.
As shipping great, built up by timbers strength,
    But iron mills their chains of greater length.
Salt, sope and glasse, Tiles, lime and bricke are made,   380
    With orders for well-ordering each Trade.
So suted hath his providence, that none
    Can contradict: envy of any one
Shall not prevaile, Justice and peace shall still,
    Perfect this worke, govern for God they will,   385
For husbandry, Corne, Cattell, wood and hay,
    Good lawes are made for all men to obey.
Listen a while, I must spend one word more,
    Some rubs remaine, are hardlier gotten o're.

Bipartior in many Court and Cause, 390
 Doth dull the edge of Justice, Sword and Lawes.
Discloseth Counsels, opens Breaches wide,
 That adverse part steps in without a guide.
Makes causes good or bad, as men affect it,
 Doth what's oppos'd, and what is lik't neglect it. 395
Tells liberty, authority will stop,
 And clip her wings, quoth she, I'le sit on top.
Tells men their cause is good, but wanting
 Lawes: or Judges are in learn'd, in sight scanting.
More yet remaines, swift speakers show but backe, 400
 So counsels lost words will not fill a sack.
And now say truth doth not great skill appear,
 Through such tempestuous seas and stormes to stere.
So swiftly one grapling with Pirats oft,
 For *England* fain'd, bearing their flag aloft. 405
To *England* yet, ungratefull they'l not be,
 That governe here, yet little help they see.
The more's to come, experience teaches sure,
 You'l pitty more, when you the like endure.
More yet you'l find our enemies are yours, 410
 You'l hurt your selves if you encrease their powers.
Forgive, that they so much your good forget,
 Lighter to truth, those they should harder it.
If *England* one as truths but one embrace,
 These tooke your name, and you will take their case. 415
If *England* say more wayes then one they will,
 Allow no more then helps reforming still.
Those that are skil'd in structures modell, make,
 A little moddel here is for you, take
What may serve turne for opposites to awe, 420
 For Kings may rule without a Bishops law.
Could Bishops keepe downe all their Lordships spoile,
 And can't highest Court awe those Gods word defile.
With blasphemous horrid interpretation,
 As only they knowing Gods explanation. 425
Ruine now men strive, with words contentious strength,
 New-Englands acts shall speak, not words at length.
While fogs arise from errour-broaching braines,
 Their justice clouded is, and what remaines.
But unto God that they commit their way, 430
 And judgment shall burst forth as sunny day.

Let *England* wait with patience for the same,
　Not drawing backe for cost, finish for shame.
Lest Prelates proud tollerating deride,
　Ye know not truth without their guide.

[*What creature man that is so apt to take*]

What creature man that is so apt to take
　His praise, who work and workman both did make
In telling of these Worthies work then I
　Own none but God, and yet his meanes I eye,
Who though nine hundred leagues at sea, hath sent
　These twenty Worthies, who their time have spent
In preaching Christ, his mind and will reveale
　From Scripture light each servants portion deale.
One opens Prophesies as yet to come,
　So ready is the Scripture in his tongue.
That word and sense his memory retaines,
　Cleare Scripture light, all by great labour gaines.
One hewes the cords of wicked works with ire,
　Full Arguments as God doth him require.
One pretious Balm from Christs deare sufferings fets,[1]
　Wounded to heale; if heale to fast, then frets
Down the proud flesh from thought of knowledge rising,
　Till Christ alone they know, him onely prizing.
One Sheppard[2] he takes restlesse pains that none
　Themselves delude with happy state as one
Belov'd of God in Christ, and therefore makes
　Cleare evidence from Gods word, whom he takes,
And wholly bent to save his flock from tearing,
　With watchfull eye 'way sheepslaying wolves is scaring.
One labours faith may get assurance fast,
　One he exhorts the anchor, hope to cast.
One follows peace, and bids all folk pursue it,
　One's for fresh love, and when it's old renew it.
One puts in minde with patience to abide,
　One cease from strife, take meeknesse on your side.
One to humility exhorts with care,
　One wills their lives may passe in godly feare.
One cheerfull bids in spirits joy to cheere.
　One would men mourn with those are mourners here.

[1] fetches.
[2] Thomas Shepard I (1605–49).

One bounty doth by his example teach,   470
    One zeal to God and's truth doth daily preach.
One heavenly mindednesse perswadeth still,
    One Christian boldnesse seated in the will.
One purity and holinesse commends,
    One for just dealing both with foes and friend.   475
One he exhorts all Christian watch to keep,
    One prayer would with sighes and groanes so deep.
One unto reading Scripture men perswades,
    One labour bids for food that never fades.
One to redeem their time exhorteth all,   480
    One looking round, for wary walking calls.
One he perswades men buy the truth, not sell,
    One would men should in moderatenesse excell.
One for renew'd repentance daily strives,
    One's for a conscience cleare in all mens lives.   485
One he exhorts all men Gods word to heare,
    One doth beseech to lend obedient eare.
One he desires evil's appearance shun,
    One with diligence would all should be done.
One shews their woe that will not God believe;   490
    One doth beseech Gods Spirit they'l not grieve.
One wishes none to deep despair do run,
    One bids beware none to presumption come.
One wils that all at murmuring take heed,
    One shewes that strife and envie should not breed.   495
One shewes the hatred God to pride doth beare,
    One covetousnesse cries down with hellish feare.
One to luke-warmnesse wishes doe grow,
    One none for feare forsake the truth they know.
One idle talk and foolish jesting shun,   500
    One bids that none unto uncleannesse run.
One sayes, none should self-seeking entertain,
    One teaches all in anger should contain.
One idlenesse dehorts with meekle[3] pains,
    One bids beware of error-broaching brains.   505
One would all men surfets excesse take heed,
    One worlds joy and sorrow doe not exceed.
One ignorance would not mens soules should slay,
    One in known sins bids men they would not stay.

[3] mickle: much.

One wishes none of Faith doe shipwrack make,   510
    One their first love in Christ, that none forsake.
One in their breast would none two hearts should beare,
    One woe of hypocrites doth oft declare.
One bids beware, hardnesse of heart will breed,
    One, to adde sin to sin that none proceed.   515
One lying tongues doth tell God hateth such,
    One bids beware, for Satans wiles are much.
One sayes gainst all, power from Christ is had,
    One bids all be with's armour ever clad.
I name but one, 'cause all as one the same,   520
    Exhort, dehort, in the Lord Christ his Name.
Minding all still it's Christ his will that all
    Depart from ill, that on Gods name doe call.
And further they professe that Christ alone,
    Works all in his, and for his every one.   525
So grace is free, and nothing we to cause
    The cords of love with which Gods Spirit drawes.
Which Spirit plainly doth appeare in all
    These preachings that from earthen lips doe fall
Like deaw on grasse, how ever some deny it,   530
    As legall they: from Gods word doe thou try it.
And neighbour *John,* yet one thing more now mind,
    Their learned counsell helps the truth to finde.
Coupling these men in Synods God hath blest,
    By his word truth is found, error confest.   535
As helpfull unto Godly learning they,
    With Schooles and Colledge, finde out learnings way.

[*Yet unto God this people feeling sayes*]

Yet unto God this people feeling sayes,
    Not unto us, but to thy name be praise.
Now must I mind what hindrances remain,   540
    To blast the fruit of all these Worthies pain.
Some would none should endevour unity,
    Tyrants (say they) do hinder liberty:
Why truth's but one, and Christ will make you free,
    Come to the Word, let that your touch-stone bee.   545
Some feare Presbytery hath too great power,
    If you are Christs, then all they have is yours.
Some odd ones say they *Independents* are,
    Therefore in others counsel they'l not share.

But now Ile end and tell you friend, what will   550
   Perswade their way doth hold with still.
Strong arguments doe papers fill each way
   With words of heat: but honest John now stay,
Unto experience let thy judgement bow,
   Let actions speake, and not mens words to you.   555
For little time, some subtile Foxes will,
   Bridle their nature, and yet Foxes still.
Lord Bishops did some errors fend from sheep,
   So beasts of prey others from preying keep.
Some new raisd errors Bishops power deny   560
   To side with truth, and yet their error eye.
Neare twenty yeares these Churches you may trace
   In godly steps, no false way they'l embrace.
Look in this glasse that thus is slubberd[1] or'e,
   And you may see foure things uneyd before.   565
No Prelate no King: that's not so, for see,
   Here Churches power and command agree,
Of civill power to which these Churches yeeld
   Humble obedience, as their duty held.
Next note, some say, Opinions none must touch,   570
   For feare they wrong the consciences of such,
With word of truth, God helping true endeavours,
   Christs Pastor here error and conscience severs.
Third, Law and Gospel at such oddes have set,
   That Rule of walking from it none may get.   575
But here experience from Gods word is found,
   Gods folk with's word walk wary, looking round.
Last, humane learning is no mean, some say;
   Blest by the Lord, to find his word and way,
But as a meanes this people found it have,   580
   Yet trust not means, its onely God must save.
But England now to thee Ile means commend,
   Make use of these before their life they end.

[Church-covenant Band brought in with liberty]

Church-covenant Band brought in with liberty,
   But causeth men to walk licentiously.   585
Some buy the truth: for conscience liberty,
   Error's brought in to blind men damningly.

[1] stained, darkened.

ROGER WILLIAMS

(c. 1603–1683)

In 1631 Governor William Bradford of Plymouth wrote down his impression of young Mr. Roger Williams, newly arrived in America. Bradford called him "a man godly and zealous, having many precious parts, but very unsettled in judgmente." Always of a gentle cast of mind, Bradford concluded that Williams was not a man to be condemned, but "to be pitied, and prayed for." Bradford himself prayed that God might "shew him his errors, and reduse him into the way of truth," and give him a constant, settled judgment as well. Contrary to the Plymouth governor's prayer, however, Roger Williams never did hold in good proportion the convictions embraced by Puritans in the Massachusetts Bay. Consequently, his life in New England was one of quarrel and controversy.

Born in 1603, Roger Williams was the son of a tailor in Cow Lane, London. His early promise won him the patronage of Sir Edward Coke, under whose influence Williams was admitted to the Charterhouse School and later to Pembroke College, Cambridge, then a seat of religious non-conformity. Two years after his graduation in 1627 Williams was ordained and also married, and in 1631 he arrived in New England with his wife. Immediately Williams was invited to officiate at the Boston Church, for his fine reputation as a godly and brilliant young minister had preceded him. But difficulties arose when Williams refused the Boston invitation. That church, he declared, was no true church because it had not separated from its corrupted mother church in England. Roger Williams had not traveled three thousand miles to affiliate with "a vessel once infected with the contagion of leprosy." In these terms the alarm was sounded, for the churches of the Bay had no intention of casting off their English brethren back home.

To the mind of most New England divines, including that of the prominent John Cotton, Roger Williams was seeking a level of purity unattainable by human beings in their churches. They believed there indeed existed God's "Church Invisible," as St. Augustine had termed it; but God alone knew who comprised that spiritually perfect church. As for men on earth, frail and depraved, they could only strive toward a purity impossible of attainment. They could screen members carefully; they could demand that each candidate for membership recite to their satisfaction his knowledge of God's having saved him; and they could refuse membership to best-intentioned, upstanding citizens unable to attest to personal knowledge of their salvation. But they knew they could not, for all their efforts, prevent a few hypocrites from slipping in to soil their "Church Visible" on earth. This was the point on which they differed from Roger Williams, who believed that the division between the "saved" and the "damned" could govern all affairs in this world.

It did not take the New Englanders long to see the implication of what Williams was saying: if the pure church was to be the only institution ordained by God, then God had no hand in the political structure through which men organized communities, built schools, and made laws. In other words, Williams was sanctioning political anarchy. Aside from members of the "pure" church, all other men could go their way and be damned, both now and hereafter. To the Puritan ministers and magistrates, who saw valid biblical parallels between Mosaic Law and their own, Roger Williams was guilty of gravest error. His four years in the Bay, from 1631 to 1635, are a record of Williams' tenacity of conscience opposed to the efforts of Puritan leaders to convince him of his wrongheadedness.

Williams' sojourn in Massachusetts took him to several towns before his banishment and removal to Rhode Island. Having refused the offer of the Boston Church, he was invited as minister to Salem, in defiance of a warning by the General Court. Ousted from Salem just two months later, he went to Plymouth, only to return to Salem briefly before being banished from Massachusetts in 1635, when he fled to Narragansett County to found Providence in 1636. Williams helped secure a charter for Providence between 1644 and 1663, and was governor of the colony from 1654 to 1657. He died in 1683.

Most of Roger Williams' writings were in prose, emerging from New England religious controversy. His best-known *Bloudy Tenent of Persecution* is a dialogue between Truth and Peace, written to refute the Massachusetts ministers' "A Model of Church and Civil Power." Williams' verses appear in a volume entitled *A Key into the*

Language of America, published in London in 1643 to "open" somewhat the language of the Narragansett Indians. Interspersed throughout the volume, the verses play on the contrast and comparison between the Indians and the English. The recurrent theme is that the faults of the savage Indians are all the more egregious when manifested by supposedly civilized "Christian" Englishmen. In such a world of sinners, the godly souls figure as "little fishes" which, pursued, are forced "To leape on driest sand, / To gaspe on earthie element."

Williams' full capabilities as a poet are not, perhaps, revealed in his slight quantity of verse. But his ability to evoke the quality of an image, both apart from and in complement to the moral meaning he assigns it, sets him apart from many early New England verse writers. It also secures his place among America's early poets.

[The Courteous Pagan shall condemne]

1. *The Courteous* Pagan[1] *shall condemne*
    Uncourteous Englishmen
    Who live like Foxes, Bears and Wolves,
    Or Lyon in his Den.

2. *Let none sing* blessings *to their soules,*
    For that they Courteous are:
    The wild Barbarians *with no more*
    Then[2] *Nature, go so farre:*

3. *If Natures Sons both* wild *and* tame,
    Humane and Courteous be:
    How ill becomes it Sonnes of God
    To want Humanity?

[Course bread and water's most their fare]

1. *Course*[1] bread *and* water's *most their fare;*
    O Englands *diet fine;*

1 Indians.
2 than.
1 coarse.

> Thy cup *runs ore with plenteous store*
> *Of wholesome* beare *and* wine.

2. *Sometimes* God *gives them* Fish *or* Flesh,
   Yet they're content *without;*
   And what comes in, they part to friends
   and strangers *round about.*

3. *Gods* providence *is rich to his,*
   Let none distrustfull *be;*
   In wildernesse, *in great* distresse,
   These Ravens *have fed me.*

[God gives them sleep on Ground, on Straw]

1. *God gives them sleep on Ground, on Straw,*
   on Sedgie Mats or Boord:
   When English softest Beds of Downe,
   sometimes no sleep affoord.

2. *I have knowne them leave their House and Mat*
   to lodge a Friend or stranger,
   When Jewes and Christians oft have sent
   Christ Jesus *to the Manger.*

3. *'Fore day they invocate their Gods,*
   though Many, False and New:
   O how should that God worshipt be,
   who is but One and True?

[The Pagans wild confesse the bonds]

> *The* Pagans *wild confesse* the bonds
> *Of* married chastitie:
> *How vild are* Nicolâitans[1] *that hold*
> *Of* Wives *communitie?*

---

[1] mentioned in Rev ii 6, 15: obscure early 'Gnostic' heretics who offended chiefly by violating the decree of the Council at Jerusalem (Acts xv 29) which forbade Christians from taking part in heathen feasts and the licentiousness which followed. Williams' allusion may be to an assertion by Irenaeus (*Against*

How kindly flames of nature *burne*
In wild humanitie?
Naturall affections *who wants, is sure*
Far from Christianity.

Best nature's vaine, he's blest that's made
A new and rich partaker
Of divine Nature of his God,
And blest eternall Maker.

[How busie are the sonnes of men?]

1. *How busie are the sonnes of men?*
   How full their heads and hands?
   What noyse and tumults in our owne,
   And eke in Pagan *lands?*

2. *Yet I have found lesse noyse, more peace*
   In wilde America,
   Where women quickly build the house,
   And quickly move away.

3. English *and* Indians *busie are,*
   In parts of their abode:
   Yet both stand idle, *till God's call*
   Mat. 20: 7 *Set them to worke for God.*

[Boast not proud E[n]glish, of thy birth and blood]

Boast not proud E[n]glish, *of thy birth and blood,*
Thy brother Indian *is by birth as* Good.
Of one blood God made Him, and Thee and All,
As wise, as faire, as strong, as personall.

By nature wrath's his portion, thine no more
Till Grace his *soule and* thine *in Christ restore*
Make sure thy second birth, else thou shalt see,
Heaven ope to Indians *wild, but shut to thee.*

Heresies): "The Nicolaitans . . . teach that it is a matter of indifference to practice adultery and to eat things sacrificed to idols" (i, 26).

[Mans restlesse soule hath restlesse eyes and ears]

Mans *restlesse soule hath restlesse eyes and ears.*
Wanders in change *of sorrows, cares and fears.*
Faine would it (Bee-like) *suck by the ears, by the eye*
Something that might his hunger satisfie:
The Gospel, *or* Glad tidings *onely can,*
Make glad the English, *and the* Indian.

[They see Gods wonders that are call'd]

They see Gods wonders that are call'd
  Through dreadfull Seas to passe,
In tearing winds and roaring seas,
  And calmes as Smooth as glasse.

I have in Europes *ships, oft been*
  In King of terrours hand;
When all have cri'd, Now, now we sinck,
  Yet God brought safe to land.

Alone 'mongst Indians *in Canoes,*
  Sometime o're-turn'd, I have been
Halfe inch from death, in Ocean deepe,
  Gods wonders I have seene.

[What Habacuck once spake, mine eyes]

What Habacuck *once spake, mine eyes*
  Have often seene most true,
The greater fishes devoure the lesse,
  And cruelly pursue.

Forcing them through Coves and Creekes,
  To leape on driest sand,
To gaspe on earthie element, or die
  By wildest Indians *hand.*

Christs little ones must hunted be
  Devour'd; yet rise as Hee.

And eate up those which now a while
Their fierce devourers be.

[Adulteries, Murthers, Robberies, Thefts]

1. *Adulteries, Murthers, Robberies, Thefts,*
   Wild Indians *punish these!*
   And hold the Scales of Justice so,
   That no man farthing leese.

2. *When* Indians *heare the horrid filths,*
   Of Irish, English *Men,*
   The horrid Oaths and Murthers late,
   Thus say these Indians *then.*

3. *We weare no Cloaths, have many Gods,*
   And yet our sinnes are lesse:
   You are Barbarians, Pagans wild,
   Your Land's the Wildernesse.

[The Indians prize not English gold]

1. *The* Indians *prize not* English *gold,*
   Nor English Indians *shell:*
   Each in his place will passe for ought,
   What ere men buy or sell.

2. English *and* Indians *all passe hence,*
   To an eternall place,
   Where shels nor finest gold's worth ought,
   Where nought's worth ought but Grace.

3. *This Coyne the* Indians *know not of,*
   Who knowes how soone they may?
   The English *knowing prize it not,*
   But fling't like drosse away.

[I have heard ingenuous Indians say]

I have heard ingenuous Indians *say,*
In debts, they could not sleepe.

How far worse are such English *then,*
Who love in debts to keepe?

If debts of pounds cause restlesse nights
In trade with man and man,
How hard's that heart that millions owes
To God, and yet sleepe can?

Debts paid, sleep's sweet, sins paid, death's sweet,
Death's night then's turn'd to light;
Who dies in sinnes unpaid, that soule
His light's eternall night.

[Our English Gamesters scorne to stake]

1. *Our* English *Gamesters scorne to stake*
    Their clothes as Indians *do,*
    Nor yet themselves, alas, yet both
    Stake soules and lose them to.

2. *O fearfull Games! the divell stakes*
    But Strawes and Toyes and Trash,
    (For what is All, compar'd with Christ,
    But Dogs meat and Swines wash?)

Phil. 3: 8

3. *Man stakes his Jewell-darling soule,*
    (His owne most wretched foe)
    Ventures, and loseth all in sport
    At one most dreadfull throw.

[The Indians count of Men as Dogs]

The Indians *count of Men as Dogs,*
It is no Wonder then:
They teare out one anothers throats!
But now that English *Men,*

That boast themselves Gods Children, and
Members of Christ to be,
That they should thus break out in flames.
Sure 'tis a Mystery.

Rev. 2: 6

> *The second sea'ld Mystery or red Horse,*
> *Whose Rider hath power and will,*
> *To take away Peace from Earthly Men,*
> *They must* Each *other* kill.

[Truth is a Native, naked Beauty; but]

Truth is a Native, naked Beauty; but
Lying Inventions are but Indian *Paints,*
Dissembling hearts their Beautie's but a Lye,
Truth is the proper Beauty of Gods Saints.

Fowle are the Indians *Haire and painted Faces,*
More foule such Haire, such Face in Israel.
England *so calls her selfe, yet there's*
Absoloms *foule Haire and Face of* Jesabell.

Paints will not bide Christs washing Flames of fire,
Fained Inventions will not bide such stormes:
O that we may prevent him, that betimes,
Repentance Teares may wash of all such Formes.

[One step twix't Me and Death]

1. *One step twix't Me and Death,* (*twas Davids speech,*)
   And true of sick Folks all:
   Mans Leafe it fades, his Clay house cracks;
   Before it's dreadful Fall.

2. *Like Grashopper the* Indian *leapes,*
   Till blasts of sicknesse rise:
   Nor soule nor Body Physick hath,
   Then Soule and Body dies.

3. *O happy* English *who for both,*
   Have precious physicks store:
   How should (when Christ hath both refresh't,[)]
   Thy Love and zeale be more?

[When Indians heare that some there are]

When Indians heare that some there are,
  (That Men the Papists call)
Forbidding Mariage Bed and yet,
  To thousand Whoredomes fall:

They aske if such doe goe in Cloaths,
  And whether God they know?
And when they heare they're richly clad,
  Know God, yet practice so.

No sure they're Beasts not men (say they,)
  Mens shame and foule disgrace.
Or men have mixt with Beasts and so,
  Brought forth that monstrous Race.

JOHN FISKE

(1608–1677)

Mention of John Fiske's name in an occasional ecclesiastical history has produced tribute to his ministerial devotion, but not one word about his verse. Like so many of New England's early poets, Fiske lay in anonymity for more than two centuries until his verses were called to public attention in 1943. Previously they had remained in manuscript in Fiske's commonplace book, deposited unread in the library of Brown University. Through the centuries an occasional peruser of his poems might well have been put off by Fiske's verse form, for rather than narrating a familiar, if perilous, sea voyage, as Richard Steere chose to do, or writing love lyrics in the manner of John Saffin, Fiske perfected a verse form alien to contemporary knowledge and taste. It is therefore not enough simply to bring Fiske's verses to light, for if they are to be appreciated, the reader must extend himself to understand the intent and method of the anagram. It is a form which in the seventeenth century needed no apology, much less explanation.

The man who concentrated his poetic efforts on the verse anagram was born in 1608 in Suffolk, England. He entered Peterhouse, Cambridge, as a sizar in 1625, received his bachelor's degree three years later, and was ordained. For the next six years, from 1630 to 1636, Fiske preached throughout England and regularly suffered the harassment non-conformists were subjected to. Frequently frustrated in the exercise of his ministerial office, Fiske at length resigned to take up medicine, for which he was publicly licensed. Married in 1635 to Anne Gipps, Fiske emigrated to New England the very next year with his bride and several family members.

Fiske's voyage to America, like that of many another seventeenth-century traveler to the New World, had its tragic aspects. Fiske's mother died on shipboard, and his infant child did not long survive arrival in America. To add to the difficulty, the family landed in Massachusetts during the most hectic months of the Pequot War, an unsettling time in which to establish a new home in a strange land. Yet Fiske rose to the challenge, took up life in New England, and began to teach school, first in Charlestown and later in Salem. In Salem Fiske also assisted the Reverend Hugh Peters, later to be accused as one of the Regicides, until 1641, when Fiske was called as pastor to a tiny church in Wenham, Massachusetts. There he served as schoolmaster, minister, and physician until 1655, when he and a majority of his parishioners removed to the newly formed town of Chelmsford. Fiske continued as minister there until his death in 1677. His unceasing ministerial devotion is attested to in a statement that although he was "visited with the severities of stone and gout[,] these occasioned him to be carried to and from the pulpit in a chair, whence, in a sitting posture, he dispensed the messages of salvation."

John Fiske was not a prolific poet, nor did he publish what he wrote. The longest of his anagrams were elegies read at gravesides and intended for no further distribution. These circumstances of limited audience and commemorative occasion imply a certain privacy and privilege of implicitness for the poet. That is, since the verses were addressed to an audience already familiar with their subject, there was no need for the poet to trace biography, or to catalogue explicitly the accomplishments of the subject. Rather than using the verse narrative or the formal elegy, then, he was able to turn to the anagram as his major structural device for revealing the character and achievements of his subject.

Historically the anagram, dating from the Middle Ages, was used (from the tenth to the seventeenth century) as an exercise for religious orders. It involved recognizing the significance of a person's name, the letters of which were used to form the anagram, a terse epigrammatic motto which became the theme of the poem following. No mere verbal game, the anagram was intended to reveal aspects of a person's character that lay hidden in the letters of his name. For the poet it was not a matter of ingenious invention, but of laying open to view what was latent and obscured.

The major poetic technique of the anagram was a focus on the one or two or perhaps three words central to the anagrammatic theme. For example, Fiske's anagram "O, Honie Knott" impells him to make the two words, "honie" and "knott," thematically pervasive of the entire poem, and relevant to John Cotton, the poem's subject.

Poetic demand was for the greatest number of meanings to be discerned from the word and yet made applicable to the person who was subject of the poem. It meant that the verse writer must construct a fugue of meanings from a single word, searching out every nuance and fitting them into a cohesive pattern. Obviously it was no simple matter, for it required of the poet considerable verbal dexterity, as well as a heightened consciousness of the extremely subtle variant meanings of a single word. In this respect, since it pushed words to the very limits of usage, the anagram can be called Baroque.

The verse anagram has, of course, lost favor since the seventeenth century, having come to be viewed more as verbal trickery than serious art. However, the reader who can suspend his contemporary cultural judgments and extend literary sympathy will find John Fiske's verse rewarding and admirable.

Upon the much-to be lamented desease
of the Reverend Mr John Cotton
late Teacher to the Church at Boston N. E.
who departed this Life 23 of 10. [16]52.

John $\begin{cases} Cotton \\ Kotton \quad \textit{after the old English writi'g} \end{cases}$

Anagr:
O, Honie knott

With Joy erst while, (when knotty doubts arose)
To Thee we calld, o Sir, the knott disclose:
But now o and alasse to thee to call
In vayne tis thou no Answer give or shall.
Could loud Shrickes, could crys recall thee back   5
From deaths estate we wold our eye ne're slack
O, this our greife it is, lament shall we
A Father in our Israel's cea'st to be
Even hee that in the Church a pillar was
A gurdeon knot[1] of sweetest graces as   10
He who set fast to Truths so clossly knitt
As loosen him could ne're the keenest witt

[1] the ingenious and intricate knot that Gordius, King of Phrygia, used to fasten the yoke to his wagon, dedicated to Jupiter.

Hee who his Flesh together bound ful-fast
No knott more sure whilest his life did last
Hee who the knotts of Truth, of Mysteries 15
Sacred, most cleerely did ope 'fore our eyes
Even hee who such a one, is ceas'd to bee
'Twixt whose life, death, the most sweete harmony
Knotts we doe meet with many a cue daily
Which crabbed anggry tough unpleasing bee 20
But we as in a honi-comb a knott
Of Hony sweete, here had such sweetenes Gott
The knotts and knobbs that on the Trees doe grow
The bitterest excressences we know.

     his soule Embalmd with grace 25
       was fit to soare on high
    and to receive its place
       above the starry skie.
    now grant O G[od that we]
       may follow afte[r him] 30
   surviving worlds ocean unto thee
       our passage safe may swim.

A vine tree seene, a plant of Gods owne hand
In it this knott of sweetest parts did stand.
The knott in place sublime: most eminent 35
As, his, no Branch could challeng like extent
The knott sometimes seems a deformity
It's a mistake, tho such be light set by
The knott it is the Joynt, the strength of parts
The bodies-beauty, so this knott out-starts 40
What others in that place, they ought to bee
Even such a knott exemplar'ly was hee
Knotts now adayes affrayd of are most men
Of Hony if expose'd feare none would then
I guesse why knotty Learning downe does goe 45
'Twould not, if as in him 'twere sweetned soe
Meeknes Humility forbearance too
This lovely knott to love the most did woe
In knotts what greate adoe to gayne the hearte
Yee had it heere, he did it free impart 50
When knotty theames and paynes some meet with then
As knotty and uncouth their tongue and pen
So 'twas not heere, he caus'd us understand

And tast the sweetnes of the knott in hand.
When knotty querks and quiddities broacht were   55
By witt of man he sweetely Breathed there.
His charity his wisdom meeknes eke
Left none that loved light, in knotts to seeke
Hee tho invincible thrô softnes did
The knottiest peeces calme and cleave amid   60
Such was hee of such use in these last dayes
Whose want bewayle, o, and alas alwaies
This knott so we have seen lien broknly
By knotts so breathlesse, so crookt, crackt, or fly
This knott thereof so surfetted we see   65
By hony surfetted we know som bee
The cause nor in the knott nor hony say
Thro Temper bad, unskilfulnes this may
O knott of Hony most delightfull when
Thou livd'st, thi death a sad presage hath ben   70
Have Ben? yea is, and is, and is alas
For woe to us, so greate a Breach when was
Woe to that knotty pride hee ne're subdude
Woe they who doe his Truthes dispenct exclude
And woe to them that factions there contrive   75
Woe them whose wayes unrighteous survive
Woe they that by him warning did not take
Woe to us all if mercy us forsake
A Mercy once New England thou hast had
(You Boston cheifly) in thi Cotton clad   80
Some 'gan to count't too meane a dresse and sought
Silk Velvetts Taffeties best could be bought
These last will soyle, if first doe soyle also
How can we think but Naked we shall goe
Must silken witts, must velvet tongues be had   85
And shall playne preaching be accounted bad
I feare a famine, pinching times t'ensue
Time Such may have, slighted mercy to Rue
My wakened muse to rest, my moystned pen
Mye eye, my hearte which powred out this have ben   90
Cease try no more, for Hee hath gayn'd his prize
His heavenly mansion 'bove the starry skie
Returne thee home and wayle the evills there
Repent breake off thi sins Jehovah feare

O Jehovah feare: this will thi wisdom bee   95
And thou his waies of mercy yet maust see
Returne thou mee;   And turned bie
Lord unto thee: even so shall I.
    Jo: Fiske

Upon the decease of Mris Anne Griffin
(the wife of Mr Richard Griffin late Ruling Elder
to the Church in Concord) departing this life
upon 23 of 10. [16]55 being about 96 yeers of Age
Anne Griffin
Anagr
In Fanne: Rig

Canst thinke the Cargoe wherewith ship is fraught
Pure wheate should bee, and shee unrig'd? And why
Should't once be thought, the Soule which Grace hath caught,
And stor'd its ship therewith, unrig'd should Lye.

Whil'st wheate in Fanne,[1] the ship in Rigging is   5
The Tackling fitt and fastned to there[2] use
When Season is, that it set forth, amisse
That nought there bee, to gayne the haven it chuse

Like to the wheate, Thy wheate appeare that't may
As twere in Fanne; thou now at last hast ben   10
Even such a Fanne, none like to it they say
Thou knew'st before; in yeeres nigh ten times ten

O're all Thy changes Chelmesford Granary[3]
Must be where Fanne caus'd Thee Repose to have
Yet still the Fanne, thy portion there doth Lye   15
Thy seas nor calme, tho Thou heere Rest didst crave

Yea that thy ship, (wherein thy soule Imbarkt)
Had heere as in a hoped safe Port, cast
Her Anchor, found fresh feares in eares were har[kt]
Heere no abode, up, Rig, to flight make hast.   20

[1] a threshing fan, for winnowing wheat.
[2] their.
[3] Chelmsford, Mass.

Time calls, be Gone, hoyse⁴ yards, out, get the⁵ home
Longer abroad tis not for Thee to bee
Deathes Summons tells thee when wilbe Thy Dome⁶
And Thou an End of weary dayes shalt see.

See! now Thou seest, Thou feel'st, Thou find'st thy Re[st]   25
The sweetest Rest, the surest Anchorage
In such a haven, in Earth as not exprest
Where Rockes endanger not nor Billowes Rage

We who surevive, hence double duty ken
Her change, her Gayne to Count: her blest to Judg[e]   30
We must the Fanning heere expect till done
Hye Time, when once in Fanne, thinke hence to Trudg[e]

When once Afflictions doe thee seaze, thinke then
Death will ere long approach, to thy long home
Thee hence to fetch: to Rest prepar'd who ben   35
Who Tyrant-like to unprepared come.

                                        J F.

But more, in Fanne of tryalls seest a saint
Yea one whose aged yeers the Deeps might know
Think't time for us to Rig, for us acquaint
Will God with Tryalls such, And lay us Low   40

Yea lay us Low, and humble us Hee will
Or first or Last ere that he us will rayse
And follow us with waves and billowes still
Ere that for aye him we in Glory prayse.

                                        J F.

What thou heere soughtst, pray'd for, hop'd for, desir'd   45
Which heere is not our portion to Enjoy
That there Thou hast more fully then requir'd
Or understood could bee whilst sin annoy

⁴ hoist.
⁵ thee.
⁶ Doom.

JOHN SAFFIN

(1626–1710)

In his later years the illustrious Judge Samuel Sewall of Boston wrote a vitriolic little verse about a contemporary barrister-merchant with whom he was feuding. Mr. John Saffin was, according to Sewall, a "Superanuated Squier, wigg'd and powder'd with pretense." While Saffin's "pretense" remains a matter for conjecture, the fact that he wore a fashionable periwig reflected the growing prosperity of the New England commerce so profitable to him. For nearly two hundred years his record in colonial legal and commercial ventures, along with the dubious distinction accorded him by Sewall, gave Mr. John Saffin a minor place in New England history. It was not until the turn of the last century that one of his descendants gave the Rhode Island Historical Society the hand-written, personal notebook that revealed John Saffin as a man of letters.

John Saffin was born in 1626 in Somerset County, "of an old English arms-bearing family." At an early age he traveled with his family to Scituate, Massachusetts, where he grew up. Unlike some of the rural, new towns, such as Captain Edward Johnson's Woburn, Scituate was well established and had long-standing affiliations with Plymouth Colony. The town prided itself on being founded by "the best class of English gentlemen of their day; men of education, many of them college graduates, and of considerable fortune." Statistics bear out this local boast, for Scituate did indeed produce much New England leadership. That he grew up in a rather sophisticated environment helps to explain why Saffin, though never attending Harvard or an English university, as did most New England leaders and literary figures, nonetheless rose in public life and displayed remarkable learning in his *Notebook*.

Saffin was a boyhood pupil of Charles Chauncy, Scituate schoolmaster who was later president of Harvard. And he was probably trained in the law by Messrs. Foster and Hoar, the only practicing attorneys in the colony. Early in his life he witnessed and drew up legal documents, laying the base for his future career as lawyer, assistant judge, councilor, and justice. Because of his sometimes volatile temper, Saffin spent substantial time as plaintiff and defendant as well.

By 1660 Saffin was in Boston and had "joyned" the church there. For several years he had plied the lucrative trade route down the coast to Virginia, where New England lumber and fish were exchanged for tobacco and hides. He had also married Martha Willet, the first and most beloved of his three wives. She bore him eight sons, all of whom died in infancy or early childhood, eliciting some of Saffin's tenderest elegies.

While in Boston Saffin engaged in several profitable commercial ventures. He held partnership in a foundry and, with others, a monopoly on drying salt from shallow ponds and producing naval stores. His engagement in the slave trade was not unusual for the time, nor, from evidence of existing records, was his profiteering from plundered French and Spanish ships. While it might be thought that Saffin's business ventures ran counter to his Puritan religious convictions, this was not the case. The Puritans believed that God's influence could be felt in every aspect of their personal lives, and it was natural to assume that He intervened in one's vocational choice. That is, He "called" the individual to his vocation, and it was tremendously important that the individual respond properly to God's call, both by recognizing and pursuing it. Of course, young children could not be expected to know immediately what God intended for them, and therefore parents were expected to guide and assist them in finding the right calling. In Judge Sewall's Diary, for example, he not only comments on his marked dislike of periwigs, but agonizes over his son's difficulty in finding the right calling. So it was that the very commerce so unsuitable to young Sewall was the kind of endeavor in which John Saffin thrived. The inference, obvious to New England Puritans, was that God intended it that way.

Saffin's mercantile and legal careers frequently won him enemies, and in 1687–88 he moved to Bristol, Rhode Island, to live on some Indian land he had claimed. The move was a kind of forced retirement, since he had lost favor with the Dudley government in Boston. It was in these later years, too, that he had his celebrated feud with

Samuel Sewall over the freeing of Saffin's slave Adam. The case was not at all an ideologically simple one, and it lingered long in the courts.

Saffin's *Notebook*, a personal miscellany of maxims and short notes, contains some fifty poems, only one or two of which were published during his lifetime. The quantity of his verse ranks him seventh or eighth among colonial poets, but it is the quality of his work, so varied as to include love poems, satires, characters, elegies, and occasional verse, that establishes his place among important poets of early America. In a period when much of the verse was of a formal, "public" nature, Saffin's voice emerges as engagingly personal.

An Acrostick on Mrs Elizabeth Hull

Elustrious Dame whose vertues rare doe shine
Like Phoebus faire in her Mirridian line
I one doth thee favour for me think I see
Zealous Dame Nature hath Adorned thee
Above the Nimphs, in fair and comely feature
Beautious-Sweet-Smileing and Heart-moveing Creature
Ere may you prosper, may Great Juno pleasure
Thee with High honour and with boundless Treasure
Heavens give thee Sweet content, when heart and hands
Hymen Shall Joyn in Sacred Nuptiall Bands
Venus, and Vesta then shall with the Graces
Lead hand in hand to Crown thy Dear Embraces.

An Acrostick on Mrs. Winifret Griffin

Within the Casket of thy Coelick[1] Breast,
Inclos'd is vertue like the Phenix Nest.
Nor can the merits of A Noble mind,
Invested be, with one more true and kind.
Fair Venus, and Minerva, both combine:[2]   5
Resplendently, to make their Graces thine:
Each in her proper Station; Witt, and Beauty

[1] heavenly.
[2] i.e. beauty and wisdom.

Take Thee for Mistris out of Bounden duty.
Great are Joves favours on thee passing Sence
Rare Master-piece of Natures Excellence.   10
Juno confer on Thee out of her Treasure,
Fresh new Supplys of riches, Honour, Pleasure:
Firme to Abide, may Hymen give consent,
In Nuptiall State, to Crown Thee with consent,
N'ere may those Joys abate, and then Endeavour   15
In your own Cupidons[3] to live forever

Consideratus Considerandus*

What pleasure can this gaudy world afford?
What true delight does Teeming Nature hoard?
In Her great Store-house, where She lays her Treasure
Alas! tis all the Shaddow of a Pleasure;
No true content in all Her works are found   5
No solled[1] joys in all Earths Spacious Round
For Labouring Man, who toyles himself in vaine
Eagerly grasping what creates his paine
How false and feeble, Nay scarce worth a Name
Are Riches, Honour Power, and Babling fame   10
Yet tis for those Men wade through Seas of Blood,
And bold in Mischief, Storm to be withstood
Which when Obtaind breed but Stupendious feare
Strife, jealousies, and Sleep-Disturbing Care;
No Beam of Comfort, not a Ray of Light   15
Shines thence to guide us thrô Fates Gloomy Night
But lost in Dismall Darkness there we Stay
Bereft of Reason in an Endless way
Vertu's the Souls true good if any bee
Tis that creats us true filicitie   20
Thô we despise, Contemn, and cast it by
As worthless, or Our fatalst Enemy
Because our Darling Lusts it dare Controule
And bound the Roveings of the wandering Soul.
Therefore in Garments poor it still appears   25
And sometimes (Naked) it no garment weares
Shun'd by the Great, and worthless deem'd by most

[3] admirers (beaux).
[1] solid.

Urg'd to be gone, or wish'd forever Lost
Yet it is Loath to leave our wretched Coast
But in Disguise does here, and there intrude,   30
Striveing to Conquer base Ingrattitude
And boldly ventures now and then to Shine
So to make known it is of Birth Divine
But clouded oft it like the Lightning plays
Looseing as sone as seen its poynted Rays   35
Which scarceness makes those that are weak in witt
For vertues Self admire its Counterfiete
With Damned Hipocrites the world Delude
As men on Indians Glass, for Gems obtrude.

*This poem, though it appears in Saffin's commonplace book, may well be by Rochester. See the "First-Line List of Poems Omitted" (p. 235) in David M. Vieth's *The Complete Poems of John Wilmot, Earl of Rochester* (Yale U.P., 1968); see also my "Notes on Editing Seventeenth-Century American Poetry" in the *Center for Editions of American Authors Newsletter*, July 1969, pp. 11–14.

A lamentation on my Dear Son Simon who dyed of the Small pox on the 23 November 1678

Simon my son, son of my Nuptiall knott
Ah! Simon's gone, Simon my son is not
Whose Heaven-born Soul in full ripe fruit appears
Wherein he liv'd an age above his years.
Whose pregnant witt, quick Genius, parts sublime   5
Facill'd his Books, made him Pernassus clime
And Dare Apelles[1] so were he alive
Who best should . . . or Rarest piece contrive
He unappall'd with humble Confidence
Could to's Superiours speak without Offence   10
So free and unconcern'd as one had been
Conversing with his Equalls Dayly seen
His Towering Fancy, and his quaint invention
Excell'd most of his Standing and pretention
Lovely in's features his Complection fair   15
Of comely Jeasture, flaxen was his haire
But that which Crowneth all the Rest
In his own language better is Exprest.

[1] Celebrated 4th century B.C. Greek painter, court artist to Philip of Macedon and Alexander the Great. His portrait of Alexander in the temple of Diana at Ephesus depicts Alexander wielding the thunderbolts of Zeus.

[Sweetly (my Dearest) I left thee asleep]

Sweetly (my Dearest) I left thee asleep
Which Silent parting made my heart to weep,
Faine would I wake her, but Love did Reply
O wake her not, So sweetly let her Lye.
But must I goe, O must I Leave her So,   5
So ill at Ease: involv'd in Slumbering wo
Must I goe hence: and thus my Love desert
Unknown to Her, O must I now Depart;
Thus was I hurried with such thoughts as these,
Yet loath to Rob the of thy present Ease,   10
Or rather senceless payn: farewell thought I,
My Joy my Deare in whom I live or Dye
Farewell Content, farewell fare Beauty's light
And the most pleasing Object of my Sight;
I must begone, Adieu my Dear, Adieu   15
Heavens grant good Tideings I next heare from you
Thus in sad Silence I alone and mute,
My lips bad thee farewell, with a Salute.
And so went from thee; turning back againe
I thought one kiss to little then Stole twaine   20
And then another: but no more of this,
Count with your Self how many of them you miss.
And now my love soon let me from the heare
Of thy good health, that may my Spirits Cheare
Acquaint me with such passages as may   25
Present themselves since I am come away
And above all things let me thee Request
To bee both Chearfull quiet and at Rest
In thine own Spirit, and let nothing move
Thee unto Discontent my Joy my Love.   30
Hopeing that all things shall at last Conduce
Unto our Comfort and a Blessed use
Considering that those things are hardly gain'd
Are most Delightfull when they are Attain'd.
Gold Crowns are heavy: Idalian Burn's[1]   35
And Lovers Days are good, and bad by turn's
But yet the Consummation will Repay

[1] Idalium, in Cyprus, was consecrated to Aphrodite, goddess of love.

The Debt that's due many a happy Day
Which that it may so be, Ile Heaven Implore
To grant the fame henceforth forever more   40
And so farewell, farewell fair Beautys light
Ten thousand times Adieu my Dear Delight.
  Your Ever loveing friend whilest Hee
  Desolved is: or Cease to bee.

A brief Elegie on my Dear Son John the second of that name of mine[1]

My Dear Son John's deceas'd ah! gone from hence,
Son of my Joy, my Strength, my Excellence,
Though the second Son, the Eldest that surviv'd,
And had allmost to seventeen years ariv'd,
Who in the Colledge Chief of Thirteen was
That then were Entered Members of his Class.[2]
Ah! he is not but gone to take his Right
Of Heritance among the Saints in Light.

An Elegie
On the Deploreable Departure of the Honered and truely Religious Chieftain John Hull Esq[r] who put off his Earthly Tabernacle to be Possessed with a Celestiall Mantion on the [30] Day of [Sept.] in the [59th] year of his Age Anno Dom. 1683

Arise faint Muse bring one heart-melting verse
To Drop upon his sweet Embalmed Herse
Arise I say, run in amongst the Throng
Of Mourners with an Epicaedian Song:[1]
Shake off the Shackles of thy Contemplation   5
And set thy Self a part for Lamentation;
Rouse up thy drooping Spirits, dull invention
That the most unconcern'd may give Attention
And Eyes burst out with teares like Jeremiah,
When they had lost their Pious King Josiah   10

[1] died in Boston, 9 December 1678.
[2] Harvard, class of 1678.
[1] funeral song.

As one bereav'd of all: thy loss Deplore
Lament the same, or never Speak no more;
Thy loss said I; alas! thy Share is Small,
In this great loss, which is a loss to all.
What shall I say? or where shall I begin   15
The Ocian is so vast I'me lanching in;
My Compass is but small, wavering unstable:
To Steer a Course Direct, I am unable
What can a Punie Muse, alas! here yeild
That is bewilder'd in so large a field;   20
But Haire of Goates was us'd among rich things
Such as I have my humble Muse here brings
As a free offering; my little Taper burn
In honour to his Odriferous Urn
T' Invoke the Sisters, or the Saddest Shee   25
The Ancients call the Muse Melpomene:[2]
Or Supplicat Minerva ayd to Daigne,
To screw my Muse up to a Mournfull Straine
Needs not alas! this, this, is cause alone,
The Dove-like Meek-Beloved John is gone;   30
Gone's that desired One, who bore the Name
Of Great Shem's Grand-Son, Aram's son of fame
He's gone he's gone! and is already prest
To keep an Everlasting Sabath-Rest.
But tis a woefull and a Gloomy-Day,   35
When Righteous men are taken thus away;
Heaven Speaks aloud to Mortalls, reads ther Doom
Such are Removed from Dire ills to Come;
O may not this, this Sad Catastrophe
Fore run the loss of our Dear Liberty.   40
Hee in his youth like Gracious Timothy
Not verst in Schooll, but Script-Divinity
Was ready in't, as Schollers con their part
Not onely in his head, but in his Heart.
His Zeal for God, love to his Countrey Dear   45
In his whole Course to all men did appear;
His house a little Church, such Celibration
Maintain'd Religion in its Reputation
He with his vertuous, and beloved Wife
Liv'd an unblamable unspotted life: 50

[2] Muse of tragedy.

So amiable, constant, to his Death
Like Holy Zachary, and Elizabeth.
O what Soul Ravishing Communion he
Had Dayly with the Blessed Trinity
For in the Throng of Busness Every Day   55
Hee'd set a part some Select times to pray
Yea He a Gap-man[3] was t' avert Heavens Rod,
He mighty was in prayer a Prince with God.
Gracious in Speech, pleasant in Conversation
Descreetly Grave, devoyd of Ostentation;   60
In all's Discourses allways Intermixt
Something of God, the Soul, or Heaven betwixt
So wining were his words, fair Collours paint
T' would make an Infidel become a Saint.
His even temper Equinimious Mind   65
Was manifest to all in Every kind:
In change of State whith'r prosperous, or Distrest
Not over lifted up, nor much Deprest;
His Bounteous Heart was large, as 'twere a kings
The liberall man deviseth Liberall things.   70
So prudently he did his gifts bestow
To all whose reall wants he came to know
Nor was his Bounty Stinted Nigh at hand
But was Deffused throughout all the Land
Even unto such poor as Scripture saith   75
Whom he in love deem'd of the House of faith
He shew'd much kindness to, oft did invite
The Prophets, like that Wealthy Shunamite;
The time would faile me to Commemorate
This worthy's worth, his Praise is in the Gate.   80
His Earthly Tabernacle hath layd Down
And hence with Joy's gone to Receive A Crown.
My lowly Muse now takes her flight on high
I am Envellop'd in an Extasie
As one Surrounded with some Dazleing Ray,   85
Mee thinkes I heare his blessed Genious say
Weep not for me, but for yourselves aright
I'me fixed in an Orbe at glorious Light
I'me Paradiz'd in unconceived Joy
Above the pitch of Envy or annoy.   90

[3] an alert man.

I Smile at Sorrows, past and am Secure
From the wrath of men and Devils to be sure
Beyond the reach of Ran-da-[4] and all those
That puff at me N-Englands open foes.
Then f[a]re well wife and Children friends and all;   95
Watch chearfully untill your Lord shall call.
By a true . . .   J. S.

One presenting a rare Book to Madame Hull Senr: his Vallintine

Here's Witts Extraction Morall and Divine
Presented to you, by your Vallintine
Here's Florid Language Suiting well your Straine
The Pallas of a Rare Mercurian Braine[1]
Appollo's Darlings[2] and the Hesperedes[3]
Doe with the Graces[4] joyntly seeke to please
Your Towering fancy and Ingenious Spirit
You by the favour of the Gods Inherit
And I in Honour of my Vallintine
Leave Her Devoted at Minerva's Shrine

To his Excellency Joseph Dudley Eqr Gover: &c[1]

Sr: My humble Muse Sad, and in lonely State
On various things doth meekly Contemplate
And now presumes to give Her sober Sence
Of what She deemes concerns your Excellence.
Yet some perhaps more gratefull might Reveale   5
What they thrô fear, or bye Respects Conseale.

[4] Rhadamanthus, judge of the infernal regions.
[1] According to Greek myth, Pallas Athena sprang from the head of her father Zeus.
[2] the Muses.
[3] the "Daughters of Evening" in Greek myth, guardians of the tree that bore the golden apples.
[4] Aglaia, Thalia, and Euphrosyne, sister goddesses who bestowed beauty and charm and were themselves the embodiment of both.
[1] When Saffin was unseated from the council by Joseph Dudley in 1703, he sent this poetic epistle, stating his rights and emphasizing that the governor had exceeded authority in his action.

When Erst that Noble Bassa dar'd to tell
The Grand Amurath[2] (plaine) he did not well
T' Omit his great Affaires of State (unarm'd)
Was by the Beauty of his Captive Charm'd;   10
On which (adds he) your Vassalls all amated,
Say you your Ancestors han't Imitated;
In Glorious Atchievements.
And now Great Sir, my loyalty Comands
Me thus to put my life into your hands: 15
To act towards me as you please at Leasure
I humbly Bow unto your Royall Pleasure.
Thus Said, the Sultan gravely did Reply,
I pardon this thy Bold Temerity;
And thee Comand forth with the Estates Convene   20
And thou shalt Shortly see another Seene.
Then why may'nt I by way of Imitation
Speak Truth to you, thô in a lower Station
And thrô unfeined love presume to Say
What may be usefull unto you this Day: 25
Who am your faithfull Servant, (thô forsaken)
Your Excellence hath not fitt Measures taken;
In the due Conduct of your Government,
Which has Occasiond so much discontent
Among your people: if you they have not hated,   30
Yet to your Self, their Love is much abated;
I need not name particulars, They Strang
In Church and Comon weale there's such a Chang
Made, and Endeavour'd, in so Short a Space
Which threatens all Our Priviledge to Rase;   35
And if Accomplished would surely then:
Cause us to Cease to be Right Englishman.

Now if you think these Hints proceed from mee
I doe assure you tis Vox Populi:
And if I miss not much in my Account   40
If you persist therein, 'Twill you Dismount;
Sure Wisest Princes all Endeavours prove
To gaine and keep their loyall Subjects Love
For as Lord Burleigh[3] to that Queen said do

[2] The allusion here is probably to Amurath (Murad III), sultan of the Turks
in the sixteenth century, a feeble, uxorious man whose rule was marked by
misjudgments and reverses.
[3] William Cecil Burleigh (1520–96), principal adviser to Elizabeth I. Lord
High Treasurer after 1572, his policy of national aggrandizement made in-

But gaine their Hearts, you've hands, and purses to.   45
And that wise Queen in working Reformation,
Wrought gradually, not Sudden Alteration.
And tis a Rule to which all men Consent,
That violent motions are not Permanent.
And he that manageth Affaires of State   50
Had need beware, he Don't Precipitate.

You know what Phoebus Said to Phaeton,
When he would Rule the Chariot of the Sun:
Me Imitate, the Tracts thy wheeles will guide
For bear the whip, and doe not over Ride.   55

And now, Sir, Thô my life's not in your hand,
Yet is my welfare much at your Comand:
Zeale me incites these Memoires (as tis meet)
To lay them at your Excellencys feet;
It may perhaps Displease, if so it do   60
Sure love and honour me Constraines thereto:
And I Remember what the Wiseman Sed,
Tis better be Reprov'd, than flattered;
And he more favouer afterwards shall finde
Than he that Sailes with Every Blast of winde   65
But if to speak the Truth be Deem'd a Crime,
We may conclude it is an Evil time.

From him who honoureth your Excellence
Thô not Regarded with that Recompence
                                        John Saffin

                    or

From him thô Aged, is not whimsey Pated,
Or prone to Dote, nor Supernnuated.

March 4th Anno 1698[/9]
A Charracteristicall Satyre on a proud upstart

Should I thee ranke with Radamanthus fell
And all those furies (Poets) faine in Hell;
Who (when incarnate) were in Sundry times

---

dustry and commerce thrive. Cautious yet decisive, Burleigh took the responsibility for the execution of Mary Queen of Scots and was largely responsible for the solidification of Protestantism in England.

The Plague of Nature, and the Forge of Crimes.
I should more Honour unto thee Impart
Ten Thousand times above thy Due Desert.
For nothing's in thee which in them was Rare
But with their villanies thou maiest Compare.
If Arrogance, and Dareing Impudence:
Bold Boysterous Rudness, Brazen Insolence;
Concomitant in thee, to all mens Sight,
Imperious outrage, and Mallicious Spite
Be such Endowments as doe merit praise
Then Let my Muse for Thee this Trophy raise.

or Thus
A Satyretericall Charracter of a proud Upstart[1]

Should I thee Ranke with Radamanthus fell,
And the other Judges Furies (Poets faine) of Hell,
Who (when Incarnate) were in Sundry times,
The Plague of Nature, and the Forge of Crimes;
I should more Honour unto thee Impart   5
Ten thousand times above thy due Desert;
For, Nothing's in thee: which in them was Rare,
But with their Villanies, thou mayst Compaire;
If Arrogance, and Dareing Impudence
Bold, Boysterous Rudness, Brazen Insolence: 10
Imperious Outrage, and malicious Spite,
(Concomitant in thee, to all mens Sight)
Be such Endowments as doe merit Praise
Then Let my Muse for thee, this Trophy raise
[If Arrogance and Dareing Impudence   15
Bold, Boysterous Rudeness Brazen Insolence
Audacious Boasting thy Pseudo-parts
Slighting detracting Others true Deserts
Imperious Outrage and malicious Spite
(Concomitant With thee to all men's Sight)   20
Be such Endowments as doe merit Praise
Then let my Muse for thee this Trophy Raise][2]

[1] a second version.
[2] another version of the conclusion [enclosed in brackets].

URIAN OAKES

(1631–1681)

Urian Oakes's literary reputation rests today on one poem, "An Elegy upon the Death of the Reverend Mr. Thomas Shepard." During his own lifetime, however, Oakes was better known as a Latinate virtuoso who used the language as if it were a living one, coining words, punning outrageously, speaking with a facility equal to his English. He had plenty of opportunities to demonstrate his Latin, for Oakes spent nearly six reluctant years as President of Harvard College, delivering numerous addresses in the classical tongue.

Born in England, Urian Oakes received his B.A. from Harvard in 1649, after which he returned to England for seventeen years as a preacher and schoolmaster. When he returned to America in 1671 he served as minister at Cambridge, and was appointed acting president of Harvard in 1675. The college had reached a low ebb that year, for poor fiscal management and the devastating King Philip's War had taken their toll, resulting in a temporary closing of the school. During the next five years Oakes fought to establish stability at Harvard, a satisfactory performance attested to by his unqualified appointment as president in 1679. He died just two years later at the age of fifty. According to Cotton Mather, Oakes "Considered as a *Scholar,* was a Notable Critick in all the Points of Learning." In his Harvard addresses Oakes deplores the philistine contempt for learning, which he saw mounting in New England. Similarly, his pattern throughout the elegy on Shepard is not only to eulogize, but to warn of the implication that God had called home his "Ambassadour," and that New England ought to "dread some grievous Inundation."

To the Reader

1

Reader! I am no Poet: but I grieve!
Behold here, what that passion can do!
That forc'd a verse, without *Apollo's* leave,
And whether th' Learned Sistters would or no.
    My Griefs can hardly speak: my sobbing Muse
    In broken terms our sad bereavement rues.

2

I wonder what the learned World still ailes,
To tune and pace their sorrows and complaints
In Rhythm and Verse! He that his crosses wailes
Indeed, would vent his griefs without restraints.
    To tye our grief to numbers, measures, feet,
    Is not to let it loose, but fetter it.

3

Is this it? that a Poets softer heart
Of great impressions susceptible is?
He wisely doth perform his mourning part
In Verse, lest grief should time and measure miss.
    But griefs unmeasurable would not be
    Curb'd, and rein'd-in by measur'd Poetry.

4

Stop, stop my Pen! lest *Israel's* singer sweet
Should be condemn'd, who, in that Song of th' Bow,
To vent his passionate complaints thought meet,
And to bewail his great Friends overthrow.
    King *David* in an Elegiack Knell,
    Rung out his dolours, when dear *Jona'than* fell.

5

No matter what's the trifling Poets Use,
Th' Imperious Law of custome we deride:

We have Diviner Warrant to produce,
The Soveraign, Sacred Poet is our guide.
    He wept his Friend in verse: then let us try,
    Now *Shepard's* faln, to write his Elegy.

U. O.

AN ELEGIE
*Upon that Reverend, Learned, Eminently Pious, and Singularly
Accomplished Divine, my ever Honoured B R O T H E R*
Mr. THOMAS SHEPARD,
*The late Faithful and Worthy Teacher of the Church of Christ
at* Charlstown *in* New-England
*Who finished his Course on Earth, and went to receive
his Crown,* December 22, 1677
In the 43rd Year of his Age

1

Oh! that I were a Poet now in grain!
How would I invocate the Muses all
To deign their presence, lend their flowing Vein,
And help to grace dear *Shepard's* Funeral!
    How would I paint our griefs, and succours borrow
    From Art and Fancy, to limn out our sorrow!

2

Now could I wish (if wishing would obtain)
The sprightli'est Efforts of Poetick Rage,
To vent my Griefs, make others feel my pain,
For this loss of the Glory of our Age.
    Here is a subject for the loftiest Verse
    That ever waited on the bravest Hearse:

3

And could my Pen ingeniously distill
The purest Spirits of a sparkling wit
In rare conceits, the quintessence of skill
In *Elegiack Strains;* none like to it:
    I should think all too little to condole
    The fatal loss (to us) of such a Soul.

4

Could I take highest Flights of Fancy, soar
Aloft; If Wits Monopoly were mine:
All would be much too low, too light, too poor,
To pay due tribute to this great Divine.
     Ah! Wit avails not, when th' Heart's like to break,
     Great griefs are Tongue-ti'ed, when the lesser speak.

5

Away loose rein'd Careers of Poetry,
The celebrated Sisters may be gone;
We need no *Mourning Womens* Elegy,
No forc'd, affected, artificial Tone.
     Great and good *Shepard's* Dead! Ah! this alone
     Will set our eyes abroach,[1] dissolve a stone.

6

Poetick Raptures are of no esteem,
Daring *Hyperboles* have here no place,
Luxuriant wits on such a copious Theme,
Would shame themselves, and blush to shew their face
     Here's worth enough to overmatch the skill
     Of the most stately Poet *Laureat's Quill*.

7

Exube'rant Fancies useless here I deem,
Transcendent vertue scorns feign'd Elogies:
He that gives *Shepard* half his due, may seem,
If Strangers hear it, to Hyperbolize.
     Let him that can, tell what his vertues were,
     And say, this Star mov'd in no common Sphere.

8

Here need no Spices, Odours, curious Arts,
No skill of *Egypt*, to embalm the Name

---

[1] broach; in a condition for yielding liquor.

Of such a Worthy: let men speak their hearts,
They'l say, He merits an Immortal Fame,
    When *Shepard* is forgot, all must conclude,
    This is prodigious ingratitude.

9

But live he shall in many a gratefull Breast,
Where he hath rear'd himself a Monument,
A Monument more stately than the best,
On which Immensest Treasures have been spent.
    Could you but into th' Hearts of thousands peep,
    There would you read his Name engraven deep.

10

Oh! that my head were Waters, and mine Eyes
A flowing Spring of Tears, still issuing forth
In Streams of bitterness, to solemnize
The *Obits* of this Man of matchless worth!
    Next to the Tears our sins do need and crave,
    I would bestow my Tears on *Shepards* Grave.

11

Not that he needs our Tears: for he hath dropt
His measure full; not one Tear more shall fall
Into God's Bottle from his eyes: *Death* stopt
That water-course, his sorrows ending all.
    He Fears, he Cares, he Sighs, he Weeps no more:
    Hee's past all storms, Arriv'd at th' wished Shoar.

12

Dear *Shepard* could we reach so high a strain
Of pure Seraphick love, as to devest
Our selves, and love, of self-respects, thy gain
Would joy us, though it cross our interest.
    Then would we silence all complaints with this,
    Our Dearest Friend is doubtless gone to Bliss.

13

Ah! but the Lesson's hard, thus to deny
Our own dear selves, to part with such a Loan
Of Heaven (in time of such necessity)
And love thy comforts better than our own.
  Then let us moan our loss, adjourn our glee,
  Till we come thither to rejoice with thee.

14

As when some formidable Comets blaze,
As when Portentous Prodigies appear,
Poor mortals with amazement stand and gaze,
With hearts affrighted, and with trembling fear:
  So are we all amazed at this blow,
  Sadly portending some approaching woe.

15

We shall not summon bold Astrologers,
To tell us what the Stars say in the case,
(Those Cousin-Germans to black Conjurers)
We have a sacred Oracle that says,
  When th' Righteous perish, men of mercy go,
  It is a sure presage of coming wo.

16

He was (ah woful word! to say he was)
Our wrestling *Israel*, second unto none,
The man that stood i' th' gap, to keep the pass,
To stop the Troops of Judgement[s p]ushing on.
  This man the honour had to hold the hand
  Of an incensed God against our Land.

17

When such a Pillar's faln (Oh such an one!)
When such a glorious, shining Light's put out,
When Chariot and Horsemen thus are gone:
Well may we fear some Downfal, Darkness, Rout,

When such a Bank's broke down, there's sad occasion
To wail, and dread some grievous Inundation.

18

What! must we with our God, and Glory part?
Lord! is thy Treaty with *New-England* come
Thus to an end? And is War in thy Heart?
That this Ambassadour is called home.
    So Earthly Gods (Kings) when they War intend,
    Call home their Ministers, and Treaties end.

19

Oh for the Raptures, Transports, Inspirations
Of *Israel's Singer*, when his *Jon'athan's* Fall
So tun'ed his mourning Harp! what Lamentations
Then would I make for *Shepards* Funerall!
    How truly can I say, as well as He?
    My *dearest Brother I'm distress'd for thee.*

20

How Lovely, Worthy, Peerless, in my view?
How Precious, Pleasant hast thou been to me?
How Learned, Prudent, Pious, Grave, and True?
And what a Faithful Friend? who like to thee?
    Mine Eye's desire is vanish'd; who can tell
    Where lives my dearest *Shepard's* Parallel?

21

'Tis strange to think: but we may well believe,
That not a few of different Perswasions
From this great Worthy, do now truly grieve
I' th' Mourning croud, and joyn their Lamentations.
    Such Powers Magnetick had He to draw to Him
    The very Hearts, and Souls, of all that knew Him!

22

Art, Nature, Grace, in Him were all combin'd
To shew the World a matchless *Paragon:*

In whom of Radiant Virtues no less shin'd,
Then a whole Constellation: but hee's gone!
    Hee's gone alas! Down in the Dust must ly
    As much of this rare Person as could dy.

23

If to have solid Judgement, Pregnant Parts,
A piercing Wit, and comprehensive Brain;
If to have gone the *Round* of all the Arts,
Immunity from Deaths Arrest would gain,
    Shepard would have been Death-proof, and secure
    From that All conquering Hand, Im very sure.

24

If Holy Life, and Deeds of Charity,
If Grace illustrious, and Virtue tri'ed,
If modest Carriage, rare Humility,
Could have brib'd Death, good *Shepard* had not di'ed.
    Oh! but inexorable Death attacks
    The best Men, and promiscu'ous havock makes.

25

Come tell me, Criticks, have you ever known
Such Zeal, so temper'd well with moderation?
Such Prudence, and such Inno'cence met in one?
Such Parts, so little Pride and Ostentation?
    Let *Momus*[2] carp, and *Envy* do her worst,
    And swell with *Spleen* and *Rancour* till she burst.

26

To be descended well, doth *that* commend?
Can Sons their Fathers Glory call their own?
Our *Shepard* justly might to this pretend,
(His Blessed Father was of high Renown,
    Both *Englands* speak him great, admire his Name.)
    But his own pers'onal worth's better claim.

[2] Greek god of ridicule.

27

Great was the Father, once a glorious Light
Among us, Famous to an high Degree:
Great was this Son; indeed (to do him right)
As Great and Good (to say no more) as He.
    A double portion of his Fathers Spirit
    Did this (his Eldest) Son, through Grace, inherit.

28

His Look commanded Reverence and Awe,
Though Mild and Amiable, not Austere:
Well Humour'd was He (as I ever saw)
And rul'd by Love and Wisdome, more than Fear.
    The Muses, and the Graces too, conspir'd
    To set forth this Rare Piece, to be admir'd.

29

He govern'd well the Tongue (that busie thing,
Unruly, Lawless and Pragmatical)
Gravely Reserv'd, in Speech not lavishing,
Neither too sparing, nor too liberal.
    His Words were few, well season'd, wisely weigh'd
    And in his Tongue the Law of Kindness sway'd.

30

Learned he was beyond the common Size,
Befriended much by Nature in his Wit,
And Temper, (Sweet, Sedate, Ingenious, Wise)
And (which crown'd all) he was Heav'ens Favourite.
    On whom the God of all Grace did command,
    And show'r down Blessings with a lib'eral hand.

31

Wise He, not wily, was: Grave, not Morose:
Not stiffe, but steady; Seri'ous, but not Sowre;
Concern'd for all, as if he had no Foes:
(Strange if he had!) and would not wast an Hour.

Thoughtful and Active for the common good:
And yet his own place wisely understood.

32

Nothing could make him stray from Duty: Death
Was not so frightful to him, as Omission
Of Ministerial work; he fear'd no breath
Infecti'ous, i'th'discharge of his Commission.
  Rather than run from's work, he chose to dy,
  Boldly to run on Death, than duty fly.

33

(Cruel Disease! that didst (like *High-way-men*)
Assault the honest Trav'eller in his way,
And rob dear *Shepard* of his life (Ah!) then,
When he was on the Road, where Duty lay.
  Forbear, bold Pen! 'twas God that took him thus,
  To give him great Reward, and punish us.)

34

Zealous in God's cause, but meek in his own;
Modest of Nature, bold as any Lion,
Where Consc'ience was concern'd: and there was none
More constant Mourners for afflicted Sion.
  So gene'ral was his care for th' Churches all,
  His Spirit seemed Apostolical.

35

Large was his Heart, to spend without regret,
Rejoycing to do good: not like those *Moles*
That root i' th' Earth, or roam abroad, to get
All for themselves (those sorry, narrow Souls!)
  But He, like th' Sun (i' th' Center, as some say)
  Diffus'd his Rayes of Goodness every way.

36

He breath'd Love, and pursu'd Peace in his day,
As if his Soul were made of Harmony:

Scarce ever more of Goodness crouded lay
In such a piece of frail Mortality.
    Sure Father *Wilsons*[3] genuine Son was he,
    New-England's Paul had such a *Timothy.*

37

No Slave to th' Worlds grand *Idols;* but he flew
At *Fairer Quarries,* without stooping down
To Sublunary prey: his great Soul knew
Ambition none, but of the Heave'nly Crown.
    How he hath won it, and shall wear't with Honour,
    Adoring Grace, and God in Christ, the Donour.

38

A Friend to Truth, a constant Foe to Errour,
Pow'erful i' th' *Pulpit,* and sweet in converse,
To weak ones gentle, to th' Profane a Terrour.
Who can his vertues, and good works rehearse?
    The Scripture—Bishops-Character read o're,
    Say this was *Shepards:* what need I say more?

39

I say no more: let them that can declare
His rich and rare endowments, paint this Sun,
With all its dazling Rayes: But I despair,
Hopeless by any hand to see it done.
    They that can *Shepards* goodness well display,
    Must be as good as he: But who are they?

40

See where our Sister *Charlstown* sits and Moans!
Poor Widowed *Charlstown!* all in Dust, in Tears!
Mark how she wrings her hands! hear how she groans!
See how she weeps! what sorrow like to hers!
    Charlstown, that might for joy compare of late
    With all about her, now looks desolate.

[3] John Wilson I (c. 1588–1667), pastor at Boston, Mass.

41

As you have seen some Pale, Wan, Ghastly look,
When grisly Death, that will not be said nay,
Hath seiz'd all for it self, Possession took,
And turn'd the Soul out of its house of Clay:
    So Visag'd is poor *Charlstown* at this day;
    Shepard, her very Soul, is torn away.

42

Cambridge groans under this so heavy cross,
And Sympathizes with her Sister dear;
Renews her Griefs afresh for her old loss
Of her own *Shepard,* and drops many a Tear.
    Cambridge and *Charlstown* now joint Mourners are,
    And this tremendous loss between them share.

43

Must Learnings Friend (Ah! worth us all) go thus?
That Great Support to *Harvards* Nursery!
Our *Fellow* (that no Fellow had with us)
Is gone to Heave'ns great University.
    Our's now indeed's a lifeless *Corporation,*
    The Soul is fled, that gave it *Animation!*

44

Poor *Harvard's* Sons are in their Mourning Dress,
Their sure Friend's gone! their Hearts have *put on Mourning*
Within their Walls are Sighs, Tears, Pensiveness;
Their new Foundations dread an overturning.
    Harvard! where's such a fast Friend left to thee!
    Unless thy great Friend, *LEVERET,*[4] it be.

45

We must not with our greatest Soveraign strive,
Who dare find fault with him that is most High?

[4]John Leverett (1616–79), governor of the Massachusetts Colony (1673–79).

That hath an absolute Prerogative,
And doth his pleasure: none may ask him, why?
    We're Clay-lumps, Dust-heaps, nothings in his sight:
    The Judge of all the Earth doth always right.

46

Ah! could not Prayers and Tears prevail with God!
Was there no warding off that dreadful Blow!
And was there no averting of that Rod!
Must *Shepard* dy! and that good Angel go!
    Alas! our heinous sins (more than our hairs)
    It seems, were louder, and out-crie'd our Prayers.

47

See what our sins have done! what Ruines wrought
And how they have pluck'd out our very eyes!
Our sins have slain our *Shepard!* we have bought,
And dearly paid for, our Enormities.
    Ah Cursed sins! that strike at God, and kill
    His *Servants*, and the Blood of *Prophets* spill.

48

As you would loath the Sword that's warm and red,
As you would hate the hands that are embru'd
I' th' Hearts-blood of your dearest Friends: so dread,
And hate your sins; Oh! let them be pursu'd:
    Revenges take on bloody sins: for there's
    No Refuge-City for these Murtherers.

49

In vain we build the Prophets Sepulchers,
In vain bedew their Tombs with Tears, when Dead:
In vain bewail the Deaths of Ministers,
Whilst Prophet-killing sins are harboured.
    Those that these Murth'erous Traitors favour, hide;
    And with the blood of Prophets deeply di'ed.

50

New England! know thy Heart-plague: feel this blow;
A blow that sorely wounds both Head and Heart,
A blow that reaches All, both high and low,
A blow that may be felt in every part.
    Mourn that this *Great Man's* faln in *Israel:*
    Lest it be said, *with him New-England fell!*

51

Farewel, Dear *Shepard!* Thou art gone before,
Made free of *Heaven,* where thou shalt sing loud *Hymns*
Of *High triumphant Praises* evermore,
In the sweet Quire of *Saints* and *Seraphims.*
    Lord! look on us here, clogg'd with sin and clay,
    And we, through Grace, shall be as happy as they.

52

My Dearest, Inmost, Bosome-Friend is Gone!
Gone is my sweet Companion, Soul's delight!
Now in an Huddling Croud I'm all alone,
And almost could bid all the World *Goodnight:*
    Blest be my Rock! God lives: Oh let him be,
    As He is All, so All in All to me.

The Bereaved, Sorrowful

URIAN OAKES.

BENJAMIN TOMPSON

(1642–1714)

Still legible on Benjamin Tompson's gravestone in Roxbury, Massachusetts, is the phrase, ". . . AND THE RENOWNED POET OF NEW ENGLAND." While Tompson's renown is questionable, even in New England, there is no doubt that he was a thoroughly native American poet. Born in 1642 in Braintree, now Quincy, Massachusetts, Tompson was one of several children of a non-conformist minister transplanted from England during the peak years of Puritan migration. When Tompson was just three months old, his father, along with two other men, answered a ministerial call from a group of non-conformists in Virginia who complained of spiritual languishing from lack of pastoral leadership. But when the three ministers arrived, after a difficult journey, they found cold reception from the Virginia governor and legislature, who made it clear that non-conformists were unwelcome in the colony. Returning once again to New England, Reverend William Tompson found that his young wife had died in his absence, leaving his children in neighboring foster homes.

The elder Tompson, a melancholic man who suffered increasingly severe fits of depression throughout his life, did not reclaim all his children from the families that had taken them in. Benjamin thus grew up with the three children of Thomas Blanchard who, at his death, bequeathed to Benjamin the means of preparing for entrance into Harvard College. This was high tribute to pay the boy, for the college was an object of regional pride and a source of religious and political leadership in the colony.

Although it might have been hoped that young Tompson would prepare for the ministry, he chose from the time of his graduation in 1662 to become a schoolmaster. After five years spent at home in Braintree with his nearly indigent family, Tompson was appointed schoolmaster at the Boston Latin School, possibly at the behest of the influential Mather family whose head, Richard Mather, had been both youthful companion and colleague of Tompson's father. Tompson remained master at the Latin school only three years, however, for when the town selectmen voted in Ezekiel Cheever, the celebrated classical pedagogue, as headmaster, Tompson resigned to teach at Charlestown and later in Braintree and at the Roxbury Latin School. Married and the father of a growing family that eventually numbered nine children, Tompson's financial situation was always difficult. The latter half of the seventeenth century was not economically prosperous, and the schoolmaster's stipend suffered accordingly.

The subject of Benjamin Tompson's best-known poem, "New-Englands Tears" and "New Englands Crisis," is the falling-away of New England from its former pious strength, and the terrible chastisement of King Philip's War that might prove to be either the undoing or strengthening of the colony. Since both works were published in 1676, at mid-point of the savage Indian Insurrection, the poet is unable to predict the result. He does, in fact, use a somewhat ambivalent tone in the poems. On the one hand, as we learn in the Prologue, the golden age of New England has been "sin'd away for love of gold." Instead of strength and piety, there is now chocolate and gossip, and comets portending ill. "The mirrour of the Christian world," he tells us, "lyes burnt to heaps in part." And yet in his forceful, vigorous narrative of the conflict, he sides uncompromisingly with the colonists. His position is that if a dreadfully brutal war is necessary to bring New England back to its pristine state, then that war is worth while. And if the colonists are to be defeated, then they must have been so hopelessly corrupt that they deserved to be.

Though Tompson's meter is somewhat unpolished, even crude in places, he has a lively, hard-driving pace and a perceptive eye for situations. For example, in his mock-epic portrait of the ludicrous attempt by a group of women to defend Boston against the Indians with a "Ruff" of "mud and turfe" he combines a gently satiric chuckle at their ineffectualness with admiration for the spirit of the endeavor. It is his ability to take a whole view of situations and events, and to fix them with graphic completeness, that makes Tompson an important poet of early America.

And he is a particularly American poet, the first to publish in America a volume of poetry about the country. He may sprinkle classical references throughout his work, but Tompson's eye is steadily on the land and its inhabitants. His Indians are American ones, not European conceptions of Indians.

After 1676, Tompson published elegies, which were often printed as broadsides for distribution at the graveside to the bereaved. Although they are not now recognized as works of high literary art, Tompson nonetheless deserves the praise offered by Samuel Mather, who called him "a Man of great Learning and Wit, who was well acquainted with *Roman* and *Greek* Writers, and a good Poet."

EDMUND DAVIE 1682[1]

annagram
AD Deum veni
To God, the Center of all Souls, I'm flown,
Having been from all eternity his own

I'm now arriv'd the soul desired Port
More pleasing far then glories of the Court:
My saviour is my only Cæsar: Here's
Instead of Nobles, Angels hosts, bright Peers,
Great Princes thronging round, thicker then swains   5
Below at publicke votes: Here each one Reigns.
Our streets are pav'd with Saphires, and wee pass
Or'e streems of Christial like to fusil glass
Heres Treasuries, the like were never seen;
All guesses at the worth have fool'ries been.   10
Mountains of Rubies safe from privateers
Within the Ramphiers of these lofty Spheres.
Here's piles of Scepters, Diadems of Gold
More then the worlds vast space at once will hold.
But that which butifies the boundless room   15
Is great JEHOVAH, unto whom I'm come.
Eternity's the highest link of Bliss;
Its sunshine never sets, nor clouded is.
I've hitt the very Place I wisht at heart,
I'm fixt for ever: Never thence to part.   20
His heart was erst inamoured with delights
In studious solitudes, in Attick Nights

[1] son of Humphrey Davie and elder brother of Sir John Davie who died in London, 1681.

To prove the greatest avarice of his minde
After the Gems of Skill his Body pin'd.
Hating the sluggards bed, and flattering sloth,   25
Nocturnal Wakes had brought him to vast growth.
His tender years were seasoned with a Juice,
Which might have provd, if spared, of gen'ral use.
He clim'd the Shrowds of Science: Now hees dead,
Hees got a Cove the verry topmast head,   30
Hearing that word which set his soul on fire
With blazing zeal of Love: Brite Soul, come higher,
All that thou seest is thine, myselfe to boot;
Heres an Eternal feast of Love: fall to it.
High, we believe, this welcome Guest was seated,   35
And in an instant all his joys compleated.

Epitaph

THE World was once in danger to drop out
Sidney's Remains, Wits universe about.
Here in Death's gripes a gemme of Art so rare
New-England's Poverty claimeth her share;   40
Since here she nurst him with a silvane teat
Untill hee's fledgd to seek a distant seat:
Gaining the naked substance, his Intent's
From statlier Halls to gain Embellishments
Of sciences profound: Twas well essayd;   45
But by that means this gallant Spark hath paid
What England, Honours Throne, his place of Birth,
Did rightly claime, his soul deserted Earth.
Hee lies among that precious Dust unknown
Which with most friendly silence huggs its own.   50
Great Gransiers of most venerable race,
Yield this their Nephew a retiring Place
In their dark Conclave, where there hands and brains,
Under the umbrage of the grave remains.

Haec genitoris amor, matris revere[n]tia poscit
    Carmina, Tutoris pauperis obsequio.[2]

                                        B. T

[2] This love of one's parent, this reverence for one's mother, requires a song,
with the indulgence of one's guardian.

To my Honoured Patron HUMPHERY Davie
A renewing the Memory of Dr Edmund Davie
Who expired at London, Anno 1681

Bereav'd Sir

Delug'd with tears, by what you heard before,
Here Unexpected meets you one stroke more.
Wave upon wave; Blows fall so thicke, so fast,
Arterial blood, I fear, will come at last
Instead of tears; Methinks I feel the smart,   5
Which in this hour of tryal cramps your heart.
A spouses Death, so wise, so Chast, so fair,
Would bring a Job himselfe next Door Despair:
Soon after that, the First fruits of your streangth;
I fear your patience will you fail at length.   10
But I recall that word, though hard no doubt
Who tends the Furnace, sure will helpe you out.
Had I an intrest where the Pair are gone,
The Vertuous Mother, with the Learned Son;
I'd beg a Balsom for your bleeding wound,   15
No where below this Climate to be found
Distance cannot be salv'd: let S'impathize
A very little space your heart suffice.

Amplitudini tuæ devinctus[1]
Benjamin Tompson
Braintry; 29 4 1682.
Samuel Sewall His Book written
July 31. 1695.

New-Englands Crisis

The
Prologue

The times wherein old *Pompion* was a Saint,
When men far'd hardly yet without complaint

[1] Overwhelmed by your greatness.

On vilest *Cates;*[1] the dainty *Indian Maize*
Was eat with *Clamp-shells* out of wooden Trayes
Under thatch *Hutts* without the cry of *Rent,*   5
And the best *Sawce* to every Dish, *Content.*
When Flesh was food, and hairy skins made coats,
And men as wel as birds had chirping Notes.
When Cimnels[2] were accounted noble bloud
Among the tribes of common herbage food.   10
Of Ceres bounty form'd was many a knack
Enough to fill *poor Robins Almanack.*
These golden times (too fortunate to hold)
Were quickly sin'd away for love of gold.
Twas then among the bushes, not the street   15
If one in place did an inferiour meet,
Good morrow Brother, is there ought you want?
Take freely of me, what I have you ha'nt.
Plain *Tom* and *Dick* would pass as currant now,
As ever since *Your Servant Sir* and bow.   20
Deep-skirted doublets, *puritanick* capes
Which now would render men like upright Apes,
Was comlier wear our wiser Fathers thought
Than the cast fashions from all *Europe* brought.
Twas in those dayes an honest *Grace* would hold   25
Till an hot puddin grew at heart a cold.
And men had better stomachs to religion
That I to capon, turkey-cock or pigeon.
When honest Sisters met to pray not prate
About their own and not their neighbours state.   30
During *Plain Dealings* Reign, that worthy Stud
Of th' ancient planters race before the flood
These times were good, Merchants car'd not a rush
For other fare than *Jonakin*[3] *and Mush.*
Although men far'd and lodged very hard   35
Yet Innocence was better than a Guard.
Twas long before spiders and wormes had drawn
Their dungy webs or hid with cheating Lawne
New-Englands beautyes, which stil seem'd to me
Illustrious in their own simplicity.   40
Twas ere the neighbouring *Virgin-land* had broke
The Hogsheads of her worse than hellish smoak.

[1] provisions, foods.
[2] simnels: biscuits.
[3] Johnnycake.

Twas ere the Islands sent their Presents in,
Which but to use was counted next to sin.
Twas ere a *Barge* had made so rich a fraight   45
As *Chocholatte,* dust-gold and bitts of eight.
Ere wines from *France* and *Moscovadoe* too
Without the which the drink will scarsly doe,
From western Isles, ere fruits and dilicacies,
Did rot maids teeth and spoil their hansome faces.   50
Or ere these times did chance the noise of war
Was from our towns and hearts removed far.
No Bugbear Comets in the chrystal air
To drive our christian Planters to despair.
No sooner pagan malice peeped forth   55
But Valour snib'd[4] it; then were men of worth
Who by their prayers slew thousands Angel like,
Their weapons are unseen with which they strike.
Then had the Churches rest, as yet the coales
Were covered up in most contentious souls.   60
Freeness in Judgment, union in affection,
Dear love, sound truth they were our grand protection.
These were the twins which in our Councells sate,
These gave prognosticks of our future fate,
If these be longer liv'd our hopes increase,   65
These warrs will usher in a longer peace:
But if *New-Englands* love die in its youth
The grave will open next for blessed Truth.
This *Theame* is out of date, the peacefull hours
When Castles needed not but pleasant bowers   70
Not ink, but bloud and tears now serve the turn
To draw the figure of *New-Englands* Urne.
New Englands hour of passion is at hand,
No power except Divine can it withstand;
Scarce hath her glass of fifty years run out,   75
But her old prosperous Steeds turn heads about,
Tracking themselves back to their poor beginnings,
To fear and fare upon their fruits of sinnings:
So that the mirrour of the Christian world
Lyes burnt to heaps in part, her Streamers furl'd   80
Grief reigns, joyes flee and dismal fears surprize,
Not dastard spirits only but the wise.
Thus have the fairest hopes deceiv'd the eye

[4] rebuffed.

Of the big swoln Expectant standing by.
Thus the proud Ship after a little turn   85
Sinks into *Neptunes* arms to find its Urn.
Thus hath the heir to many thousands born
Been in an instant from the mother torn.
Ev'n thus thine infant cheeks begin to pale,
And thy supporters through great losses fail.   90
This is the *Prologue* to thy future woe,
The *Epilogue* no mortal yet can know.

New-Englands Crisis

In seventy five the *Critick* of our years
Commenc'd our war with *Phillip* and his peers.[1]
Whither the sun in *Leo* had inspir'd
A feav'rish heat, and *Pagan* spirits fir'd?
Whither some Romish Agent hatcht the plot?   5
Or whither they themselves? appeareth not.
Whither our infant thrivings did invite?
Or whither to our lands pretended right?
Is hard to say; but *Indian spirits* need
No grounds but lust to make a Christian bleed.   10

And here methinks I see this greazy *Lout*
With all his pagan slaves coil'd round about,
Assuming all the majesty his throne
Of rotten stump, or of the rugged stone
Could yield; casting some bacon-rine-like looks,   15
Enough to fright a Student from his books,
Thus treat his peers, and next to them his Commons,
Kennel'd together all without a summons.
My friends, our Fathers were not half so wise
As we our selves who see with younger eyes.   20
They sel our land to english man who teach
Our nation all so fast to pray and preach:
Of all our countrey they enjoy the best,
And quickly they intend to have the rest.
This no wunnegin,[2] so big matchit[2] law,   25

[1] the Indian War (1675–76) known as King Philip's War.
[2] some of Tompson's words today are difficult to provide exact meanings for; some of them, indeed (e.g. *wunnegin, matchit, sneep*) may be Anglicized American Indian words for which we have no English equivalent. See M. M. Mathews, *Dictionary of American English.*

Which our old fathers fathers never saw.
These english make and we must keep them too,
Which is too hard for them or us to doe,
We drink we so big whipt, but english they
Go sneep,[2] no more, or else a little pay.   30
Me meddle Squaw me hang'd, our fathers kept
What Squaws they would whither they wakt or slept.
Now if you'le fight Ile get you english coats,
And wine to drink out of their Captains throats.
The richest merchants houses shall be ours,   35
Wee'l no more on matts or dwell in bowers
Wee'l have their silken wives take they our Squaws,
They shall be whipt by virtue of our laws.
If ere we strike tis now before they swell
To greater swarmes then we know how to quell.   40
This my resolve, let neighbouring *Sachems* know,
And every one that hath club, gun or bow.
This was assented to, and for a close
He strokt his smutty beard and curst his foes.
This counsel lightning like their tribes invade,   45
And something like a muster's quickly made,
A ragged regiment, a naked swarm,
Whome hopes of booty doth with courage arm,
Set forthwith bloody hearts, the first they meet
Of men or beasts they butcher at their feet.   50
They round our skirts, they pare, they fleece they kil,
And to our bordering towns do what they will.
Poor Hovills (better far then *Caesars* court
In the experience of the meaner sort)
Receive from them their doom next execution,   55
By flames reduc'd to horror and confusion:
Here might be seen the smoking funeral piles
Of wildred towns pitcht distant many miles.
Here might be seen the infant from the breast
Snatcht by a pagan hand to lasting rest: 60
The mother *Rachel*-like shrieks out my child
She wrings her hands and raves as she were wild.
The bruitish wolves suppress her anxious moan
By crueltyes more deadly of her own.
Will she or nill the chastest turtle must   65
Tast of the pangs of their unbridled lust.
From farmes to farmes, from towns to towns they post,

They strip, they bind, they ravish, flea[3] and roast.
The beasts which wont their masters crib to know,
Over the ashes of their shelters low.   70
What the inexorable flames doe spare
More cruel *Heathen* lug away for fare.
These tidings ebbing from the outward parts
Makes trades-men cast aside their wonted Arts
And study armes: the craving merchants plot   75
Not to augment but keep what they have got.
And every soul which hath but common sence
Thinks it the time to make a just defence.
Alarums every where resound in streets,
From west sad tidings with the *Eastern* meets.   80
Our common fathers in their Councels close
A martial treaty with the pagan foes,
All answers center here that fire and sword
Must make their *Sachem* universal Lord.
This armes the english with a resolution   85
To give the vaporing *Scab* a retribution.
Heav'ns they consult by prayer, the best design
A furious foe to quel or undermine.
RESOLV'D that from the *Massachusetts* bands
Be prest on service some *Herculean* hands   90
And certainly he wel deserv'd a jerke
That slipt the Collar from so good a work.
Some Volunteers, some by compulsion goe
To range the hideous forest for a foe.
The tender Mother now's all bowels grown,   95
Clings to her son as if they'd melt in one.
Wives claspe about their husbands as the vine
Huggs the fair elm, while tears burst out like wine.
The new-sprung love in many a virgin heart
Swels to a mountain when the lovers part.   100
Nephews and kindred turn all springs of tears,
Their hearts are so surpriz'd with panick fears.
But dolefull shrieks of captives summon forth
Our walking castles, men of noted worth,
Made all of life, each Captain was a *Mars*,   105
His name too strong to sta[n]d on waterish verse:
Due praise I leave to some poetick hand
Whose pen and witts are better at command.

[3] flay.

Methinks I see the *Trojan-horse* b[u]rst ope,
And such rush forth as might with giants cope: 110
These first the natives treachery felt, too fierce
For any but eye-witness to rehearse.
Yet sundry times in places where they came
Upon the Indian skins they carv'd their name.
The trees stood Centinels and bullets flew 115
From every bush (a shelter for their crew)
Hence came our wounds and deaths from every side
While skulking enemies squat undiscri'd,
That every stump shot like a musketeer,
And bowes with arrows every tree did bear 120
The swamps were Courts of Guard, thither retir'd
The stragling blew-coats when their guns were fir'd,
In dark Meanders, and these winding groves,
Where Beares and panthers with their Monarch moves
These far more cruel slily hidden lay, 125
Expecting english men to move that way.
One party lets them i[n], the other greets
Them with the next thing to their winding-sheets;
Most fall, the rest thus startled back return,
And from their by past foes receive an urn. 130
Here fel a Captain, to be nam'd with tears,
Who for his Courage left not many peers,
With many more who scarce a number left
To tell how treacherously they were bereft.
This flusht the pagan courage, now they think 135
The victory theirs, not lacking meat or drink.
The ranging wolves find here and there a prey,
And having fil'd their paunch they run away
By their Hosts light, the thanks which they return
Is to lead Captives and their taverns burn. 140
Many whose thrift had stor'd for after use
Sustain their wicked plunder and abuse.
Poor people spying an unwonted light,
Fearing a Martydom, in sudden fright
Leap to the door to fly, but all in vain, 145
They are surrounded with a pagan train;
Their first salute is death, which if they shun
Some are condemn'd the Gauntelet to run;
Death would a mercy prove to such as those
Who feel the rigour of such hellish foes. 150
Posts daily on their *Pegasean* Steeds

Bring sad reports of worse than *Nero's* deeds,
Such brutish Murthers as would paper stain
Not to be heard in a Domitians Reign.
The field which nature hid is common laid,   155
And Mothers bodies ript for lack of aid.
The secret Cabinets which nature meant
To hide her master piece is open rent,
The half formd Infant there receives a death
Before it sees the light or draws its breath,   160
Many hot welcomes from the natives arms
Hid in their sculking holes many alarms
Our brethren had, and weary weary trants,
Sometimes in melting heats and pinching wants:
Sometimes the clouds with sympathizing tears   165
Ready to burst discharg'd about their ears:
Sometimes on craggy hills, anon in bogs
And miery swamps better befitting hogs,
And after tedious Marches little boast
Is to be heard of stewd or bakt or roast,   170
Their beds are hurdles, open house they keep
Through shady boughs the stars upon them peep,
Their chrystal drink drawn from the mothers breast
Disposes not to mirth but sleep and rest.
Thus many dayes and weeks, some months run out   175
To find and quell the vagabonding rout,
Who like inchanted Castles fair appear,
But all is vanisht if you come but near,
Just so we might the *Pagan* Archers track
With towns and merchandize upon their back;   180
And thousands in the *South* who settled down
To all the points and winds are quickly blown.
At many meetings of their fleeting crew,
From whom like haile arrows and bullets flew:
The *English* courage with whole swarms dispute,   185
Hundreds they hack in pieces in pursuit.
Sed haud impune,[4] English sides do feel
As well as tawny skins the lead and steel
And some such gallant Sparks by bullets fell,
As might have curst the powder back to Hell: 190
Had only Swords these skirmishes decided
All *Pagan Sculls* had been long since divided.

[4] but not safely.

The lingring war out-lives the Summer sun,
Who hence departs hoping it might be done,
Ere his return at *Spring* but ah hee'l find   195
The Swo[r]d still drawn, men of unchanged mind.
Cold winter now nibbles at hands and toes
And shrewdly pinches both our friends and foes.
Fierce *Boreas* whips the *Pagan* tribe together
Advising them to fit for foes and weather: 200
The axe which late had tasted Christian bloud
Now sets its steely teeth to feast on wood.
The forests suffer now, by waight constrein'd
To kiss the earth with souldiers lately brain'd.
The lofty oakes and ash doe wagge the head   205
To see so many of their neighbours dead;
Their fallen carcasses are carried thence
To stand our enemies in their defence.
Their Myrmidons inclos'd with clefts of trees
Are busie like the ants or nimble bees: 210
And first they limber poles fix in the ground,
In figure of the heavens convex: all round
They draw their arras-matts and skins of beasts,
And under these the Elves do make their nests.
Rome took more time to grow then twice six hours,   215
But half that time will serve for indian bowers.
A Citty shall be rear'd in one dayes space
As shall an hundred english men out-face.
Canonicus[5] precincts there swarmes unite,
Rather to keep a winter guard then fight.   220
A dern[6] and dismal swamp some Scout had found
Whose bosome was a spot of rising ground
Hedg'd up with mighty oakes, maples and ashes,
Nurst up with springs, quick boggs and miery plashes,
A place which nature coyn'd on very nonce   225
For tygers not for men to be a sconce.
Twas here these Monsters shapt and fac'd like men
Took up there Rendezvouz and brumal[7] den,
Deeming the depth of snow, hail, frost and ice
Would make our Infantry more tame and wise   230
Then by forsaking beds and loving wives,
Meerly for indian skins to hazzard lives:

[5] Narragansett Indian chief (c. 1565–1647), friend of the early colonists.
[6] drear.
[7] winter.

These hopes had something calm'd the boiling passion
Of this incorrigible warlike nation.
During this short *Parenthesis* of peace   235
Our forces found, but left him not at ease.
Here english valour most illustrous shone,
Finding their numbers ten times ten to one.
A shower of leaden hail our captains feel
Which made the bravest blades among us reel.   240
Like to some ant-hill newly spurn'd abroad,
Where each takes heels and bears away his load:
Instead of plate and jewels, indian trayes
With baskets up they snatch and run their wayes.
Sundry the flames arrest and some the blade,   245
By bullets heaps on heaps of Indians laid.
The Flames like lightening in their narrow streets
Dart in the face of every one it meets.
Here might be heard an hideous indian cry,
Of wounded ones who in the Wigwams fry.   250
Had we been *Canibals* here might we feast
On brave Westphalia gammons ready drest.
The tauny hue is Ethiopick made
Of such on whom *Vulcan* his clutches laid.
There fate was sudden, our advantage great   255
To give them once for all a grand defeat;
But tedious travell had so crampt our toes
It was too hard a task to chase the foes.
Distinctness in the numbers of the slain,
Or the account of Pagans which remain   260
Are both uncertain, losses of our own
Are too too sadly felt, too sadly known.
War digs a common grave for friends and foes,
Captains in with the common souldier throws.
Six of our Leaders in the first assault   265
Crave readmission to their Mothers Vault
Who had they fell in ancient *Homers* dayes
Had been enrol'd with *Hecatombs* of praise.
As clouds disperst, the natives troops divide,
And like the streames along the thickets glide.   270
Some breathing time we had, and short God knowes
But new alarums from recruited foes
Bounce at our eares, the mounting clouds of smoak
From martyr'd townes the heav'ns for aid invoke:
Churches, barns, houses with most ponderous things   275

Made volatile fly ore the land with wings.
Hundreds of cattle now they sacrifice
For aiery spirits up to gormandize;
And to the *Molech* of their hellish guts,
Which craves the flesh in gross, their ale in butts.   280
Lancaster, Medfield, Mendon wildred *Groton,*
With many Villages by me not thought on
Dy in their youth by fire that usefull foe,
Which this grand cheat the world will overflow.
The wandring Priest to every one he meets   285
Preaches his Churches funeral in the streets.
Sheep from their fold are frighted, Keepers too
Put to their trumps not knowing what to doe.
This monster Warre hath hatcht a beauteous dove
In dogged hearts, of most unfeigned love,   290
Fraternal love the livery of a Saint
Being come in fashion though by sad constraint,
Which if it thrive and prosper with us long
Will make *New-England* forty thousand strong.
But off the Table hand, let this suffice   295
As the abridgment of our miseryes.
If Mildew, Famine, Sword, and fired Townes,
If Slaughter, Captivating, Deaths and wounds,
If daily whippings once reform our wayes,
These all will issue in our Fathers Praise;   300
If otherwise, the sword must never rest
Till all New-Englands *Glory it divest.*

On
A Fortification
At *Boston* begun by Women
Dux Foemina Facti[1]

A Grand attempt some Amazonian Dames
Contrive whereby to glorify their names,
A Ruff for *Boston* Neck of mud and turfe,
Reaching from side to side from surfe to surfe,
Their nimble hands spin up like Christmas pyes,   5
Their pastry by degrees on high doth rise.

[1] Virgil *Aeneid* I. 364: The leader is a woman. A motto used on medals struck in 1588 after Elizabeth I's victory over the Spanish Armada.

The wheel at home counts it an holiday,
Since while the Mistris worketh it may play.
A tribe of female hands, but manly hearts
Forsake at home their pasty-crust and tarts   10
To knead the dirt, the samplers down they hurle,
Their undulating silks they closely furle.
The pick-axe one as a Commandress holds,
While t'other at her awkness gently scolds.
One puffs and sweats, the other mutters why   15
Cant you promove your work so fast as I?
Some dig, some delve, and others hands do feel
The little waggons weight with single wheel.
And least some fainting fits the weak surprize,
They want no sack nor cakes, they are more wise.   20
These brave essayes draw forth Male stronger hands
More like to Dawbers than to Martial bands:
These do the work, and sturdy bulwarks raise,
But the beginners well deserve the praise.

Marlburyes *Fate*

When *Londons* fatal bills were blown abroad
And few but Specters travel'd on the road,
Not towns but men in the black bill enrol'd
Were in *Gazetts* by *Typographers* sold:
But our *Gazetts* without *Errataes* must   5
Report the plague of towns reduct to dust:
And feavers formerly to tenants sent
Arrest the timbers of the tenement.
Ere the late ruines of old *Groton's* cold,
Of *Marlbury's* peracute disease we're told.   10
The feet of such who neighbouring dwellings urnd
Unto her ashes, not her doors return'd.
And what remaind of tears as yet unspent
Are to its final gasps a tribute lent.
If painter overtrack my pen let him   15
An olive colour mix, these elves to trim;
Of such an hue let many thousand thieves
Be drawn like Scare-crows clad with oaken leaves,
Exhausted of their verdant life and blown
From place to place without an home to own.   20
Draw Devils like themselves, upon their cheeks

The banks for grease and mud, a place for leeks.
Whose locks *Medusaes* snakes, do ropes resemble,
And ghostly looks would make *Achilles* tremble.
Limm them besmear'd with Christian Bloud and oild   25
With fat out of white humane bodyes boil'd.
Draw them with clubs like maules and full of stains,
Like *Vulcans* anvilling *New-Englands* brains.
Let round be gloomy forrests with crag'd rocks
Where like to castles they may hide their flocks,   30
Till oppertunity their cautious friend
Shall jogge them fiery worship to attend.
Shew them like serpents in an avious[1] path
Seeking to sow the fire-brands of their wrath.
Most like AEneas in his cloak of mist,   35
Who undiscover'd move where ere they list
Cupid they tell us hath too sorts of darts.
One sharp and one obtuse, one causing wounds,
One piercing deep the other dull rebounds,
But we feel none but such as drill our hearts.   40
From Indian sheaves which to their shoulders cling,
Upon the word they quickly feel the string.
Let earth be made a screen to hide our woe
From Heavens Monarch and his Ladyes too;
And least our Jealousie think they partake,   45
For the red stage with clouds a curtain make.
Let dogs be gag'd and every quickning sound
Be charm'd to silence, here and there all round
The town to suffer, from a thousand holes
Let crawl thees fiends with brands and fired poles,   50
Paint here the house and there the barn on fire,
With holocausts ascending in a spire.
Here granaries, yonder the Churches smoak
Which vengeance on the actors doth invoke.
Let *Morpheus* with his leaden keyes have bound   55
In feather-beds some, some upon the ground,
That none may burst his drowsie shackles till
The brutish pagans have obtain'd their will,
And *Vulcan* files them off then *Zeuxis* paint
The phrenzy glances of the sinking saint.   60
Draw there the Pastor for his bible crying,
The souldier for his sword, The Glutton frying

[1] twisting.

With streams of glory-fat, the thin-jaw'd Miser
Oh had I given this I had been wiser.
Let here the Mother seem a statue turn'd   65
At the sad object of her bowels burn'd.
Let the unstable weakling in belief
Be mounting Ashurs horses for relief.
Let the half Convert seem suspended twixt
The dens of darkness, and the Planets fixt,   70
Ready to quit his hold, and yet hold fast
By the great *Atlas* of the Heavens vast.
Paint Papists muttering ore their apish beads
Whome the blind follow while the blind man leads.
Let *Ataxy*[2] be mounted on a throne   75
Imposing her Commands on every one,
A many-headed monster without eyes
To see the wayes which wont to make men wise.
Give her a thousand tongues with wings and hands
To be ubiquitary in Commands,   80
But let the concave of her skull appear
Clean washt and empty quite of all but fear,
One she bids flee, another stay, a third
She bids betake him to his rusty sword,
This to his treasure, th'other to his knees,   85
Some counsels she to fry and some to freeze,
These to the garison, those to the road,
Some to run empty, some to take their load:
Thus while confusion most mens hearts divide
Fire doth their small exchequer soon decide.   90
Thus all things seeming ope or secret foes,
An Infant may grow old before a close,
But yet my hopes abide in perfect strength,
New England will be prosperous once at length.

The Town called Providence
Its Fate

Why muse wee thus to see the wheeles run cross
Since *Providence* it self sustains a loss:
And yet should *Providence* forget to watch
I fear the enemy would all dispatch;

[2] disorder.

Celestial lights would soon forget their line,   5
The wandering planets would forget to shine,
The stars run all out of their common spheres,
And quickly fall together by the eares:
Kingdoms would jostles out their Kings and set
The poor Mechanick up whome next they met,   10
Or rather would whole kingdoms with the world
Into a *Chaos* their first egge be hurl'd.
Ther's none this Providence of the Most High
Who can survive and write its Elegie:
But of a solitary town I write,   15
A place of darkness yet receiving light
From pagan hands, a miscellanious nest
Of errors Hectors, where they sought a rest
Out of the reach of Lawes but not of God,
Since they have felt the smart of common rod.   20
Twas much I thought they did escape so long,
Who Gospel truth so manifestly wronge:
For one *Lots* sake perhaps, or else I think
Justice did at greatest offenders wink
But now the shott is paid, I hope the dross   25
Will be cashiered in this common loss.
Houses with substance feel uplifting wings,
The earth remains, the last of humane things:
But know the dismal day draws neer wherein
The fire shall earth it self dissolve and sin.   30

Seaconk Plain *Engagement*

On our *Pharsalian Plaines*, comprizing space
For *Caesars* host brave *Pompey* to outface,
An handfull of our men are walled round
With Indian swarmes; anon their pieces sound
A *Madrigal* like heav'ns artilery   5
Lightning and thunderbolts their bullets fly.
Her's hosts to handfulls, of a few they leave
Fewer to tell how many they bereave.
Fool-hardy fortitude it had been sure
Fierce storms of shot and arrows to endure   10
Without all hopes of some requital to
So numerous and pestilent a foe.
Some musing a retreat and thence to run,

Have in an instant all their business done,
They sink and all their sorrows ponderous weight   15
Down at their feet they cast and tumble straight.
Such who outliv'd the fate of others fly
Into the Irish bogs of misery.
Such who might dye like men like beasts do range
Uncertain whither for a better change,   20
These Natives hunt and chase with currish mind,
And plague with crueltyes such as they find.
    When shall this shower of Bloud be over? When?
    Quickly we pray oh Lord! say thou Amen.

Seaconk *or* Rehoboths *Fate*

I once conjectur'd that those tygers hard
To reverend *Newmans* bones would have regard,
But were all *SAINTS* they met twere all one case,
They have no rev'rence to an Angels face:
But where they fix their griping lions paws
They rend without remorse or heed to laws.
Rehoboth here in common english, Rest
They ransack, *Newmans* Relicts to molest.
Here all the town is made a publick stage
Whereon these *Nimrods* act their monstrous rage.
All crueltyes which paper stain'd before
Are acted to the life here ore and ore.

Chelmsfords *Fate*

Ere famous *Winthrops* bones are laid to rest
The pagans *Chelmsford* with sad flames arrest,
Making an artificial day of night
By that plantations formidable light.
Here's midnight shrieks and Soul-amazing moanes,   5
Enough to melt the very marble stones:
Fire-brands and bullets, darts and deaths and wounds
Confusive outcryes every where resounds:
The natives shooting with the mixed cryes,
With all the crueltyes the foes devise   10
Might fill a volume, but I leave a space

For mercyes still successive in there place
Not doubting but the foes have done their worst,
And shall by heaven suddenly be curst.

> *Let this dear Lord the sad Conclusion be*   15
> *Of poor* New-Englands *dismal tragedy.*
> *Let not the glory of thy former work*
> *Blasphemed be by pagan Jew or Turk:*
> *But in its funeral ashes write thy Name*
> *So fair all Nations may expound the same:*   20
> *Out of her ashes let a Phœnix rise*
> *That may outshine the first and be more wise.*
> B. Tompson.

A Supplement

What meanes this silence of *Harvardine* quils
While *Mars* triumphant thunders on our hills.
Have pagan priests their Eloquence confin'd
To no mans use but the mysterious mind?
Have Pawaws[1] charm'd that art which was so rife
To crouch to every Don that lost his life?
But now whole towns and Churches fire and dy
Without the pitty of an *Elegy.*
Nay rather should my quils were they all swords
Wear to the hilts in some lamenting words.
I dare not stile them poetry but truth,
The dwingling products of my crazy youth.
If these essayes shall raise some quainter pens
Twil to the Writer make a rich amends.

[1] Powah, Powaw: an Indian religious figure with chief responsibility for conjuring up the devil and for curing the sick and wounded.

RICHARD STEERE

(1643-1721)

Many poets of early New England are—or have been until recently—known best for activities other than their verse writing. For instance, John Saffin's historical niche is established from records of his business career, and Captain Edward Johnson's part in the founding of Woburn, Massachusetts, is fully documented in that town's records. In any case, biographical data for these writers can frequently be gleaned from extant genealogical or historical papers. One poet whose life is still difficult to trace, however, is Richard Steere. In fact, were it not for extant copies of his printed poems, Steere would have virtually no place at all in American history or letters.

We do know that Richard Steere was born in 1643 in England, and that he was a "citizen of London," which title would accord him official respectability and probably indicate that he was a member of one of the great Guilds or Companies of London. Quite probably he was a merchant. By 1690 Steere was in New London, Connecticut, and two years later he married Elizabeth Wheeler, a widow. It is possible that he had been in America for several years prior to 1690, perhaps having joined several members of his family in Providence, Rhode Island, as a supporter of Roger Williams.

Richard Steere's political and religious leanings can be inferred from a libel suit brought against him in 1695 when, together with two other men, he formally protested the imprisonment of Reverend John Rogers. Rogers and his followers, called Rogerenes, had separated from the Newport Church after the minister had significantly altered the church service. Rogers' ultimate imprisonment aroused Steere and his colleagues to accuse government and colony of persecution, narrowness of principle, self-interest, and a domineering spirit. Further, they protested that compelling persons to pay Presbyterian ministerial fees was contrary to the laws of England and constituted "rapine, robbery and aggression." For this they were arrested, found guilty, and fined five pounds each, a penalty not unduly harsh for the time. Although there were threats of appeal to the English throne, the case went no further. At some later date Richard Steere crossed into Long Island and died at Southold in 1721.

Not only is Steere's personal history in large part lost to us, but his poetry has been ignored in most discussions of early American verse. His poems have escaped all anthologies, and his name has gone unmentioned by literary historians. Nevertheless, Richard Steere deserves attention for several reasons: he wrote the only Nativity poem composed in seventeenth-century America; he wrote one of the few early American poems whose theme is esthetic attitude; he wrote perhaps the most sharply satirical anti-Catholic verse narrative of the era; and he wrote at least one poetic description of an approaching storm, in which the drama is heightened by unusual verse form and tight rhyme.

Steere's celebration of the Nativity in "Upon the Caelestial Embassy Perform'd by Angels, to the Shepherds on the Plains of Bethlehem, at the Birth of our Redeemer," represents a noteworthy departure from standard Puritan view. Christmas in New England was assigned no religious significance. Roman Catholic observation of the Feast Day, including veneration of the Virgin, gorgeous pageants, burning incense, and decorated statuary, was to the Puritans idolatrous, and New Englanders had no intention of permitting such heresy. They railed against "Christmas-keeping" at every turn, and did not elevate the Nativity to thematic stature in their literature.

Although Steere departed from strict Puritan theology in his Nativity poem, he held firmly to it in *Antichrist Display'd*, published first as a broadside in 1682. The poem illustrates in part the Puritan interpretation of the prophetic Book of Revelation. Because history to the Puritans was God's working-out of events in both Old and New Testaments, they believed that they needed only to consult Scripture to learn the course of world events. Difficulties arose when these events, symbolically stated, were variously interpreted. There could be, in truth, only one correct interpretation, and most Puritan divines applied their skill and knowledge to discern it. Thus the pouring out of the "Seven Vials" in Revelation was a subject of frequent learned discourse, including that of John Cotton. If there was one aspect of Revelation on which all Puritans agreed, however, it was that the "Whore of Babylon" was indisputably the Roman

Catholic Church. Accordingly, the Pope was Antichrist whose fall was imminent. This is the theme of Steere's narrative, and one in which he exercises a wickedly acrid wit. He calls the Protestants true Christians who "would not own a *Breaden God;*" that is, they could not accept the Catholic doctrine of transubstantiation. Throughout the poem Steere envisions the fall of Rome and depicts dire consequences for its followers.

It is to Richard Steere, also, that we owe a poetic denial of the stereotype of the pleasure-hating Puritan mistrustful of all sensuous pleasure. "Earth Felicities, Heavens Allowances," one of the first blank verse poems written in America, reveals Steere's delight in nature and society. Overwritten and at times awkward, its focus is important in a period where esthetic attitude is seldom stated or thematically central, and frequently misunderstood.

Richard Steere at his worst is long-winded, as in his political fable *The Daniel Catcher,* which is modeled after Dryden's *Absolom and Achitophel.* But when he sheds convention to state his own perceptions, his poetic imagination is evident in verse form and imagery.

A
Monumental Memorial
Of
Marine Mercy &c.

Since Every *Quill* is silent to Relate
What being known must needs be wonder'd at
I take the boldness to present your *Eye*
With Safty's *Prospect* in Extremity,
Which tho not Cloath'd with *Academick* Skill,   5
Or lofty Raptures of a *Poet's* Quill;
But wrapt in *raggs,* through which your eyes may see
The *Naked* Truth in plain simplicitee.
  I without further prologue *Lanch with* ink[1]
With Captain *Balston*[2] in th' *Adventure Pinck;*[3]   10

[1] launch a written account.
[2] [Joshua Boylston?].
[3] A pinck is, loosely, a small ship. No ship with the name *Adventure Pinck* has been found in contemporary records, though *Adventures* by the dozen appear (see John Hotten, *Original Lists of Persons of Quality* . . . [New York, 1874], pp. 345–418).

Who in *December* on the fourteenth day,[4]
His Anchors *weigh'd* in *Massachusets BAY,*
New-England's Chiefest *Port,* and *sayling* on,
Soon *lay'd the Land* below the *Horizon.*

    The *Sea* was kind, the Sky serene and clear,   15
All seem to smile, no threating Frowns appear;
Yet sometimes Clouds of Rain, of Hail, of Snow,
Sometimes the *winds* more lofty, sometimes low,
    The *Mariners* and *Passengers* a'board,
Enjoying what the Vessel did afford   20
With Satisfaction, and in full Content:
This good beginning was Encouragement
Of good success, in hope and expectation
The Ship might prove an *Ark* of preservation;
Her *swelling sayls* gave her a nimble motion,   25
Making her *Keel* to *plough* the Yeilding *Ocean,*
Whose little *Billows* still her *Bow* out braves,
Glideing Tryumphant o're the *Curled waves.*

    Thus for five weeks the gentler winds did play
Upon the *Oceans* Surface to convey   30
Our little *Pinck,* filling her plyant Sayles
With easie *Breezes,* sweet *Topgallant Gailes:*[5]
And now the *Mariners* by Judgment found
We did approach nigh to *Great Brittains* ground
And therefore *heav'd* the *Deep-sea lead* to *sound,*   35
Which tho they *Fathom'd* not did Truth afford;
For the same night a *Land bird* came *a'board,*
And the next morning we beheld two more
Which made the Judgment good they gave before[.]

    Had we continu'd *thus* upon the Deep   40
We had bin Charm'd into a drowsie sleep
Of calme Security, nor had we known
The Excellence of *PRESERVATION;*
We had been Dumb and silent to Express
Affectedly the Voy'ges good success.   45

    But to awake and Rowse our sleepy minds,
The *Po'wrs* above let loose th' unruly winds,
Heav'ns milder *Puffs* with violence at last
Let fly more fierce, and *blow* a stronger *Blast:*
The dark'ned Sky with gloomy *Clouds* o're spread,   50

---

[4] 1683.
[5] a breeze of roughly 34 m.p.h. in which a square-rigger can carry her top-gallants.

Whose moist'ned *fleeces* have *Enveloped*
Tempestous Flaws which Issue more and more
In *Thunder's* Language, or as *Cannons* roar:
The weighty Seas Roul from the *Deeps* beneath.
Hill stands on *hill* by force of Heav'n blown breath,   55
And from the *rocks foundations* do arise
As tho resolv'd to *storm* th' *Impending* Skyes;
Flaws from those lofty *Battlements* are hurld,
As to a *Chaos* they would shake the world:
Thus as between a warr of *Sea* and *Heaven*,   60
From place to place our little *Ship* is driven;
And by the Seas tost like a ball in sport,
From *wave* to *wave* in *Neptunes Tennis Court.*
   While thus the *winds* and *seas* their pow'rs dispute
A neighb'ring object did our Eyes salute,   65
A *Sayle to windward;* (in Distress no doubt)
Who *Fir'd a Gun* and *heav'd* their *Colours* out;
We *made* her *English,* but no help could give,
The Lofty Seas found each enough to *live*
But in the morning we to *windward* were   70
And *Bearing down* resolv'd to *speak with her,*
And understood she from *East India* came,
Under Command of Captain *Hide* by Name,[6]
Burden *six hundred Tuns* and *Ninety Men*
Having about ten *months* from *India* been,   75
And had bin *Beating* six *weeks* on the *Coast*
Wanting *Provision,* almost spent and Lost:
An Interval of *storms* became their friend,
And gave us leave some little help to lend:
The *storm* renewing its *Impetuous* Force   80
Did Each from Other further off Divorce,
Yet we might see them two or three dayes more,
But since have heard that they were drave *a'shore*
Somewhere in *Cornwall,* on the *Western Coast,*
And ev'ry *Soul* except two *Boyes* were lost.   85
   Still the restless *winds* rebellious grow,
As they the *Universe* would Overthrow,
The pondrous *seas* like Rowling *Mountains* still,
Each *Billow* seeming an *Alpean* hill
By its prodigious Altitude: Despair   90
And fear of Danger, moves all lips to *pray'r*

[6] so far unidentified.

Mixt with *Industry,* but *Industry* failes,
The *Pumps* are now in use but not the *Sayles,*
The Artist's *Quadrants*[7] now are useless grown,
For *Darkness* dwells upon our *Horizon;*   95
Thus we for sev'ral days upon the *Ocean*
Did *Ly a Hull,*[8] keeping our *Pumps* in motion;
Till *January twenty sixth* at night,
A mighty *Sea* did *Overwhelm* us quite,
Which falling down with a resistless stroke   100
Both our Ships *Waste*[9] (or well built *Gunwalls*)[10] broke
And carr'd away: now seeming like a *Wreck*
From the *Fore-castle* to the *Quarter Deck,*
The *Long boat, Windless,*[11] *Captstern,*[12] with the blow
Besides two weighty *Anchors* from the *Bow,*   105
With *Ropes,* and *Ring-bolts* (where ye *Boat* was fast,
And we constrain'd to cut our *Mizen mast,*)[13]
All lost at once: Afflictions now prevail,
And each mans heart and strength begins to fail;
Sometimes we seem to *sink* sometimes to *float,*   110
The *Masters mate* tear's from his back his Coat
And stuffs between the *Timbers;* then they cry
For *Bedding, Ruggs, and Blankets* eagerly,
Which when obtain'd they Crowd into each place
Where *streams of water* Issu'd in apace: 115
But all Industry seems without success,
The *Rageing storm* grows rather more than Less;
Over those *Ruggs* they added *skins* of *Bears,*
And two new *Clothes*[14] which our new *mainsail* spares;
Here may the hand of providence be Ey'd,   120
The *sayl* was made by those two *clothes* too wide,
Which by so much, we had made so much less
But a few dayes before our great Distress;
Ropes *Fore and Aft* were *streched* to secure
The *Mariners,* who scarcely could endure   125

[7] early navigational instruments for measuring latitude and longitude; fore-runner of sextant.
[8] situation of a ship with all sails furled and lying with her side to the wind.
[9] waist.
[10] gunwales: where deck and topsides meet.
[11] windlass: winch for hauling in anchor cable.
[12] capstan: rotating drum around which anchor cable is wound.
[13] mizzenmast: mast aft or next aft the mainmast.
[14] lengths of canvas or duck that are sewn together to make the sail.

Those *Big-swel'd Billows,* (what are feeble men?)
So oft wash'd in, and out and in agen,
Sometimes upon, sometimes within the Ocean;
The *Pumps* nev'r *sucking* tho in Constant motion;
Whilst all the men and women then *on board*   130
With earnest Cryes did call upon the *LORD*
The *Seas* did frequently *o'erflow* the *ship,*
And we were often buri'd in the *Deep:*
The Chests *between Decks swim* as in a *flood,*
Where men up to their *knees* in water stood,   135
Expecting ev'ry Moment *grim look'd Death*
With that cold Element would stop their breath.
    When suddenly a voice salutes our ears,
With Joy unspeakable amidst our Fears,
One of the PUMPS *does* SUCK! who can believe   140
What unexpected Comfort a *Repreive*
Brings a Condemned *Convict:* So that Voice
Caused each Cast down spirit to Rejoyce.
    But on the *Fifth* of *February* we
Ship'd a prodigious *Mountain of a sea,*   145
Which with a pondrous and resistless Stroke
The Fixed *Table* and the Benches broke,
And with its Force Op'ned the *Cabbin* Door.
A weighty *Chest of Tooles* away it bore,
Then with loud Ecchos ev'ry Tongue declares   150
Our Period come, our Hopes were now Despaires,
For we lay *buri'd* in the *Oceans Womb,*
And might conclude it was our *wat'ry Tomb;*
But an Almighty power became our Freind,
Causing our *buri'd Vessel* to Ascend,   155
And by degrees climb up the *Mountain waves,*
From whence our *eyes* might view our *fluid Graves;*
Thus the Great God did Snatch us from below,
Unto whose pow'r we all our safeties owe.
    Some few dayes after we a Ship might see,   160
Which *Coming up with* understood to be
For *England bound,* and from *Virginia* came,
Gregory Sugar was her *Captains* Name;
So *Leaky* (that tho they did what they could)
Sh' had *six* or *sev'n foot water in the Hould,*   165
The Safety of their *Lives* they only sought,
For to preserve their *Vessel* they could not,

And *Hoysting* out their *Boat* to come *a'board*
Which could not Safety to them all afford,
Yet *Thirteen* of them soon into it prest: 170
And *putting off*, promis'd to fetch the Rest:
When they came nigh our *Side* such fear was shown,
None sought the good of *others* but his *own*,
Each striving to preserve himself with hast,
without regard to *make the Painter*[15] *fast;*   175
(Had they Endeavour'd, it had bin in vain)
The *Boat* such wrong and dammage did sustain:
In *Laying us aboard*[16] her *Bows* were *Stav'd,*
That t'was meer *Mercy* any man was sav'd:
Soon the Disabled *Boat was gon a drift,*   180
And now no hope of preservation left
For those behind, who were in number five,
For 'twas not possible the Ship should *Live,*
Nor with our Vessel did we dare come nigh,
For still the troubled Sea *ran mountains high,*   185
Tho their Intreaties, Peircing Cries and Grones,
Might even draw Remorsness out of Stones;
And now because of the approaching night,
We did advise them to *hang out a Light,*
Which but till eight a Clock appear'd in Sight,   190
After which time it did no more appear,
And we concluded (as we well might fear)
They then went down: Tho we could not *relieve*
Their *wants*, their *loss* we could not choose *but grieve.*
    And now some Comfort we begin to find,   195
The *winds* are *Calmer* and the *Seas* more kind,
Now Heav'ns alscourging hand its strokes withdrew
And former Consolations did Renew,
By giving us at length the *Sight* of *Land,*
By an Or'e ruling providential hand: 200
Our Cloudy cares appear to fly apace,
And Comforts seemingly supply their place;
The fourteenth day at *Plymouth* we Arrive,
With those thirteen we had preserv'd alive:
The nineteenth day for *London* we *set sayle,*   205
With not too much *wind,* but a mod'rate Gale.
But as if *Heav'n* with anger should reprove,

[15] a rope attached to the bow of a longboat.
[16] in approaching the ship.

That we those mercies did not well Improve;
Its *Breath* comes forth with *Fury* as before,
And we tho in the *Downes*[17] and nigh the *Shore*,   210
Must feel more *strokes* of the chastising *Rod*
Of our offended of our angry GOD.

The Two and twentieth day much *wind* did blow,
When in the *Downs* we let our *Anchor* goe,
But it *came home:* we our *Shift Anchor Cast*,[18]   215
Which (*insignificant*) *came home* as fast,
And we were driven up *alongst* the *Side*
Of a *Ship* there, which did at *Anchor ride*,
Our *Anchor* took her *Cable*, and did pass
Up with a speedy motion to her *Hass*,[19]   220
Which at their *Bows* they *Cutting* from the *Cable*,
And t'other *Anchor* being too unable
To bring us up, broke in the *shank*, and we
Again (by Violence) *Drove out to Sea;*
We thought to *Anchor* then in *Poulstone Bay*,   225
And let our *small Bower*[20] go without delay,
Which like a rotten stick was quickly broke
(When once it came to strain) both *flewks* & *stock*,[21]
Neither *Shift-Anchor*, *Best* nor yet *Small Bower*
To *Bring us up* had strength enough or power;   230
And in the Afternoon the *winds* Restrain
Their furious *Blasts*, now only did remain
Our small *Cedge Anchor*,[22] (unto which we must
Our *Lives*, our *Ship*, and all her *Cargo* trust,)
Which *Letting go*, Heav'ns care did so provide,   235
That we that *Ebb* secure in safety *Ride;*
From which our apprehensions may Inspect,
How the *Great* God by *Small* meanes doth protect,
Whose strength can make our strongest *cables* weak,
Our *Cobwebs* strong, no earthly strein can break,   240
That we might put no Trust in *Earthen* Powers:
For weak is all the *Fortitude* of Ours.
An *Anchor* we that night from *Shore* obtain.

[17] famous shipping route along eastern coast of Kent from Dover to the North
Foreland; excellent anchorage, shelter from westerly gales.
[18] spare anchor.
[19] hawse, hawser: heavy rope.
[20] small bow anchor.
[21] hooks and crosspiece of anchor.
[22] another small anchor kept in reserve on a square-rigger.

And so Return into the *Downs* again,
And *weighing* thence, favour'd with *winds* and *floods*,   245
Our *selves* in Safety with our *ship* and *goods*,
The *Twenty fifth* (assisted by the Lord)
Arriv'd at *London* and at *Ratcliff Moor'd*.
    Thou God of this great Vast, *that aloft Command*
              With thy Almighty Hand,   250
            Water, Earth, Air, and Fire
    (*The Elements:*) *the* Sun, *the* Moon, *and* Stars
            Act not their own affaires,
            But what thou dost require:
O who can view thy pow'r, *and not thy* pow'r *admire.*   255
Tis thou Alone art our alone support,
            Thy Mercy's our strong fort,
            Thou giv'st us length of dayes,
To thee th' Almighty *and* Tri-une *JEHOVE,*
            Dwelling in Heav'en *above;*   260
            Be Everlasting Praise;
O who can tast thy Good, *and not* Thanksgiving *Raise.*

Earth Felicities,
Heavens Allowances.
A
Blank Poem

    Upon the Earth there are so many Treasures
Various Abounding objects of Delight,
That to Enumerate, would be a Task
Too ponderous for my Imperfect Skill,
Or Pen, to Charactise Effect'ally.   5
    Yet these felicities may be Reduc'd
Under three heads; As, *Riches, Honours, Pleasures:*
Whence as from fountains, All External good
Riseth, and flows to us in many Streams;
And whosoe'er possesseth these, Enjoys   10
The fulness of all Temporary good.
    The good Effects which doth from *Riches* spring
Are not a few, nor of a mean Account;
As Education, Friends Acquaintance, Lovers.
With Dignity, Authority, Command,   15
And many other worthy our Esteem.

From *Honour* comes Renown and Reputation,
Which when from worthy Actions it proceeds,
It's still accompanied with inward Joy;
And brighter shines in men of Noble birth;   20
When they shall not Degenerate from those,
Their worthy Ancestors, whose virt'ous Acts
Lifted them to those Honours, and that trust,
Which gives these titles to the Name of great;
Nothing can more Imbellish noble Souls,   25
Than when their merits challenge honours crown.
   Pleasures are many and of Divers Kinds,
Riches and *Honour* only serve to *please;*
And ev'ry good seems to this end ordain'd;
How many sweet felicities are found   30
Contributing to pleasure ev'ry scence
Visus, Auditus, Gustus, and Olfactus.[1]
   To please the *Eye* how many various Sights?
The fair and glorious Aspect of the *Heav'ns,*
The Darling brightness of the *Sun Moon Stars,*   35
The naked *Air,* the Curled Silver *Streams,*
The *Birds* Enamel'd with their Divers *Plumes;*
Orchards, whose *Trees,* with *blossoms, leaves and fruit*
Of various Kinds, all pleasing to the Eye,
The ev'n *Meadows,* in their Tap'stry green,   40
All Diapred with beauty blooming flow'rs;
The spacious *Ocean,* spreads her wat'ry vail
From shore, to shore, out of whole bowels come
Of sundry Creatures, Infinite in number,
As doth the Land afford, of Diff'rent *figures:*   45
Ships, Cities, Towns, Castles, and *Monuments:*
Gold, Pearls, and Rare Inestimable *Jems;*
Do all Contribute to delight the *Opticks.*
   Likewise to please, and charm the List'ning *Ears,*
Sweet Musicks pleasant and harmonious Sounds;   50
The chirping notes of winged *Choresters,*
And Purling Murmurs of the Gliding *brooks,*
Modulate Accents of a *well Tun'd voice,*
Joyn'd with the Sweet *Allurements* of the *Lute,*
The Gallant noise of Manly Musick, *Bells*   55
Belonas[2] voice of *Trumpets, Fifes* and *Drums,*

[1] sight, sound, taste, smell.
[2] Bellona: in Roman myth, goddess of war and wife of Mars.

Pleasing discourses, *Histories* and *Novals,*
Am'rous Converse, when Innocent and clean,
All give a Charming Sweetness to the Muse.
    Also to Gratifie the sence of *Tasting,*   60
Are various sorts of *Flesh, Fish, Fowl,* and *Fruits;*
Delicious Banquets, with their pleasing *Sauces,*
With Life refreshing neat brisk Sparkling *Wines,*
Of Divers kinds, both Simple and Compound;
And many more unite to please the *Taste.*   65
    So, the *Olfactal* faculty's Supply'd,
With Oderiferous, and Choice *perfumes,*
Of *Myrrh,* of *Cassia,* and of *Bruised Spices;*
Sweet Smelling *Gums,* from the Arabian Coast,
Or our Domestick *Violets, Pinks,* and *Roses;*   70
With Fragrant *Herbs,* and *Blossoms* of our *Gardens.*
In fine, the pleasures of the Earth are such,
So good, so many, Common, yet so Sweet,
That should I Dwell for ever on Discourse,
It would surpass the skill of Tongue or Pen,   75
Sufficiently their value to relate.
    Yet let me add to these a pleasure more,
Of Loving *Parents,* Counter Loving *Children;*
Husband and *Wife,* in Mut'al one-ness knit;
Friends, during Life sharing each others Joys   80
Injoying Each the Others happy Love,
With Delectation: When we make our selves
Sensible, of the sweetness all affords;
We may perceive a Possibility
By bounteous Heav'ns Allowance, on the Earth,   85
To find in Temp'ral good felicity.
    Having thus Transciently, in brief Survey'd,
Wherein all Earthly Happiness consists;
To the intent we may therein be safe,
We with Content must fortify our minds,   90
That in all Stations, Accidents, Conditions,
We may Enjoy this worlds felicities,
Abstracted from the Ills that do accrue.
    He is the Richest, and most happy man,
Who is most moderate in his Desire: 95
Can be Content and sweetly satisfy'd
In ev'ry State, Condition, and degree;
For he that Covets not possesseth all,
And may be truely call'd the Richest man;

When he that has abundance, and yet fears   100
The loss or want of them, is truely poor,
By his Ambitious and Intemp'rate mind,
Grieving for want of what his heart Desires,
Is in more Poverty, than he that wants,
Yet is Content to want. It grieves not him,   105
Who makes his little with Content Enough:
Whoso lets Loose th' unruly Appetite,
Desiring first a *Lordship* to possess
Then next a *Kingdom;* After that a *World*
Which if he had, he would Account too Little   110
Or grieve, and pine, because it was no better,
Troubling his Restless mind still with desire;
Such in no State can meet with Satisfaction:
Mind with how little nature is supply'd,
If we that little always have at hand,   115
We have as much in our Sufficiency,
As if possess'd with all the world affords.
   The silent Shade, the Quiet Country life
Free from the Troubles of the *Crowded Town,*
Or the Perplexing Cares of State affairs,   120
And deep Projections of great *Politicians;*
Under that bush where *Tityrus*[3] did Sing,
Amidst the sweets of satisfy'd Delights,
With no more wealth than Riseth from Content
This is a happy State: We often hear   125
The unperplexed plowmans Thoughtless note,
Tuneing his whistle to his working Teame,
In him behold the Emblem of Content,
A state of Happiness which we should seek,
Tho' Troubles cross the Road that leads thereto.   130
   Crosses and *Troubles* Common are to men,
No one is free: *Crosses* sometimes he needs
To mix with pleasures, Pleasures else were bitter,
And wou'd grow Stale, and Cloy the Appetite,
But relish sweeter when with *Crosses* mixt;   135
And tho our Troubles should be very Tart,
Yet being past we relish pleasures better.
   Wisdom and fortitude will us assist,
To raise our minds to such a noble Temper.

[3] poetic surname for a shepherd; Spenser calls Chaucer Tityrus in *The Shep-heard's Calendar* (February, June, December).

And fix such Peace, and Courage in our Souls,   140
That we shall dare to slight the *world* when't *frowns,*
And with Contempt shall look on its Insults;
Scorning those Stroaks that Conquer feeble minds,
And thereby Crown our selves with Happiness.
   True Piety will Equally Contribute,   145
To make us face adversity with boldness,
Yielding to *God* Depend on him alone,
Who always what is best for us, will give;
Subject our wills to his, Let the world frown,
We shall from all Afflictions be releas'd.   150
And relish Joy, when Sorrow's gone the better.
   Since there's a kind of happiness in Crosses,
Let no Condition find us discontent:
None can more Earths Felicities Enjoy,
Than doth the fearless free Contented man,   155
Who whether want, or have, or Loss, or gain,
He's of an even temper in all States,
All are alike to him, he's always happy.
   Would we on Earth be happy, we must then
Use Earthly happiness without abuse;   160
All our Intemperate desires will prove,
Disturbers of our Peace and happiness,
Griefs, Cares Distemp'red Passions, Anguish, Fears,
Are very Incident to vicious men;
They'r not Content with vice, tho it seem pleasant;   165
None like the virt'ous man can live Content,
He's most secure, lives Healthy, Happy, Free,
Pleasantly Chearful always Dwells in peace;
The Treasures, Riches, pleasures of his mind
Are Durable: In all things he delights,   170
His way to Heaven seems a pleasant path,
And all his Jo[ur]ney as in Summer time.
   Let virtue guide us then in Earth Enjoyments,
Let *Temp'rance* teach us how to measure all,
Consult to use a mean, without abuse,   175
Both in the manner, measure, and the time,
While Justice leads us in the paths we tread,
Temp'rance (is like a Razour) Takes away
Those vicious Superfluities, that grow
Up to abuses, were they not Correct   180
By the Incision of its pruning virtues.

In all things we Enjoy, remember still
To send our thanks, to, whence the blessing came,
And let the Earths felicities Excite,
To move with Chearfulness in worthy Acts,   185
Raising our Thankful minds up to the fountain,
And with Divine and hearty Love Rejoyce,
That lo by Looking up to heav'n above,
From whence these Lower joys to us descend,
We may a Heav'nly Paradice possess,   190
Of sweet and Comforting delights on Earth.
    That we in Earths Delights may find a joy,
Let's banish Superstition from our minds.
Could we Religions Excellency see,
We should be much Enamour'd with its Beauty,   195
Whose strict Injunctions no way does Impede
The Temp'rate Right and Consolating use
Of Heav'ns Allowance; Earths Felicities.
    However Superstitious *Stoicks,* may
Refuse those blessings which are freely giv'n: 200
As if not making use of Earthly good,
Were to obtain Heav'ns Glory in Exchange,
And by a Solitary Ridged Fear,
Deprive themselves of Temp'ral Consolations,
Consulting all those Comforts to despise,   205
And seeming fearful of their sweets to taste,
As if within their good were Lodg'd infection:
And so deny themselves their harmless use;
By which their fear, thro' weakness they have made
The world a grief and burthen to their minds.   210
Whereas without abuse we may, nay ought,
Freely Enjoy Earths good in its good use.
Nature Invites, and Reason bids us tast;
Temp'rance, as well Condemns Stupidity,
As Glut'ny and Excess it disallows,   215
Since both prohibit and deny us Comfort;
We may Receive them, we are call'd to do 't,
They were Created only for our sakes;
God freely gives them with a bount'ous hand,
To our necessities, while here we live;   220
With mod'rate delectation, we may then
Freely Enjoy, what God hath given Gratis:
Those who Reject a Joy so good as this,
(Which Heav'n so freely offers) are to blame.

Such who Condemn the free and Chearful use   225
Of Earths Injoyments, do it for this cause:
All Temporary Honours, Riches, Pleasures,
Are vain, uncertain, short, and Transitory,
And in comparison of Heavenly joys,
They are not worthy of the least Esteem,   230
But rather to be scornfully despis'd.
   Tis True those Souls who often Contemplate,
The Heav'nly glories of Eternal Bliss,
Are above Earthly pleasures lifted up:
Such count Earths Joys comparatively none,   235
Or at the least not worthy their Esteem:
While their Blest Souls aspire to heav'nly joys,
With sweet desires they do forget the Earth.
And Ravished with Supersweet Delights,
Seeming to feed upon heav'ns Joys already.   240
And when their Souls are raised to that pitch
They seem to Trample underfoot the World.
'Tis certain no comparison can be,
'Twixt Heav'ns Eternity and Earthly time,
And in Comparison of Heav'nly joys,   245
Earth's best of Blessings, scarce deserve a name:
Yet in themselves, and in Respect to us,
And our necessities, to disesteem 'em.
Would make us guilty of a heinous Crime.
They are in worth and time to be Regarded,   250
As they're free gifts to us giv'n by the hand
Of God himself as Tokens sent from Heav'n
Not only for our needs, But to delight us,
Which may appear, because unto our sense,
They do afford us various Delectations,   255
Beyond necessity to Satiate.
Nor is this all, God doth not only give,
But lovingly Commands us to Enjoy,
Those Gracious Earnests of his future Love.
So that without abuses we may use them;   260
In their true use and moderate Enjoyance;
Which may Attract, Encourage, and Invite,
To all commendable and worthy Acts,
And raise our Souls to God from whence they came.
   Tis certain there are many Dangers, hid   265
In Temporary, *Riches, Honours, Pleasures,*
Terrestrial Greatness, greatly may provoke

To all Ambition, and Intemp'rate Vice,
Yet guided by an Alsufficient Grace,
All those Impediments we may avoid,   270
And all into Felicity Convert.
When our Affections to those ills incline,
We ought with Reason, and with Grace consult
Such ill Desires to conquer and subdue.
It is more praise and glory to do well,   275
When in the middest of Greatest Temptations,
Than to be good for meer necessity;
(Who in an Eunuch Chastity admires?)
And as the Dangers greater, so we shall
Greater Rewards gain by such Victory;   280
Whereas to bind our selves by Sequestration,
Thereby to shun things Lawful and Expedient,
Which may, and ought with moderate Delight,
By us be us'd, because there's danger there,
Argues a feeble and distrustful mind.   285
    But for a man to know the highest joys
This World affords, and yet without offence;
To Live therein, and as a Master use them,
In all Respects, and yet without abuse;
One, who can as he list Compel the World   290
To be his Servant, and will then do well,
When he's hedg'd round about with great Temptations,
Certainly such a man in Heav'n, shall be
Crown'd with the brighter Diadem of Glory:
What tho' no man can serve two Masters well,   295
The Supream God, and the Inferiour Mammon,
He's not concern'd, as being not the Man;
This Man subjects to one, Commands the other,
Owns God his Master, makes the World his Slave.
    'Tis further yet Objected, Abstinence   300
Suits best, and fittest to prepare the mind.
For Divine Exercise and Contemplation;
And next that many vicious Men Enjoy,
The Earth's Felicities, which Good men want,
Which shews they are Impediments to Goodness   305
Also our Saviour doth expresly say,
'Tis hard for Rich men to Inherit glory,
And that the Meek, the Mournful, and Deject
Are rather Blessed than Voluptuous men.

Tis true, that Fasting best prepares the mind,   310
'Tis therefore requisite to Fast and Pray,
Retiring from the Pleasures of the World;
This is a Duty pleasing unto God,
And beneficial to the mind and body;
Purging our natures clean from sloth and dulness   315
Making us more Angelick, free and quick,
In the performance of our good Devotion;
It Aptifies our Souls, to Entertain
More Heav'nly and Divine Illumination.
But let Convenient Order be observ'd,   320
As there's a time to Mourn and be Deject,
A time from lawful Comforts to refrain;
So there's a time wherein we may Rejoyce,
May use and not refuse those Creature Gifts,
And Blessings, which our God so freely offers: 325
But in good order too, and times convenient
Using a Temp'rate Custom in their use,
That in their use we may attain their Blessing.
When by assistance of the Heav'nly Grace,
We can our minds unto that temper bring,   330
While in the fulness of all Earthly joys,
Which like our vassals wait on our Commands;
That how, and at our pleasure we may use,
And yet contemn them, when they intervene
Our heav'n born Souls, and our approach to Heav'n   335
Then notwithstanding all their Vanities,
Their Real Dangers, and Impedements,
We to their End may use them, and as such
May with content, with Chearfulness, and freedom,
Extract their sweetness with a Heavenly mind.   340
Can we with *Lot* in *Sodom* live untainted?
Or with our Saviour Temp'rate mong sinners
When *Quires* of *Syrens* Tempt to ill Designs,
Yet in the midst of all Allurements Chaste,
Is worth the name of Conquest, and Obtains   345
Vice-victors wreaths of Laurel: for whose brows
Crowns of Immortal honour are prepar'd,
Among those Heav'nly Inexhausted Treasures.
Then Blessed are the Rich, the Great and Noble,
Whose Stations are above those Cob-web Laws,   350
Which keeps in Awe the Low and vulgar Crowd,
Yet can withstand the strongest of Temptations,

Provoking, and Enchanting, with Allurements;
Such who have Pow'r to Sin without Controul;
Yet in the Throng of all those Charming baits,   355
Can overcome Temptation in its pow'r,
Such Heroes Trampling on the Tempters head,
May sweetly Triumph as victorious Souls.
    That many good men want, what bad Enjoy.
May be to Quicken and Refine their Souls,   360
With Heav'nly Graces, and Increase their Glory:
In that Cælestial Happiness to Come.
That vicious men have what the Vertuous want,
May be to make their Misery the Greater,
With Greater punishment for Misimprovement: 365
Or for what other causes, only known,
To the free Donor of all kinds of Good.
Yet many Regular, and Pious men,
As *Abrah'm*, *Job*, and divers others, have
Possessed, and Enjoy'd Terrestrial Comforts;   370
Not few, but in great Plenty, and Abundance;
And *Christ* Himself, did at the Marriage Feast,
Approve, and use them; least we should mistake,
And count those Evils, which our God calls Good:
Good in themselves, indeed, and yet they are   375
But of indifferent natures, unto us,
Both Good, and Ill, as used, or abus'd;
Those who these high Felicities Enjoy,
In their most true and useful Excellence,
Can use them and contemn them as they please;   380
This shews of Stronger Sanctity and Grace,
Then by Recluseness to Abandon all,
And will, by consequence, be best Rewarded.
    Then doubtless 'tis Erronious to maintain,
Religion should deject, or cast us down,   385
Which rather Quickens, and with Comfort Chears
The Mourning and Dejected, Lifting up
Their drooping minds, to view their Kingdoms Glory,
Filling their Souls with perfect joy and peace;
It makes Earth's Happiness appear the sweeter,   390
When we enjoy the same, with Heav'nly minds.
    When we're Commanded to forsake the World,
'Tis understood its Vices and Abuses;
For certainly its good is not intended.
So to forsake our Parents, Wives, and Children,   395

Nay hate them; can it justly be suppos'd,
He who Commands, to Honour, and to Love,
Such our Relations, contradicts him self;
No doubtless, but our all to Disesteem,
When it with Christ in Competition stands,   400
And seek to be preferr'd in our Affections,
To those Exalted Joys Compris'd in him.
    When in these Comforts we receive Delight.
Through them, as Perspects, we Direct our Eye
Above the *Spheres,* viewing that bount'ous hand,   405
That free Disposer of all kinds of good,
From whom they come, and Contemplate in them,
A Glimpse of that Eternal weight of glory,
God, and in him the fulness of all Pleasures.
    By the dim Eye of Reason we may view,   410
Through this Perspective of our Earthly joy,
As t'were, a glance of Heav'ns Felicity;
These are but Invitations to that fulness,
Of which by help of Faith we gain a Taste,
If we Consider but these Earthly Things,   415
Reason will tell us, if in Creatures are
Such Worth, and Excellency, how much more
May we Conceive of the Creators Worth,
From whom, as little Droppings, these descend.
If we perceive some pleasure in these Drops,   420
What will that Ocean of Delight afford.
    When we the Azure Cannopy Survey,
Deck'd *with those bright* and Glorious Rouling *Torches;*
It mounts our minds in Raptur'd Contemplation,
With Rev'rence, up to the Admired Author,   425
With Awe, *with* Joy, *with* Fear, with Love to think
How great their Lord is, who above 'em dwells;
These but by Reason view'd, will make us own,
He is all Wisdom and Immence in Pow'r.
We with our Corp'ral Eye, can gaze unto   430
The *Spangled* Spheres, and *view those* Lights *of* Heav'n,
Whose dazling, glorious, silver brightness, gives
A pleasant delectation; higher thence
Our Sprightly Souls, by winged Reason mounts,
To view the Impartial Throne, and Contemplate   435
Those Sence-Surpassing glories that attend it:
So that through Earthly Comforts, our dull Eyes
By Reasons Light, as through a Tellescope

May look to Heav'n, To God himself, and see
Some Glimpses of his Goodness, and his Pow'r,   440
And in some measure may already Taste,
Of those Reserved Sweets of Heav'nly Pleasures.
    But when we add Faiths Light, to Reasons Eye,
We far more plain, and clearly, can discern
God, in the mid'st of his Reserv'd Rewards,   445
Touching the Longing Palates of our Souls,
With fuller Cups of those Cælestial Joys,
And by a Spiritual conveyance feasts,
Our Ravish'd Souls with symptomes of his Love.
    How frequent may we find in Sacred Writ,   450
Metaphors, Similies, Comparisons,
Drawn from these Temp'ral Things that are in sight,
To signify to us Heav'ns unseen Glory,
As Riches, Honours, Pleasures, Kingdoms, Crowns,
Speaks to our sense the Highest State of Glory,   455
By such known Language Heav'n conveys to us,
High Apprehensions of Eternal Bliss;
Faith Exercis'd on these is of such force,
As to present our minds with future things,
Faith Soars aloft, and thence (preventing time)   460
Descends with Samples of those Joys to come.
    Let's often then by Faith and Reason Climb,
From Earthly Comforts up to Heav'nly Joys,
And Ruminate upon those Glorious Mansions,
Treasures, Crowns, Kingdoms, That Eternal Joy   465
Which we Expect hereafter to possess,
In him, in whom alone all fulness Dwells.
    The Poor, Despis'd, and Miserable man,
Hopes all his Comfort in the World to come,
Hopes to be Rich and Honourable there.   470
The Rich and Prosp'rous man with Reason thinks,
If he Enjoys Prosperity below,
And finds some Happiness consists therein,
He shall be much more happy, when posses'd
With Riches, whose duration never Ends.   475
Mount Contemplating Souls, a lofty pitch,
Upon the Soaring Wings of Faith and Reason,
To the Imperial Heav'n, To God on High,
Where of true pleasure thou may'st take thy fill.
    The Worlds vast Palace we may freely dwell in,   480
And let our Eyes, our Ears, and all our Senses,

Enjoy its Comforts with a chearful mind;
Since we have toleration from Above;
Still keeping pace with Time and Moderation.
Her lowest of Delights, are for that End   485
Created and Ordain'd; The Chirping Birds
Instructed in their warbling notes by nature,
Do Sing to please our Ears; whose Harmony
Affords to us a more Excelling use,
When we Contemplate on those Heav'nly Joyes,   490
Which are prepar'd for us, where our Ears
Shall be more Bless'd with an Angelick Quire
Of Heav'nly Musicks Lofty Rapid Aires,
Will Charm our Souls into an Extasy.
    The Senceless Fountains also seem to strive,   495
With their Soft purling Murmurs to Delight,
And Catch the Senses with their pretty pleasures;
Inviting us to think of those pure Streams,
Whose sweet Refreshings glads our Heav'nly City,
And of that Springing, Inexhausted fountain,   500
That whosoever Tasts, shall never thirst.
    When we Behold those Glorious Lights above,
And shining Beauties of the Starry Orb,
Think of that Glory, so Surpassing this,
That could we Spy the Gl[i]tt'ring of one Ray,   505
'Twould Dazle *with* its brightness *our weak* opticks,
And we with *Peter* should desire to Dwell,
Where we such Glorious Excellence behold.
    Or when we *Pallet*[4] those Delicious wines,
And Curious Dainties of most pleasing fruits,   510
Let them Excite our Appetites, to Taste
Of those Celestial feasts, of Love and pleasure,
Whose Endless sweetness is beyond our thoughts
This Heav'nly Manna, This Angelick Bread,
This Divine Nectar, is so sweet, so pure;   515
Did we but truly Taste thereof, we should
Be wholly Charm'd into a *Rapsody*,
Of Heav'nly Pleasures, Pleasures past Compare,
And in some small degree, our Souls might Relish
The sweetness of Eternal Joys on Earth.   520
    If thus the Earths Felicities we use,
Looking through them up to those joys beyond,

    [4] palate: taste.

And so Enjoy them with a heav'nly mind,
We may in them feel heav'nly joys below,
That when our days shall Terminate, we may 525
From Heav'n on Earth, to Heav'n in Heav'n ascend,
Where our Felicities can know no
                    End.

On a Sea-Storm nigh the Coast

All round the Horizon black Clouds appear;
                    A Storm is near:
Darkness Eclipseth the Sereener Sky,
                    The Winds are high,
Making the Surface of the Ocean Show 5
Like mountains Lofty, and like Vallies Low.

The weighty Seas are rowled from the Deeps
                    In mighty heaps,
And from the Rocks Foundations do arise
                    To Kiss the Skies 10
Wave after Wave in Hills each other Crowds,
As if the Deeps resolv'd to Storm the Clouds.

How did the Surging Billows Fome and Rore
                    Against the Shore
Threatning to bring the Land under their power 15
                    And it Devour:
Those Liquid Mountains on the Clifts were hurld
As to a Chaos they would shake the World.

The Earth did Interpose the Prince of Light,
                    'Twas Sable night: 20
All Darkness was but when the Lightnings fly
                    And Light the Sky,
Night, Thunder, Lightning, Rain, and *raging* Wind,
To make a Storm had all their forces joyn'd.

A POEM,
Upon the Caelestial Embassy Perform'd by Angels,
to the Shepherds on the Plains of Bethlehem,
at the Birth of our Redeemer

Angels in Heav'n, as we may say,
Keep one Eternal Holy-Day;
No *Fasts* there are, nor *Vigils* there,
But Triumphs are their constant cheer
Yet when their King vouchsaf'd to come,   5
And make this lower world his home,
    They were so kind we know,
To come and keep one holy day below,
Sent on a solemn Embassy, to tell
The world, how great a guest was coming there to dwell.   10

New Robes of Light, Heav'ns Liv'ry, they
Assume, more bright (by far) than day.
Yet not so bright as those, that there
The meanest Saint is us'd to wear;
For they foresaw, it might undo   15
The lower world, to view them so:
    The Luster of so bright
And shining presence, would but scare and frigh[t]
The Guilty world into Astonishment,
And fear they come to bring deserved punishment.   20

But on a milder Errand these
Are sent, an Embassy of Peace,
Therefore they take a milder flame,
And with their beams unpointed came
Having Communion from above,   25
To Publish universal Love;
    And being thus prepar'd,
That mortals at their sight might not be scar'd
Drest in their Trav'ling cloaths; Direct the way
Unto *that distant place where their great Sov'reign lay.*   30

Through rouling spheres and floods of flame,
Swifter than sight or thought they came
Toward the last, and lowest rounds,
Of the Etherial spreading bounds,

Which parts the high, from lower world,   35
And from those battlements they hurld
    Their Glances, to Survey
The lower Regions, and where *Bethle'm* lay
They spy a little round black spot, call'd Earth
This they conclude the place of their great Sov'reigns birth.   40

Cry they, Admiring then, is that!
(Pointing to Earth) that mighty Plat[1]
Where are those spacious Lands and Seas
Those mighty States and Monarchies
That mortals brag of, where's that pride   45
Which has so often Heav'n defy'd?
    And is the place so small?
What are the dwellers that about it Crawl?
Our Prince made *one of* them; how great above
How *small art thou below!* How *low the steps of Love.*   50

Down they decend, the clouds give way,
Those Regions all in darkness lay,
Until their Presence made it day;
In spite of th' interviewing shade.
They by their beams discov'ries made: 55
The Earth seems greater to their Eye,
As they draw nearer, Seas they spy,
    What space the Oceans fill,
And *how the lofty* tow'ring mountains, swell
Above the surface of those works of fame,   60
To *which the* lower worlds Inhabitants lay claim.

Cities, and Towns they spy, and amongst them
Juries[2] Metropolis *Jerusalem,*
In Fertile *Palestine,* nigh which they view
Bethle'm a little Town; to which they flew,   65
This *is the place* they'r sent to, here they cease
Their *long fetch'd Journey, to make known the peace.*
    Which their great Sov'reign now,
Was come himself in Person to bestow;
Such matchless condescention as that,   70
Makes all the heav'nly host amaz'd *with* wonder at.

[1] plot: piece of ground.
[2] Jewry's.

Amaz'd, twixt scorn and wonder, they
Smile to see how mean he lay;
That he, whom Heav'ns Immencitie
Could not contain, should crowded be,   75
And shrink into the central point,
Of the vast universe, and stint
   His greatness to a Place,
Of but a span amidst the Aiery space.
Will here, cry they, our Monarch keep his Court?   80
Must *this be now the place to which* we must Resort?

Then to the Plains of *Bethl'em* they move,
There to Proclaim this universal love,
Not to the Prince at Court, but to the Swains,
Who *watch their* flocks by night *upon those* Plains: 85
To them this Gracious Embassy is told,
Begining to Proclaim it thus BEHOLD;
(Amazing brightness drives away the dark.
Hark! Fellow Shepherds, Hark!
The Proem is an Exce. Exces are   90
Ushers to things most Admirably Rare.)
GLAD NEWS, OF UNIVERSAL JOY WE BRING;
THIS DAY IS BORN MANS ONLY SAVIOUR, CHRIST THE KING.

Gloria in Excelces

NICHOLAS NOYES

(1647–1717)

The bookseller, John Dunton, spoke fondly of Nicholas Noyes as "a hale, lusty man," one who was *all that's delightful in Conversation*." Indeed, Dunton's appraisal was in full accord with the opinion of Noyes's colleagues and acquaintances dating back to his student days at Harvard, where he was remembered for his verse writing. Yet Noyes, who enjoyed the warm regard of his parishioners at Salem, as well as the respect of his senior ministerial colleague John Higginson, is a man best remembered today for his part in the most infamous period of New England history, that of the Salem witchcraft trials.

Nicholas Noyes was born in Newbury, Massachusetts, in 1647. His father, a deacon at the Newbury Church, had emigrated from England a few years before the birth of his son. In 1663 Noyes entered Harvard College, graduating four years later with first-class honors. Subsequently he moved to Connecticut and was chosen by the General Court to preach at Haddam, though he was not ordained there. Noyes took part in King Philip's War as a chaplain, a service he rendered so well that he was offered two hundred acres of land in thanks at the close of the savage Indian insurrection. Perhaps it was Noyes's ambition that motivated his refusal of the gift, for he accepted soon afterward a position as assistant to the Reverend John Higginson of Salem, and was ordained there in 1683.

Noyes's pastorate promised to be a quietly satisfying one. His relationship with Higginson was excellent, and his preaching well received. As a college man, which his senior colleague was not, Noyes could expound upon the difficult scriptural passages whose explication required formal, classical education. In addition, Noyes's personal friendships included some of New England's most illustrious men, among them the Mathers and Samuel Sewall.

Noyes's part in condoning the Salem witchcraft trials and executions is, while despicable to contemporary minds, in full accordance with seventeenth-century attitudes. Witchcraft, defined as the devil's work effected through a human agent, had been accepted belief throughout Europe since the Middle Ages. Numerous trials and executions are recorded, among which the Salem affair is not outstanding. Viewed from a perspective of nearly three centuries, the Salem trials appear hysterical and barbaric, but they can be understood, if not sympathized with, as the product of a psychology that saw life on earth as a very real enactment of the divine drama. The Puritans felt that God's forces often had to take drastic steps to rid the world of insidious diabolical powers. In approving purgation of the devil's agents, Reverend Nicholas Noyes was exercising his prerogative as a man of God.

Unlike several of his contemporaries involved in the trials, Noyes never publicly regretted his acts once the furor died down. We have no way of knowing, however, what restitution he may have made privately to the survivors of "witches'" families. Noyes did not in his later years enjoy good health, and he died after a brief illness in 1717.

In his time Nicholas Noyes enjoyed prestige as a writer both of prose and verse. Among his works are sermons, anagrams, elegies, prefatory poems, and consolatory pieces. Working within traditional seventeenth-century forms favored by Puritans, Noyes showed no penchant for radical departure from current literary practice. His strongest theme is Puritan orthodoxy and the affirmation of tenets of New England Puritanism both in thematic statement and in literary execution. Unlike many of his contemporaries, Noyes did not lament in poetic stanzas the Puritan decline, the impending wrath of an increasingly impatient God, or the events portending New England's doom if she did not immediately mend her ways. Rather, his voice spoke positively of the Puritan pathway to God. His elegiac tone emphasizes the deceased's certain attainment of heaven rather than New England's irreparable loss. For Noyes the truly alchemical philosopher's stone for achievement of grace is "none, save pious *Meditation*."

A
Præfatory POEM
To the Little Book, Entituled,
Christianus per Ignem[1]

The *Fire* of *Meditation* burns
What *Sense* into the *Fancy* turns.
And all is Grist that comes to Mill
Where *thinking* is with *grace* and *skill*
For all men know the busie mind   5
Into one Object not confin'd.
The touch, the taste, Eye, Ear and Smell,
Matter provide for *musing* well.
Invention, Judgment, Memory,
And Conscience have a faculty,   10
To make *all* praise him that made *all:*
The *Sanctify'd thus bless Him shall.*
There is a *Stone* (as I am told)
That turns *all Metals* into *Gold:*
But I believe, that there is none,   15
Save pious *Meditation.*
Yet if there be, sure *this* excels,
That m[ade] them *Gold,* and all things else.
The *Brass,* the *Iron Doggs* and *Tongs,*
And *Bellows* that have *leather Lungs*   20
Fire, Wood, Brands, Ashes, Coals and *Smoke,*
Do all to *Godliness* provoke:
The *flame,* the *sparks, light, heat* and *motion,*
Are *Metamorphosed* to *Devotion.*
If *Godliness* be *greatest gain,*   25
And doth when Gold is dross, remain;
Conclude then this Cœlestial *Stone.*
Out does the *Philosophick One.*
    The *thoughts* are like a swarm of *Bees,*
That fly both *when* and *where* they please;   30
Those little folks both *work* and *play,*
About a *thousand flow'rs* a day.
Yet in their *lawless range* contrive,
To bring in *Honey* to their *Hive.*

[1] by Cotton Mather (Boston, 1702).

Who look for *method* in their march,   35
At *Honey making* are not arch.
The Sally's of our *Author's* Soul
So fly about without controul:
Sometimes they clamber *Heavens* steep,
And sometimes into *Hell* do peep.   40
Good meditation *both* improve,
For *both* to Godly living move.
Methinks I see him climb the *Sky*,
Viewing the *Flaming Fires* on High,
And how the *will of God, they do*,   45
That we on *Earth* may do so too.
And then to *Hell* he doth descend,
To know the Sinners woful end:
He stands aloof, and hears the cry
Of *Guilty worms* that *cannot die*,   50
But live in Lakes of *flaming Fire*,
That *never! Never!* shall Expire.
Then *fir'd* with *zeal*, like *Lion* bold,
Roars out, and *tells* what can't be *told;*
Warns men to *fly from Wrath to come*,   55
Before the Judge pronounce their doom.
So snatching *brands* from *Fire* and *Death*,
He may his *Fingers* burn therewith;
Yet better so, than *burn* our *Souls*,
By vexing God, and pleasing fools.   60
Our Author judg'd such thoughts as these
Would profit *men*, and *God* would please:
If so, he gets his Souls desire,
And spent his *time* well by the *Fire*.
Who live nigh to the *Frigid Zone*,   65
In *Pænitentials* may bemoan,
The loss of many precious hours,
The *Fire side* day and night devours:
For of all *loss* the *Fire* does bring
The *loss of time's* the saddest thing.   70
We have no cause to grudge at *him*,
Who fills his *time* up to the brim,
And works for God, himself, and friends,
Ev'n whilst he *warms his fingers ends.*
  Come Reader if thou dost aspire   75
To warm thy self by *Holy Fire*,
Come set by *this*, or take a *Coal*,
Which will both *light* and *heat* thy Soul:

And will perfume, and purifie
Thy mind, and make it heavenly. 80
It will not *scorch* thine eyes nor skin,
Nor will it *Carbonade* thy *Shin:*
Yet *Bones* and *Marrow* penetrates,
And like to like it generates.
Thine *Hearth* to make an *Altar* tries, 85
Thy self a *Living Sacrifice;*
And turns the use of common things
To *Incense* and *Burnt offerings.*
It will digest thy *Crudityes,*
And save from slander, chat, and lyes. 90
And will redeem the *time* thou hast
[On] other *Fire* been wont to wast.
[Pr]eacheth the *Refining trade,*
And of what *metal* thou art made;
[It] takes away the *dross* and *tin,* 95
Makes *Gold* without, and *Gold* within;
It makes a *New man* of the *Old,*
And cast's him in another mould.
  Now if thy *musing burn* not thus,
Thy *Fire's* an *Ignis fatuus.* 100
Fear lest the *Founder* melt in vain,
With but his labour for his pain:
Lest thou prove *Silver reprobate,*
Which God and man *reject,* and *hate,*
And when the *Great Refiner* come, 105
Thou prove a *Caput mortuum.*[2]
  Excuse me, Reader, I have *done,*
But thou hast scarcely yet *begun:*
Come, read the Book, and by and by,
Thou wilt commend it, what need *I?* 110
And if the Authors *Fire* but burn,
Praise or *dispraise* will serve his turn.
But if *these thoughts* to thee seem vile,
Produce thine *own,* thou hadst the while;
If thine *burn purer,* I design, 115
To leave *his Fire,* and set by *thine:*
For I am *cold,* and need the *best,*
Mean while what *warms* me I have *blest.*

              Nicholas Noyes.

[2] literally, dead head.

The Rev. Nicholas Noyes to the Rev. Cotton Mather
Salem Aug: 15. 1706[1]

You plant like Paul, you Water like Apollos,
You set fair Coppyes, happy he that follows
You bid fair for it, let Heaven make it doe;
And by your hands, wash the Æthiopean toe.
Christs grace and blood applyed, makes white within,   5
And clenseth from the Guilt and Stain of Sin.
The resurrection whiten will the Skin;
The great refiner and the blessed Fuller,
Will one day make the Saints all of a coler.
And all be blacker then the Sons of Cham,   10
That are not Whitned by the Spotless Lamb.
And they of all men only shall be free,
Christ bought, and brought out of Captivity.
The Slaves of Sin and Satan then shall stand
Bound hand and foot, though here they did command.   15
The pious Master and the pious Slave,
The Liberty of Sons of God shall have.
But these are riddles unto Mammons fooles,
That use their Slaves as if they had no Soules;
For want of saving theres their own lose will;   20
If you shall make them Wise more Wonders still,
New-Englands Thaumatorgos[2] you shall be,
And have the thanks, both of the bond and Free.

---

[1] Addressed "To Mr. C:M: in Boston," these lines are written on the same
sheet on which Noyes wrote to Cotton Mather on the question of Negro servants.

[2] an allusion to the title Cotton Mather assigned to Book VI of his *Magnalia*,
and to Mather as "miracle worker."

A Prefatory Poem,
On that Excellent Book, Entituled,
Magnalia Christi Americana:
Written by the Reverend
Mr. *COTTON MATHER, Pastor of a Church at*
Boston, New-England

To the Candid Reader

Struck with huge Love, of what to be possest,
I much despond, good Reader, in the *quest;*
Yet help me, if at length it may be said,
Who first the *Chambers of the South* display'd?
Inform me, Whence the *Tawny People* came?   5
Who was their Father, *Japhet, Shem,* or *Cham?*
And how they straddled to th' *Antipodes,*
To look *another World* beyond the Seas?
And when, and why, and where they last broke ground,
What Risks they ran, where they first Anchoring found?   10
Tell me their Patriarchs, Prophets, Priests and Kings,
Religion, Manners, Monumental things:
What *Charters* had they? What Immunities?
What Altars, Temples, Cities, Colonies,
Did they erect? Who were their publick Spirits?   15
Where may we find the *Records* of their Merits?
What Instances, what glorious Displayes
Of Heav'ns high Hand, commenced in their dayes?
These things in *Black Oblivion* covered o'er,
(As they'd ne'er been) lye, with a thousand more.   20
A vexing Thought, that makes me scarce forbear
To stamp, and wring my Hands, and pluck my Hair,
To think, what Blessed *Ignorance* hath done,
What fine Threads *Learnings* Enemies have spun,
How well Books, Schools, and Colledge may be spar'd,   25
So *Men* with *Beasts* may fitly be compar'd!
Yea, how *Tradition* leaves us in the lurch,
And who, nor stay at home, nor go to Church:
The *Light-within-Enthusiasts,* who let fly
Against our *Pen and Ink Divinity;*[1]   30

[1] Anne Hutchinson and others insisted on their "inner light," instead of the learned Puritan sermon, as a guide to God.

Who boldly do pretend (but who'll believe it?)
If *Genesis* were lost, they could retrieve it;
Yea, all the *Sacred Writ;* Pray let them try
On the *New World,* their *Gift of Prophecy.*
For all them, the *New Worlds Antiquities,*   35
Smother'd in everlasting Silence lies;
And its *First Sachims* mention'd are no more,
Than they that *Agamemnon* liv'd before.
The poor *Americans* are under blame,
Like them of old, that from *Tel-melah*[2] came,   40
Conjectur'd once to be of *Israel's* Seed,
But no *Record* appear'd to prove the Deed:
And like *Habajah's* Sons,[3] that were put by
The *Priesthood,* Holy things to come not nigh,
For having lost their *Genealogy.*   45
Who can past things to memory command,
Till one with *Aaron's Breast-plate* up shall stand?
Mischiefs Remediless such Sloth ensue;
God and their Parents lose their Honour due,
And Childrens Children suffer on that Score,   50
Like Bastards cast forlorn at any Door;
And they and others put to seek their Father,
For want of such a *Scribe* as COTTON MATHER:
Whose Piety, whose Pains, and peerless Pen,
Revives *New-England's* nigh-lost Origin.   55
    Heads of our *Tribes,* whose *Corps* are under ground,
Their Names and Fames in *Chronicles* renown'd,
Begemm'd on *Golden Ouches*[4] he hath set,
Past Envy's Teeth, and Times corroding Fret:
Of *Death* and *Malice,* he has brush'd off the Dust,   60
And made a *Resurrection of the Just:*
And clear'd the Lands Religion of the Gloss,
And *Copper-Cuts* of *Alexander Ross.*[5]
He hath related *Academic* things,
And paid their *First-Fruits* to the King of Kings;   65
And done his *Alma Mater* that just Favour,

[2] a town in Babylon, of uncertain location.
[3] Neh vii 73–74.
[4] brooches, ornaments.
[5] Alexander Ross (1591–1654), Anglican clergyman, wrote voluminously in English and Latin, and through Laud's influence was appointed Chaplain to Charles I. The allusion here is to the portraits of Ross prefixed to several of his books, e.g. *Medicus Medicatus* (1645), owned by the Mather family.

To shew *Sal Gentium*[6] hath not lost its Savour.
He writes like an *Historian,* and *Divine,*
Of *Churches, Synods, Faith,* and *Discipline.*
Illustrious Providences are display'd,   70
Mercies and Judgments are in colours laid;
Salvations wonderful by Sea and Land,
Themselves are *Saved* by his Pious Hand.
The *Churches Wars,* and various *Enemies,*
Wild *Salvages,* and wilder *Sectaries,*   75
Are notify'd for them that after rise.
  This *well-instructed Scribe* brings *New* and *Old,*
And from his *Mines* digs richer things than Gold;
Yet freely gives, as *Fountains* do their Streams,
Nor more than they, Himself, by giving, drains.   80
He's all *Design,* and by his *Craftier Wiles*
Locks fast his Reader, and the Time beguiles:
Whilst *Wit* and *Learning* moves themselves aright,
Thro' ev'ry line, and *Colour* in our sight,
So interweaving *Profit* with *Delight;*   85
And curiously inlaying both together,
That he must needs find Both, who looks for either.
  His *Preaching, Writing,* and his Pastoral Care,
Are very much, to fall to one Man's share.
This added to the rest, is admirable,   90
And proves the Author *Indefatigable.*
Play is his Toyl, and *Work* his Recreation,
And his *Inventions* next to Inspiration.
His *Pen* was taken from some *Bird of Light,*
Addicted to a swift and lofty Flight.   95
Dearly it loves *Art, Air,* and *Eloquence,*
And hates *Confinement,* save to *Truth* and *Sense.*
  Allow what's known; they who write Histories,
Write many things they see with others Eyes;
'Tis fair, where nought is feign'd, nor undigested,   100
Nor ought, but what is credibly attested.
The Risk is his; and seeing others do,
Why may not I speak mine Opinion too?
  The *Stuff* is true, the *Trimming* neat and spruce,
The Workman's good, the Work of publick use;   105
Most piously design'd, a publick Store,
And well deserves the publick Thanks, and more.

  Nichólas Noyes, Teacher of the Church at *Salem.*

[6] salt of the race.

May 28th. *1706.,*
To my Worthy Friend,
Mr. James Bayley,
Living (if Living) in Roxbury   *A   POEM*

My Old Companion! and my Friend!
I cannot Come, and therefore send.
Some pity should be shown to One
That's heavy laden with the Stone;
That's wearied out with fits of pain   5
Returning like Clouds after Rain.
Alas! my Brother, what can I
Do for thee, more than Pray and Cry,
To Counsel, and to comfort try,
And bear a part by Sympathy?   10
Excuse me, though I Write in Verse,
It's usual on a Dead mans Hearse:
Thou many a Death hast under-gone,
And Elegies made of thine own.[1]
    Our Saviours Funeral Obsequies,   15
One Celebrates before His eyes;
And He the Oyntment kindly takes,
That for His Burial she makes.
Two Saints array'd in glorious dress,
Appear, and talk of His Decease;   20
Whose Death from thine did take the Sting,
And wholsome make that Poyson thing.
And I have seen thine hand, and Pen,[2]
Play on that Cockatrices[3] den
In measur'd Lines, as if inspir'd,   25
And *Paroxisms* had only fir'd
An holy Soul with flaming zeal,
That flesh-pains it could scarcely feel.
What, in one breath, both Live and Dye,
Groan, Laugh, Sigh, Smile, Cry, Versifie?   30
Is this the Stone? are these the pains

[1] Noyes alludes to poems Bailey wrote but which are apparently no longer extant.

[2] another allusion to Bailey's verse.

[3] a serpent, identified with the Basilisk, said to have the power of killing by mere glance, and to be hatched from a cock's egg.

Of that Disease that plagues the Reins?⁴
That slyly steals into the bladder?
Then bites, and stings like to the Adder.
Is this the Scourge of Studious men?   35
That leaves unwhipt scarce five of ten
And Whips them once, and over again.
In Christs School there's smart Discipline,
To make His Scholars more divine;
Blest they who do not take offence,   40
Whose joy lyes in the Future Tense;
Who when they are in most distress,
Love Christ the more, and not the lest.
His Yoke is easy, burthen light,
To them that understand things right;   45
And none will afterward complain,
Who Hell escape, and Heaven obtain.
     Well, if this Stone should do its worst,
It cannot make thee be accurst:
For if thou shouldst be Ston'd to Death,   50
And this way Pelted out of Breath,
Thou wilt like *Stephen* fall asleep,
And free from pain for ever keep.
     Great Pains, with as great Patience, may
Fall little short of *Martyrs* Pay: 55
For Christs Rewards are all of Grace,
No Merit but His, in either case.
Our Lord thee good Example offer'd,
Who learn'd Obedience while He suffer'd,
Who for the joy was set before Him,   60
Endur'd the Cross He bore, and bore Him,
Who though He Pray's it might be gone,
Yet also said, Thy will be done.
That Stone which builders did refuse,
For thy Foundation choose, and use.   65
     Think also when thine Agonies
Are most intense, and force loud cryes,
They are not worthy to compare
With those that Christ for thee did bear:
Yea, think what Christ for thee hath done,   70
Who took an harder, heavyer Stone
Out of thine *Heart* and it is gone.

⁴ kidneys.

Who did thy Wo[und]ed *Spirit* cure
Of Soul-pains, that none can endure,
And this is easyer to be borne,   75
For in the *Flesh* abides this thorne:
And if Christ do not it remove,
Sufficient is His Grace, and Love,
To give thee comfort, and Support,
Because this pain is light, and short;   80
And works for thee the Glory great,
That doth exceed in length, and weight.
Besides, these Torments cant compare,
With Torments that *Eternal* are:
For they are utterly undone,   85
That rowl the *Sisyphean* Stone;[5]
Not they whose pains are limited,
And are releas'd, as soon as dead.
Add one thought more; that this distress
Makes thee partake of *Holiness:*   90
The more the flesh is hack'd, and hew'd,
The more Corruption is subdu'd.
Life is to thee the less endear'd,
And *Death* by thee is the less fear'd:
For it's but once thou hast to dye,   95
And then Live to Eternity.
The weary Body shall have Rest,
Thy Soul from thence forth shall be blest;
Thy dust be Life; for Christ shall find it,
And leave this cruel Stone behind it.   100
One Stone God's truth doth bring to light;
Another makes Iron sharp, and bright:
A third our grain doth Pulverize,
And Separate the chaff likewise.
Thine, all these profits bring to thee,   105
In nobler sense than th' other three.
Thine proves thy Grace to be Sincere;
Of rust, and dulness, doth thee clear.
And makes thee Watch, and Pray, and long
To change thy groans, for *Simeon's* Song.[6]   110

[5] In Greek myth, Sisyphus was punished by being forced eternally to roll a stone up a mountain in Hades, only to have the stone roll back to the foot of the hill ere reaching the summit.

[6] Luke ii 29: "Lord, now lettest thou thy servant depart in peace, according to thy Word."

Though grinding pains thy nature bruise,
They fit thee for thy Masters use:
And when thy dust shall be refin'd;
Thou shalt be neither pain'd, nor pin'd;
Nor full of petrifying juice,   115
Hard Studies, Heats, and Colds produce.
Then shall hid Manna be thy fare,
In which no gritt, nor gravel are;
Yea, Christ will give thee a *White Stone*,
With a *New Name* engrav'd thereon,   120
To the Enjoyer only Known.
Lord, once thou saidst, Arise and Walk;
Thy Words were Works; Mine are but Talk;
Be pleas'd to bid thy son, Good chear!
And say, Thy Sins forgiven are!   125
Then, Sink, or Swim; or Live, or Die,
He will thee greatly Glorifie.
Say so to me too, so will I.
A Man of Sorrow once Thou wast,
And still a fellow-feeling hast,   130
So to Thy Pity, I commend
My self, and my afflicted Friend.

Nicholas Noyes.

A Consolatory POEM
Dedicated unto Mr. COTTON MATHER;
Soon after the Decease of his Excellent
and Vertuous WIFE, that well-accomplished
Gentlewoman, Mrs. Abigail Mather,
Who Changed Earth for Heaven, Dec. 1. 1702
In the Thirty Third year of her Age

Sir, After you have wip'd the Eyes
Of *Thousands* in their Miseries,
And oft condol'd the heavy Fates
Of those that have Surviv'd their *Mates,*
Its come at length to your own Turn   5
To be *One half within an Urn.*
(Your Christ would have it so be done!)
Your *other Self's* torn off, and *Gone.*
Gone! Said I. Yes, and that's the worst:

Your Wife's but *gone to Heaven first*.   10
   You do *run fast*, but she *out run*,
Hath *Made* her self, not you *Undone;*
Pray, let her *Wear* what she hath *Won!*
Grudge not her *Happiness* above;
You Live by *Faith*, and she by *Love*.   15
To *live* is *Christ*, to *Dy* is *Gain;*
Betwixt you *both*, you have the *Twain*.
She was prepar'd for her Release;
And so prepar'd *Departs in Peace*.
And who would *Live*, that God makes fitt   20
To *Dy*, and then gives a *Permitt?*
And who would choose a World of Fears,
Ready to fall about their Ears,
That might get up above the Spheres?
And leave the Region of dread Thunder   25
To them that Love the World that's under:
Where *Canker'd Breasts* with Envy broyle,
And *Smooth Tongues* are but *dipt in Oyle;*
And *Cain's* Club only doth ly by,
For want of Opportunity.   30
Yea, who would Live among *Catarrhes,*
Contagions, Pains, and *Strifes*, and *Wars?*
That might go up above the Stars;
And live in *Health*, and *Peace*, and *Bliss,*
Had in that World; but *Wish'd* in this?   35
   Disturb not then her precious Dust,
With *Threnodies* that are unjust.
Let not cross'd *Nature* now repine;
Sir, *Grace* hath taught you to resign
To *Christ*, what *Nature* called, *Mine!*   40
To call for *Mourners* I came not;
There are too many on the Spott.
Already all the Neighbourhood
Have *Wept* as much as *Weepings* good,
Nor to Embalm her Memory;   45
She did *That*, e're she came to dy;
'Tis done to long Eternity!
   This *Phoenix* built her *Nest of Spice,*
Like to the *Birds of Paradise;*
Which when a [*Feaver*] sett on *Fire,*   50
Her Soul took Wing, and soared higher;
But left choice *Ashes* here behind,

Christ will for *Resurrection* find.
   My Muse, pass by her *Out Side Grace;*
Say *nothing* of a Comely Face;   55
Nor what most Lovely pleasancies
Dwelt Chastly on her Charming Eyes.
These and such *Lilly-Glories* fade,
Absconded all in *Deaths* dark shade.
Yet these again shall Rise and Shine,   60
Ten Thousand times more bright and fine;
   Say *little* of her *Inside Grace;*
For this World is a Spiteful place;
And takes it self for Injured
If Saints are Prais'd, *Alive* or *Dead;*   65
And they for *Witts* are in Esteem,
That *Heavens Dwellers* do blaspheme.
I hate their Humour, I profess,
It Smells of such rank Wickedness.
Yet this Saint shall not go her wayes,   70
Without a Sprig or two of *Bayes;*
Who well deserv'd far greater Praise.
   Her *Maiden Vertues* rendred her,
A *Meet-Help* for a Minister.
For the *best Women*, the just *Jewes*   75
(*You* know) this proper phrase would use;
A Woman worthy for to be
Wife to a Priest: And such was She.
Good; Studying that her Husband too
Nothing but *Good* might always do.   80
How *Frugal,* yet how *Generous!*
How *Modest,* yet how *Courteous!*
How *Silent,* yet how *Affable!*
How *Wise,* how *Pure,* how *Peacable.*
As *Child,* her *Parents Joy;* as *Wife,*   85
Her *Husbands Crown,* and Heart, and Life.
As *Mother* She, a *Fruitful Vine,*
Her *Offspring* of an Holy Line,
By Holy Nurture made them Shine.
   More might be said: But lest I vex   90
And stir the Envy of her Sex,
I'le not proceed in Commendation,
But leave her to their Imitation;
Who having her bright vertue kept
In Lustre; *Thus* at length She slept.   95

A Sickness full of *Mysteries,*
With Violence did on her Sieze.
She *Thirty Weeks* felt Deaths Attack,
But *Fervent Pray'r* still kept her back.
Her *Faith* and *Patience* t'was to Try,   100
And Learn *Us* how to *Live* and *Dy.*

At Last, all Thoughts of *Life* were null'd;
For *Earth* by *Heaven* was out-pull'd
And She straight way must thither go,
Whether her good Friends would or no.   105
So with the *Wings* of *Faith* and *Love,*
And Feathers of an Holy *Dove,*
She bid this Wretched World adieu,
And Swiftly up to *Heaven* flew.
Yet as She flew, let this World fall,   110
Heav'n, Heav'n will make amends for all!

NICHOLAS NOYES

PHILIP PAIN

(c. 1647–c. 1667)

So little is known about Philip Pain that even his first name is in doubt. Among the many Pain[e]s in seventeenth-century New England there appears no Philip on any registry, leaving the possibility that a printer's error is responsible for the initial "P." It appears that in 1667 or 1668 Pain, "suffering Shipwrack was drowned," probably in his twentieth year. Beyond these sparse data, Pain's brief life remains a mystery.

The collection of Pain's extant verses, entitled *Daily Meditations,* contains his poetic prologue "The Porch" and sixty-four "Meditations." Their recurrent theme is stated in Pain's subtitle, "Quotidian Preparations for, and Considerations of Death and Eternity," and restated in "The Porch," where the poet suggests that the individual break through his sense of sin and guilt to overcome fear of death. It is preparation for death that is the central theme of Pain's collection of verses.

Pain's choice of the meditative poem was altogether consistent with seventeenth-century poetic usage and with the particularly Puritan adaptation of it. Previous to and throughout the first half of the seventeenth century a meditative poetic tradition gradually was formed of which Donne, Crashaw, Vaughan, Herbert, Quarles, and, later, Edward Taylor were part. Their poems grew from a broad cultural acceptance of the individual's duty to make spiritual meditation a part of his daily life.

In general the meditative process followed a consistent pattern. It began with an intellectual consideration of the relationship of an individual to his God. Aided by memory, the individual's faculty of understanding brought him closer to God, whereupon his will began to work on his affections until, at length, every part of him was involved in the meditation. This was not just recitation of prayer, or emotional rhapsodizing, or cold theological speculation. Rather, in meditation, all of the individual's faculties co-ordinated to give him a better understanding of his man-God relationship.

Puritan divergence from the Catholic and Anglican meditation was more of degree than kind. In the Catholic view the ultimate meditation purpose was to gain understanding through an imaginative similitude with the object of meditation. Thus an individual meditating on the crucifixion of Christ would ultimately gain an appreciation for his Redeemer's trials if he himself used his senses and imagination to enter into those trials. Expectedly, the Puritans rejected such sensuous extension of the individual toward a mystical experience they did not believe in. For them the individual ought always to maintain a marked spiritual distance from the object of his meditation.

In poetry the Catholic-Anglican-Puritan meditative spectrum is reflected in use of imagery. The sanguine images the Catholic poet Crashaw used without reservation were abhorrent to the Puritan, who found them uncontrolled and tasteless. Even the rich sensuous images of Herbert sometimes displeased the Puritans, who did not approve of lengthy dwelling upon a particular image. An acknowledged artist such as Edward Taylor could strike a balance inviolate of his Puritan beliefs while yet maintaining his artistic integrity. Philip Pain, however, is frequently unable to work his images into a cohesive thematic pattern, and is therefore too often forced into flat thematic statement. Another of his poetic limitations is an inability to accommodate diction to rhythm, resulting in lines stuffed with verbal feet which contribute little to meaning.

Pain's "Porch" deserves mention because its historical significance is relevant to Pain's theme throughout the "Meditations." Traditionally it was the portico from which the ancient Stoics taught that true happiness lay in freedom from the bondage of human appetites. Pain's "Porch" functions similarly to remind his reader that only through transcendence of the carnal state in death can an individual find eternal happiness. His "Porch" also refers to the church portico, onto which he invited the reader before retiring into the church proper for the "Meditations."

The Porch[1]

To live's a Gift, to dye's a Debt that we
Each of us owe unto Mortality.
What though the dead do ghastly look, and we
Like Children frighted are even but to be
Spectators of a dying man or woman?   5
Yet nothing's to be fear'd that is so common.
It is not *Death* that we in them do see;
It's but the *Mask* wherewith 'twill vailed be.
Yet where's the man or woman that can look
Death in the face, as in some pleasing book?   10
Can we contented be to view our face
In such a dreadful, doleful Looking-glass?
O where's the man or woman that can cry,
Behold I Come, Death I desire to dye?
O where's the man or woman that can say,   15
Lord, I desire my dissolution day?
And what's the reason 'tis so hard to dye,
To leave this world so full of vanity?
What makes it terrible? naught but the sense
Of *guilt* and *sin:* Break down this potent fence,   20
And then be sure for aye you shall enjoy
Joyes everlasting, Everlasting joy.

Meditations for July 19, 1666 (*Fifth day*)

Meditation 1

Great God, how short's mans time; each minute speaks
He is but dust, and that his Vessel leaks.
Each moment of my momenta[r]y time,
Does plainly tell me 'tis not mine, but thine.
   He gives me time to live, and verily
   Ere long I shall have likewise time to dye.

[1] prefatory poem to Pain's *Daily Meditations; or, Quotidian Preparations for and Considerations of DEATH AND ETERNITY* . . . *begun July 19, 1666.*

Meditation 2

After the time of Life is ended, then
Oh there's *Another Time* for sons of men;
A great ETERNITY will surely come,
Of blessed Happiness, or cursed Doom.
    Lord, grant I may be one of those that may
    Enjoy the first with thee another day.

Meditation 3

Down to the grave I must ere long descend,
Leave all my friends behinde; thither I bend,
And steer my wearied Course unto that Port,
To which all sorts of Nations do resort.
    When I cast Anchor, grant, O Lord, that I
    May safely ride where Christ himself did lye.

Meditation 4

This World a Sea of trouble is, and Man
Is swimming through this vast wide Ocean.
The billows beat, the waves are angry, and
'Tis seldome that he spies a helping hand
    To buoy his head up. O great God, let me
    Be kept from sinking into misery.
This day is past; but tell me, who can say
That I shall surely live another day.

Meditations for July 25, 1666 (Fourth day)

Meditation 25

Alas poor Death, where does thy great strength lye?
'Tis true, I'me mortall, yet I cannot dye.
I tell thee, If I dye in Christ, it is
The way thou shew'st me to eternal bliss.
    By death I live if that I live to Christ,
    And then thou'lt say the mark I have not mist.

Meditation 26

Alas, what's Sorrow? 'tis our portion here;
The Christian's portion, Trouble, Grief, and Fear:
He is *The* Man of Sorrows here below
Of all the men on earth; yet let us know,
 Christ left his Grave-clothes, that we might when grief
 Draws tears, or blood, not want an Handkerchief.

Meditation 27

Is Death so formidable? Can the chance
Of one poor day change our fresh Countenance?
Is there so much in Death, that we should be
Like Children frighted at our destiny?
 Of Heaven give me assurance (Lord) and I
 Shall ne're believe Death looks so dreadfully.

Meditation 28

Could I in greatness farre surmount the skie,
Or yet in glory could the Sun out-vie;
Could I be more then any man that lives,
Great, Fair, Rich, Wise, all in Superlatives:
 Yet if I were still mortal, there would be
 A debt still to be paid to death by me.
Lord, as thou givest me more hours to live,
So with it, Oh do thou thy grace me give.

Meditations for July 26, 1666 (*Fifth day*)

Meditation 29

How mutable is every thing that here
Below we do enjoy? with how much fear
And trouble are those gilded Vanities
Attended, that so captivate our eyes?
 Oh, who would trust this World, or prize what's in it,
 That gives, and takes, and changes in a minute?

Meditation 30

Sure every soul in this world hath its day
Of grace, and if he will improve it, may.
The time will come when it shall have an end,
Ev'n when we must unto the grave descend.
    Lord, help me now to know the things that do
    Belong unto my peace, and them pursue.

Meditation 31

We have no License from our God to waste
One day, one hour, one moment, that do haste
So swiftly from us in our sinful pleasures,
But rather to lay up for lasting treasures.
    Lord, spare me yet a little, that I may
    Prepare for Death, and for the Judgement-day.

Meditation 32

The damned now in Hell, that there do ly
In endless flames, that howl, and weep, and cry
For anguish great, this is their deepest Crime,
Heart-vexing trouble, *Oh Mispence of Time!*
    Oh who would rush into those flames of Fire,
    That of mis-spending time they may enquire?
Lord, let thy Terrours every day cause me
To prepare for my end, and ready be.

Meditations for August 1, 1666 (*Fourth day*)

Meditation 53

How often should we think of this, that we
Must ere long yield to Death's supremacie?
The time ere long will come, when we shall be
No more; and shortly we no time shall see.
    O that I might be then prepar'd for this
    So great a Change, and be receiv'd to Bliss.

Meditation 54

The sons of men are prone to forget Death,
And put it farre away from them, till breath
Begins to tell them they must to the grave,
And then, Oh what would they give but to have
    One year of respite? Help me, Lord, to know
    As I move here, so my time moves also.

Meditation 55

Whilst we live here, we have the blessed voice
Of God by Ministers, the blessed noise
And sound of Aarons Bells:[2] the time will be
When we no more of this shall hear or see.
    Help, Lord, that I may then improve the fame
    Unto the praise and glory of thy Name.

Meditation 56

The time will be, when we shall be *No more:*
Where will the World be then? 'Twill be *No more.*
Where will our Comforts be? They'll be *No more.*
Where will our Friends be then? They'll be *No more.*
    Lord, grant me then thy grace, lest that *No more,*
    Do seize upon me, and I be *No more.*
No More! *O solemn sound: This night I may*
Be struck by Death, and never see the day.

\aron was the patriarch of the Jewish church, and as such, gave his name
1 pastoral leaders.

FRANCIS DANIEL PASTORIUS

(1651–1720)

Francis Daniel Pastorius, born in Sommerhausen, Franconia, and educated at Strassburg, Basel, Jena, and Altdorf, traveled widely in Europe before being engaged by a Pietist group in Frankfurt as agent for fifteen thousand acres of land the group had purchased in the Colony of Pennsylvania to establish a settlement. Pastorius arrived in Philadelphia in 1683, founded the village of Germantown, and became successively bailiff, scrivener, justice of the peace, and founder of two schools, one in the new village and the other in Philadelphia.

A meticulous and energetic man, Pastorius kept full records of everything he did, from his day-to-day activities at home and in public life to a detailed list of his reading and writing in seven languages. We know, for example, precisely what he brought with him to Pennsylvania in August 1683: which books, which particular scientific instruments, what sorts of sponge, clothes brush, garden tools, and quill pens. We know who his traveling companions were, and his estimates of their characters and qualities. We know from his elaborate account of the founding of "Germanopolis" on October 24, 1683, the kind of soil, the quality of pasturage, and the varieties of trees and flowers and herbs in the district. And we know much from Pastorius' observant jottings about each of the twelve families —a total of 41 persons—that composed the first settlement of the new town.

Of most interest to students of literature is the record of Pastorius' reading and writing, in prose and verse, chiefly contained in his huge folio manuscript, *The Beehive*, begun by Pastorius in 1696 as a sort of encyclopedia for his two sons, John Samuel and Henricus, and today preserved in the Library of the University of Pennsylvania. Written in English, Latin, German, French, Dutch, Low German, and Greek, it contains philosophical, religious, and sociological commentary; agricultural and horticultural observations, formulae, and advice; accounts of Pastorius' comings and goings, projects and plans; opinions of current books purchased and sent to him by acquaintances; and, most important, lyrics, epigrams, rhymed proverbs, hymns, dedicatory and prefatory verses—poetry in an astonishing variety of forms, styles, and meters composed on an equally astonishing range of subjects.

In his elegies, anagrams, and verse paraphrases of Scripture, Pastorius stands well within the mainstream of seventeenth-century American poetry. His wealth of garden and herbal imagery, his rollicking humor, his regularly gentle but occasionally sharp satire, and his experiments in rhythms, structures, and rebus effects establish him not only as the first poet of consequence in Pennsylvania but also as one of the most important poets of early America.

[When I Solidly Do Ponder]

When I solidly do ponder,
How *Thoughts wander;* I must wonder,
 And for Shame exclaim, and own,
 Mine are ranging up and down.
Now on Eagle's Wings ascending   5
Far above the Skies, there spending
 Some good Minutes in a Song;
 But, alas! this lasts not long.
Unawares they are departing,
And themselves (like Arrows,) darting   10
 In the very Depth of Hell,
 Where the Damned wail and yell.
Weari'd with this frightful Crying,
They in haste from thence are flying,
 And as giddy-headed hurl'd   15
 Fore- and back-ward in the World.
Thro' Great Britain, France and Holland,
Denmark, Moscovy, Spain, Polland,
 Portugal and Italy,
 Oft'ner yet thro' Germany.   20
Hence returning to Braganza,
To the Cape of Bon Speranza;
 So, by way of Africa,
 Home to Penn Silvania.
Here I bid them to be quiet,   25
They deny: however try it,

Go to bed, and sleep almost;
But soon starting, take the Post,
And afresh begin to travel,
Not regarding Mire nor Gravel,   30
River, Valley, Swamps nor hill,
Presently light where they will.
Tripping, traping still the faster
Like a Cur, that lost his Master,
To and fro, from place to place,   35
Stir their Stumps, and run a Race.
Some times in the Garden ramble
From the Tulip to the Bramble:
From the Rose and Eglantine
To the Nep[1] or Columbine.   40
Then retiring leave these Flowers,
Sit a while in Shady Bowers,
With a Book to meditate,
And, as if it were, abate.
In a moment, loath to tarry,   45
Swiftly, as their feet can carry
Their small Bodies, whip away
In the Woods to seek a Stray.
Here they hith'r and thither straggle,
Gad, fig, f[r]isk, stir, waver, waggle   50
Course and roam, and rove about,
Till there is no Coming out.
Justly I may call them Gropers,
Gypsies, Runnagates, Landlopers,
Vagrants, Fugitives and Rogues,   55
That deserve the Stocks and Strokes.

Animus sine pondere velox.   *Horat.*[2]

[On His Garden Book]

I first would have him understand,
Whoever takes the same in hand,

[1] nepeta, catnip.
[2] Horace *Epistles* I. xii. 13: "miramur, si Democrati pecus edit agellos / cultaque, dum peregre est animus sine corpore velox" (We wonder that Democritus' herds ate up his fields and meadows, while his fast-moving mind wandered off by itself without his body).

That by my Contemplations
His mind should not
(Some seeming nought)
Be *drawn from any better Thought.*   5
And then, before he doth slight this,
Pray, Let him grant me Sight of his
Rare Garden Meditations;
Perhaps we shall be One at once.   10

If any be pleased to walk into my poor Garden, I heartily bid him or her welcome, *thus*

Friend, Coming in a friendly wise,
From East, West, North or South,
Take here the Owner's own advice:

Put nothing in thy mouth;
But freely Fill thy Nose and Eyes   5
With all my Garden's growth.
For, if thou imitate the Apes,
And Clandestinely steal my grapes,
One wishes thee the Belly-Gripes,
An other hundred Scaffold-Stripes, &c.   10
Therefore, Pray, Curb thy appetite,
And mind what I hereunder write:
    Do not Covet,
    Though thou Love it;
    But without any Bluster,   15
    Go Buy a lusty Cluster.
Now, On those Terms, I give thee leave to Enter,
And Penetrate from both Ends to the Center:
But do not Break, nor Take Stalks, Fruit, or Seed,
For We hereby are Otherwise agreed.   20
Such-like Contracts bind without Seal and hand,
A good man's Word exceeds a bad ones Bond.

[Most Weeds, whilst young]

Most Weeds, whilst young,
An easy hand can pluck;
But when grown strong,

Men then must pull and tuck.
This thus apply, Friend,   5
To thine Inward State,
What thoughts should die,
With speed eradicate:
Make no Delay
That Quick grass to destroy,   10
Before it may
The best of Plants annoy;
When once it sets
Its running Strings about,
And deep ground gets,   15
'Tis hard to Root it out.

[If thou wouldest *Roses Scent*]

If thou wouldest *Roses Scent*
Mend, and make more excellent,
Then thou formerly hadst them,
Plant but Garlick to their Stem;
Likewise, if a Friend of thine
Should to Goodness so incline,
As to lead a Vertuous life,
Let him take a Scolding Wife:
Thus Natura works, you see
Sometimes by Antipathy.

[When one or other rambles]

When one or other rambles,
To Fishermen and Shambles,
To Pothecaries Shops:
For Physick and for Vittles,
Which they cut with their Whittles,   5
And play the dainty Fops,
Then I go to my Garden,
But no flesh, nor Pope's Pardon,
Now in the time of Lent;
But herbs and Eggs there gather,   10
Whereon I'm feeding rather
Than on such graisement.

How be it a good Cony,
Young Chickens, Chees and honey,
I heartily do own,   15
Distasting likewise never
What Roots and Fruits soever
In Fields are sown and grown.
The best things for my Palat
Are parsnips, Corn and Sallet,   20
And sugar'd Apple-pyes,
For Med'cine I use Lillies:
They cure most all what ill is
In man's heart, brain, and Eyes.
Next Sage with hyssop rises,   25
Preferred to those Spices,
Fetcht from the East and West.
My pen now waxing weary,
I leave off to be airy:
Short Follies are the best.   30

[As often as some where before my Feet]

As often as some where before my Feet
I with a fine, rare, and fair Object meet,
I shut my Outward Eyes,
And bid my Inward rise
To Him, who made, and does uphold that Thing
So that my heart (whilst I His praises sing,)
To the Creator cleaves
And that quaint Creature leaves.
Concluding thus: If this, which is but vain,
Appears to men so handsom, deft and clean,
How beautiful must he
Pure, Bright, and Glorious be
Whose wondrous works I see.

[Thy Garden, Orchard, Fields]

Thy Garden, Orchard, Fields,
And Vinyard being planted
With what good Nature yields,
Brave things to thee are granted;

Besides the Gifts of Grace,
Therefore go on and gather,
Use each kind in its place,
And Bless our God and Father.
Who gives so liberally,
What's needful for our Living,
And would us have Reply
In bowed-down Thanks-giving
To him, to whom belongs
All Praise in Prose and Songs.

[Extract the Quint-essence]

Extract the Quint-essence
Of *Time* and *Patience*
Which grow not in all Gardens;
It makes hard cases soft,
And when applied oft,
Faint, weak and soft hearts harden's.
None of the World's Produce
Hath such a gen'ral Use
As this quaint Quint Essence
Of Time and Patience.

[*To God alone*, the Only donour]

To God alone, the Only donour
Of all our good and perfect Gifts,
Be Glory, Thanks, Renown and Honour,
That He my Mind ay upwards lifts;
For tho' stern Death does cut asunder
The Body, Spirit and the Soul,
Yet keeps he not the latter under:
To him belongs nought but the Foul.

[Delight in Books from Evening]

Delight in Books from Evening
Till mid-night when the Cocks do sing;
Till Morning when the day doth spring:

Till Sun-set when the Bell doth ring.
Delight in Books, for Books do bring
Poor men to learn most every thing;
The Art of true Levelling:
Yea even how to please the king.
Delight in Books, they're carrying
Us so far, that we know to fling
On waspish men (who taking wing
Surround us) that they can not sting.

[I have a pretty Little Flow'r]

I have a pretty Little Flow'r,
Which in the woods I found,
The same I hundred times an hour
May take out of the Ground,
And keep it dry as long's I will   5
In either of my hands;
But finally Replant it still,
And there full Fresh it stands.
Nay! when I set it on a Roof,
It even then does grow,   10
For me and mine Assigns behoof,
As formerly below.
Its Colour is Vermillion red,
Go, give it now a Name;
Tho' small, yet was't for man's sake bred,   15
To men at last it came.
In likeness of a Skipper's Cap,
Or Hat of Cardinal;
Here th' *Persian Tarbant* gives a tap
To both and bids me call   20
It after him, hap what may hap,
So therefore we say all.

[Learn, Lads and Lasses]

Learn, Lads and Lasses, of my Garden,
That Time doth Thorns and Thistles harden,
And that ill Weeds make no good hay;
Why then should any of you say

We will be better, *when we're older*[?]
I am afraid, you shall be Colder
In Soul, in Spirit, and in Flesh:
Therefore mend, mend! whilst young and fresh.

Epigrams

At ten a Clock, when I the Fire rake,
I then a *Verse* of twice ten words do make;
And in the Morning, when for Coals I look,
One of twice nine I in the Ashes hook.
Turn but five Leaves, and there you'll surely find
Some of the first, and some of th'other kind.

He certainly is in the Right
Who *mingles Profit with Delight.*

Men of Learning, Sense, and Reason
Have *to ev'ry thing a* Season;
As the Summer serves the Mason,
And the Winter time the Thrasher,
Market-days the Haberdasher,
Sun-shine Hay-harvest and the Washer.

Dear Children! Come and look
Often in your Father's book;
Not only look, but understand,
For Learning's more than house and land.
A house may burn, the land be spent,
True Learning never has an end:
True Learning is most excellent.

From Poetry Poverty in all ages arose;
Therefore, my Children, content you with Prose.

Cowslips never hurted none;
But let Girls' Lips alone:
Thereby many were undone.

If *Patience* in the heart be planted,
It may be found as soon as wanted;
But this Per Force ought to be granted,
That that kind, which our garden breeds,
Is often over run by Weeds.
Then men must do what they must needs.

Whatever in my *garden grows,*
God's Goodness, Might, and Wisdom shows;
This threefold Attribute I see
In ev'ry Herb, Flow'r, Shrub and Tree:
Each Tree, Shrub, Herb, and Flower cries,
He's bounteous, powerful and wise.

My *hopes* and *hops* do grow together,
And both exceeding brave.
However, if God change the weather,
For Ought I nought may have.

These *Garden-Tricks,* how men may render
Their Pompions thick, their Salads tender,
Their Turnips large, their Vines to teem,
To Madcaps do like Witchcraft seem.

My garden's fruitful womb is *always breeding,*
When one thing dies, another is succeeding;
It's never barren, but sends ever forth
Flow'rs, herbs and Roots, admir'd for their Worth.

The English can eat flesh both without herbs and bread,
Flesh without herbs and bread to Germans is black Lead.

The more men tread on *Chamomil,*
The quicklier it revives;
The sorer they of Truth speak ill,
The better it still thrives.

Tho' *Thorns* be prickly, and *Nettles* sore burning,
Hair brained men ticklish, fool hardy ones spurning,
Yet none of all these so much given
To Secret Sins and Inward Evil,
As Counterfeited Friends, who're driven
By a hypocritical Devil.

Let Kings and Princes keep the wide Earth-Ball,
I would not change my Garden with them all.

Men and their Garden-*mould* are of the selfsame stuff,
What reason have they then to hector and to huff?
As if their bodily terrestrial Descent
Of high-breath'd AEther were, that purest Element;
Whenas Experience does Convince them, that they must
Revolve back whence they came, and so resolve to Dust.

My Jolly *Columbines:* some white, some red, some blue,
Are Emblems of Man's Age, significant and true;
For Childhood favours milk, Youth's fiery, tough as glue,
Decrepits, old and cold, are of a with'red hue.

A man us'd to the Spade, or such like Instrument,
Oft to the Purpose speaks Things very congruent;
But Doctors frequently do miss, and cannot hit
The Nail upon the head: are talking more than 't's fit.

The Lust of Flesh and Eyes, The Pride of Life,
Are three most noisome weeds, which rankly thrive
In Rich men's well dung'd grounds; mine being poor,
Thanks be to God, they are kept out of door.

The *hours for Sleep* I thus prefix:
To Students five; to Merchants six,
To Gentlemen I do grant seven,
To Sluggards eight, to Fools eleven.

Hans Sachs[1] and *David Lindsay*[2] write,
And all is Verse what they indite,
But Verse per verse, which Modern's loath.
Pray! tell me WHO is best of both?
The German doubtless will say Sachs,
The English of his Lindsay cracks.

White Lillies yield the sweetest Smell
When Virgin like they stand;
I mean, when (understand me well)
Untouched by humane hand.
So is the Sacred Writ of old
Without the Newish Gloss,
Of Glossers, and of Glossers bold,
Away with all their Dross!

IF ev'ry man, or reasonable Creature,
Would only use what's requisite by Nature,
They all might feed on Wheaten Flow'r most fine,
Drink Beer and Ale, yea nothing else than Wine;
BUT, a great BUT! the richest and the greatest

---

[1] Hans Sachs (1494–1576), author of 34 manuscript volumes containing 208 plays, 1,700 comic tales, and 450 lyrics; sometimes called the "cobbler-poet."
[2] David Lindsay (1490–1555), Scottish poet and usher to Prince James (later James V), author of "Complaynt to the King" (1529).

Amongst mankind do prove Degeneratest,
Misspend and waste their Liquor and their Food:
What's left for us? Scarce any thing that's good.
Brass almost looks like *Gold,* and still it is but Brass,
So English Pewter may with Fools for Silver pass:
Oh! hoh! what Diff'rence between Ox and Ass!

SAMUEL SEWALL

(1652–1730)

Samuel Sewall was a classmate of Edward Taylor's at Harvard, tutor to undergraduates after he received his B.A. in 1671, judge at the Salem witchcraft trials of 1692, and Chief Justice of Massachusetts. One of the busiest of men throughout his life, he was an equally busy author, composing not only judicial opinions, essays, tracts, and a voluminous *Diary* but also more than fifty poems and translations in English and Latin. He delighted in sending scribbled verses to his friends for comment, and in receiving similar offerings from them, many of which we know today only because Sewall industriously copied them into his commonplace book, preserved in the New York Historical Society.

WEDNESDAY, January 1. 1701
A little before Break-a-Day, at Boston *of the* Massachusets

ONCE more! Our GOD, vouchsafe to Shine:
Tame Thou the Rigour of our Clime.
Make haste with thy Impartial Light,
And terminate this long dark Night.

Let the transplanted ENGLISH Vine   5
Spread further still: still Call it Thine.
Prune it with Skill: for yield it can
More Fruit to Thee the Husbandman.

Give the poor INDIANS Eyes to see
The Light of Life: and set them free;   10
That they Religion may profess,
Denying all Ungodliness.

From hard'ned JEWS the Vail remove,
Let them their Martyr'd JESUS love;
And Homage unto Him afford,   15
Because He is their Rightful LORD.

So false Religions shall decay,
And Darkness fly before bright Day:
So Men shall GOD in CHRIST adore;
And worship Idols vain, no more.   20

So ASIA, and AFRICA,
EUROPA, with AMERICA;
All Four, in Consort join'd, shall Sing
New Songs of Praise to CHRIST our KING.

The Humble Springs of stately Sandwich Beach[1]

The Humble Springs of stately Sandwich Beach
To all Inferiours may observance teach,
They (without Complement) do all concur,
Praying the Sea, Accept our Duty, Sir,
He mild severe, I've (now) no need: and when—
As you are come: go back and come agen.

Upon the Springs issuing out from the foot of Plimouth Beach, and running out into the Ocean.[2]

The humble Springs of stately Plimouth Beach,
To all Inferiours, due Observance teach.
Perpetually Good Humour'd they concur,
Praying the Sea, Accept our Duty, Sir!
He, mild severe, I've now no need: and When . . .
As you are come, Go back, and come agen.

This morning Tom Child, the Painter, died[1]

Tom Child had often painted Death,
But never to the Life, before:
Doing it now, he's out of Breath;
He paints it once; and paints no more.

[1] first version in Sewall's *Diary*, October 28, 1676.
[2] revised version in *Diary*, February 1723; printed in *The Boston News-Letter*, March 28, 1723.
[1] Thomas Child, painter-stainer, who died Nov. 10, 1706.

To be engraven on a Dial[1]

Keep in God's way; keep pace with evry hour
Hurt none; do all the Good that's in your Power.
Hours can't look back at all; theyl stay for none
Tread sure, keep up with them, and All's your own.

To the Rev'd Mr. Jno. Sparhawk on the Birth of His Son, Augt. or Sept. 1713

Hath God, who freely gave you his own Son,
Freely bestowed on you one of your own?
You certainly can justly do no less
Than thankfully own yours to be his.
Your doing so, may very much conduce
To love him well, and yet not love too much.
Don't love so much; you cannot love too well.
Love God for all, your Love will then excell.
Love not so much, lest you too soon should lose.
Our comforts wither may, upon abuse.
May Father, Mother, Son be always blest
With all the Blessings purchased by Christ!
Sic tibi corde suo ferventior optat amicus,
Omnia qui tua vult sua gaudia semper habes.[1]

[1] i.e. a sundial.
[1] Thus the intimate friend desires in his heart for you,
That you may always have all his joys as your own.

JOHN DANFORTH

(1660–1730)

The most prolific and well published in a family of poets, John Danforth was born in Roxbury, Massachusetts. Like his father Samuel I and his brother Samuel II, he attended Harvard and entered the ministry, accepting a call to the Church at Dorchester in 1682, in which post he served till his death in 1730.

In comparison with other members of his family Danforth lived a rather drab life, brightened only by occasional high marks of interest such as his Dighton Rock involvement. In October 1680 Danforth visited Assonet Neck near Dighton, Massachusetts, and made a drawing of the strange inscriptions carved on an eleven-foot rock. His transcription evoked considerable interest: Sewall asked for a copy, and Cotton Mather trekked out to Dighton to see and record for himself these odd carvings. John Danforth's manuscript came eventually into the holdings of the British Museum, where it is today.

Danforth was an active and assiduous writer of verse, composing elegies, almanac verse, epigrams, anagrams, didactic poems, dedicatory verse, and lyrics—and all but one of which we have record were published during his lifetime. (Even the epitaphs were published in the broad sense by being carved on appropriate gravestones.) He experimented with various lengths, meters, and verse forms, and valued responses provided by Samuel Sewall, and perhaps Edward Taylor, with whom he exchanged verse in manuscript. He was widely read, as is evidenced not only in his poetry but also in his large library, in part inherited from his father Samuel I and added to judiciously by Danforth throughout his life.

At his poorest, as in the epitaph on Miriam Wood (1706), Danforth adheres to the form and style for funerary verse current among his contemporaries—the matter and manner so effectively satirized by Benjamin Franklin in his "Receipt to make a New-England Funeral Elegy" (Silence Dogood Paper, No. 7, *New-England Courant*, 25 June 1722). At his best, as in the verse selected below, he has a keen sense of the right word, an ear for rhythms and sounds, and a control of imagery and structure that earn him a respectable place among America's early poets.

On my Lord Bacon[1]

My mind i th' mines of rich Philosophy
Did sweetly sweat, t' inrich all standers by;
Mean time, my Blades did want their masters [eye]
Filtched Royall Cash, then in my custody;
 The Deed was Theirs, The fault was mine,
 Or His who did me imploy;
  So lurch'd was I,
 Reduc'd to outward penury;
Tho' rich in Tongues, Arts, Parts, and Fame
And every Thing that's High.

Posuit J. D.

Two vast Enjoyments *commemorated, and two great* Bereavements *lamented, in two excellent Persons, viz. the Reverend Mr. PETER THACHER, Pastor of the Church of CHRIST in Milton, who was born into this World July 18. Anno Dom. 1651. and ascended to a better World, December 17. Anno Dom. 1727.* AEtatis *77. and in the 47th of his Pastorate And the Reverend Mr. SAMUEL DANFORTH, Pastor of the Church of CHRIST in Taunton, whose Nativity was December 18. Anno Dom. 1666. and his Translation to the heavenly Paradise, November 14. Anno Dom. 1727. Fifteen Days after the first Shock of the great Earthquake in New-England*

WHAT! Without Feeling? Don't we make Pretense,
In some Degree, unto that vital Sense?
Dumb too! and would be press'd to Death as Mutes?[1]
Angels use speaking Arts: but rarely Brutes.

[1] written in Danforth's hand in his signed copy of Lord Verulam's *Sylva Sylvarum, or A Naturall Historie* (London, 1626), now in the possession of Professor Harold S. Jantz, and printed here with his kind permission.

[1] an accused who refused to plead, i.e. stood mute, was "pressed" by having stones piled upon him until he did plead guilty or not guilty.

Lisp we no Ecchoes to the dismal Sound,   5
From Caverns and Convulsions under Ground?
To th' Peals from the charg'd Chambers of the Skies?
To th' Voice from Temples of the LORD Most High?

To th' Shrieks from the bereav'd BRITANNICK THRONE,
And Realms; Great GEORGE'S Death that loudly groan?   10
When Warning-Pieces great are fired and shot;
When shook, and struck, and call'd, answer we not?

Blind Eyes, deaf Ears, hard Hearts, bind fast the Tongue;
What frightful Maladies upon us throng?
O SON of *David* Mercy on us shew!   15
Restore our Souls! Our spiritual Sense renew!
From Blindness, Deafness, Hardness, instantly
LORD! If thou wilt, Thou can'st our Souls set free.

We'll then with Thanks review Enjoyments past,
For poor Improvements we will be abas'd.   20
Our late Bereavements we will lay to Heartt;
But most of all, GOD'S Wrath, and our Desert.

We long enjoy'd a *Sky*, that did refrain;
An *Earth*, that *Terra Firma* did remain;
And not *Infirma*, but a quiet Seat;   25
Groan'd not so loud, to make our Hearts to beat.

Long were we bless'd with GEORGE's Influence,
By whom GOD gave us great Deliverance,
Th' ascended LORD long favour'd us with Lights
To Shine vile Rebels into Favourites.   30
The Council-Board, the Bench, the sacred Desk
Long shone with Heroes, who are now at Rest.
CHRIST's two last *aged Shepherds* tarried long,
His dear, (but now bereaved) Flocks among.

View their paternal and maternal Lines,   35
Both of them sprang from many great Divines,
Honour'd in *England,* and *New England* too,
For Service they for CHRIST, and's Church did do.

Angels, *per Saltum,*[2] took their high Degree,
Commencing Spirits, from *Non-Entity,*   40
These Angels of our Churches, Babes first were;
How excellent the Mothers that them bare?

2 with a leap.

Again they both were *New-Born* of the SPIRIT:
And both great double-Portions did inherit,
Of the rare *Spirit* of the bless'd ELIJAHS,   45
Whose Mantles fell to these good young ABIJAHS.[3]

What Man (since Miracles are ceas'd) e're gains,
Without the Teachers, and the Learners Pains,
And th' Blessing upon both, from GOD most High,
Sufficient Knowledge in the Mystery   50
Of Arts, of Languages, and of Religion
To qualify for the Prophetick-Vision?

GOD bless'd the Pains, (bless'd be His glorious Name!)
To both of these, that quickly they became
(Like well-taught *Pegasuss*) thorow-pac'd;   55
Before they were with College-Laurels grac'd.

Their Temper far from Injucundity;
Their Tongues and Pens from Infacundity.
Solid and Grave, yet pleasant they were each;
Lest any should of Starch'dness them impeach.   60

In Med'cine, and in civil Laws, well read
Were *Luke* and *Zenas;* for their Neighbours Need.
Each, on Occasion, might few Minutes lend,
To Advise a Sick or an exposed Friend:
Both these our Pastors very Skilful were,   65
Like *Luke* the one, th' other like *Zenas* rare.
Their Usefulness thence flowing, by the by,
How full of Piety and Charity!
All to their Office-Work subordinated;
A Work unrivall'd, not to be check-mated.   70
A Work, upon the Wheels forever going;
A Work (whatever else was done) still doing.
A Work for which they left no Stone unturn'd;
A Work for which the Indian-Tongue they learn'd,
Th' Indians in their own Language had their Lectures,   75
All full of CHRIST, and Grace, and Heav'nly Nectars.
But th' English mainly had their Pains and Care,
To th' English they were Angels Tutelar.
High in Employments, but not high in Pride,
Their HIGH-EMPLOYER was their Guard and Guide.   80

[3] I Kings xiv: son and successor of Reheboam.

To batter Sin they mighty were; For Zeal
Chariots and Horsemen of our Israel,
Their Churches were by them (as Bulwarks strong)
From Vice (thank the MOST HIGH) defended long:
While the Resistless Sword was in their Hand,   85
Agags[4] were hewn to Pieces in their Land.
'Gainst Sin did Lions in GOD's Cause appear,
But in their own, they Lambs for Meekness were.

They left a sacred Stamp, where e're they trod;
Their Lives-Right-Steps shew'd Men the Way to GOD: 90
They both were to their Flocks unblotted Paterns;
And of all Godliness and Virtue Patrons.

Shepherds they were, the Sheep who right did guide;
And who seducing Wolves could not abide.
Both wrought *with* GOD, and wrought by Faith and Prayer,   95
Both wrought *for* GOD, and were His tender Care.

Both many thousand sacred Sermons preach'd,
That th' Ears and Hearts of many Hundreds reach'd.
Most bounteously GOD answered their Desire,
Hard Hearts would melt by their seraphick Fire.   100

Their Prayers and Prophecyings (by Heav'ns Might)
Rais'd up dead Souls, restor'd the Blind to sight.
Right noble Wisdom thus each of 'em had;
Wise to win Souls, to make their SAVIOUR glad.

Careful they were CHRIST's Sheep should never feed   105
On *Arian*, *Popish* or *Arminian* Weed.
Careful lest worldly Lusts should hot pursue 'em,
Bad Company and Pleasures should undo 'em.
Careful to bring 'em from destructive Things,
To the safe Shelter of bless'd JESUS'S Wings.   110

For Foresight and good Forecast, few their Match:
Were ever on their Guard, and on their Watch.
Both Men and Things they studied well, and knew;
Their Bow they seldom at Adventure drew.
In Councils frequent and in Travels oft;   115

[4] I Sam xv 8: "And he took Agag the king of the Amalekites alive, and utterly destroyed all the people with the edge of the sword." In Dryden's *Absolom and Achitophel*, Agag is Sir Edmund Berry Godfrey, the magistrate before whom Titus Oates made his declaration, and whose mutilated body was afterwards found in a ditch.

Success (like joyful Streamers) seen aloft.
But I omit whole Volumes yet behind;
So great Enjoyments tell us GOD is kind.
Lustres of Years (though fit for Heaven) they stood,
By CHRIST continued, for His Churches good.   120
Their precious useful *Memory* remains,
For wise Improvers everlasting Gains.
Who gain'd no Gold by these Aurifick-Stones,
Have Reason now to make their doleful Moans.
Our Loss in their Remove is far from small,   125
Who were such copious Blessings unto all.

May Heaven, that takes our Treasures, make Retrievements!
Else Bankrupts are undone by such Bereavements.
Levi'thans they who do not (for their Part)
The wounding-Warnings duely lay to heart.   130
Portended Ills prevent! most gracious GOD!
Make all take Warning, by thy speaking Rod!
Bereaved Famalies, and Flocks with Tears,
Ask tender Sympathy, and fervent Prayers:
May Heav'ns kind Ears receive their Lamentations!   135
Give, LORD! Their weakned Hearts strong Consolations.

Amen.

Ita humillime precatur[5]

J. D.

THE MERCIES Of the YEAR, COMMEMORATED: A SONG for Little CHILDREN IN NEW-ENGLAND December 13th 1720

[1]

Heaven's MERCY shines, *Wonders* and *Glorys* meet;
Angels are lost in sweet *surprize* to see't.
The *Circle* of the *Year* is well near Run
Earth's-*Conflagration* is not yet begun.

[5] Thus most humbly prayed.

[2]

Heaven spares the *Bulwark* of our *Peace*, King GEORGE;[1]
Our CHARTER holds; and *Privileges* large.
Our GOVERNOUR and SENATORS can meet;
And Greet, and *Join* in Consultation sweet.

[3]

Though Great our Loss in GREENWOOD'S bless'd Translation;[2]
Yet well fill'd *Pulpits* bless the *Little Nation*.
New Churches Gather'd; Th' *Eastern Peace* not lost;[3]
And *Satan's* overthrown with all his Host.

[4]

Sickness from Distant Lands Arrives, and Fears;
JEHOVAH in the *Mount* as oft *Appears*.
Contagion stops with Precious *Captain* GORE;[4]
How *Great* our *Loss?* But *Heav'n* will draw no more.

[5]

Tho' ripening HEAT came *late*, yet *Frost* held off,
We Reap the *Harvest*, and have *Bread* enough.
Provision's dear, Goods high, Bills low, Cash none;
And yet the *Suffering Tribe* is not *Undone*.

[6]

A *Miracle!* That Ocean-Seas of Sin,
Have not prevail'd to let a Deluge in!
That Earth's upheld to bear the heavy Load!
Adore the *Grace* of a Long suffering GOD!

[1] George I, crowned 1714.
[2] Thomas Greenwood of Cambridge, died 1720.
[3] i.e. with the Indians.
[4] On Sept. 30, 1716, Samuel Sewall wrote in his *Diary* (III, 104) of a Captain Gore who "was come in from Barbados."

[7]

Some Vices in the Church not yet subdu'd;
Old Barren Vines and Trees, not yet down hew'd.
Sinners, not sent to their Deserved Place;
A YEAR is added to their DAY of Grace.

[8]

The Fugitive may be returned home;
The Foe to GOD, a Favourite become:
Who have no shelter from Thy Jealous Eye,
JESUS! for shelter to thy Wounds may Fly.

[9]

The *whole Years space* for Faith, Repentance, Prayer;
The *Most* have not improved well, I Fear:
Look then, *with broken Hearts*, upon your ways;
And see, your *Future Lives*, JEHOVAH *Praise*.

Profit and Loss: AN ELEGY Upon the Decease of
Mrs. Mary Gerrish,
Late Vertuous Wife of Mr. Samuel Gerrish, *and Daughter*
of the Honourable Judge SEWALL.
Who on Novemb. *17. 1710. the Night after Publick*
Thanksgiving, Entred on the Celebration of
Triumphant Hallelujahs, to her Profit, and our
Loss. Aged *19.* Years *and 20.* Days

MARY, the Blessed *VIRGINS* Name,
 EXALTED, Signifies:
ARMY, was once the *Anagram,*
 a Poet did devise.[1]
Behold! How her *Exaltedness*   5
 an *Army* justly Boasts:

---

[1] Danforth alludes to George Herbert's anagram on the Virgin Mary:

$$Ana\text{-}\left\{ \begin{array}{c} \text{Mary} \\ \text{Army} \end{array} \right\} gram$$

How well her name an *Army* doth present,
In whom the *Lord of Hosts* did pitch his tent!

Because within her, *HE* Incamp'd,
  who was the *LORD OF HOSTS.*
To many a Precious *MARY*, since,
  great *Exaltation's* Given;
Fill'd with the Spiritual *Presence* of
  the Eternal *LORD* of Heav'n.
Our beauteous *MARY* too, She was
  (of *Honourable* Race;)
Besides all other Brightnesses,
  enobled most by Grace.
By Grace she chose the better Part;
  ne're to be taken from her:
Her Heart, *Rabboni,* cry'd to Christ
  whose Love did overcome her.
WHO 'twas that pitch'd His Tabernacle
  within her sacred heart,
Her *Letters, Carriage,* and *Discourse,*
  unto her Friends impart.
Her PARENTS dear, will nev'r Repent
  her *Pious Education:*
Or wish their Prayers unpray'd, that sped
  so well, in her Salvation.
They'l Joy, Because Eternal Life,
  (the Crown of Righteousness,)
She Carries, notwithstanding Deaths
  Hereditariness:
Armies of Merits, All Her LORD's,
  (while she her own deny'd;)
Prevailing for her, and all Such,
  as in whose stead He Dy'd.
By *Faith* she dy'd, depending still
  upon the Grace Divine,
That thro' the *Mediator,* would
  in her Salvation shine.
She has Attaind now, with Advance,
  what she desir'd below;
(Joyn'd to the Church in Heav'n,) She doth
  to Full Communion go.
Her Place is Empty; bear't you must,
  She's on a *Visit* gone,
To better Friends, than any here;
  and will Return anon.

The Raising-Day hastens apace;
   her Second Coming too;   50
Twill dazzle all such Eyes as ours,
   her Beauty then to view.
Now, for her Absence, and her Stay,
   She need no Pardon ask;
Commanded hence; but not before   55
   She first had done her task.
Onely she craves, by Friends here left
   for to be Visited;
And would Rejoyce to see them all
   at th' Heav'nly Table fed: 60
Yet is content they stay a while;
   while 'tis for th' *Churches* gain:
For which; we, (with Submission,) Pray
   they here may long Remain.
She's satisfy'd, her Relatives   65
   can never be Undone,
By the departure of a star,
   while they enjoy the *Sun.*
Good is the Country she has left;
   it is *IMMANUEL's.*   70
But HEAVEN the *Better* Country is;
   and there her *SPIRIT* dwells.
The more of *Excellence* in her
   your ravish'd Eyes did fill;
Your Resignation shines the more   75
   to Heav'ns Remanding Will.
You grieve, the Time's so short; but yet
   had you Enjoy'd her longer,
The Bands of Love had Faster grown,
   and Bands of Grief much stronger.   80
You'd but short warning of her Death,
   its suddenness is Trying;
Yet ben't surpriz'd to see that Dead,
   you always knew was Dying.
Your sweetest Terrene Hopes are cross'd   85
   by disappointment sad:
That your Eternal Hope's secure,
   your Souls may yet be glad.
Who *Gave* her, He has *Taken* her;
   this is beyond Dispute: 90
Indisputable Sov'raignty
   then binds you to be Mute.

Partings are Grief: Happy the Hearts
  here, made Bereavement-Proof;
In Times of need, you know WHERE there   95
  is Grace and Help enough.
A *Daughter, Sister, Spouse,* is tak'n;
  whom dear Relations miss;
Much of their Worldly *Comfort's* gone,
  now she is gone to *Bliss.*   100
Stop your Pursuing Griefs for her,
  your *Hue-en-crys* forbear;
You want her Much: SEEK HER IN CHRIST
AND YOU WILL FIND HER THERE.

Maestus Composuit J. D.

A few Lines to fill up a Vacant PAGE

Wo worth[1] the Days! The Days I spent
  I' th' Regions of Discontent;
  Where I nought rightly understood,
  But thought Good, Evil; Evil, Good;
Friends I deem'd Foes; Wrong I conceiv'd was done me;   5
I Swell'd and Rage'd; whole Heaven could not Atone me:
My Soul ('tis known) was not my Own, so far it had undone me.

  Health, Fame, and Wealth were full of Stings;
  Children, and Friends were no such Things;
  My wholesome food was Poison'd all,   10
  And Hony did but Swell my Gall;
God was no God, Christ was no Christ to me,[2]

While thus I Drave in Discontentments Sea:
Thank this first Vice, that *Adam* e're lost Paradice, and me.

  Thus being Lost, wrong Course I steerd,   15
  While neither Sun, nor Stars appear'd;
  Instead of Heav'n's Land, I made Hell,
  I knew't by its Sulphureous Smell:

[1] archaic for woe betide or befall.
[2] cf. *Bartas His Devine Weekes and Workes 1605,* trans. Joshua Sylvester (Gainesville, Florida, 1965), p. 10:
  All, All was void of beauty, rule, and light;
All without fashion, foule, and motion, quite.
Fire was no fire, the water was no water,
Aire was no aire, the Earth no earthly matter.

Coming on Waters, strait my LORD spy'd I;
Avaunt, Foul Fiend! Avoid, fell Foe! Cry'd I;[3]   20
So vilely I mistook, and therefore spake foul Blasphemy.

    'Tis I, quoth He, Be not Afraid.
    Which Words He had no sooner said,
    But all my Discontents resil'd;[4]
    The Rustling Winds, and Waves were still'd;   25
By what Time, Faith and Hope my Sailes could hoise,[5]
I got safe and firm Anch'rage in a trice,
Within the very inmost Bays of blissfull Paradice.

A POEM
Upon the Triumphant TRANSLATION
of a Mother in Our ISRAEL, Viz.
Mrs. ANNE ELIOT.
From This Life to a Better.
on March 24th, 1687. Aetatis Suae. 84

All Hallelujahs, Oh ye *Heav'nly Quires*,
Ye *Powers*, ye Winged and Immortal *Fires!*
    Redouble to the *Highest ONE:*[1]
Here's Joy, to your Eternal *Jubile*[2]
Advanc'd, by th' New come welcome Company   5
    of a *Bright Soul*, but lately flown.
        Congratulate
        Eternally,
     With Sacred *Symphony*,
     Her happy State.   10

Haile! *Happy Soul!* In Luster excellent
Transcending far the *Starry Firmament*,
    Which is thy *Footstool* now become:
With all the World, *America* shall Vye,
For to Produce thy Peer: Now cast thine Eye   15
    All round about that Spacious Room,
        None shalt thou see
        Of *Blest Women*,
     Much more *Triumphant* than
     Thy self to be.   20

[3] "Avaunt" and "Avoid" are equivalent archaics for "begone."
[4] recovered, regained.
[5] hoist.
[1] in music, to add a note two octaves higher than the given note.
[2] cf. Lev xxv 8–17: "Jubile," from Yobel, a ram's horn.

Haile! Thou *Sagacious* and *Advent'rous* Soul!
Haile, *Amazon!* Created to Controll
  Weak Nature's Foes, and t' take her part,
The King of Terrours,[3] Thou, ('till the Command
Irrevocable came to Stay thy Hand,)   25
    Didst oft *Repel,* by thy *Choice Art:*[4]
      By *High Decree,*
      Long didst thou stand
     An Atlas, in *Heav'n's Hand*[5]
     To th' *World* to be.   30

All Hallelujahs to His bounteous *Care,*
That such a *Peerless* Consort did Prepare[6]
  For HIM, whom *Sacred Things* with held
From *Seculars;* Who was to *Gospellize,*
And *Preach Redemption* to GODS *Enemys*[7]   35
    Beyound all *Memory,* Rebell'd:
      For *his sake,* sure,
      Thine *Aged Life*
     It did with *Death* in Strife
     So long endure.   40

Heav'n's Richest Spices, Choicest Graces were
[*Queen Esther* like,] allotted to *Thy Share,*
  For to *Prepare* Thee for Thy KING:
Thee, to *Pay Table,* for *Full Recompence,*
With Interest, for all thy Vast *Expense,*   45
    Angels, on Wings of Grace, strait, bring:[8]
      As *Phaltiel,*[9]
      Thy CONSORT Dear
     Mourning, Thee follow'th near,
     To bid FAREWEL.   50

J. D.

[3] cf. Job xviii 14.
[4] Anne Eliot's choice art was that of healing.
[5] As Atlas, Anne Eliot was a bearer of burdens, a mainstay.
[6] As John Eliot's betrothed, Anne Mumford came to New England for their wedding in Oct. 1632, a year after Eliot had arrived.
[7] Indians.
[8] note pun on Angels (as coins) and on Grace ("Anne" means "grace").
[9] II Sam iii 14–16. In *Magnalia Christi Americana* Cotton Mather wrote a moving account of the aged Eliot weeping over the coffin of his wife.

COTTON MATHER
(1663–1728)

In *Manuductio ad Ministerium*, a handbook for young ministers, Cotton Mather advised that the writing of poetry might "sharpen your sense, and polish your style for more important performances." He added that "you may . . . all your days make a little recreation of poetry in the midst of your painful studies." Disciplined Puritan that he was, Mather hastened to warn against the excesses of poetizing, which, if indulged too much, could lead a young man away from the godly purposes of life and into sensuous carnality. To Mather balance and proportion ought to be strived for in all aspects of life, including letters. His own literary balance is reflected in the enormous variety of his writings, and in the catholicity of his interests. Yet no other figure of Puritan New England has been so frequently and consistently accused of excess as the Reverend Cotton Mather of Boston.

Mather's New England family was so illustrious that it frequently has received the designation dynasty. Both grandfathers, Richard Mather and John Cotton, were patriarchs in the Bay Colony during the early years of its formation. Cotton Mather's father, Increase, who served as minister to the Second Boston Church, and as President of Harvard College, was recognized as the leading intellect in a colony which placed high value on intellectual attainment. Expectedly, Cotton Mather felt deeply the responsibility of his lineage. He strove to uphold it in his lifetime, though not without censure from others and pain to himself.

Born in 1663 in Boston, Cotton Mather was a precocious child who at the age of twelve could read, write, and speak fluently both Greek and Latin. Further, he had read most of the New Testament in Hebrew. Since these linguistic attainments were considered sufficient preparation for college, Cotton Mather entered Harvard in his thirteenth year. He was, understandably, not popular with his fellow students, who harassed him. But scholastically he excelled, graduating in 1678 and receiving his Master's degree just three years later. As a child Mather had been afflicted by stammering, and had therefore thought himself unfit for the ministry. He had settled instead on medicine, which was then more superstition than science. However, with effort he overcame his speech impairment and decided on a ministerial career.

After his graduation Mather was invited to a pastorate in New Haven. He declined, preferring instead to assist his father at the Second Boston Church. It was at this church, known throughout the colony as the ecclesiastical domain of the Mather family, that Cotton spent his life. From there he preached, exerted political influence, corresponded with the most learned men of Europe, and sought unceasingly to restore the great zeal which he felt was no longer to be found in New England Puritanism. His efforts at restoration, sometimes querulous and ranting, earned him the title of pedant, and the label "Puritan" in the most pejorative sense of the word. However, an objective glance at his life reveals Cotton Mather to be much more, for his election to the Royal Society, his advocacy of inoculation to prevent smallpox, his tolerance of other churches, and his moderation during the Salem witchcraft trials prove him to be otherwise than a caricature of a stern, narrow-minded, otherworldly, pleasure-hating New Englander.

Cotton Mather was a victim of history even in his own time. The zealous strength of that first generation willing to risk the ocean and live in wilderness for the sake of religious conviction was waning fast. Their children were not flocking to the churches to offer personal narratives of their conversions, as the parents had assumed they would. Consequently, though the churches were full, their official membership was dwindling. To compensate, ministers held synods at which they agreed to baptize the members' children and grandchildren. The agreement was called—at first derogatively—the Half-Way Covenant. It meant that rather than an individual being compacted with God in the two sacraments, baptism and the Lord's Supper, he could be baptized in the hope of later experiencing conversion. Then the Lord's Supper would be open to him to make the Covenant whole. But when the youth of the second generation failed still to cite their conversion experiences, some ministers began to extend more widely the Lord's Supper. Rather than a confirmation of salvation, that sacrament now became a promise of it. Here was proof-positive that Puritanism was on the wane.

Yet a few ministers, most notably Cotton Mather, sought desperately to stem a tide they saw as utterly sinful. As the colony became more and more remiss, Mather redoubled his efforts from the pulpit and through his writings to alert New England that God would not restrain His wrath much longer, and to assure them that they yet had a strong place in Christian and classical tradition.

Mather's life was one of frustration and affliction. All three of his wives died within a few years of marriage, and his third wife became insane. Of Mather's fifteen children, only two were living when he retired from his church career in 1728. In public life he saw his father forced to resign as president of Harvard, and Mather, who so hoped to make the college an instrument for restoring godly ways to New England, never held the presidency he so longed for.

Yet Cotton Mather studied and wrote tirelessly throughout his life. His publications include sermons, tracts, observations on natural history, biographies, fables, treatises, and, of course, verses. Many of the poems formerly attributed to him, notably the longer poems and short snatches of verse in his *Magnalia Christi Americana,* are not of his authorship. But there remains enough of his verse for critical evaluation. His relentless display of erudition in some verses vitiates poetic quality. But Mather was capable at times of successfully fitting appropriate imagery with good rhythms. Learned man of letters that he was, he spoke in the widely varied poetic forms he knew.

See also Grindall Rawson, "To the Learned and Reverend Mr. Cotton Mather, on his Excellent *Magnalia,*" p. 478; and Nicholas Noyes.

Vigilantius

OR,

A Servant of the LORD
Found READY for the
Coming of the LORD
A Discourse
Occasioned by the EARLY DEATH
of SEVEN Young
MINISTERS,[1]
Within a Little while One of another:
With some ESSAY, upon their
very Commendable and Imitable
CHARACTER

And an ELEGY upon them

On the GRAVES
OF MY
YOUNG BRETHREN,
Carent quia vate Sacro[2]

Graves! Where in Dust are laid our dearest *Hopes!*
Pay, *Passengers,* your *Tributary Drops,*
Your *Tears* Allow'd, yea, *Hallowed* now become,
Since *Tears* were drop't by JESUS on a *Tomb.*
Churches, Weep on; and Wounded yeild your *Tears;*   5
Tears use to flow from hack't *New-English Firrs.*
  Zion, Thy *Sons* are gone; Tho' men might see
This and that Man, brave Men, were *born in thee.*
Tell, what they were; Let thy *True Trumpet* tell
Truth of the *Sons of Truth,* and how they fell.   10
Sure, when our *Sev'n* did to their Seats retire,
Th' Harmonious *Nine* did not with them expire.
Smooth Numbers first were form'd for *Themes* like these;
T' immortalize deserving *Memories.*

  [1] Edward Tompson (1665–1705); John Morse (1646?–1704?); [Joseph?]
Wakeman (d. 1704); John Hubbard (d. 1705); [Nathaniel?] Wade (d. 1704);
Andrew Gardner (1674–1704); John Clark (1670–1705). Only Hubbard and
Clark are named in this elegy; the other five men are discussed in the *Discourse*
which precedes the poem.
  [2] "Because they lack a sacred bard" (Horace *Carmina* iv. 9. 28).

First, *What they were not,* Say; For they were *Not*   15
Such as their *Mother* might account a *Blot.*
Not such as to the *Sacred Priest-hood* fly,
Meerly as to a *Craft,* to Live thereby.
Not, who at *Church* seem *Serious* and *Demure,*
But out of it, no *Strictness* can Endure,   20
Not those who dare *Jest* with Gods awful Word
And lewdly can *Play* with the *Flaming Sword.*
Not the *Black* Folks, where nothing *White* we know
But what as *Open'd Mouth* may chance to show.

Not Snuffs,[3] instead of *Stars;* (the Room, no doubt,   25
Would Sweeter be, if *Such* were turned out.)
Not Blind-men (So the *Talmuds* reckon them!)
Who *Dark* themselves, hold *Lights* to other men.
Not Lads, whom for their *Levity* alone
The Punning Tribe, *De Tribu Levi,* own.   30
Not who to *Pulpits* hop Unfledg'd and there,
Talk twice a *Week,* and *Preach* not once a year.
Not those who do the *Pious Neighbour* Shun,
But to the Wicked *Sons of Belial* run.
Not those who hate their Work, as Boyes the *Rod,*   35
And hate and flour *Laborious* Men of *God.*
    If such there are; *Take, Lord, thy Holy Scourge,*
    And from such Nusances, thy Temple Purge!

Not such my Sons; by *Zion* so we're told;
Sons comparable to the Finest Gold.   40
    But, *What they were,* Fair Lady, canst thou say,
What thy Lost *Seven,* and not faint away!
    For with her *Seven Sons,* and such as these,
    Dy'd the brave Mother of the *Maccabees.*[4]
Mirrours of Piety they were, and knew   45
Betimes, how to be Wise and Good and True.
Early the *Larks* Praise to their Maker Sung;
So Saint *Macarius,*[5] *Old* while very *Young,*
The Towns to which they did their Toyls dispense
Them their Bright *Glory* thought, and Strong *Defence.*   50

The *Tears* of their Bereaved Flocks Proclaime
More than could Marble *Pyramids* their Name.

[3] candles; in comparison, therefore, feeble.
[4] The full story is told in the apocryphal book, 2 Maccabees, vii.
[5] Aemilius Macer, an Augustan poet older than Ovid, author of *Orinthogonia.*

These were *N. England's Pride;* But Humbly Show'd
Men might be *so,* and not *themselves* be *Proud.*
Dryden Sayes, *Look the Reformation round,*   55
No Treatise of HUMILITY IS FOUND.
Dryden, Thou Ly'st; They *Write,* and more than so,
They *Live Humility;* they can be *low.*
Low these were always in their own *Esteem,*
But the more *highly* we Esteemed them.   60
Low-roof'd the *Temples,* but more Stately than
St. *Sophy's,* built by Great *Justinian,*
The *Proud* might trample on them as on *Earth,*
But glorious *Mines* of *Worth* lay underneath.

    First they did all to *Kiriath-Sepher* go;[6]   65
And *then* a *Church* did Heav'n on them bestow.
By Learning first their *Lamps* were made to Blaze,
And *Incense* each *then* on the *Altar* layes.
The *Liberal Arts* they knew; but understood
Most Thine, Great *Antonine;*[7] That, (*To be Good.*)   70
And *Good to Do,* This was their main Delight;
For *This* they did all *Youths* vain Pleasure Sleight.

    While such rare Youths must Dy, no *Lawyers* wit
    (Not *Asgils*)[8] can *abate Death's Fatal Writ,*
    Must such see but a *Finger* of the *Span*   75
    That is to measure the Frail *Life* of man!
    Yet we'l demand *Eternity* for them;
    And they shall Live too in *Eternal Fame.*

Reckon, O Jews, your *Priestly Blemishes,*
Forty above an *Hundred,* if you please: 80
A *Priest* for each of these did lose his call:
But *Ours,* to all appear'd still free from all.
The Power of your fine *Loadstones,* wondrous Great,
Report, ye *Masters of the Cabinet:*
Loadstones in weight a *Dram;* well-Shodden they   85
Pull up what near *Two Hundred Drams* will weigh.
Our *Potent Loadstones* more *attractive* were;
And more the *Sphere of their Activity* extended far.

[6] the town of Debir, conquered by Joshua.
[7] Antoninus Pius (A.D. 86–161) dispensed "nine liberalities."
[8] John Asgill (1659–1738), English lawyer noted for a treatise (1700) which sought to prove that, the penalty for original sin having been paid by Christ, death was no longer legal, and Christians would thus pass to eternity by "translation."

Now, *Pancirol*,[9] upon my honest Word,
The Lost *Sepulchral Lamps*, are Now Restor'd. 90
Our *Saints*, to whom do Serve as *Oyl*, our Tears,
Bright *Lamps*, they glare still in their *Sepulchres*.

My CLARK was One. And such a *Clark* as he
Synods of *Angels* would take *Theirs* to be.
Faintly to Praise a Youth of such Desert, 95
Were but to Shoot indeed vile *Slanders* Dart.
See but his *Wasted Flesh:* T'was Flaming *Zeal*
That Melted him: The Flame is burning still.
Methinks I see his Ravish'd Hearers wait
And long to hear still his next *Heav'nly Treat*. 100
Look; The Fat Cloud, what *Oracles* he pours
On Thirsty Souls in most *Expedient Showres!*
His *Preaching* much, but more his *Practice* wrought;
A *Living Sermon* of the Truths he *Taught*.
So all might *See* the *Doctrines* which they *Heard*, 105
And way to *Application* fairly clear'd.

Strong were the *Charms* of that Sinceritie
Which made his *Works* well with his *Words* agree.
Painter, Thy Pencils take. Draw first, a *Face*
Shining, (but by himself not seen) with *Grace*. 110
An Heav'n touch'd *Eye*, where (what of *Kens* is told)
One might, MY GOD, in *Capitals* behold.
A *Mouth*, from whence a *Label* shall proceed,
And (O LOVE CHRIST) the *Motto* to be Read.
An *Hand* still open to relieve the Poor, 115
And by *Dispersing* to *increase* the Store.
Such was my CLARK; so did he Look, and so
Much more than *Look*, or *Speak*, so did he *Do*.
Botanists, Boast your *Palm-Tree*, whence arise
More than three Hundred rich Commodities. 120
Write, *Persian Poet*, that brave Tree to Praise,
As many *Songs* as in the year be *Dayes*.
My CLARK more *Vertues* had; So must the Tree
Too rich for Earth, to Heav'n transplanted be.

HUBBARD Another. When the Youth they saw, 125
So *Wise*, Their *Love* he challeng'd, and their *Awe*.
Older Spectators fed their wondering Eyes,

[9] Guido Panciroli (1523–99), erudite Italian lawyer, antiquarian, and translator; author of *The History of Many Memorable Things* . . . (London, 1715).

With *Love*, to see Young Children grow so *Wise*.
Envy her self grew weary of her *Gall*,
And gave Consent, he should be *Lov'd* by all.   130
The *Pastoral* of *Gregory* the Great,
Won't Say how well he fill'd the *Pastors* Seat.
In Saving Souls his Happy Hours he spent,
And Preach'd *Salvation* wheresoe're he went.
A *Cassius*,[10] whom the Hearers did attend,   135
With constant *Fear*, that he would make an *End*.

His *Life* a *Letter*, where the World might Spell
Great *Basils Morals*,[11] and his Death the *Seal*.
The *Graces* which were *Sparks* on *Earth* below,
To Glorious *Flames* in *Heav'n* they now do grow.   140
Oh! Should a *Star* drop from the Sky to us,
We should with Reverence admire it thus!
For such a Child of *Jacob* there Unite
Th' *Egyptian* Weeping with the *Israelite*.
So has his *After-Beams* the Setting *Sun;*   145
Tho' he be *Set*, his splendor is not gone.
    Adieu, My CLARK; my HUBBARD, thus Adieu;
    A *Pair* well *Parallel'd* we had in you.
    Grave *Plutarch*,[12] Hadst thou Liv'd till now, the *Pair*
    Would have engross'd thy Pen, they Look so fair.   150
    Such Gifts as these by Heav'n bestow'd on Men,
    Must just be *Show'n*, and then call'd back agen!
Lord, Why so soon, such *Fruitful Trees* cut down!
No *Wood* of Such, was on the *Altar* known.
Trees not cut down, (the Glorious Answer is,)   155
But all Translated into *Paradise*.
From the *Quick Seizure* of the greedy *Grave*
Her Darling *Sons* my Country cannot Save.
But, *Grave*, Thou shalt not so thy Prey consume,
As ever *Buried* in *Oblivions* Womb.   160
Thus *Thetis* Comforted her *Short-Liv'd* Son,[13]
Dy Young, Long shalt thou be Admir'd when Dead and Gone.

[10] Cassius Severus, brilliant Augustan orator (died A.D. 34).
[11] St. Basil (A.D. 329–379), supporter of the orthodox faith against Arianism, and author of scriptural commentaries, liturgies, and homilies.
[12] (c. A.D. 46–120), who composed biographies of soldiers and statesmen, mainly in pairs (first a Greek, then a Roman, then a comparison).
[13] Thetis was a sea goddess, mother of Achilles.

One of the *Pleiades* long since withdrew.[14]
And Heav'n but *Six,* does of the *Seven* shew.
If all the rest should chance to hide their Face,   165
My *Seven Stars* may well Supply their Place.
Now, hold, my Pen; Plato of old would have
But *Four Heroick Lines* upon a Grave.

Help me, my God, at Work like them to be;
And take their Deaths as Watch-words unto me.   170

Ex *Paulini* Panegyrico in Oblitum *Celsi.*

Heu, quid agam? Dubia Pendens Pietate Laboro,
    Gratuler an Doleam? Dignus utroque Puer.
Cujus Amor Lacrymas et Amor mihi Gaudia Suadet;
    Sed Gaudere Fides, Flere jubet Pietas.   175
Tam Modicum Patribus, tam dulci e pignore Fructum
    Defleo in Exiguo Temporis esse datum.
Laetor Obisse brevi functum Mortalia Seclo,
    Ut cito divinas Consequeretur Opes.[15]

[14] Merope, one of the seven daughters of Atlas and Pleione, married a mortal
and thus surrendered her own immortal nature.

[15] Here Mather quotes, but takes liberties with, *Carmen 31* by Paulinus of
Nola (A.D. 355–c. 431), which F. J. E. Raby suggests is probably the first
Christian elegy (*A History of Christian Latin Poetry* [Oxford, 1958], p. 105).
Mather omits two of Paulinus' lines, which in the original follow line 6 of
Mather's quotation,

Rursus ut aeternae bona volvo perennia vitae,
Quae deus in caelo praeparat innocuis,

and he has substituted *Consequeretur* [attain to] for *perfrueretur* [enjoy fully]
in the final line. The full passage may be translated:

Alas, what shall I do? Pondering, I suffer in fluctuating love;
Should I rejoice or grieve? The boy [Celsus] is worthy of both [joy and
    sorrow],
Love for him moves me to tears, love moves me to joy;
But faith urges me to rejoice, piety impels me to weep.
I weep that so little enjoyment of so sweet a child was
Given to the parents in this trifle of time.
As I meditate in turn the perpetual good things of eternal life
Which God prepares in Heaven for the innocent.
I rejoice that having lived his brief life he has passed beyond mortal affairs,
So that he may rapidly and fully enjoy divine riches.

Epitaph

169v

DUMMER¹ the Shepherd *Sacrific'd*
By Wolves, *because the* Sheep *he priz'd.*
The Orphans *Father, Churches* Light,
The Love of Heav'n, *of* Hell *the* Spight.
The Countries Gapman,² *and the* Face   5
That Shone, *but knew it not, with* Grace.
Hunted by Devils, *but Reliev'd*
By Angels, *and on high Receiv'd.*
The Martyr'd Pelican, *who Bled*
Rather than leave his Charge Unfed.   10
A *proper* Bird of Paradise,
Shot, and Flown thither in a Trice.

Lord, *hear the Cry of* Righteous DUMMER's *Wounds,*
Ascending still against the Salvage Hounds,
That Worry thy dear Flocks; *and let the* Cry   15
Add Force to Theirs *that at thine* Altar *lye.*

To Compleat the *Epitaph* of this Good Man there
now needs no more than the famous old *Chaucer's* Motto,

*Mors mihi ærumnarum Requies.*³

[Go then, my Dove, but now no longer mine]

Go *then,* my DOVE, but now no longer *mine;*¹
Leave *Earth,* and now in *heavenly Glory* shine,
Bright for thy Wisdome, Goodness, Beauty here;
Now *brighter* in a more *angelick Sphære.*
JESUS, with whom thy Soul did long to be,
Into His *Ark,* and Arms, has taken thee.
Dear *Friends,* with whom thou didst so dearly live,
Feel thy *one Death* to *them* a *thousand* give.

¹ Shubael Dummer (died York, Maine, 25 January 1691/2, *aet.* 56), victim of
an Indian attack.
² an alert man.
³ Death for me is a respite from hard labor.
¹ Abigail, Mather's wife, died in November 1702.

Thy *Prayers* are done; thy *Alms* are spent; thy *Pains*
Are *ended* now, in *endless* Joyes and Gains.
    I faint, till thy last Words to Mind I call;
    Rich Words! HEAV'N, HEAV'N WILL MAKE AMENDS
                            FOR ALL.

[O Glorious CHRIST of GOD; I live]

O Glorious CHRIST of GOD; I live
    In Views of Thee alone.
Life to my gasping Soul, oh! give!
    Shine Thou, or I'm undone.

I cannot live, my GOD, if thou
    Enlivnest not my Faith.
I'm dead; I'm lost; oh! Save me now
    from a lamented Death!

For the Return of my Health, I added:

My glorious Healer, thou restore
    My Health, and make me whole.
But this is what I most implore;
    Oh, for an Healed Soul!

BENJAMIN COLMAN

(1673–1747)

Benjamin Colman was the Puritan minister whose tract on "The Government and Improvement of Mirth" demolished for perceptive posterity the cliché of New England Puritans as a humorless lot. But Colman's career, beginning at the turn of the eighteenth century, also reflects significant, if subtle, changes in New England Puritanism, and in literary taste as well.

Born in 1673 in Boston, Benjamin Colman later attended Harvard, graduating in 1692. Subsequently he traveled to England, where he served as minister at Bath. His return to Boston to assume pastoral duties at the Brattle Street Church was no simple response to ministerial calling in New England, however, for Colman's acceptance of the position allied him with Thomas Brattle and William Leverett, whose opposition to the Mathers was developing steadily into a feud.

Brattle and Leverett, who had been tutors at Harvard while Increase Mather sojourned in England for four years, were later chastised by Mather in an Epistle reminding them that they, younger than he, were his protégés and ought not to assert themselves independent of him. An undercurrent of dissension continued until a group of Boston merchants, supported by Brattle and Leverett, proposed the founding of a liberal Congregational Church in Boston. At this point lines of opposition against the Mathers were explicitly drawn. The Brattle-Leverett faction urged that Colman be invited to officiate at the new church, for Colman had been a favorite pupil of the former Harvard tutors. Knowing that the Mathers would probably attempt to prevent Colman's ordination in the usual Congregational way, the organizers of the new church saw to it that he obtained a Presbyterian ordination before leaving London for New England in 1699.

Within a month of assuming his new duties, Colman issued for his church a "Manifesto" of its principles. Although there was no professed variance from Puritan theology, Colman's manifesto enumerated changes in church policy. The personal narration of individual conversion experience, previously requisite for admission to the Lord's Supper, was to be abolished. In addition, the children of all professed Christians, whether communicants or not, were to be baptized. There were other innovations in the church service as well, but these two were the salient points which violated the traditional New England Congregational way so staunchly supported by the Mathers. In their view, it was one thing to tolerate the presence of other, erring, sects in the colony, but quite another to be faced with insurrection from within one's own ranks. Colman's manifesto, detestable to the Mathers, marked a distinct step in the breakdown of exclusive and restrictive Puritanism in New England.

The Brattle Street Church Manifesto found no immediate widespread popularity, however, nor was it adopted by any other congregation. Indeed, a street ballad ridiculed the ecclesiastical innovations. But Colman's career did not suffer, for after a time the controversy quieted, and he continued his pastoral duties unimpaired. Upon John Leverett's death, Colman was invited to assume the presidency of Harvard, but his congregation prevailed upon him to remain with them in the Brattle Street Church whose reputation was that of the intellectually elite.

Just as Colman's career reflects change in New England Puritanism, so do some of his verses reveal new literary trends soon to be dominant in England and the colonies. His verses, like his manifesto, assert traditional Puritan theology, but his manner of execution departs from that of many of his predecessors. The rough cadence characteristic of earlier seventeenth-century verse has yielded in Colman to a much greater syntactic smoothness, and to a clarity that permits immediate and full perception of his narrative progression. It is no surprise, therefore, that Colman's last poem is dedicated to Alexander Pope, whose verse manner Colman so sympathized with.

A Quarrel with Fortune[1]

So have I seen a little silly Fly
Upon a blazing Taper dart and die.
The foolish Insect ravish'd with so bright
And fair a Glory, would devour the Light.

[1] written for Miss Ashurst, daughter of Sir Henry Ashurst, at her request, c. 1697.

At first he wheels about the threatning Fire,   5
With a Career as fleet as his Desire:
This Ceremony past, he joins the same
In Hopes to be transform'd himself to Flame.
The fiery, circumambient Sparkles glow,
And vainly warn him of his Overthrow,   10
But resolute he'll to Destruction go.
  So mean-born Mortals, such as I, aspire,
And injure with unhallowed Desire,
The Glory we ought only to admire.
  We little think of the intense fierce Flame,   15
That Gold alone is Proof against the same;
And that such Trash as we like drossy Lead,
Consume before it, and it strikes us dead.

[To "Philomela"][1]

So Paradise was brightened, so 'twas blest,
When Innocence and Beauty it possest.
Such was it's more retired Path and Seat,
For Eve and musing Angels a Retreat.
Such Eden's Streams, and Banks, and tow'ring Groves;
Such Eve her self, and such her Muse and Loves.
Only there wants an Adam on the Green,
Or else all Paradise might here be seen.

To Urania
On the Death of her first and only Child

Why mourns my beauteous Friend, bereft?
Her Saviour and her Heav'n are left:
Her lovely Babe is there at Rest,
In Jesus' Arms embrac'd and blest.
  Would you, Urania, wish it down   5
From yon bright Throne, and shining Crown?
To your cold Arms, and empty Breast,
Could Heaven indulge you the Request;

[1] extempore poem on Miss Elizabeth Singer ("Philomela") of Agford near Frome who had "a Volume of Poems then in Print, being about her twenty-fourth Year."

Your Bosom's neither warm nor fair,
Compar'd with *Abraham's:* leave it there.
   He, the fam'd Father of the Just,
Beheld himself but Earth and Dust,
Before the Will of God most High,
And bid his Darling *Isaac* die.
   When Heav'n requir'd in Sacrifice
The dear Desire of his Eyes;
And more to prove his Love commands
The Offering from the Father's Hands;
See how th' illustrious Parent yields,
And seeks *Moriah's* mournful Fields.
   He bound his lovely only Child
For Death; his Soul serene and mild:
He reach'd his Hand, and grasp'd the Knife,
To give up the devoted Life.
Less Heaven demands of thee, my Friend;
And less thy Faith shall recommend.
All it requires, is to resign,
To Heaven's own Act, and make it thine
By Silence under Discipline.
   The least we to our Maker owe!
The least, *Urania,* you did vow!
The least that was your Saviour's Claim,
When o're your Babe his glorious Name
Was call'd in awful Baptism! Then
You gave it back to Heaven again.
   You freely own'd that happy Hour,
Heaven's Right, Propriety and Power,
The Loan at Pleasure to resume,
And call the pretty Stranger Home.
   A Witness likewise at its Birth
I stood, that Hour of Joy and Mirth:
I saw your thankful Praises rise,
And flow from pleas'd, uplifted Eyes:
With rais'd Devotion, one Accord,
We gave the Infant to its Lord.
   And think, *Urania,* 'ere that Day,
While the fair Fruit in secret lay,
Unseen, yet lov'd within the Womb,
(Which also might have been its Tomb)
How oft, before it blest your Sight,

In secret Prayers with great Delight,
You did recognize Heaven's Right.
    Now stand to these blest Acts, my Friend:
Stand firmly by them to the End:
Now you are try'd, repeat the Act;   55
Too just, too glorious to retract.
    Think, dear *Urania*, how for thee,
God gave his *only* Son to be,
An Offering on the cursed Tree.
    Think, how the *Son of God* on Earth;   60
(The spotless Virgins blessed Birth)
Our lovely Babes took up, and blest;
And them high Heirs of Heaven confest!
    Think, how the Bless'd of Women stood,
While impious Hands, to th' cursed Wood   65
Nail'd down her only Son and God!
    Learn hence, *Urania*, to be dumb!
Learn thou the Praise that may become
Thy lighter Grief; which Heaven does please
To take such wondrous Ways to ease.   70
    Adore the God, who from thee takes,
No more than what he gives and makes:
And means in tenderest Love, the Rod
To serve to thy eternal Good.

Another to Urania, &c

    Attend, ye mournful Parents, while
I sing, a *Mother* in *Israel;*
The fam'd, the gracious *Shunamite*,
Whose beauteous Story would invite
A Saint to yield her only one,   5
Almost without a Tear or Groan.
    A wondrous Son she did embrace,
Heaven's signal Work, and special Grace;
Nor long embrac'd, but on her Knees
Arrested by a fierce Disease,   10
Scarce could he cry, *My Head, My Head!*
E'er the dear Parent saw him dead:
She laid him breathless on the Bed.
    Deep was her Anguish, yet her Peace
She held, and went to God for Ease.   15

No Signs of Grief distort her Face,
Nor cloud its wonted Beams of Grace.
No Moans, no Shrieks, no piercing Cries;
No wringed Hands, or flowing Eyes
Distressed the House in that Surprize.   20
   She hastes her to the Man of God,
Hastes to the Place of his Abode:
Mildly denies the Cause to tell
To her dear Spouse; all would be well
She trusts: So did her Faith excell.   25
Elisha, with a tender Fear,
Saw his illustrious Friend draw near:
'Twas not one of the Holy-Days
Sacred to publick Prayer and Praise;
Why then the *Shunamite* from Home?   30
On what great Errand was she come?
Her Speed bespoke some weighty Care,
Which generous Friendship long'd to share.
   It struck him, something had befell
The Husband, Child,—*All was not well*—   35
Go, run *Gehazi*, said the Seer,
Enquire, with Earnestness sincere;
"Say, generous Host, if all be well?—
"*All's well;* my Lord! she said, and fell   40
At her great Intercessor's Feet:
There vents her Grief in Accents sweet,
Mild in her Anguish, in her Plaints discreet.
   Such dear *Urania,* you to me!
O might I be but such to thee!
   Mind, gracious Friend, the Word she said, 45
All well, and yet the Child was dead.
   What God ordains is *well* and best.
Well 'tis with ours, when gone to Rest.
It's *well* with us, who stay behind,
If more from Earth and Sense refin'd   50
W' are patient, pray'rful, meek, resign'd.

A POEM On ELIJAHS Translation,
Occasion'd by the DEATH of the
Reverend and Learned,
Mr. SAMUEL WILLARD[1]

I Sing the MAN, by Heav'ns peculiar Grace,
The *Prince of Prophets,* of the *Chosen Race,*
Rais'd and Accomplisht for *degenerate Times,*
To Stem the *Ebb* with Faith and Zeal
       Sublime;
T' assert forsaken *Truth,* to *Check* the Rage   5
Of rampant Vice, and cure a Wicked *Age.*
Such *Times* need such a *Prophet,* and in his
       Death
Is quencht the Light of *Israel,* and their
       Breath.

Plain was the *Saint,* his Soul by Grace
       refin'd,
His *Girdle* mean, but much adorn'd his *Mind:*   10
In Face, as well as Mind, above the Toyes
Of this vain World, and all its sensual Joyes:
Simple in *Diet,* negligent of *Dress,*

2 *Kings* i. 8   Hairy and rough his Robe, meet to express
St. *Mat.* iii. 4   One Mortify'd to things of Time and Sense,   15
        To Truth and things Divine a Love Intense.

1 *Kings* xix. 10   *Jealous* for *Israel,* and the LORD OF
          HOSTS,
        Disdain'd to see HIM Rival'd by a *Post,*
        Mourn'd his *forsaken Covenant,* and Worship
           lost.
        Courageous, dar'd Alone to stand the Shock,   20
1 *Kings* xviii. 22, 27   Of num'rous *Priests* of *Baal,* and to deride
          their *Stock.*
        Fac'd feirce Tyrannous *Powers,* told their
          Crimes,
        And shames deserv'd, the Judgments of their
          Times.

[1] (1639–1707), vice-president of Harvard College (1701–7).

His and Truths *Triumphs* Glorious: Strange to
say!

1 *Kings* v. 39, 40   A debaucht Nation Convert in a Day,   25
And sham'd, enrag'd *Impostures* fled away!

A wondrous *Saint;* Inspir'd, Imploy'd and
Led
1 *Kings* xvii. 6, 9,   By Heav'nly Love; by many *Wonders* fed.
16; xix. 5, 7   The *Care* of Heav'n, the *Darling* of his GOD,
Signally *Sav'd*, cheer'd by his *Staff* and *Rod.*   30
Voracious *Ravens* yield Him up their Prey:
Glad *Angels* to his Succour wing away:
And Heav'n, to show its Empire more,
commands
Hopeless Relief from famishing *Widows*
hands.

St. *James* v. 17   *He Pray'd*, the *Sealed Heav'ns* withheld
their *Rain:*   35
He Pray'd, the op'ned Clouds discharge again.
2 *Kings* i. 10   Provokt, *He* askt; *strange* blazing show'rs of
St. *Luk* ix. 54   Flame
Stream down, and *Sodoms Day* renewed
came.
2 *Kings* ii. 8   He struck the *Floods*, the refluent Waves
divide,
His *Mantles* Breath drove back the flowing
Tyde.   40
What aild thee, O astonisht Sea, to fly?
Jordan! from *Joshua's* dayes thy Banks not
dry!
1 *Kings* xvii. 22, 24   Yet Greater Wonders view: He spake, the
Dead
In *Sin*, or *Grave*, lift up their fallen Head:
Witness the happy *Mother*, fully won   45
To Heaven as she receiv'd her raised *Son:*
Blest Work of *Grace!* the Mercy of the *Mean*
Illustrious, as the Saving *Change*, is Seen.

Not less Miraculous the *Prophets Fasts*,
1 *Kings* xix. 8   *Labours* and *Travels* glcriously Surpast: 50
His Strength and Application, as his Trust
Noble and vast, Angelick and August:
In publick Toils consum'd, of Life profuse,

Exhausted in retired holy Muse,
On the deep things of God, and *Mysteries*
      Abstruse. 55

Such Labours *Bounteous Heav'n* is wont to
      Crown
With Heav'nly *Visions*, Light and Joyes
      unknown.

Exod. xxxiv. 6 So Heav'nly Glories dazled *Moses* Eyes
2 *Cor.* xii. 4 And Lab'ring *Paul* was caught to *Paradise*.
No less *Elijah* to his *Saviour* dear, 60
No less his Cares and Toils, his Pray'rs and
      Tears;
Nor less wou'd Heav'n his suff'ring Soul to
      cheer.

1 *Kings* xix. 11, 12, The GOD of *Israel* past before the *Cave*
13; *Exod.* xx. 18, In Majesty, as 'erst the *Law* he gave,
19 And frightned Nature seem'd to seek a Grave. 65
Tempests and *Flames*, and *Earthquakes*
      marcht before,
Speaking the Terrors of Almighty Pow'r;
These usher'd in the *small still Voice* of
      Grace;
His Soul grew Calm, Serene the troubled
      Place:
Husht as the Winds were all his boist'rous
      Fears, 70
The Humble *Saint*, call'd forth by God,
      appears;
With Mantle *wrapt* about his face he stood,
Afraid to *hear*, nor wisht to *see* his GOD.

Yet lest the *Hero* as his GOD we show,
2 *Cor.* xii. 7 Or He Elate with Visions, vain shou'd grow, 75
At times his *Passions* did the *Man* betray,
That Saints have *Sin*, and Prophets are but
      Clay.
1 *Kings* xix. 3, 9 Too *Tim'rous* midst his Triumphs; left to *fly*
St. *James* v. 17 A *Womans* Rage and Threats, and wish to
      die.
St. *James* v. 14, 18 *Desponding* moan'd Christ of his Church
      bereft, 80
And not a single Saint in *Israel* left.

344

Psal. xxxix. 5	All to hide Pride from Man, to show how
	<div align="right">*Vain*</div>
	We are at *Best,* and undue Tho'ts restrain.
1 *John* i. 5	GOD is the *Light,* in whom's no *Shade at*
	<div align="right">*all,*</div>
	To *Him* in prostrate Adorations fall. 85
	Created Brightness ever has its Blots,
	And even *Persia's Idol* has its *Spots.*
	Yet Admiration, Reverence and Love
	Are due to Saints on Earth, or those Above.
	Sure the *curst Spirit* that hates is born of Hell, 90
	Nor is less *Monster* then foul *Jezebel:*
1 *Kings* xix. 2	*She* Murd'rous sought his Blood: *Ahab* his
	<div align="right">Name</div>
1 *Kings* xviii. 21	(*Dearer* than Life) with sland'rous lies
	<div align="right">defames:</div>
	And both invet'rate *Hate,* and deadly *War*
	<div align="right">proclaim.</div>
	Yet Spite of *Envy,* Spite of *Malice* curst, 95
	VERTUE shall live: see *Bloated Fiend,* and
	<div align="right">burst!</div>
	See the *fair Name* Immortal in my *Verse!*
	See the *Strew'd Glories* on the *Hero's Herse!*
	A *Name imbalm'd* shall be the *Just* Mans lot,
	While Vicious *Teeth* shall *gnash,* and *Names*
	<div align="right">shall *rot.* 100</div>
	Return, *my Muse,* and Sing his faithful
	<div align="right">Care,</div>
2 *Kings* ii. 2, 3	And noblest *Trust,* in happy *Bethels Chair.*
Gen. xxviii. 12, 17,	*Hail,* Venerable Seat! from *Jacobs* dayes
19	Sacred to *Israels* GOD, and to his Praise!
	Blest evermore with Visions! the Resort 105
	Of Holy Angels! Heav'ns Inferior Court!
	Hail dreadful Place! th' *Eternals* blest Abode!
	The Gate of Heav'n, and the House of GOD!
	Blest place of Inspiration! ——
	Here stood the Spacious *Colledge,*[2] *Israels*
	<div align="right">*pride:* 110</div>
	And here th' Illustrious *Seer* did preside.

[2] Harvard.

Stately the *Dome,* worthy the Beauteous
Train,
Religion pure devoted to Maintain,
And to the Age to come the Laws Divine
explain.
Richly *Endow'd* by every pious *Zeal,*   115
Studious of *Zions* Glory and her Weal:
Blest *Tribute!* dear to Heav'n: A pious *Aid*
Given to Christ, and liberally repaid
In richer Blessings to the *Church* and *State;*
So *He* returns us what we *Consecrate.*   120

Hence *Israels Chiefs,* and hence her
Teachers came;
Hence *Truth* and *Grace,* hence issu'd *Light*
and *Flame;*
Hence Men Renown'd, and of Celebrious
Fame.
Micaiah one: from foul *Illusion* free,
Faithful to God, and *Ahab* true to thee!   125
Kings trembled as he Spake and Homage
paid,
Of *Truth* and the *Superior Man* afraid.
Elisha too, to greater *Glories* born,
Was hence: and high exalted is his *Horn!*

These *beauteous Sons* were the blest
Prophets pride,   130
Under *his Wing* they bloom'd, and flourisht
by his Side:
Paid him a Reverence profound and true,
To Heav'ns Election, *Israels* Suffrage due.

Them, as by Office bound, He did Inspect,
Taught heav'nly Truth, and Errors did
correct: 135
Cherisht the Good, and form'd their Manners
well,
But searcht out Vice, th' Infection to expel.
Meek and Majestick, Affable and Grave,
Lowly and Good; and all that's Great and
Brave.
He Overaw'd and Charm'd: Base hearts he
won,   140
And perfected where Goodness was begun.

1 *Kings* xxii. 8, 19,
28

To *them* His *Lectures* on the Holy Law,
Sublime they were, new *Mysteries* they saw:
Like Him with Heav'nly Light and Joyes
Inspir'd,
Their ravisht Minds the *Sacred Deeps*
admir'd.   145

St. John viii. 56   They saw the promised MESSIAH's *dayes,*
And the Glad *Schools* resounded with his
Praise.

Mal. iv. 5   They Sang the *Baptist* in their *Prophets*
Mat. xvii. 12, 13   *Spirit,*
Luke i. 17   And blest the *Saint Elect* that shou'd Inherit.

St. Mat. xvii, 2, 3   They Sang of the *Transfigur'd Saviours*
Luke ix. 31   *Rayes,*   150
What *Fav'rite Saints,* from Heav'n it self, to
gaze,
On Glories yet Unknown; and Talk of High
Mysterious Truths; into which *Angels Pry,*
And pass in Transports *Immortality.*

Psalm lxviii. 18   They Sang his High Ascent, and Gifts
Act ii. 3, 4   Ineffable,   155
Designed to   The *Cloven Tongues of Fire* on *Pentecost*
resemble the   that *fell,*
Ascent *meditated*   And what *Great Type* shou'd all these Wonders
on, and to represent   *Figure* and *Foretell.*
the Poverty of
Number *and*   Thus *taught,* they waited long the *Great*
Rhime   *Event,*
to express the   Foresaw the Day, Amaz'd at the Portent:
unspeakable Gifts.   Stupendous *Grace* and *Power* they View'd,
Ador'd   160
The Sov'rain GOD, and Pry'd into his Word.

And now the *Saint* had his *Last Visit* made,
His Solemn *Charge,* and final *Blessing* said.
His Weeping *Sons* receiv'd his last *Adieu,*
With eager Eyes their *Breath* departing View,   165
2 Kings ii. 7   *And following far behind to Jordans Brink*
they drew.
Each Emulous to *Succeed,* but well prepar'd
To welcome Him whom Heav'n had *Heir*
declar'd.

1 Kings xix. 16, 19   *ELISHA* He! The Wisdom of the choice
Applauded with United Hearts and Voice.   170

Un-envy'd in the *Schools,* had long out-shone
In Gifts Divine, and *Rival* there was none.
Glorious the *Seers* Fidelity was here,
And Heav'ns Good Conduct Splendid did
          appear.
Nor *Blood,* nor *Name,* his upright Zeal retard,   175
Gods *Choice* and *Will* he simply did regard;
Whom Heav'n accomplishes it will reward.

The happy *Youth* cleav'd to his *Fathers*
          feet,
Ministring to Him with a *Duty* meet;
    2 Kings iii. 11, 12
From his *Oraculous* Lips askt Counsel
          Sage,   180
And had the Pray'rs and Blessings of his *Age.*

Yet there remain'd the last and *dy'ng*
          Bequest,
And the Wise *Son* had ready his Request.
"Say, now at Parting, what I shall bequeath:"   *2 Kings ii. 9*
Trembling He fell the *Prophets* feet beneath,   185
Grieved to part, afraid to speak his Tho't,
Conscious how vast the Blessing was he so't:
With Mouth in dust he said,—"May I inherit
"A *double Portion* of thy Blessed *Spirit!*
"O might my last and highest *Wish* have
          place,   190
"An *Em'nent Measure* of thy *Gifts* and
          Grace!"

Divine *Ambition!* to be *Wise* and *Good!*
So he his *Fame* and Interest understood.
Modest his Wish, He only askt *a part,*
And Heav'n gave *all,* even an *Equal Heart:*   195
    1 Kings iii. 5, 9, 10, 12
Obvious the Truth, from *Sacred Record*
          known,
None came so near *Elijah* as his wondrous
          Son.

'Twas at *high Noon,* the Day serene and
          fair,
Mountains of Lum'nous Clouds roll'd in the
          Air,
When on a sudden, from the *radiant* Skies,   200
Superior Light *flasht* in *Elijah's* Eyes:

The Heav'ns were *cleft*, and from th'
     Imperial Throne
A *Stream* of Glory, *daz'ling Splendor*, Shone:
Beams of ten Thousand *Suns* Shot round
     about,
The Sun and every blazon'd Cloud went out: 205
Bright Hosts of *Angels* lin'd the Heav'nly
     Way,
To guard the *Saint* up to Eternal Day.
Then down the *Steep Descent*, a *Chariot*
     Bright,
And *Steeds of Fire*, swift as the Beams of
     Light.
Wing'd Seraphs ready stood, *bow'd low* to
     greet 210
The *Fav'rite Saint*, and *hand* him to his *Seat*.

Enthron'd he Sat, *Transform'd* with Joyes
     his *Mein*,
Calm his *gay Soul*, and like his Face *Serene*.
His Eye and burning Wishes *to his* GOD,
Forward he bow'd, and on the *Triumph* rode. 215
*"Saluted, as he past the Heav'nly Croud,
"With Shouts of Joy, and *Hallelujahs* laud.
"Ten thousand thousand *Angel Trumpets*
     Sound,
"And the vast Realms of Heav'n all eccho'd
     round.

Acts i. 9, 10 They Sang of *Greater Triumphs* yet to come, 220
Their next Descent to wait the SAVIOUR
     Home:

St. Mat. xxiv. 31 And the *glad Errand* of the *Final Day*,
The *raised Dust* of Saints to bring away
In equal *Triumph*, and in like *Array*.

Thus midst Inspir'd, Sublime, Prophetick
     Songs, 225
(Sweet Melody) the *Vision* past along.
The *Prince of Air* Accurst fled swift the *Light*,
And heav'nly *Sounds*, more grating than the
     Sight;
Blaspheem'd, and rag'd and gnasht in furious
     Spite.

* Mr. *Standen.*

2 Kings ii. 12 Elisha saw: "My Father, loud he cry'd,   230
"My Father! Israels Safety! and her Pride!
"More wer't Thou our Defence and Glory far,
"Than all our Chariots and strong Troops of
War.
"Thy Pray'rs and Pow'r with God did more
secure
"Our Tott'ring State, and naked Coasts
immure,   235
"Than all our Arms. ————

He said: Nor more cou'd see: Immense the
space!
The Flying Glory now had gain'd the Place
1 Tim. vi. 16 Of Light ne're to be seen by Mortal Eye:
Acts i. 11 Nor longer gaz'd he on the closing Skie.   240
2 Kings ii. 12 With Anguish seiz'd his goodly Robes he
rent,
Himself, the Church, and Schools did sore
lament.
The Prophets Bliss cou'd not his Tears
restrain,
He wept their Loss, in His Eternal Gain.
Nor yet in Useless tears staid he to vent   245
His mighty Griefs, on Greater things Intent:

2 Kings v. 13 The Mantle faln with Joy surprizing spy'd,
Laid the dear Pledge close to his panting Side;
Sov'rain Receipt! his fainting heart reviv'd.
By it Install'd in the blest Prophets Place!   250
With it receiv'd his Spirit and his Grace!
The Sacred Banner flying in his Hand,
Display'd his Empire, on the distant Strand;
Nature Obsequious, to his dread Command.
Triumphant-wise, the pensive Conqu'ror
stood,   255
The precious Relick wav'd, and smote the
flood:
2 Kings v. 14 "Where is the LORD, Elijahs GOD?" He
cry'd.
Th' Obedient Waves again in haste divide.
He pass'd: the ravisht Prophets saw; confest
The Miracle of Grace, and thankful blest   260
2 Kings v. 15 Th' Eternal SPIRIT, and his Glorious Rest.

2 Kings v. 15

O'rejoy'd they run the Saint Elect to meet,
And *bow* beneath the bright *Successors* feet.
They breathe their Pray'rs and Blessings in
his Arms,
Cheer his sad Soul, and their own Passions
charm.   265

St. Luke xxiv. 32

Their Hearts within 'em *glow*, their *Graces*
burn;
Each speak Mysterious *Oracles* in their turn:

Exod. xxxiv. 30

Inspir'd their Mind, *Transform'd* their very
Mein,
In Both *Superior Grace* and *Beauty* seen.
In Holiness and Truth sweet their *Accord*,   270
And Faith their *Consolation* did afford,

St. Mark ix. 4

Elijahs more Illustrious *Second Coming* with
his Lord.

A Hymn of Praise,
on a recovery from sickness

1

God of my life! What Songs of praise
To thy great name I owe?
Praise, like thy mercies, thro' my days
Should swift and freely flow.

2

Fast to the grave I sank: My life
Down to the dust flow'd fast:
Thy pow'r and grace to my relief
Came down with equal haste.

3

Thy word which kills and makes alive,
Rebuk'd the mortal foe.
My Saviour came, bid me revive,
Take up my bed and goe.

4

Lord! at thy word I live: The Dead
 At the same word shall rise:
The rising just thy praise shall spread,
 And rend with Songs the skies.

5

Like them, My Saviour, with my Song
 Of thanks I gladly come:
This does of right from them belong
 Thou callest from the Tomb.

6

Lord! To thy praise I consecrate
 My spar'd, renewed time:
Take hence my life an happier State,
 More Heav'nly, more Sublime.

THE BAY PSALM BOOK

The first book written and printed in America, *The Whole Booke of Psalmes Faithfully Translated into English Metre* (Cambridge, 1640) and more familiarly known as the Bay Psalm Book, represents the work of a group of leading New England clergymen—perhaps as many as twelve or thirteen men—who undertook to provide "a plaine translation . . . [of] the hebrew words into english language, and Davids poetry into english meetre; that soe wee may sing in Sion the Lords songs of prayse according to his owne will . . . ."

At its worst, as in Psalm 137, the Bay Psalm Book is "utter rhythmic and syntactic wreckage"; at its best, as in the four selections printed below, it demands that we come to terms with the verse in recognition of its place in American literary history and of the fact that it was composed by some of the most learned and respected men of the era.

Psalme 1

[1]   O Blessed man, that in th' advice
        Of wicked doeth not walk:
        Nor stand in sinners way, or sit
2   In chayre of scornfull folk.
        But in the law of Jehovah,
        Is his longing delight:
        And in his law doth meditate,
        By day and eke by night.
3   And he shall be like to a tree
        Planted by water-rivers:
        That in his season yeilds his fruit,
        And his leafe never withers.
4   And all he doth, shall prosper well,
        The wicked are not so:
        But they are like unto the chaffe,
        Which winde drives to and fro.

5   Therefore shall not ungodly men,
        Rise to stand in the doome,
        Nor shall the sinners with the just,
        In their assemblie *come*.

6   For of the righteous men, the Lord
        Acknowledgeth the way:
        But the way of ungodly men,
        Shall utterly decay.

Psalme 19

To the chiefe musician a psalme of David

[1]   The heavens doe declare
        The majesty of God:
        Also the firmament shews forth
        His handy-work abroad.

2   Day speaks to day, knowledge
        Night hath to night declar'd.

3   There neither speach nor language is,
        Where their voyce is not heard.

4   Through all the earth their line
        Is gone forth, and unto
        The utmost end of all the world,
        Their speaches reach also:
        A Tabernacle hee
        In them pitcht for the Sun.

5   Who Bridegroom like from's chamber goes
        Glad Giants-race to run.

6   From heavens utmost end,
        His course and compassing;
        To ends of it, and from the heat
        Thereof is hid nothing.

2

7   The Lords law perfect is,
        The soule converting back:
        Gods testimony faithfull is,
        Makes wise who-wisdome-lack.

8   The statutes of the Lord,
        Are right, and glad the heart:

The Lords commandement is pure,
  Light doth to eyes impart.
9 Jehovahs feare is cleane,
  And doth indure for ever:
The judgements of the Lord are true,
  And righteous altogether.
10 Then gold, then much fine gold,
  More to be prized are,
Then hony, and the hony-comb,
  Sweeter they are by farre.
11 Also thy servant is
  Admonished from hence:
And in the keeping of the same
  Is a full recompence.
12 Who can his errors know?
  From secret faults cleanse mee.
13 And from presumptuous-sins, let thou
  Kept back thy servant bee:
Let them not beare the rule
  In me, and then shall I
Be perfect, and shall cleansed bee
  From much iniquity.
14 Let the words of my mouth,
  And the thoughts of my heart,
Be pleasing with thee, Lord, my Rock
  Who my redeemer art.

Psalme 103
A psalme *of David*

[1] O Thou my soule, Jehovah blesse,
  And all things that in me
Most inward are, in humblenes
  His Holy-Name blesse ye
2 The Lord blesse in humility,
  O thou my soule: also
Put not out of thy memory
  All's bounties, thee unto.
3 For hee it is who pardoneth
  All thine iniquityes:
He it is also who healeth
  All thine infirmityes.

4 Who thy life from destruction
  Redeems: who crowneth thee
 With his tender compassion
  And kinde benignitee.

5 Who with good things abundantlee
  Doth satisfie thy mouth:
 So that like as the Eagles bee
  Renewed is thy youth.

6 The Lord doth judgement and justice
  For all oppressed ones.

7 To Moses shew'd those wayes of his:
  His acts to Isr'ells sonnes.

2

8 The Lord is mercifull also
  Hee's very gracious:
 And unto anger hee is slow,
  In mercy plenteous.

9 Contention he will not maintaine
  To perpetuity:
 Nor he his anger will retaine
  Unto eternity.

10 According to our sins *likewise*
  To us hee hath not done:
 Nor hath he our iniquityes
  Rewarded us upon.

11 Because even as the heavens are
  In height the earth above:
 So toward them that doe him feare
  Confirmed is his love.

12 Like as the East and West they are
  Farre in their distances:
 He hath remov'd away so far
  From us our trespasses.

13 A fathers pitty like unto,
  Which he his sonnes doth beare
 Like pitty doth Jehovah show
  To them that doe him feare.

14 For he doth know this frame of ours:
  He minds that dust wee bee.

15 Mans dayes are like the grasse: like flowrs
  In field, so flourisheth hee.

16 For over it the winde doth passe,
  And it away doth goe;
  Also the place wheras it was
  Noe longer shall it know.

3

17 But yet Gods mercy ever is,
  Shall be, and aye hath been
  To them that feare him; and's justice
  Unto childrens children.

18 To such as keepe his covenant,
  That doe in minde up lay
  The charge of his commandement
  That it they may obey.

19 The Lord hath in the heavens hye
  Established his throne:
  And over all his Royallty
  Doth beare dominion.

20 O yee his Angells that excell
  In strength, blesse yee the Lord,
  That doe his word, that harken well
  Unto the voyce of's word.

21 All yee that are the Lords armies,
  O blesse Jehovah *still:*
  And all yee ministers of his,
  His pleasure that fullfill.

22 Yea, all his works in places all
  Of his dominion,
  Blesse yee Jehovah: o my Soul,
  Jehovah blesse *alone.*

Psalme 107

[1] O Give yee thanks unto the Lord,
  Because that good is hee:
  Because his loving kindenes lasts
  To perpetuitee.

2 So let the Lords redeem'd say: whom
  Hee freed from th' enemies hands:

3 And gathred them from East, and West,
  From South, and Northerne lands.

4   I'th desart, in a desart way
        They wandred: no towne finde,
5   To dwell in. Hungry and thirsty:
        Their soule within them pinde.
[6] Then did they to Jehovah cry
        When they were in distresse:
    Who did them set at liberty
        Out of their anguishes.
7   In such a way that was most right
        He led them forth also:
    That to a citty which they might
        Inhabit they might go.
8   O that men would Jehovah prayse
        For his great goodnes *then:*
    And for his workings wonderfull
        Unto the sonnes of men.
9   Because that he the longing soule
        Doth throughly satisfy:
    The hungry soule he also fills
        With good abundantly.

2

10   Such as in darknes' and within
        The shade of death abide;
    Who are in sore affliction,
        Also in yron tyde:
11   By reason that against the words
        Of God they did rebell;
    Also of him that is most high
        Contemned the counsell.
12   Therefore with molestation
        Hee did bring downe their heart:
    Downe they did fall, and none their was
        Could help them to impart.
13   Then did they to Jehovah cry
        When they were in distress:
    Who did them set at liberty
        Out of their anguishes.
14   He did them out of darknes bring,
        Also deaths shade from under:
    As for the bands that they were in
        He did break them asunder.

15   O that men would Jehovah prayse
         For his great goodness *then:*
     And for his workings wonderfull
         Unto the sonnes of men.

16   For he hath all to shivers broke
         The gates that were of brasse:
     And he asunder cut each barre
         That made of yron was.

3

17   For their transgressions and their sins,
         Fooles do affliction beare.

18   All kinde of meate their soule abhorres:
         To deaths gate they draw neare.

19   Then did they to Jehovah cry
         When they were in distress:
     Who did them set at liberty
         Out of their anguishes.

20   He, sent his word, and therewithall
         Healing to them he gave:
     From out of their destructions
         He did them also save.

21   O that men would Jehovah prayse,
         For his great goodnes *then:*
     And for his workings wonderfull
         Unto the sons of men.

22   And sacrifices sacrifice
         Let them of thanksgiving:
     And while his works they doe declare
         Let them for gladnes sing.

4

23   They that goe downe to 'th sea in ships:
         Their busines there to doo

24   In waters great. The Lords work see,
         I'th deep his wonders too.

25   Because that he the stormy winde
         Commandeth to arise:
     Which lifteth up the waves thereof,

26   They mount up to the skyes:

Downe goe they to the depths againe,
   Their soule with ill doth quaile.
27 They reele, and stagger, drunkard like,
   And all their witt doth faile.
28 Then did they to Jehovah cry
   When they were in distress:
And therupon he bringeth them
   Out of their anguishes.
29 Hee makes the storme a calme: so that
   The waves therof are still.
30 Their rest then glads them; he them brings
   To 'th hav'n which they did will.
31 O that men would Jehovah prayse
   For his great goodnes *then:*
And for his workings wonderfull
   Unto the sons of men.
32 Also within the peoples Church
   Him let them highly rayse:
Where Elders are assembled, there
   Him also let them prayse.

5

33 He rivers to a desart turnes,
   To drought the springing well:
34 A fruitfull soyle to barrennes;
   For their sin there that dwell.
35 The desart to a poole he turnes;
   And dry ground to a spring.
36 Seates there the hungry; who prepare
   Their towne of habiting,
37 Vineyards there also for to plant,
   Also to sow the field;
Which may unto them fruitfull things
   Of much revenue yield.
38 Also he blesseth them, so that
   They greatly are increast:
And for to be diminished
   He suffers not their beast.
39 Againe they are diminished
   And they are brought downe low,
By reason of their pressing-streights,
   Affliction and sorrow.

6

40   On Princes he contempt doth powre;
        And causeth them to stray
I'th solitary wildernes,
        Wherin there is no way.

41   Yet hee out of affliction
        Doth make the poore to rise:
And like as if it were a flock
        Doth make him families.

42   The righteous shall it behold,
        And he shall joyfull bee:
In silence stop her mouth also
        Shall all iniquitee.

43   Who so is wise, and who so will
        These things attentive learne:
The loving kindenes of the Lord
        They clearely shall discerne.

Other Representative Writers

THOMAS DUDLEY

(1576–1653)

Thomas Dudley, Anne Bradstreet's father, was born in Northampton, England, and was successively page, lawyer's clerk, soldier, and steward to the Earl of Lincoln before he sailed to the New World. From his daughter's poetry we know that Dudley had written at least two poems of considerable length, one as early as King James's reign, and the other in the 1630s in America, but the only text of Dudley's extant today is the "paper of verses found in his pocket after his death," printed below.

Verses found in [Thomas Dudley's] pocket after his death

Dimme eyes, deaf ears, cold stomach shew
My dissolution is in view
Eleven times seven near lived have I,
And now God calls, I willing dye.
My shuttle's shut, my race is run,   5
My sun is set, my deed is done.
My span is measured, [my] tale is told,
My flower's faded and grown old.
My life is vanish'd, shadows fled,
My soul's with Christ, my body dead.   10
Farewell, dear wife, child[re]n and friends,
Hate heresy, make blessed ends,
Bear poverty, live with good men,
So shall we meet with joy agen.
Let men of God, in courts and churches watch   15
O'er such as do a toleration hatch,
Least that ill egg bring forth a cockatrice,[1]
To pay you all with heresy and vice.
If men be left and otherwise combine,
Mine epitaph's—I did no hurt to thine.   20

[1] fabulous monster with the wings of a fowl, tail of a dragon, and head of a cock, produced from a cock's egg hatched by a serpent.

NATHANIEL WARD

(1578–1652)

For the last three centuries Nathaniel Ward, the English-born "Simple Cobler of Aggawam," has been more widely known than many of his contemporary New England verse writers. Using the satirical pose of the *naif*, Ward primarily castigates toleration of the very sects he and his New England contemporaries had traveled three thousand miles to escape.

Born in England in 1578, Ward emigrated to America in 1634 and became minister at Ipswich, Massachusetts, a community whose Indian name was Aggawam. Retiring from the ministry two years later, he worked to formulate for Massachusetts a body of laws spiritually sympathetic with the Old Testament Mosaic Law, yet viable in the seventeenth-century New England colony. The resultant "Body of Liberties" is regarded as fundamental to American judicature. In 1647 Ward returned to England, resuming duties as a clergyman. He did not again journey to America.

Aside from his *Simple Cobler*, Nathaniel Ward wrote the less well-known (but equally ingenious) *Simple Coblers Boy*, and several verses, including one prefatory to the 1678 edition of Anne Bradstreet's poems. Consistently adopting the satirical view of a world where appearance and reality are topsy-turvy, Ward reveals his perceptions of inversion in a thoroughly Baroque manner. He even goes so far as to warn in his verse commending Anne Bradstreet that "Men look to't, least Women wear the Spurrs." That, Ward satirically implies, would be the ultimate violation of proper degree and order.

[Mercury shew'd *Apollo, Bartas* Book][1]

Mercury shew'd *Apollo, Bartas* Book,[2]
Minerva this, and wisht him well to look,
And tell uprightly, which did which excell,
He view'd and view'd, and vow'd he could not tel.
They did him Hemisphear his mouldy nose,   5
With's crackt leering-glasses, for it would pose
The best brains he had in's old pudding-pan,
Sex weigh'd, which best, the Woman, or the Man?
He peer'd, and por'd, and glar'd, and said for wore
I'me even as wise now, as I was before: 10
They both 'gan laugh, and said, it was no mar'l
The Auth'ress was a right *Du Bartas* Girle.
Good sooth quoth the old *Don*, tel ye me so,
I muse whither at length these Girls will go;
It half revives my chil frost-bitten blood,   15
To see a woman once do, ought, that's good;
And chode by *Chaucers* Boots, and *Homers* Furrs,
Let Men look to't, least Women wear the Spurrs.

[The world's a well strung fidle, mans tongue the quill][1]

The world's a well strung fidle, mans tongue the quill,
    That fills the world with fumble for want of skill,
When things and words in tune and tone doe meet,
    The universall song goes smooth and sweet.

[Poetry's a gift wherein but few excell][1]

Poetry's a gift wherein but few excell;
    He doth very ill, that doth not passing well.
But he doth passing well, that doth his best,
    And he doth best, that passeth all the rest.

[1] to Anne Bradstreet: this poem and others preface *Several Poems* (1678), the
second edition, corrected and enlarged, of *The Tenth Muse* (1650).
[2] Guillaume du Bartas, whose *La semaine* was translated by Joshua Sylvester
in 1605–7 as *Devine Weekes and Works.*
[1] from *The Simple Cobler of Aggawam in America* (London, 1647).

Mr. Ward of Anagrams thus[2]

We poor Agawams
are so stiff in the hams
that we cannot make Anagrams,
But Mr John Wilson[3]
the great Epigrammatist
Can let out an Anagram
even as he list.

[2] in Thomas Weld III's commonplace book, Massachusetts Historical Society. Text from Jantz, p. 12.
[3] John Wilson I (c. 1588–1667), Ward's good friend.

THOMAS MORTON

(c. 1580–1646)

Thomas Morton, born in England and trained in law at Clifford's Inn, came to New England between 1622 and 1624, promptly set a record for being driven out of town, and earned himself the reputation of being America's first rascal. Governor Bradford's account of the famous, or infamous, May Day celebration held in 1627 by Morton and his followers at Ma-re Mount (Mount Wollaston) reports in stern tones the "frisking togither" with Indian women, the "beastly practieses of the madd Bacchinalians," and the repeating of "sundry rimes and verses, some tending to lasciviousness, and others to the detraction and scandall of some persons. . . ."

Morton's account of the celebration is understandably different in his *New English Canaan,* published in Amsterdam in 1637, but his polemic in response to his Puritan detractors does not bar him from high praise of the virgin wilderness of America, which, says Morton, lacks only a lover with whom to share her wealth. Like William Wood's *New Englands Prospect* (1634) and other narratives before and after, *New English Canaan* is in prose interspersed with verses.

New English Canaan,
or
New Canaan

The Authors Prologue

If art and industry should doe as much
As Nature hath for Canaan, not such
Another place, for benefit and rest,
In all the universe can be possest,
The more we proove it by discovery,
The more delight each object to the eye
Procures, as if the elements had here
Bin reconcil'd, and pleas'd it should appeare,

5

Like a faire virgin, longing to be sped,
And meete her lover in a Nuptiall bed,   10
Deck'd in rich ornaments t' advaunce her state
And excellence, being most fortunate,
When most enjoy'd, so would our Canaan be
If well imploy'd by art and industry
Whose offspring, now shewes that her fruitfull wombe   15
Not being enjoy'd, is like a glorious tombe,
Admired things producing which there dye,
And ly fast bound in darck obscurity,
The worth of which in each particuler,
Who list to know, this abstract will declare.   20

New Canaans Genius
Epilogus

Thou that art by Fates degree,[1]
Or Providence ordain'd to see,
Natures wonder, her rich store,
Ne'-r discovered before,
Th' admired Lake of Erocoise,[2]   5
And fertile Borders now rejoyce,
See what multitudes of Fish,
Shee presents to fitt thy dish,
If Rich furres thou dost adore,
And of Beaver Fleeces store,   10
See the Lake where they abound,
And what pleasures els are found,
There chast Leda[3] free from fire,
Does enjoy her hearts desire,
Mongst the flowry bancks at ease,   15
Live the sporting Najades,[4]
Bigg lim'd Druides[5] whose browes,
Bewtified with greenebowes,
See the Nimphes how they doe make,
Fine Meanders from the Lake,   20

[1] decree.
[2] Lake Champlain.
[3] swan: while bathing, Leda was seen by Zeus, who made love to her in the guise of a swan.
[4] Naiads: water nymphs.
[5] probably dryads, not druids.

Twining in and out as they,
Through the pleasant groves make way,
Weaving by the shady trees,
Curious Anastomases,[6]
Where the harmeles Turtles breede,   25
And such usefull Beasts doe feede,
As no Traveller can tell,
Els where how to paralell,
Colcos[7] golden Fleece reject,
This deserveth best respect,   30
In sweete Peans[8] let thy voyce,
Sing the praise of Erocoise,
Peans to advaunce her name,
New Canaans everlasting fame.

Epitaph 1637

Time that bringes all things to light,
Doth hide this thinge out of sight,
Yet fame hath left behinde a story,
A hopefull race to shew the glory:
For underneath this heape of stones,
Lieth a percell[1] of small bones,
What hope at last can such impes have,
That from the wombe goes to the grave.

Carmen Elegiacum

Melpomene[1] (at whose mischeifous tove,[2]
The screech owles voyce is heard; the mandraks gro[v]e)
Commands my pen in an Iambick vaine,
To tell a dismall tale, that may constraine,
The hart of him to bleede that shall discerne,   5
How much this foule amisse does him concerne,

6 Anastomoses: branches, interconnected channels.
7 Colchis: Medea's kingdom, site of the Golden Fleece.
8 Paeans: hymns of praise.
1 parcel.
1 Muse of Tragedy.
2 chat, babble.

Alecto[3] (grim Alecto) light thy tortch,
To thy beloved sister next the porch,
That leads unto the mansion howse of fate,
Whose farewell makes her freind more fortunate.   10
A great Squa Sachem[4] can shee poynt to goe,
Before grim Minos,[5] and yet no man know.
That knives, and halters, ponds, and poysonous things,
Are alwayes ready when the Divell once brings,
Such deadly sinners: to a deepe remorse,   15
Of conscience selfe accusing that will force,
Them to dispaire like wicked Kain, whiles death,
Stands ready with all these to stopp their breath,
The beare comes by; that oft hath bayted ben,
By many a Satyres whelpe unlesse you can,   20
Command your eies to drop huge milstones forth,
In lamentation of this losse on earth,
Of her, of whome, so much prayse wee may finde,
Goe when shee will, shee'l leave none like behinde,
Shee was too good for earth, too bad for heaven.   25
Why then for hell the match is somewhat even.

The Poem

Rise Oedipeus, and if thou canst unfould,
What meanes Caribdis underneath the
                                      mould,
When Scilla sollitary on the ground,
(Sitting in forme of Niobe) was found;
Till Amphitrites Darling did acquaint,   5
Grim Neptune with the Tenor of her plaint,
And causd him send forth Triton with the
                                      sound,
Of Trumpet lowd, at which the Seas were
                                      found,
So full of Protean formes, that the bold shore,
Presented Scilla a new parramore,   10

[3] the "Unresting": one of the Furies.
[4] Indian Queen, possibly the widow of Nanepashemet, who was sought by Miles Standish.
[5] King of Crete, son of Zeus and Europa, who became chief justice of Tartarus after his death.

The man who brought her over was named Samson Job.

So strange as Sampson and so patient,
As Job himselfe, directed thus, by fate,
To comfort Scilla so unfortunate.
I doe prof[e]sse by Cupids beautious mother,
Heres Scogans[1] choise for Scilla, and none
              other;   15
Though Scilla's sick with greife because no
              signe,
Can there be found of vertue masculine.
Esculapius come, I know right well,
His laboure's lost when you may ring her
              Knell,
The fatall sisters doome none can withstand,   20
Nor Cithareas powre, who poynts to land,
With proclamation that the first of May,
At Ma-re Mount[2] shall be kept hollyday.

The Songe

Drinke and be merry, merry, merry boyes,
Let all your delight be in Hymens joyes,
Io to Hymen now the day is come,
About the merry Maypole take a Roome,
    Make greene garlons,[1] bring bottles out;
    And fill sweet Nectar, freely about,
    Uncover thy head, and feare no harme,
    For hers good liquor to keepe it warme.
Then drinke and be merry, &c.
Io to Hymen, &c.
    Nectar is a thing assign'd,
    By the Deities owne minde,
    To cure the hart opprest with greife,
    And of good liquors is the cheife,
Then drinke, &c.
Io to Hymen, &c.
    Give to the Mellancolly man,
    A cup or two of't now and than;

[1] Thomas Scogan, 15th-century English poet, author of *Scoggins Jests.*
[2] Merrymount: "Bacchanalian" settlement founded by Morton et al. (1625) in what is now Quincy, Mass., and dispersed by Miles Standish (1628).
[1] garlands.

This physick' will soone revive his blood,
And make him be of a merrier moode.
Then drinke, &c.
Io to Hymen, &c.
Give to the Nymphe thats free from scorne,
No Irish; stuff nor Scotch over worne,
Lasses in beaver coats come away,
Yee shall be welcome to us night and day.
To drinke and be merry, &c.
Io to Hymen, &c.

The Poem

Master Ben:
Johnnson

I sing th' adventures of mine worthy wights,
And pitty 't is I cannot call them Knights,
Since they had brawne and braine and were
right able,
To be installed of prince Arthures table,
Yet all of them were Squires of low degree, 5
As did appeare by rules of heraldry,
The Magi tould of a prodigeous birth,
That shortly should be found upon the earth,
By Archimedes art, which they misconster,[1]
Unto their Land would proove a hiddeous
monster, 10
Seaven heades it had, and twice so many
feete,
Arguing the body to be wondrous greate,
Besides a forked taile heav'd up on highe,
As if it threaten'd battell to the skie,
The Rumor of this fearefull prodigy, 15
Did cause th' effeminate multitude to cry,
For want of great Alcides aide and stood,
Like People that have seene Medusas head,
Great was the greife of hart, great was the
mone,
And great the feare conceived by every one, 20
Of Hydras hiddeous forme and dreadfull
powre,

[1] misconstrue.

Doubting in time this Monster would
devoure,
All their best flocks whose dainty wolle
consorts,
It selfe with Scarlet in all Princes Courts,
Not Jason nor the adventerous youths of
Greece,   25
Did bring from Colcos any ritcher Fleece,
In Emulation of the Gretian force,
These Worthies nine prepar'd a woodden
horse,
And prick'd with pride of like successe
divise,
How they may purchase glory by this prize,   30
And if they give to Hidraes head the fall,
It will remaine a plat forme unto all,
Theire brave atchivements, and in time to
comme,
Per fas aut nef[2] as they'l erect a throne.
Cloubs are turn'd trumps: so now the lott
is cast,   35
With fire and sword, to Hidras den they
haste,
Mars in th' assendant, Soll in Cancer now,
And Lerna Lake to Plutos court must bow,
What though they rebuk'd by thundring
Jove,
Tis neither Gods nor men that can remove,   40
Their mindes from making this a dismall day,
These nine will now be actors in this play,
And Sum on Hidra to appeare a non,[3]
Before their witles Combination,
But his undaunted spirit nursd with meate,   45
Such as the Cecrops gave their babes to eate,
Scorn'd their base accons, for with Cecrops
charme,
Hee knew he could defend himselfe from
harme,
Of Minos, Eacus, and Radamand,[4]
Princes of Limbo who must out of hand,   50

[2] by good or ill.
[3] anon.
[4] Minos, Aeacus, and Rhadamanthus sat as judges of the dead in Tartarus.

Consult bout Hidra what must now be done,
Who having sate in Counsell one by one,
Retorne this answere to the Stiggean
                                    feinds,
And first grim Minos spake: most loving
                                    freinds,
Hidra prognosticks ruine to our state,   55
And that our Kingdome will grow desolate,
But if one head from thence be tane away,
The Body and the members will decay,
To take in hand, what Eacus this taske,
Is such as harebraind Phaeton did aske,   60
Of Phebus to begird the world about,
Which graunted put the Netherlands to rout,
Presumptious fooles learne wit at too much
                                    cost,
For like and laboure both at once hee lost,
Sterne Radamantus being last to speake,   65
Made a great hum and thus did silence
                                    breake,
What if with ratling chaines of Iron bands,
Hidra be bound either by feete or hands,
And after being lashed with smarting rodds,
Hee be conveyed by Stix unto the godds,   70
To be accused on the upper ground,
Of Lesæ Majesta⁵ is this crime found,
T'will be unpossible from thence I trowe,
Hidra shall come to trouble us belowe,
This sentence pleasd the friends exceedingly,   75
That up they tost their bonnets and did cry,
Long live our Court in great prosperity.
The Sessions ended some did straight devise,
Court Revells antiques and a world of joyes,
Brave Christmas gambals, there was open
                                    hall,   80
Kept to the full: and sport the Divell and
                                    all,
Labours despised the loomes are laid away,
And this proclaim'd the Stigean Holliday,
In came grim Minos with his motly beard,
And brought a distillation well prepar'd,   85

⁵ laesa mājestas, "injured sovereignty": a crime or offense against the sovereign
power of a state.

And Eacus who is as suer as text,
Came in with his preparatives the next,
Then Radamantus last and principall,
Feasted the Worthies in his sumptuous hall,
There Caron Cerberous and the rout of
                feinds,   90
Had lap enough and so their pastims ends.

The Poem

What ailes Pigmalion? Is it Lunacy;
Or Doteage on his owne Imagery?
Let him remember how hee came from Hell,
That after ages by record may tell,
The compleate story to posterity;
Blazon his Coate in forme of Heraldry.
    Hee bearth argent alwaies at commaund;
    A barre betweene three crusty rolls at hand:
    And for his crest with froth there does appeare,
    Dextra Paw Elevant a Jugg of beare.

CAPTAIN JOHN SMITH
(1580–1631)

One of the most popular figures in American history, Captain John Smith was the author of "the first book in American literature," *A True Relation of such Occurrences and Accidents of Note as hath happened in Virginia* (1608), which contains the first version of the Pocahontas story, since elevated to mythic stature.

Smith has not been considered as a poet, possibly because much of the verse he inserted in his prose narratives was not his own, and because modern estimates of his well-known "Sea Marke" have been unjustly harsh. But Smith wrote at least two other poems in the early seventeenth century, one to John Taylor in 1627 and one in honor of Robert Norton in 1628.

The Sea Marke[1]

Aloofe, aloofe, and come no neare[2]
    the dangers doe appeare;
Which if my ruine had not beene
    you had not seene:
I onely lie upon this shelfe   5
    to be a marke to all
    which on the same might fall,
That none may perish but my selfe.

If in or outward you be bound,
    doe not forget to sound;   10
Neglect of that was cause of this
    to steare amisse.
The Seas were calme, the wind was faire,
    that made me so secure,[3]
    that now I must indure   15

[1] marker buoy.
[2] i.e. nearer.
[3] heedless.

All weathers be they foule or faire.

The Winters cold, the Summers heat,
    alternatively beat
Upon my bruised sides, that rue
    because too true   20
That no releefe can ever come.
  But why should I despair
  being promised so faire
That there shall be a day of Dome.

John Smith *of his friend Master* John Taylor *and his Armado*[1]

Arme, Arme, Arme, Arme, great *Neptune* rowze, awake
And muster up, thy monsters speedily:
Boreas unto thy blustering blasts betake,
Gard, guard your selves from *Taylors* policy,
Rockes, shoales, Lee-shores, oh helpe them *Goodwin* Sands
For this new Fleete runs over Seas and Lands.
And's now so victu'led, Riggd and yarely plyes
It threatens all the waters, ayre and skyes,
Truth in his Navy such a power doth leade
The Devill, Hell, vice, and all, the Fleet may dreade.
And well it may, if well you understand,
So rare a Fleet, was never made nor man'd.

In the due Honor of the Author Master Robert Norton, *and his Worke*[1]

Perfection, if't hath ever been attayned,
In *Gunners* Art, this Author hath it gayned,
By Study and Experiences, and he
The Fruite of all his Paynes hath offered Thee,
A Present well befitting this our Age,   5
When all the World is but a Martiall Stage:

[1] prefatory poem to John Taylor, *An Armado, or Navye of 103. Ships and Other Vessels* (London, 1627).
[1] prefatory poem to Robert Norton, *The Gunner: Shewing the Whole Practise of Artillery: With all the Appurtenances thereto belonging . . .* (London, 1628).

Let sweeter Studies lull a sleepe and please
Men, who presume security, but these
Thy Labors practi'zd, shall more safely guard
Those that foresee the Danger, th'other bar'd   10
This benefite: Wee *Soldiers* doe imbrace
This Rare and usefull Worke, and o're the face
Of all the World, let thy Fames Echo sound,
More then that roaring *Engin,* and redound
To th'Honor of our Nation, that thy Paynes   15
Transcends all former, and their glory staines.

Captaine *John Smith,*
Hungariensis.[2]

[2] Smith fought in Hungary during the early years of the seventeenth century and wrote about his exploits in the *True Travels.* The appellation "Hungariensis" here confirms Smith's authorship of the verse.

JOHN COTTON

(1584–1652)

John Cotton, summoned to appear before Archbishop William Laud because of his non-conformist preaching and practices, disappeared into the well-organized Puritan underground in England in 1632, and a year later took ship for New England to become Teacher of the Church at Boston. Soon there followed the first exchange between Cotton and Roger Williams that was to occasion the famous controversy over Williams' *The Bloudy Tenent of Persecution* (1644), answered by Cotton in *The Bloudy Tenent, Washed and Made White in the Bloud of the Lambe* (1647).

Of his seven preserved sets of verses, the three printed below best represent Cotton's range, tone, and style.

See also Benjamin Woodbridge, "Upon the Tomb of the Most Reverend Mr. John Cotton" p. 410 and John Fiske, "Upon the much-to be lamented desease of . . . John Cotton," p. 187.

To my Reverend Dear Brother,
M. Samuel Stone,
Teacher of the Church at Hartford[1]

How well (dear Brother) art thou called
Stone?

John 1: 42   As sometimes Christ did *Simon Cephas* own.
A *Stone* for solid firmness, fit to rear
A part in *Zions* wall: and it upbear.

Josh. 15: 6   Like *Stone of Bohan*, Bounds fit to describe,   5
& 18: 17   'Twixt Church and Church, as that 'twixt
Tribe and Tribe.

[1] prefaced to Stone's *A Congregational Church Is a Catholike Visible Church. Or an Examination of M. [Samuel] Hudson his Vindication concerning the Integrality of the Catholike Visible Church. Wherein also satisfaction is given to what M. [Daniel] Cawdrey writes touching that subject, in his Review of M. [Thomas] Hooker's Survey of Church Discipline* (London, 1652).

1 Sam. 7: 12	Like *Samuel's Stone*, erst *Eben-Ezer* hight;
	To tell the Lord hath helpt us with his might.
1 Sam. 17: 49, 50	Like *Stone* in *Davids* sling, the head to wound

1 Sam. 7: 12   Like *Samuel's Stone*, erst *Eben-Ezer* hight;
To tell the Lord hath helpt us with his might.
1 Sam. 17: 49, 50 Like *Stone* in *Davids* sling, the head to wound
        Of that huge Giant-Church, (so far renownd) 10
        Hight the Church-Catholike, Oecumenical,
        Or at the lowest compass, National;
        Yet Poteck,[2] Visible, and of such a fashion,
        As may or Rule a world or Rule a Nation.
        Which though it be cry'd up unto the Skys, 15
        By Philistims and Isralites likewise;
        Yet seems to me to be too neer a kin
        Unto the Kingdom of the *Man* of *Sin:*
        In frame, and state, and constitution,
Rev. 13   Like to the *first beast* in the *Revelation.* 20
        Which was as large as Roman empire wide,
        And Ruled Rome, and all the world beside.
        Go on (good Brother) Gird thy Sword with
            might,
        Fight the Lord's Battels, Plead his Churches
            Right.
        To Brother *Hooker*, thou art next a kin, 25
        By Office-Right thou must his pledge
            Redeem.
        Take thou the double portion of his spirit,
        Run on his Race, and then his Crown inherit.
        Now is the time when Church is militant,
        Time hast'neth fast when it shall be
            Tryumphant. 30

In Saram

Farewel, Dear Daughter *Sara;* Now Thou'rt gone,
(Whither thou much desiredst) to thine Home:
Pray, my Dear Father, Let me now go Home!
Were the Last Words thou Spak'st to me Alone.
 Go then, Sweet *Sara*, take thy *Sabbath Rest,*
  With thy Great Lord, and all in Heaven Blest.

[2] potent [?].

A Thankful Acknowledgment of God's Providence

In mothers womb thy fingers did me mak,
And from the womb thou didst me safely take:
From breast thou hast me nurst my life throughout,
That I may say I never wanted ought.

In all my meals my table thou hast spread,   5
In all my lodgings thou hast [made my] bed:
Thou hast me clad with changes of array,
And chang'd my house for better far away.

In youthful wandrings thou didst stay my slide,
In all my journies thou hast been my Guide: 10
Thou hast me sav'd from many-an-unknown danger,
And shew'd me favour, even where I was a stranger.

In both my Callings thou hast heard my voice,
In both my matches thou hast made my choice:
Thou gav'st me sons, and daughters, them to peer,   15
And giv'st me hope thoul't learn them thee to fear.

Oft have I seen thee look with Mercy's face,
And through thy Christ have felt thy saving-grace.
This is the Heav'n on Earth, if any be:
For this, and all, my soul doth worship Thee.   20

JOHN WILSON

(c. 1588–1667)

Educated at King's College, Cambridge, John Wilson came to America in 1630 with John Winthrop and the first group of Massachusetts Bay colonists. Teacher of the first church established in Charlestown, Wilson became widely known for his piety and learning, his acute prophetic pronouncements, and his skill at composing anagrams. Cotton Mather remarked that no one since Adam had anagrammatized so nimbly, and the irrepressible Nathaniel Ward expressed his opinion of Wilson's talent in a choice bit of friendly wit (see p. 368).

A Copy Of Verses

Made by that Reverend Man of God Mr. John Wilson, *Pastor to the* first Church in *Boston;* On the sudden Death of Mr. Joseph Brisco, Who was translated from Earth to Heaven Jan. 1. 1657

> *Not by a Fiery Chariot as* Elisha *was,*
> *But by the Water, which was the outward*
> *   cause:*
> *And now at Rest with* Christ *his Saviour*
> *   dear,*
> *Though he hath left his dear Relations here.*
>
> Joseph Briscoe ⎱
> Job cries hopes. ⎰ Anagram   5
>
> There is no *Job* but cries to God and hopes,
> And God his ear in Christ; to cries he opes,
> Out of the deeps to him I cry'd and hop'd,
> And unto me his gracious ear is op'd:
> Doubt not of this ye that my death bewail,   10
> What if it did so strangely me assail:
> What if I was so soon in Waters drown'd,

And when I cry'd to men, no help I found:
There was a God in Heaven that heard my
cry:
And lookt upon me with a gracious eye,   15
He that did pity *Joseph* in his grief,
Sent from above unto my soul relief:
He sent his Angels who did it conveigh
Into his Bosom, where poor *Laz'rus* lay:
Let none presume to censure my estate,   20
As *Job* his Friends did stumble at his Fate.
All things on Earth do fall alike to all,
To good Disciples, which on God that call;
To those that do Blaspheme his Holy Name,
And unto those that reverence the same: 25
He that from nature drew me unto Grace,
And look'd upon me with a Fathers face:
When in my blood upheld me to the last,
And now I do of joyes eternal tast.
Remember how *Job's* precious children Dy'd,   30
Jonah As also what the Prophet *did* betide:
What was the end of good *Josiah's* life,
And how it fared with *Ezekiels* Wife:
Remember what a Death it was that Christ
(Suffered for me) the Darling of the highest;   35
His Death of Deaths hath quite remov'd the
sting,
No matter how or where the Lord doth bring
Us to our end, in Christ who live and die
And sure to live with Christ eternally.

Claudius Gilbert[1]
Anagram. Tis Braul I Cudgel

[Tis Braul I Cudgel,] Ranters, Quakers Braul,
Divels, and Jesuites, Founders of them all.
Their Brauling Questions whosoever reades
May soone perceive, These are their proper heades.
What Better Cudgels, then Gods holy word,

[1] Pastor of Limerick, Ireland, and author of *The Libertine School'd* (London, 1657), a defense of the old religion and an attack on Quakerism, which he sent to Wilson. Delighted, Wilson wrote the above poem on the verso of the title page. Text from Jantz, p. 117.

(For Brauls so cursed,) and the Civil sword?
By God Ordained to suppresse such evils,
Which God Abhorreth, as he doth the Devils.
Oh! Lett these blessed Cudgels knocke them downe.
Lett Sathan fall, that Christ may weare the Crowne.
Let Baal pleade for Baal; who are Christs,
Abhorr, oppose, Confound these Antichrists.
Yea Lett the Lord confound them, who with spight
Against his Truth maliciously Fight.

J W.

WILLIAM BRADFORD

(1590–1657)

The author of the most famous early history of an American settle-
ment, *Relation or Journall of the Beginning and Proceedings of the
Plantation Settled at Plymouth* (London, 1622), William Bradford
was elected as the second governor of the Plymouth Colony in 1621,
and was re-elected thirty times for a total term of thirty-three years.
He was the most prolific poet of Plymouth, composing more than a
thousand lines of verse, narrating "Gods merciful dealing with us in
this wilderness." But his purest poem is the Epitaph he composed for
himself in gratitude to God for a fruitful life—a poem first printed by
Nathaniel Morton in his *New Englands Memoriall* (Cambridge,
1669).

A Word to New England

O New England, thou canst not boast;
Thy former glory thou hast lost.
When Hooker, Winthrop, Cotton died,[1]
And many precious ones beside,
Thy beauty then it did decay,   5
And still doth languish more away;
Love, truth, good-men, mercy and grace,
And wealth and the world take their place.
Thy open sins none can them hide,
Fraud, drunkenness, whoredom and pride.   10
The great oppressors slay the poore,
But whimsic errors they kill more.
Yet some thou hast who mourne and weep,
And their garments they unspotted keep;
Who seek God's honour to maintaine   15
That true Religion may remaine.

[1] Thomas Hooker, John Winthrop I, and John Cotton all died within the
period 1647–52.

These doe invite and sweetly call
Each to other, and say to all,
Repent, amend, and turn to God
That we may prevent his sharp rod,   20
Time yet thou hast, improve it well,
That God's presence may with you dwell.

Of Boston in New England

O Boston, though thou now art grown
To be a great and wealthy town,
Yet I have seen thee a void place,
Shrubs and bushes covering thy face;
And house then in thee none were there,   5
Nor such as gold and silk did weare;
No drunkenness were then in thee,
Nor such excesse as now we see.
We then drunke freely of thy spring
Without paying of any thing;   10
We lodged freely where we would,
All things were free and nothing sold.
And they that did thee first begin
Had hearts as free and as willing
Their poor friends for to entertaine,   15
And never looked at sordid gaine.
    Some thou hast had whome I did know,
That spent theirselves to make thee grow,
And thy foundations they did lay
Which doe remaine unto this day.   20
When thou wast weak they did thee nurse,
Or else with thee it had been worse;
They left thee not, but did defend
And succour thee unto their end.
    Thou now hast growne in wealth and store,   25
Doe not forget that thou wast poore,
And lift not up thyselfe in pride,
From truth and justice turne not aside.
Remember thou a Cotton[1] had,
Which made the hearts of many glad;   30
What he thee taught bear thou in minde,

[1] John Cotton (1584–1652); see pp. 381–83.

It's hard another such to finde.
A Winthrop[2] once in thee was knowne
Who unto thee was as a crowne.
Such ornaments are very rare   35
Yet thou enjoyed this blessed pair.
But these are gone, their work is done,
Their day is past, set is their sun:
Yet faithful Wilson[3] still remains,
And learned Norton[4] doth take pains.   40
   Live ye in peace. I could say more.
Oppress ye not the weake and poore.
The trade is all in your own hand,
Take heed ye doe not wrong the land,
Lest he that hath lift you on high,   45
When, as the poore to him doe cry
Doe throw you downe from your high state,
And make you low and desolate.

[*Epitaphium Meum*]

From my years young in dayes of Youth,
God did make known to me his Truth,
And call'd me from my Native place
For to enjoy the Means of Grace.
In Wilderness *he did me guide,*   5
And in strange Lands *for me provide.*
In Fears *and* Wants, *through* Weal *and* Woe,
As Pilgrim *past I to and fro:*
Oft left of them whom I did trust;
How vain it is to rest on Dust!   10
A man of Sorrows *I have been,*
And many Changes *I have seen.*
Wars, Wants, Peace, Plenty *have I known;*
And some advanc'd, *others* thrown down.
The humble, poor, cheerful *and* glad;   15
Rich, discontent, sower *and* sad:

<hr>

[2] John Winthrop (1588–1649), Governor of Massachusetts Bay Colony twelve times between 1630 and 1649.

[3] John Wilson (c. 1588–1667); see pp. 384–86.

[4] John Norton (1606–63), teacher of the Church at Boston and chief instigator of the persecution of the Quakers in New England. For his son's "A Funeral Elogy Upon . . . Mrs. Anne Bradstreet" see p. 460.

When Fears *with* Sorrows *have been mixt,*
Consolations *came betwixt.*
Faint not, poor Soul, *in God still trust,*
Fear not the things thou suffer must;   20
For, whom he loves he doth chastise,
And then all Tears wipes from their eyes.
Farewell, dear Children, *whom I love,*
Your better Father *is above:*
When I am gone, he can supply;   25
To him I leave you when I dye.
Fear him in Truth, *walk in his* Wayes,
And he will bless you all your dayes.
My dayes are spent, Old Age *is come,*
My Strength *it fails, my* Glass *near run:*   30
Now I will wait when work is done,
Untill my happy Change *shall come,*
When from my labours I shall rest
With Christ *above for to be blest.*

SAMUEL GORTON

(1592–1677)

More infuriating to the Puritan oligarchy than Roger Williams or Thomas Morton was the man John Cotton called "arch-heretic," Samuel Gorton, author of the polemic *Simplicities Defence against Seven-Headed Policy* (1647). Politically and theologically radical, Gorton used the acid of his pen to accuse New England leaders of establishing a church state embodying the very qualities most Puritans vituperated in their attacks on prelacy and the Pope.

A Lover of peace, and one of eminent respect, viewing this Treatise at the Presse, kindly added this verse prefixed,[1] which Hath both sodainly, and unexpectedly drawn from my thoughts as here followeth, as a testimony of my kind respects unto the party, though but a stranger unto him; it may also serve as an intelligencer, what was the only ground of controversie in acting unto, and publishing of, this Treatise

The serpent w[i]th a voyce, so *slie* and *fine*
Consults with *nature*, as though he were *divine*,
Whil'st she doth seek for glory, wealth, and love
In things that are *below*, and not *in that above*;
Lending *an ear*[a] to listen unto him,   5
The *fruit looks fair*, the tree seems nothing grim:
And thence doth he, at *first begin t'arise*
Through earthly projects, for to make *man wise:*
Whereas the *light of heaven*, GOD *himself ordain'd*
To be that *thing*, whereby man is *maintain'd*   10
In wisdom, honor, happiness, and peace,
That doth from *serpent* (sin, death, hell) release;

[1] see p. 395 for this poem by "R. B."
[a] Hence doth arise the way of *Solomons* harlot, set out in the way of this woman—Gen. 3. Prov. 7. who may not speake in the Church, but usurpeth—1 Tim. 2.

And no *conjectural*, doubtful, subtil notion
Set forth, *by art*, with sign of great devotion.

Come from the *Prelates*,[b] your persecuting foes;   15
Our Church (as *Primitive*) Christ Jesus doth disclose.
Her Ordinances pure, a Church erected here
Where you may worship, voyd of care or fear,
Our Land is large; Our Magistracy good;
Come o're to save that innocent-like blood   20
From such as are to cruelty so bent,
Our ways are meek and humble, to give all content;
Thus he appears, *apparrelled in white*
To snare in that, wherein he takes delight.
An earthly Kingdom, he would fain erect   25
Then *spiritual honor,* he must needs reject.

That when that woman,[c] appeareth in her glory
With him in womb, of whom intreats all story.
Then's he *a dragon red,* for to devour
That *child,* to whom is given, *all the power*   30
In heaven, and in earth, to rule as King and Lord.
None to the serpent, no, heaven cannot afford
A *place of residence,* he must hence depart
Down to the earth, full sore against his heart,
That he a place cannot *devise to frame*   35
Which from the *heavens* may seem to take its fame.
Cruel, Raging, Carnal, now he cometh forth
His *slie,* and *subtil wisdom,* now proves nothing worth.

This woman, *now in travel,*[2] finds not *time*
To listen unto him, *nought but the child is mine:*   40
Which *child in her,* can nothing else confesse,
But *Throne of glory,*[d] and *bare Wildernesse:*
Which *twain together,* give all praise to one;
Then fury's in the Serpent, smooth policy is gone:
No *middle place,* for Satan now is found,   45
Not *one with th' manchild;* down he goes to ground:
His cunning cannot now intice so far,
But *Michael,* and *his Angels* wil make War

[b] The serpents voyce transmits into *new-England,* speaking there in way of
Ministery, as at the beginning.

[c] In this woman is set out the way of King *Lemuels* mother, that teacheth
prophecie, Rev. 12. Prov. 31. who may pray and prophecy in the Church with-
out usurpation, 1 Cor. 11.

[2] travail.

[d] For the one betakes it self to heaven, the other to the wilderness.

With *Dragon*, and with all his *Angels* great,
Yea overcome him, never sound retreat.   50

Most of his skil he useth,[e] he knows how
To talk of benefits to receive, although not now,
And so from place, and person still delights to wend,
Where's outward peace, there's Christ, doth he pretend;
And if so be that troubles do arise,   55
Himself he saves, *the serpent is so wise:*
No tye, *to fold, nor flock,* he then wil know;
Christ in an earthly peace, he'l have, where'er he go.

Whereas *our Lord,* his voyce doth sometimes teach
Go to *Decapolis,*[f] and there thou shalt me preach   60
Unto ten[g] Cities, great the number bee;
My Word shal reach them, and *I am with thee.*

For I am *truth,* and truth thou goest to show
Which makes thee free, my presence thou dost know
No place can, *scant thee off, then walke at large,*   65
Doubt not, *I'm with thee,* doe but keepe my *Charge,*
The nations shall come forth at *once,* yea at one birth,[h]
Truth in the change of *one,* reneweth all the *earth;*
Else, were *not perfect good,* in every one erect,
Nor *sinne were full,* through th' fall, that great defect,   70
If change of *one* were not a world renew'd,
What *Nation then,* not brought in, and subdu'd,
When truth is publisht, though but unto *one*
Imbrac't, receiv'd? oh happy State of man,
All Gentile Jewels, *brought in,*[i] who can want;   75
The world's in darknesse, else could ne're be scant.

But Hypocrites cannot this thing digest,
In places, times, and persons, they seek wealth and rest,
And see not how *the mighty LORD above*
Hath cast his skirt o're Ruth, yea fild her lap in love,   80
Of whom comes Christ, that world of GODS *goodwill,*

[e] He ever puts off the day of the Lord as not yet time to build the Temple,
but would live in his own seiled (or artificial) house of his own framing and
device.
[f] Though he desired to be with Jesus, yet Jesus understanding his desire to
be but nature (that is) to injoy him according to the flesh, denies him that, that
so he might be with him according to the spirit. Matt. 28. 20.
[g] For so the word *Decapolis* signifies ten Cities.
[h] See Isa. 60. 21, 22, and 66. 8.
[i] See Isa. 61. 6 and 60. 11. 16.

What can she want, that heaven or earth doth fill?
All keepe their stations, *attend* as they have done,
Neglect no *homage,* or service to the *Son,*
All bring their *vertues,* treasures, and their glory   85
Centring them all in him, a World of Princely Dowry,
Then walke through Sea, of Land, by friends or foes
Let prisons fast, hard irons thee inclose,
All take thy part, yea plead thy cause for thee
The world vents its malice, *in Christs love thou art free.*   90

    The Spirit of this world by these things come to light
Its pomp, and glory, which earst did shine so bright
Appears grosse darknesse, unto Christian eyes
Down comes its Kingdome, up goes its plaints and cryes,
Helpe *Sword and Gun,* else doth our Kingdome fall   95
Court, fire, Gangrena,[j] we tast worm-wood and gall,
No marvell, for, Christ in his native kind
Set forth, declar'd unto a carnall mind,
Appears as odious unto such a wight
As sinne to him, in whom is found the light: 100
What sentence shall be given then by sons of men,
When truth appears, if power were found in them?

    No power but that of darknesse then, let us to them ascribe
What's in the Church's *our Lord's,* all unto them deny'd;
Take heed, yee Judg of *Blasphemies* aright,   105
For Light discerns, the darknesse hath no sight.
If Light, and Candlesticke, you know not how, t'make one
Suspend your judgement, *all your skill is gone,*
And let the Judge of all, his Circuit passe apace,
Who comes *not to destroy,* such is his grace,   110
And let that man his own destruction be,
Who breaks that *faith with God,* cannot be peec'd by thee:
Cease then your prosecutions, seek yee to do good:
Save life in any, in *Church wayes* spill not blood:
In Christ, if you consider, the *Covenant* of God.   115
Youle find that all compulsion, is nought but that *Nim-rod.*[k]

S. G.

[j] Books so intituled written upon uncertain reports, tales, and conjectures to cure the Church.

[k] A meer hunting of men to worry your own hind; (or rather that hind of the morning, see Psa. 22. in the title) thirsting after the precious life. Compare Gen. 10. 8, 9, with Jer. 16. 16.

R. B.[1]

Upon an occasionall view, of this unexpected, and much unwished for Story[2]

This Story's *strange*, but altogether *true;*
Old *England's* Saints are banisht out of *New:*
O Monstrous *Art*, and *cunning* of the Devill,
What *hidden* paths he goes, to *spread* his *evill!*
The *Man* of *Sin's* the *same*, his eldest *Son;*   5
Both have more *shapes* than be *moats* in the Sun.
Hence *disappointed*, are the most of *men;*
When trouble's *past* (some thinke) they *rise* agen.
Thus it befell these *Pilgrims*, in that *Land*,
To *which* they fled, from *persecutions* hand,   10
This *Indians* note, with *Papists, Jews* and *Turks*,
For in *them all*, the selfe same *spirit* works:
Thus is the *Name* of *Christ*, blasp[h]em'd, by these,
Who burthen *them*, to whom they promise ease.

    Oh *Christ* arise, and *spread* thy *glorious* fame,   15
That all may *know*, the *sweetnesse* of thy *Name:*
As—*Affric, Europe*, and *America*
Expect! and *waite* the *dawnings* of that *day*,
That *Papists, Greeks*, and we the *Protestants*
Of *Calvins Sect*, those too, the *Lutherans*,   20
And *they* that are a *streine* above them *all*,
At *Jesus* feet, at *length* may *humbly* fall,
That so such *Christs*, which, *most* in fancy *make*
(When tis (Men think) that Christendome doth *shake*)
May at th' *appearing* of the *Lord* depart,   25
And *all* may *worship* him ev'n with *one heart:*
That so the *Nations* may this *glory see;*
And into *it*, at length *transformed* be:
This to *effect*, can't be by *sword* of *man*,
But that which to *with-stand*, no *Kingdomes* can.   30
For 'tis the *Lords* owne *might*, the *sword* that doth

[1] "R. B." remains unidentified: it is more than likely he was an Englishman. His verse is included here principally because it evoked Gorton's poem (see p. 391).
[2] Prefixed to Samuel Gorton, *Simplicities Defence against Seven-Headed Policy* (London, 1647).

Ev'n with *two edges* flow out of *Gods* mouth,
By which are *slaine* the *wicked* of each *Land,*
And will sure *breake* each persecutor's *band:*
    Then *England* and *Yee Nations* round *about,*   35
That are now so lofty, and so *stout:*
At length *downe fall* to *him* that's *Lord* of you:
And *learne* with *him,* like *meeknesse* for to *show:*
If you, with *iron Rods, Saints breake* and *bruise,*
Know then *your selves,* that *Christ* you *so* will *use.*   40

THOMAS TILLAM

(16? –post 1668)

Thomas Tillam was not the only traveler to America in the early
seventeenth century to feel a sense of dedication mixed with wonder
as he viewed the land that was to be shaped into the modern Ca-
naan. But none other recorded his response in lines so unmistakably
inspired and genuinely lyrical.

For reasons not altogether clear—perhaps disillusionment at the
rigidity of religious controls exercised in New England as a result of
the Antinomian Controversy—Tillam did not remain long in Amer-
ica, and by 1661 had established himself and his followers in a com-
munal religious society in Heidelberg, Germany.

Uppon the first sight of New-England
June 29, 1638

Hayle holy-land wherin our holy lord
Hath planted his most true and holy word
Hayle happye people who have dispossest
Your selves of friends, and meanes, to find
some rest
For your poore wearied soules, opprest of late   5
For Jesus-sake, with Envye, spight, and hate

Math. 19: 29   To yow that blessed promise truly's given
Of sure reward, which you'l receve in heaven
Methinks I heare the Lambe of God thus
speake
Come my deare little flocke, who for my sake   10
Have lefte your Country, dearest friends, and
goods
And hazarded your lives o'th raginge floods
Posses this Country; free from all anoye
Heare I'le bee with you, heare you shall
Injoye
My sabbaths, sacraments, my minestrye   15

And ordinances in their puritye
But yet beware of Sathans wylye baites
Hee lurkes amongs yow, Cunningly hee
waites
To Catch yow from mee; live not then secure
But fight 'gainst sinne, and let your lives be
pure   20
Prepare to heare your sentence thus
expressed

Math. 25: 34   Come yee my servants of my father Blessed

Thomas Tillam

WILLIAM WOOD

(1606–post 1637)

Among the numerous descriptive-promotional accounts of America published early in the seventeenth century, William Wood's *New Englands Prospect* (London, 1634) is one of the most entertaining and imaginative, if not in every respect the most accurate. Wood's enthusiasm for the natural beauties of the northeastern region of the New World, and his sharp sense of the wealth at hand for those who had the vision to finance trading and exploring companies are reflected in every page of his narrative, not only in the prose but also in the verses Wood composed to catalogue the trees and shrubs, animals (specifically the fur bearers), birds, and fish he saw or heard tales of during his two visits to America in the 1620s and 30s.

[Trees both in hills and plaines, in plenty be]

Trees both in hills and plaines, in plenty be,
The long-liv'd Oake, and mourneful Cypris tree,
Skie towring pines, and Chesnuts coated rough,
The lasting Cedar, with the Walnut tough;
The rozin dropping Firre for mast in use,   5
The boatmen seeke for Oares light, neate grown sprewse,
The brittle Ash, the ever trembling Aspes,
The broad-spread Elme, whose concave harbours waspes,
The water spungie Alder good for nought,
Small Elderne by the *Indian* Fletchers[1] sought,   10
The knottie Maple, pallid Birtch, Hawthornes,
The Horne bound[2] tree that to be cloven scornes;
Which from the tender Vine oft takes his spouse,
Who twinds imbracing armes about his boughes.
Within this Indian Orchard fruites be some,   15
The ruddie Cherrie and the jettie Plumbe,

[1] arrow makers.
[2] hornbeam.

Snake murthering Hazell, with sweet Saxaphrage,[3]
Whose spurnes[4] in beere allayes hot fevers rage.
The Diars Shumach,[5] with more trees there be,
That are both good to use, and rare to see.   20

[The kingly Lyon, and the strong arm'd Beare]

The kingly Lyon, and the strong arm'd Beare
The large lim'd Mooses, with the tripping Deare,
Quill darting Porcupines, and Rackcoones bee,
Castelld in the hollow of an aged tree;
The skipping Squerrell, Rabbet, purblinde[1] Hare,
Immured in the selfsame Castle are,
Least red-ey'd Ferrets, wily Foxes should
Them undermine, if rampir'd but with mould.
The grim-fac't Ounce,[2] and ravenous howling Woolfe,
Whose meagre paunch suckes like a swallowing gulfe.
Blacke glistering Otters, and rich coated Bever,
The Civet sented Musquash smelling ever.

[The Princely Eagle, and the soaring Hawke]

The Princely Eagle, and the soaring Hawke,
Whom in their unknowne wayes there's none can chawke:
The Humberd for some Queenes rich Cage more fit,
Than in the vacant Wildernesse to sit.
The swift wing'd Swallow sweeping to and fro,   5
As swift as arrow from *Tartarian*[1] Bow.
When as *Aurora's* infant day new springs,
There th' morning mounting *Larke* her sweete layes sings.
The harmonious Thrush, swift Pigeon, Turtle-dove,
Who to her mate does ever constant prove: 10
The Turky-Phesant, Heathcocke, Partridge rare,

[3] Saxifrage, a dwarf herb whose ground root added to wine "cureth the pestilence."
[4] outward-growing roots or rootlets.
[5] Chopped sumach leaves are used in tanning.
[1] almost blind.
[2] lynx.
[1] of Tartary; Tartar bowmen were famed for their skill.

The carrion-tearing Crow, and hurtfull Stare,[2]
The long liv'd Raven, th' ominous Screech-Owle,
Who tells as old wives say, disasters foule.
The drowsie Madge[3] that leaves her day-lov'd nest,   15
And loves to rove when day-birds be at rest:
Th' Eele-murthering Hearne,[4] and greedy Cormorant,
That neare the Creeke in morish[5] Marshes haunt.
The bellowing Bitterne, with the long-leg'd Crane,
Presaging Winters hard, and dearth of graine.   20
The Silver Swan that tunes her mournefull breath,
To sing the dirge of her approaching death.
The tatling Oldwi[v]es,[6] and the cackling Geese,
The fearefull Gull that shunnes the murthering Peece.
The strongwing'd Mallard, with the nimble Teale,   25
And ill-shape't Loone who his harsh notes doth squeale.
There Widgins, Sheldrackes and Humiliteers,[7]
Snites,[8] Doppers,[9] Sea-Larkes, in whole million flees.

[The king of waters, the Sea shouldering Whale]

The king of waters, the Sea shouldering Whale,
The snuffing Grampus, with the oyly Seale,
The storme presaging Porpus, Herring-Hogge,
Line shearing Sharke, the Catfish, and Sea Dogge,
The Scale fenc'd Sturgeon, wry mouthd Hollibut,   5
The flounsing[1] Sammon, Codfish, Greedigut:[2]
Cole, Haddocke, Ha[k]e, the Thornebacke, and the Scate,
Whose slimie outside makes him selde in date,
The stately Basse old Neptunes fleeting post,
That tides it out and in from Sea to Coast.   10
Consorting Herrings, and the bony Shad,
Big bellied Alewives, Machrills richly clad

2 starling.
3 barn owl.
4 heron.
5 peaty, sedgy.
6 long-tailed ducks.
7 localism for birds of family *Scolopacidae*.
8 snipes.
9 diving birds.
1 plunging.
2 voracious fish of all sorts.

With Rainebow colours, th' Frostfish[3] and the Smelt,
As good as ever lady Gustus felt.
The spotted Lamprons, Eeles, the Lamperies,   15
That seeks fresh water brookes with Argus eyes:
These waterie villagers with thousands more,
Do passe and repasse neare the verdant shore.

Kinds of Shel-fish

The luscious Lobster, with the Crabfish raw,
The Brinish Oister, Muscle, Periwigge,   20
And Tortoise sought for by the Indian Squaw,
Which to the flats daunce many a winters Jigge,
To dive for Cocles, and to digge for Clamms,
Whereby her lazie husbands guts shee cramms.

[3] tomcod.

JOHN JOSSELYN

(c. 1610–post 1692)

John Josselyn, born in Essex, England, is best remembered today for his *New-England's Rarities Discovered,* published in London in 1672. Keenly interested in natural phenomena of all kinds, Josselyn came to America aboard the *New Supply* in 1637/8 to visit his brother Henry in Boston, to pay his respects to Governor Winthrop and Reverend John Cotton, and to "ramble about the country." Josselyn also asserts that at this time he delivered to Cotton the translation of the Psalms "into English meeter" done by Francis Quarles.

Josselyn's rough voyage across the North Atlantic provided the subject for his carefully worked lines on a sea storm, and his "ramble" in the New World countryside materials for his poems on an Indian squaw and a New England spring.

Verses made sometime since upon the Picture of a young and handsome Gypsie, not improperly transferred upon the Indian Squa

The Poem

Whether White or Black be best
Call your Senses to the quest;
And your touch shall quickly tell
The Black in softness doth excel,
And in smoothness; but the Ear,   5
What, can that a Colour hear?
No, but 'tis your Black ones Wit
That doth catch, and captive it.
And if Slut and Fair be one,
Sweet and Fair, there can be none: 10
Nor can ought so please the tast
As what's brown and lovely drest:

And who'll say, that that is best
To please one sense, displease the rest?
Maugre then all that can be sed   15
In flattery of White and Red:
Those flatterers themselves must say
That darkness was before the Day;
And such perfection here appears
It neither Wind nor Sun-shine fears.   20

[And the bitter storm augments; the wild winds wage]

And the bitter storm augments; the wild winds wage
War from all parts; and joyn with the Seas rage.
The sad clouds sink in showers; you would have thought,
That high-swoln-seas even unto Heaven had wrought;
And Heaven to Seas descended: no star shown;
Blind night in darkness, tempests, and her own
Dread terrours lost; yet this dire lightning turns
To more fear'd light; the Sea with lightning Burns.
The Pilot knew not what to chuse or fly,
        Art stood amaz'd in Ambiguity.

[*Description of a New England Spring*]

Swift is't in pace, light poiz'd, to look in clear,
And quick in boiling (which esteemed were)
Such qualities, as rightly understood
Withouten these no water could be good.

THOMAS THATCHER

(1620–1678)

Son of the famous Peter Thatcher, Rector of St. Edmund's in Salisbury, England, Thomas Thatcher came to Boston in June 1635, and settled in Ipswich. He wed Elizabeth Partridge of Duxbury, Massachusetts, in 1643, and the couple had five children before Elizabeth died in 1664. In 1643 also, Jacob Sheafe married Margaret Webb of Boston, but then died in 1659, leaving her a widow with two daughters. Thomas Thatcher paid court to the widow Margaret Sheafe, and on the occasion of the death of one of her daughters while he was away from Boston on "publick work" wrote Margaret the lines printed below.

Thomas Thatcher's great grandson Thomas copied out the lines, added the title "A Love Letter to My Great Grandmother Elizabeth Thatcher," but erred in his identification of which great grandmother received the poem—as can be seen in the closing couplet.

A Love Letter to Elizabeth Thatcher

My Crown desired, my true love and Joy,
    All hail. Grace, Mercy, Peace to thee
From Jesus Christ our Lord and God above
    Most high, continually vouchsafed be.

        All hail Dear Soul, whose presence makes me glad
        All hail True Love, whose absence makes me sad.

Love dropping lines—of thine oft have I read,
Distilling sweetness that by far out Excells
The purest Nectar from the honey bed
Of heavenly liquor stord in curious Cells.
I read them oft, my Solace now they are,
    Still near my heart though now respect to[o] far
Whilst at this distance I am fill'd with Care.

Am filld with care, whilst Sadly I Revolve
In mine inflamd Breast the tender love
I to the[e] Bear, wherein I do Resolve   10
To spend my days Sith such to me you prove.
   Oh happy I whilst your Affection Rare
   You so discover as to ease my Care.

I want your words oft, Words convey the Mind.
Words deeds interpret and do satisfie   15
The heart wherein they credit due do find.
Words raise, Words fell the heart, words amplifie
   The kind expressions of more Silent Signs.
   Words potently sad hearts to Joy inclines.

O why should you me of those Joys debarr?   20
   Why with such sad Aspect, Such fixed Eye—
In other Objects, seem you at a [   ]
   What motions are they? what doe you descry?
   What holds you in suspence? Or plainly tell
   What doth displease? What is't you like not Well?   25

Those Manifold Temptations what are they
   That excersise your Thoughts, barr up your Speech
   Cause Sadness in my Presence? Oh mi Joy,
Tell me then Plainly I do thee beseech.
   Thy Joy I seek, thy comfort's my desire   30
   Whilst to enjoy thy bosom I aspire;
   Thy person for my Portion would acquire.
If kept I cannot nor remove it then
   Let me the Sadness bear, conceale it not;
Plunge not yourself in ruefull Sorrows when   35
   Foreseing would prevent. If tis my lot,
     Let me my Burden bear, and bear 't alone;
     What God lays on me must be undergone

What tho twere like to kill me, better dye
   By Gods wise hand, than not to bear his hand.   40
Ill trust him with my life (my Dear) and trye
   If heel not help to be at his command;
     He'l doubtless save the poor that in him trust
     And Raise the Lowly from the very Dust.

Oh let not then the Burden lay on thee   45
   Which I alone should bear, but your heart,
   Your Bosom freely open unto me,

Unlocke your cares. Ile in your griefs take part,
   If I can help it or remove it Sure
      Then that your Sadness shall not long endure.   50

To do, to Suffer, for your welfare I
Resolved am the utmost that presents
As requisite or in my power doth lie.
   These are my Secret Thoughts, my True intent.
      Banish sad damps then. Cloath your love with Joy.   55
      Hearts Secrets to me open, Be not coy

I Know your loves Entire so is mine;
   And yet assaulted it Shall be, I know.
Men will expose to tryall purest myne,
   And Satan ever was loves deadly foe.   60
      Temptations wisely God himself permits
      And by them his for farther solace fits.

We must be try'd. I look for't; nothing New
   Therein befall can. Onely arm we Must
With Christian Armour, that most firm and true,   65
   And in our great Commander Still must trust.
      He'll ne'r forsake him that up rightly Shall
      Commit to him their heart contentment [   ].

My heart still ravish'd with your love, to be
   In the glad duty whereto I am bound,   70
And true Solaces therein I Shall see
   Whilst interchanged joys with us abound.
      And we in one do laugh and weep together,
      Firmly conjoyned in both, disjoynd in neither.

My musing heart thus, in thy love must wander.   75
   Oh blame me not! thou art the Object dear
Of well fixt thoughts, true love is the Commander
   That bids be glad, or Sad, Rejoice or fear.
      Be constant in this kind,
      Upon thy constant kindness I rely.   80

Think it not much that I cannot now See thee
   As I resolved when I last took leave;
The fast or hast thoughts I would fain be with thee.
   Swift time me of that solace doth bereave;
      Tho near in heart, tho far apart, I am   85
      Joying in this that you are just the Same.—

Yet Gods Sharp visit of your family
  Would urge my coming, could I but dispence
With Publick work, So that I might be by
  To counsell, comfort, against Sorrows Sense.   90
    Excuse my Absence, Dearest, I pray,
    And with a Letter these my Lines repay.

God the Physician great now undertake
  To heal your Sick, your Well for to preserve,
And this Sad Rod unto us usefull make,   95
  Not dealing with us as our Sins deserve.
    He blessing, bless you to his grace Commanding,
    You and your branches dear my love now Ending.

These present lines of love, with thankfull heart,
  Gladly accepting what you last me sent,   100
I must conclude you are my Choicest Part:
  My dearest delight on Earth, my Hearts Content,
    Who longing, longing, longing am to Match her
    Whose my Dear Sheaf, and I her only

                      Thatcher.   105

BENJAMIN WOODBRIDGE
(1622–1684)

Benjamin Woodbridge, brother of the Reverend John Wood-
bridge and brother-in-law of Anne and Mercy Bradstreet, was born
in Wiltshire, England. He left Magdalen College, Oxford, to come to
Harvard and became not only Harvard's first graduate but also the
author of the first work to be published by a Harvard graduate.

Woodbridge's two extant poems are the graceful "Upon the Au-
thor; by a known Friend," prefixed to Anne Bradstreet's *Tenth Muse*,
and the elegy to John Cotton, printed first as a broadside soon after
Cotton's death and then reprinted by both Nathaniel Morton in
New Englands Memoriall and Cotton Mather in *Magnalia Christi
Americana*.

Upon the Author;[1] by a known Friend

Now I believe Tradition, which doth call
The Muses, Virtues, Graces, Females all;
Only they are not nine, eleven nor three;
Our Auth'ress proves them but one unity.
Mankind take up some blushes on the score;
Monopolize perfection no more;
In your own Arts, confess your selves out-done,
The Moon hath totally eclips'd the Sun,
Not with her sable Mantle muffling him;
But her bright silver makes his gold look dim:
Just as his beams force our pale lamps to wink,
And earthly Fires, within their ashes shrink.

[1] Anne Bradstreet: this poem and others preface *Several Poems* (1678), the
second edition, corrected and enlarged, of Bradstreet's *The Tenth Muse* (1650).

Upon the TOMB of the most Reverend Mr. John Cotton, late Teacher of the Church of Boston in New-England

Here lies magnanimous Humility,
Majesty, Meekness; Christian Apathy
On soft Affections: Liberty in thrall;
A Noble Spirit, Servant unto all.
Learnings great Master-piece; who yet would sit   5
As a Disciple at his Schollars feet.
A simple Serpent, or Serpentine Dove,
Made up of Wisdome, Innocence, and Love.
Neatness Embroider'd with *it self* alone;
And Civils Canonized in a Gown: 10
Embracing old and young, and low and high;
Ethicks imbodyed in Divinity:
Ambitious to be lowest, and to raise
His Brethrens Honour on his own Decayes.
Thus doth the *Sun* retire into his bed,   15
That being gone, the *Stars* may shew their head.
Could wound at Argument without Division;
Cut to the quick, and yet make no Incision;
Ready to Sacrifice Domestick Notions
To Churches Peace, and Ministers Devotions.   20
Himself indeed (and singular in that)
Whom all admired, he admired not.
Liv'd like an Angel of a Mortal Birth,
Convers'd in Heaven while he was on Earth:
Though not (as *Moses*) radiant with Light,   25
Whose Glory dazell'd the beholders sight;
Yet so divinely beautifi'd, youl'd count
He had been born and bred upon the Mount.
A living breathing Bible: Tables where
Both Covenants at large engraven were;   30
Gospel and *Law* in's Heart had each its Colume
His Head an Index to the Sacred Volume.
His very Name a *Title Page;* and next,
His Life a *Commentary* on the Text.
O what a Monument of glorious worth,   35
When in a *New Edition* he comes forth
Without *Errata's,* may we think hee'll be,

In *Leaves* and *Covers* of Eternitie!
A man of Might at Heavenly Eloquence,
To fix the Ear, and charm the Conscience,   40
As if *Apollos* were reviv'd in him,
Or he had learned of a *Seraphim*.
Spake many Tongues in one: one Voice and Sense
Wrought Joy and Sorrow, Fear and Confidence.
Rocks rent before him, Blinde receiv'd their sight,   45
Souls levell'd to the dunghil, stood upright.
Infernal Furies burst with rage to see
Their Pris'ners captiv'd into Libertie.
A *Star* that in our Eastern *England rose,*
Thence hurry'd by the Blast of stupid foes,   50
Whose foggy Darkness, and benummed Senses,
Brook'd not his daz'ling fervent Influences.
Thus did he move on Earth from East to West;
There he went down, and up to Heaven for Rest.
Nor from himself, whilst living doth he vary,   55
His death hath made him an *Ubiquitary:*
Where is his Sepulchre is hard to tell,
Who in a thousand Sepulchres doth dwell;
(Their *Hearts,* I mean, whom he hath left behind,)
In them his Sacred Relique's now Enshrin'd.   60
But let his Mourning Flock be comforted,
Though *Moses* be, yet *Joshua* is not dead:
I mean Renowned *NORTON;*[1] worthy hee
Successor to our *MOSES* is to bee,
O happy Israel in *AMERICA,*   65
In such a *MOSES* such a *JOSHUA.*

                                        B. W.

[1] John Norton (1606–63); see p. 389, n. 4.

JONATHAN MITCHELL
(1624–1668)

Nathaniel Morton's *New Englands Memoriall,* Cotton Mather's *Magnalia Christi Americana,* and Michael Wigglesworth's *Day of Doom* preserved the only verse of Jonathan Mitchell extant today. Mitchell's elegy on John Wilson was printed in full in the *Memoriall,* and a selection of five 4-line stanzas from Mitchell's tribute to Henry Dunster was included by Cotton Mather in his sketch of Dunster's life in the *Magnalia.* Mitchell's most finished verse, however, is the prefatory piece prefixed to *The Day of Doom.* See also Francis Drake, "To the Memory of the Learned and Reverend, Mr. Jonathan Mitchell," p. 457.

On the following Work and Its Author[1]

A verse may find him who a sermon flies,
Saith Herbert[2] well. Great truths to dress in Meter,
Becomes a Preacher, who men's Souls doth prize,
That Truth in Sugar roll'd may taste the sweeter.
    No cost too great, no care too curious is   5
    To set forth Truth and win men's Souls to bliss.

In costly[3] Verse, and most laborious Rhymes,
Are dish'd up here Truths worthy most regard:
No Toys, nor Fables (Poets' wonted crimes)
Here be, but things of worth, with wit prepar'd.   10
    Reader, fall to, and if thy taste be good,
    Thou'lt praise the Cook, and say, 'Tis choicest Food.

David's affliction bred us many a Psalm,
From Caves, from mouth of Graves that Singer sweet
Oft tun'd his Soul-felt notes: for not in 's calm,   15

---

[1] prefatory poem to Wigglesworth's *Day of Doom.*
[2] George Herbert (1593–1633), "The Church-porch," lines 5–6: "A verse may finde him, who a sermon flies, / And turn delight into a sacrifice."
[3] of great value.

But storms, to write most Psalms God made him meet.
   Affliction turn'd his Pen to Poetry,
   Whose serious strains do here before thee lie.

This man with many griefs afflicted sore,
Shut up from speaking much in sickly Cave,   20
Thence painful seizure hath to write the more,
And send thee Counsels from the mouth o' th' Grave.
   One foot i' th' other world long time hath been,
   Read, and thou'lt say, His heart is all therein.

Oh, happy Cave, that's to mount Nebo[4] turn'd!   25
Oh, happy prisoner that's at liberty
To walk through th' other World! the Bonds are burn'd,
(But nothing else) in Furnace fiery.
   Such fires unfetter Saints, and set more free
   Their unscorch'd Souls for Christ's sweet company.   30

Cheer on, sweet Soul, although in briny tears
Steept is thy seed; though dying every day;
Thy sheaves shall joyful be when Christ appears,
To change our death and pain to life for aye.
   The weepers now shall laugh; the jovial laughter   35
   Of vain ones here shall turn to tears hereafter.

Judge right, and his restraint is our Reproof.
The sins of Hearers Preachers' Lips do close,
And make their Tongue to cleave unto its roof,
Which else would check and cheer full freely those   40
   That need. But from this Eater comes some Meat.
   And sweetness good from this affliction great.

In those vast Woods a Christian Poet sings
(Where whilom Heathen wild were only found)
Of things to come, the last and greatest things   45
Which in our Ears aloud should ever sound.
   Of Judgment dread, Hell, Heaven, Eternity,
   Reader, think oft, and help thy thoughts thereby.

J. MITCHEL.

[4] a mountain not far from the Dead Sea, near Moses' grave.

SAMUEL DANFORTH I

(1626–1674)

Born in Suffolk, England, in 1626, Samuel Danforth emigrated to New England at the age of eight, receiving his B.A. from Harvard in 1643. Subsequently he became a minister at Roxbury, Massachusetts. While a college student Danforth was thought "unwholesomely pious," but by the time he wrote verses for the Almanac of 1647, he had clearly learned to enjoy and to imitate such "heathen" poets as Virgil. Particularly interested in astronomy, Danforth wrote a treatise on comets which was well known at the time.

Samuel Danforth's almanac verses contain topical references to current events in Massachusetts, as well as the more conventional classical and mythological allusions. The preponderance of homely images in his verse reveals his concern with everyday life in the wilderness colony.

[Almanac Verse][1]

[March]

A Coal-white Bird appeares this spring
That neither cares to sigh or sing.
This when the merry Birds espy,
They take her for some enemy.
Why so, when as she humbly stands
Only to shake you by your hands?

[April]

That which hath neither tongue nor wings
This month how merrily it sings:
To see such, out for dead who lay

[1] from *An Almanack for . . . 1647 . . . By Samuel Danforth of Harvard Colledge . . .* (Cambridge, 1647).

To cast their winding sheets away?
Freinds! would you live? some pils then take
When head and stomack both doe ake.

[May]

White Coates! whom choose you! whom you list:
Some Ana-tolleratorist:[2]
Wolves, lambs, hens, foxes to agree
By setting all opinion-free:
If Blew-coates doe not this prevent,
Hobgoblins will be insolent.

[June]

Who dig'd this spring of Gardens here,
Whose mudded streames at last run cleare?
But why should we such water drink?
Give loosers what they list to think,
Yet know, one God, one Faith profest
To be New-Englands interest.

[July]

The wooden Birds are now in sight,
Whose voices roare, whose wings are white,
Whose mawes are fill'd with hose and shooes,
With wine, cloth, sugar, salt and newes,
When they have eas'd their stomacks here
They cry, farewell untill next yeare.

[August]

Many this month I doe fore-see
Together by the eares will bee:
Indian and English in the field
To one another will not yeild.
Some weeks continue wil this fray,
Till they be carted all away.

[2] one in favor of tolerance [?]; perhaps a slighting reference to Anabaptists.

[September]

Four heads should meet and counsell have,[3]
The chickens from the kite to save,
The idle drones away to drive,
The little Bees to keep i' th hive.
How hony m[a]y be brought to these
By making fish to dance on trees.

[October]

If discontented Bellyes shall
Wish that the highest now might fall:
Their wish fulfilled they shall see,
Whenas within the woods they bee.
Poor Tinker think'st our shrubs will sing:
The Bramble here shall be our King.[4]

[November]

None of the wisest now will crave
To know what winter we shall have.
It shall be milde, let such be told.
If that it be not over cold.
Nor over cold shall they it see,
If very temperate it bee

[December]

It maybe now some enemy—[5]
Not seen, but felt, will make you fly.
Where is it best then to abide:
I think close by the fier side.
If you must fight it out i' th field,
Your hearts let woolen breast-plates shield.

[3] the confederacy of the four New England colonies.
[4] Judges ix 8–15. Verses 14–15: "Then said all the trees unto the bramble, Come thou, and reign over us. And the bramble said unto the trees, If in truth ye anoint me king over you, then come and put your trust in my shadow. . . ."
[5] winter.

[*January*]

Great bridges shall be made alone
Without ax, timber, earth or stone,
Of chrystall metall, like to glasse;
Such wondrous works soon come to passe,
If you may then have such a way,
The Ferry-man you need not pay.

[*February*]

Our Lillyes which refus'd to spin
All winter past, shall now begin
To feel the lash of such a Dame,
Whom some call Idlenes by name.
Excepting such who all this time
Had reason good against my rime.

[Awake yee westerne Nymphs, arise and sing]

Awake yee westerne Nymphs, arise and sing:
And with fresh tunes salute your welcome spring,
Behold a choyce, a rare and pleasant plant,
Which nothing but it's parallell doth want.
T'was but a tender slip a while agoe,   5
About twice ten years or a little moe,
But now 'tis grown unto such comely state
That one would think't an Olive tree or Date.

A skilfull Husband-man he was, who brought
This matchles plant from far, and here hath sought   10
A place to set it in: and for it's sake,
The wildernes a pleasant land doth make,
And with a tender care it setts and dresses,
Digs round about it, waters, dungs and blesses,
And, that it may fruit forth in season bring,   15
Doth lop and cut and prune it every spring.

Bright Phoebus casts his silver sparkling ray,
Upon this thriving plant both night and day.
And with a pleasant aspect smiles upon
The tender buds and blooms that hang theron.   20

The lofty skyes their chrystall drops bestow;
Which cause the plant to flourish and to grow.
The radiant Star is in it's Horoscope:
And there't will raigne and rule for aye, we hope.

At this tree's roots Astraea[1] sits and sings   25
And waters it, whence upright JUSTICE springs,
Which yearly shoots forth Lawes and Libertyes,
That no man Will or Wit may tyrannize.
Those Birds of prey, who somtime have opprest
And stain'd the Country with their filthy nest,   30
Justice abhors; and one day hopes to finde
A way to make all promise-breakers grinde.

On this tree's top hangs pleasant LIBERTY,
Not seen in Austria, France, Spain, Italy.
Some fling their swords at it, their caps some cast   35
In Britain 't will not downe, it hangs so fast.
A loosnes (true) it breeds (Galen ne'r saw)
Alas! the reason is, men eat it raw.
True Liberty's there ripe, where all confess
They may do what they will, but wickednes.   40

PEACE is another fruit; which this tree bears,
The cheifest garland that this Country wears,
Which over all house-tops, townes, fields doth spread,
And stuffes the pillow for each weary head.
It bloom'd in Europe once, but now 't is gon: 45
And's glad to finde a desart-mansion.
Thousands to buye it with their blood have sought
But cannot finde it; we ha't here for nought.

In times of yore, (some say, it is no ly)
There was a tree that brought forth UNITY.   50
It grew a little while, a year or twain,
But since 'twas nipt, 't hath scarce been seen again,
Till some here sought it, and they finde it now
With trembling for to hang on every bough.
At this faire fruit, no wonder, if there shall   55
Be cudgells flung sometimes, but 't will not fall.

Forsaken TRUTH, Times daughter, groweth here.
(More pretious fruit, what tree did ever beare?)

[1] goddess of justice, or of innocence and purity.

Whose pleasant sight aloft hath many fed,
And what falls down knocks Error on the head.   60
Blinde Novio[2] sayes, that nothing here is True,
Because (thinks he) no old thing can be new.
Alas poor smoaky Times, that can't yet see,
Where Truth doth grow, on this or on that Tree.

Few think, who only hear, but doe not see,   65
That PLENTY groweth much upon this tree.
That since the mighty COW her crown hath lost,
In every place shee's made to rule the rost:
That heaps of Wheat, Pork, Bisket, Beef and Beer,
Masts, Pipe-staves, Fish should store both farre and neer: 70
Which fetch in Wines, Cloth, Sweets and good Tobacc-
O be contented then, you cannot lack.

Of late from this tree's root within the ground
Rich MINES branch out, Iron and Lead are found,
Better then Peru's gold or Mexico's   75
Which cannot weapon us against our foes,
Nor make us howes, nor siths, nor plough-shares mend:
Without which tools mens honest lives would end.
Some silver-mine, if any here doe wish.
They it may finde i' th' bellyes of our fish.   80

But lest this Olive plant in time should wither,
And so it's fruit and glory end togither,
The prudent Husband-men are pleas'd to spare
No work or paines, no labour, cost or care,
A NURSERY to plant, with tender sprigs,   85
Young shoots and sprouts, small branches, slips and twigs;
Whence timely may arise a good supply
In room of sage and aged ones that dye.

The wildest SHRUBS, that forrest ever bare,
Of late into this Olive, grafted are.   90
Welcome poor Natives, from your salvage fold.
Your hopes we prize above all Western gold.
Your pray'rs, tears, knowledge, labours promise much,
Wo, if you be not, as you promise, such.
Sprout forth, poor sprigs, that all the world may sing   95
How Heathen shrubs kisse Jesus for their King.

[2] perhaps Novius, the "upstart newcomer" in Horace *Satires* I. vi. 40. Here
Novio represents blindness to truth because of sophistical reasoning.

JOHN ROGERS

(1630–1684)

John Rogers, born in 1630 in England, emigrated to New England at age six and later attended Harvard, where he studied divinity and medicine. Never ordained, he practiced medicine at Ipswich and refused the Harvard presidency the first time it was offered to him in 1677. Rogers finally accepted the post in 1682 after the death of President Urian Oakes, and held it until his death in 1684.

Related by marriage to Anne Bradstreet, Rogers may have written by invitation the only one of his verses extant today, a prefatory commendation for the Boston edition of Mistress Bradstreet's poems. Heavily dependent upon the reader's familiarity with mythical characters, Rogers' verse traces the experience of the mortal reader taken into the "Muses Grove" of Anne Bradstreet's poetry.

Upon Mrs. Anne Bradstreet Her Poems, &c[1]

MADAM, twice through the Muses Grove I walkt,.
Under your blissfull bowres, I shrowding there,
It seem'd with Nymphs of Helicon I talkt.
For there those sweet-lip'd Sisters sporting were,
Apollo with his sacred Lute sate by,
On high they made their heavenly Sonnets flye,
Posies around they strow'd, of sweetest Poesie.

2

Twice have I drunk the Nectar of your lines,
Which high sublim'd my mean born phantasie,
Flusht with these streams of your *Maronean*[2] wines
Above my self rapt to an extasie:

---

[1] This poem and others preface *Several Poems* (1678), the second edition, corrected and enlarged, of Bradstreet's *The Tenth Muse* (1650).
[2] Virgilian (Publius Virgilius Maro, 70–19 B.C.).

Methought I was upon mount *Hiblas* top,
There where I might those fragrant flowers lop,
Whence did sweet odors flow, and honey spangles drop.

3

To *Venus* shrine no Altars raised are,
Nor venom'd shafts from painted quiver fly,
Nor wanton Doves of *Aphrodites* Carr,
Or fluttering there, nor here forlornly lie,
Lorne Paramours, not chatting birds tell news
How sage *Apollo, Daphne* hot pursues,
Or stately *Jove* himself is wont to haunt the stews.[3]

4

Nor barking Satyrs breath, nor driery clouds
Exhal'd from *Styx*, their dismal drops distil
Within these *Fairy*, flowry fields, nor shrouds
The screeching night Raven, with his shady quill:
But Lyrick strings here *Orpheus* nimbly hitts,
Orion on his sadled Dolphin sits,
Chanting as every humour, age and season fits.

5

Here silver swans, with Nightingales set spells,
Which sweetly charm the Traveller, and raise
Earths earthed Monarchs, from their hidden Cells,
And to appearance summons lapsed dayes,
There heav'nly air, becalms the swelling frayes,
And fury fell of Elements allayes,
By paying every one due tribute of his praise.

6

This seem'd the Scite of all those verdant vales,
And purled springs, whereat the Nymphs do play,
With lofty hills, where Poets rear their tales,
To heavenly vaults, which heav'nly sound repay

[3] brothels.

By ecchoes sweet rebound, here Ladyes kiss,
Circling nor songs, nor dances circle miss;
But whilst those Syrens sung, I sunk in sea of bliss.

7

Thus weltring in delight, my virgin mind
Admits a rape; truth still lyes undiscri'd,
Its singular, that plural seem'd, I find,
'Twas Fancies glass alone that multipli'd;
Nature with Art so closely did combine,
I thought I saw the Muses trebble trine,
Which prov'd your lonely Muse, superiour to the nine.

8

Your only hand those Poesies did compose,
Your head the source, whence all those springs did flow,
Your voice, whence changes sweetest notes arose,
Your feet that kept the dance alone, I trow:
Then vail your bonnets, Poetasters all,
Strike, lower amain, and at these humbly fall,
And deem your selves advanc'd to be her Pedestal.

9

Should all with lowly Congies[4] Laurels bring,
Waste *Floraes* Magazine to find a wreathe;
Or *Pineus* Banks 'twere too mean offering,
Your Muse a fairer Garland doth bequeath
To guard your fairer front; here 'tis your name
Shall stand immarbled; this your little frame
Shall great *Colossus* be, to your eternal fame.

I'le please my self, though I my self disgrace,
What errors here be found, are in *Errataes* place.

[4] congees, curtseys.

RICHARD CHAMBERLAIN

(c. 1632–post 1698)

Many a seventeenth-century American was moved to respond to manifestations of witchcraft. Richard Chamberlain's *Lithobolia* (1698) is an "Exact and True Account . . . of the various Actions of Infernal Spirits, or (Devils Incarnate) Witches . . . and the great Disturbance and Amazement they gave to George Waltons Family in . . . New-England" for three months during 1682. Chamberlain was a graduate of Trinity College, Cambridge, and was trained in the law at Gray's Inn. He traveled to America in 1680 to become Secretary of the Province of New Hampshire, and was rooming at George Walton's home in Great Island when the "Stone-Throwing Devil" undertook his "Diabolick Inventions."

To the much Honoured R. F. Esq[1]

To *tell strange feats of* Daemons, *here I am;*
Strange, but most true they are, ev'n to a Dram
Tho' Sadduceans[2] *cry, 'tis all a Sham.*

Here's Stony Arg'uments of persuasive Dint,
They'l not believe it, told, nor yet in Print: 5
What should the Reason be? The Devil's *in't.*

And yet they wish to be convinc'd by Sight,
Assur'd by Apparition of a Sprite;
But Learned Brown[3] *doth state the matter right:*

[1] Dedicatory poem in Chamberlain's *Lithobolia: or, the Stone-Throwing Devil* (London, 1698), a narrative of supernatural phenomena in New Hampshire in 1682. "R. F." has not been identified.

[2] Members of a religious-political group who denied the existence of spirits.

[3] Sir Thomas Browne (1605–82), who had testified at a trial of witches in 1664. See his *Religio Medici*, Part 1.

Satan *will never Instrumental be*   10
Of so much Good, to Appear to them; for he
Hath them sure by their Infidelity.

But you, my Noble Friend, know better things;
Your Faith, mounted on Religions Wings,
Sets you above the Clouds whence Error springs.   15

Your Soul reflecting on this lower Sphear,
Of froth and vanity, joys oft to hear
The Sacred Ora'cles, where all Truths appear.

Which will Conduct out of this Labyrinth of Night,
And lead you to the source of Intellect'ual Light.   20

Which is the Hearty Prayer of
Your most faithful Humble Servant
R. C.

JOHN JAMES

(c. 1633–1729)

In addition to his three published elegies, a group of John James's manuscript verses has recently come to light, handwritten on the margins of an edition of William Drummond's poems of 1616. James was born in London and, after emigration to America, became the first minister of Haddam, Connecticut, between 1686 and 1689. Four years later in 1693 he was appointed as minister at Wethersfield, Connecticut, where he served also as town clerk and schoolmaster. His learning was recognized by the award of an honorary M.A. from Harvard in 1710.

James's best poem is a ten-line elegy on John Bunyan, in which Bunyan's vocation of tinker hammering metals for repair is a departure point for James's theme of spiritual alchemy, in which brass is transmuted into "Gold Grace." Throughout all James's verses, in fact, alchemical imagery consistently appears—a rhetorical tactic well within standard practice, for in the seventeenth century alchemy was linked both to medicine and religion.

Of John Bunyans Life &c

Wel mended Tinker![1] sans dispute
Brasse into Gold Grace can transmute.
Its hammer rings upon thy breast
So sanctifyed wert and blest
In thee an happy change was made
And thou becamest an other blad
Unswaupt,[2] instampt[3] and meliorate
By such means was thy wretched state
So sovereigne a Mastery
Has Grace to cure debauchery.

Nov-8-1702

[1] Bunyan was a tinsmith.
[2] unswapt: unsmitten.
[3] unmarked.

On the Decease of the Religious and Honourable
Jno Haynes Esqr, Who made his Exit off
the Stage of this world: Nov—1713

Strong rods for Scepters to bear Sway
How will Connecticutt display,
If thus they go unto their grave,
And we their Monuments but have,
Inscrib'd whereon their Vertues are   5
Twere better Such did in them Share,
Who cant alass therewith compare,
Devout and Conscientious Haynes
Under this Toomb Sleeps his Remains!
It would Assur'dly better Sound,   10
His goodness could in all be found,
And that did circulate around.
If such were heavens influence
Then with his loss we could dispence,
And deem Ourselves not So bereft,   15
For one, were thousand Haynes's left.
But among thousand oh how few
Survive, that do his Steps pursue,
And those hereatt who cry not Oh
Are Unconcerned it is So.   20
Let me my wishes on them Spend
That they poor Souls may live and mend.
                          Amen. Jno James
Brookfield Decembr 7–1713

SAMUEL BRADSTREET

(c. 1633–1682)

Samuel Bradstreet, eldest son of poet Anne Bradstreet and Governor Simon Bradstreet, graduated from Harvard in 1653 and shortly thereafter traveled to London, probably for the study of medicine. Returning to Boston, he practiced as a physician until 1670 when he moved to Jamaica. Bradstreet remained in the West Indies until his death in 1682.

Two of his verses for the almanac of 1657 have survived. Following convention, Bradstreet tells the story of Apollo wooing the earth goddess Tellus in springtime. With well-measured rhythms and frequent alliteration, he invests the narrative with all mythical trappings familiar to the broad audience of almanac readers.

An Almanack for the Year of Our Lord, 1657

Aspice venturo latentur ut omnia Seclo[1]

It was, when scarce had rang the morning bells
That call the dead to rise from silent tombes,
Whilst yet they were lockt up in darker Cells,
Ne had the light posses'd their shady roomes,
    That slumbring Tellus[2] in a dream did see   5
    Apollo come to cure her Lethargee.

Strait shee awoke, and lifting up her eyes
To top of tall Mount-Æthers[3] burning brow;
From flaming Globes, the Titans Herauld spies
Herward approach; Then 'fore her shrine to bow;   10
    Who bids her in great Phæbus name to cheer,
    For he was coming, and would soon be heer.

[1] All that lies hidden will be manifest in due time.
[2] ancient goddess of fertility and marriage.
[3] i.e. heaven.

Now rapt with joy, she takes her mantle soft,
On colder Couch ne longer will shee lie;
But decks her self by christall glass aloft   15
That hangs above her spangled Canopie,
    With pearly drops that fall from Limpid stilles
    She dights her too, and then with pleasance smiles.

Whilst fleet-fire-foming-steeds from farre appear
In speedy race the lofty hills to stride: 20
They Scout the smoaking Plaines, and then draw near
With burning Carre, that none but he can guide
    Who baulks their course with curb and gars⁴ them bound
    Whilst he steps down to Sublunary-round:

To greet his Tellus then he hies apace,   25
Whom sprusely deckt he findes i'th verdant gown
He whilom sent. Each other doth embrace
In loving armes, and then they sitten down
    Whilst high-born states, and low Tellurean bands
    Rejoyce to see sage Hymen joyn their hands.   30

Eftsoones Apollo gives a Girlond rare
With flowers deckt (for Tellus front alone)
To her: and sayes in mind of me this weare
And Babyes deft will thence arise anon.
    She dons it strait: And buds that erst were green   35
    Now sucklings at her milkey papps they been.

⁴ holds.

HENRICUS SELYNS

(1636–1701)

Henricus Selyns, born in Amsterdam and educated for the ministry, accepted a call to the church at Breukelen, New Netherland, and was installed as minister in 1660. He went back to Holland in 1664, a few days before New Netherland became English, but returned to New York in 1682 to become minister there. Selyns corresponded with John Wilson, Cotton Mather, Samuel Willard, and James Allen in New England, exchanged anti-Quaker and anti-Roman verses with Wilson, and wrote a dedicatory poem which was printed in the front matter of Cotton Mather's *Magnalia* (1702).

On Mercenary and Unjust Bailiffs

If they true bailiffs be, who for the law maintaining,
    Do orphans overwhelm, and widows terrify,
And hamlets gobble up, the poor with sport disdaining,
    I know not; but, I trow, a schout[1] should ever try
To have the law of God and sovereign rights possess him,
The wrong with power by right and not by wrong suppressing.

Of Scolding Wives and the Third Day Ague

Among the greatest plagues, one is the third day ague;
    But cross and scolding wives the greatest evil are;
With strong and pray'rful minds the first will cease to plague you,
But for the last I know not what advice to dare;
        Except with patience all to suffer,
        And ne'er the first assault to proffer.

[1] bailiff or sheriff (Dutch).

Upon the Bankruptcy of a Physician

That war should bankrupts make of merchants is no wonder:
But what, alas! was it that brought the doctor under?
Was 't warfare with his wife? or did he get no patients?
Or suffered he great loss from some who do not pay rents?
The one outside the house freely expends the treasure,
The other wastes, within, the goods beyond all measure.
Behold the man and wife, by squandering so flagrent,
Are rotten in the box and mothy in the raiment.

Reasons for and against
Marrying Widows

Pro.

Fears any one his bride lest she a virgin be not,
 Or what he would, I know not;
Let him a widow choose, and let the spinsters tarry,
 Ere in such doubts he marry.

Con.

To wed a widow, is it not to marry trouble,
 And *woe with woe* to double?
But be this so or not, who can take water down him
 Another had to drown in?

On Maids and Cats

A nimble cat and lazy maid,
Breed household feuds and are no aid;
But lazy cats and nimble maids,
Beyond all doubt, are greater plagues.
Once, now and then, the cat may eat,
But snoops the maid in ev'ry plate,
And makes the purse and cellar low.
How e'er it hits, *there is no dough.*

Nuptial Song
for Aegidius Luyck and Judith van Isendoorn,
Married the Second Day of Christmas

Air—O Christmas Night

1. O Christmas night! day's light transcending;—
   Who no beginning had or ending
      Until He man became, was God.
   Then He who ne'er before was human
   Was born in Bethlehem of woman,
      When nips the frost the verdant sod.

2. This richest babe comes poor in being,
   More pearled within than to the seeing
      With diadem and royal power;
   He takes no heed of greater places,
   But that small spot alone embraces,
      Where light illumes the midnight hour.

3. A maid remaining is the mother
   Of our salvation-working author,
      Who so defends us by his grace,
   We either death or devil fear not,
   For God in Him became incarnate,
      And wrestles with that hellish race.

4. This Prince,—do they desire to find him?
   They're worn-out swaddling clothes that bind him.
      A manger, spread with hay, 's his bed.
   His throne is higher than the highest,
   Yet he among the cattle lieth.
      What Him, to such a lot, has led?

5. And as they bring this child before them,
   Luyck comes and marries Isendooren,
      Standing before this Christlike crib;
   And stands when her consent is shewn,
   Flesh of his flesh, bone of his bone,
      For Judith is his second rib.

6. Now seeks he God with chaste affection.
   Who take before such crib direction,

Are better than his Bethlehem,
Which Christ no resting place will give;
For they, the after-life, shall live
With Him in New Jerusalem.

Epitaph
for Peter Stuyvesant, Late General of New Netherland

Stir not the *sand* too much, for there lies Stuyvesant,
Who erst commander was of all New Netherland.
Freely or no, unto the foe, the land did he give over.
If grief and sorrow any hearts do smite, his heart
Did die a thousand deaths and undergo a smart
Insuff'rable. At first, too rich; at last, too *pauvre*.

ICHABOD WISWALL

(1637–1700)

Ichabod Wiswall's "Judicious Observation of that Dreadful Comet" chronicles in verse the path and implications of a comet seen throughout New England in 1680 and thought certainly portentous. Wiswall's credentials for such thoroughgoing astronomical-astrological tracery in verse were those of any seventeenth-century educated man. Born in England in 1637, Wiswall emigrated to New England with his family in 1642. He later attended Harvard, refusing, however, to remain for the fourth year that had just been added to the three-year curriculum. Ordained for the ministry, Wiswall served as pastor at Duxbury, Massachusetts, from 1676 until his death in 1700, involving himself frequently in civic affairs. His efforts to secure for Plymouth a charter from the court of William and Mary were overshadowed by the more adept political machinations of Increase Mather, who saw Plymouth brought under jurisdiction of the Bay.

It was Mather, too, who wrote the best-known account of the comet Wiswall observes in verse. Yet Mather's prose narrative, while more comprehensive, lacks the forcefulness of Wiswall's poem in which he reads the comet as portending "certain draughts of Joy and Pain, / Which mortal Men must undergo."

A
Judicious Observation
Of That
Dreadful Comet
Which
Appeared on November 18, 1680, and
continued until the 10th of Fe-
bruary *following*

Wherein is shewed the manifold Judg-
ments that are like to attend upon
most parts of the World

Written by *I. W.* in *New-England*

Nunquam futilibus excanduit ignibus Æther[1]

Heavens face such Comets ne're did stain,
But mortal Men felt grievous pain.

Heavens face with Flames was never fill'd,
But Sorrows great Mens hearts soon thrill'd.

Such Comets when Heav'ns face they cover,
Bespeak aloud that Changes hover.

LONDON, Printed by *J. Darby, Anno* 1683.

Silence all Flesh, your selves prepare
To read these Lines which written are
In Heavens large *folio,* with the hand
Of him that doth all things command.
My *Genius*[2] moves me to declare,   5
And to relate what Changes are,
Like raging Waves of th' Ocean great,
Rouling themselves upon the seat
Of *Vesta*[3] now, whereon we dwell,
And must go hence to Heaven or Hell.   10
I'le not besmear my Paper with
Volatile Megrim-Fancies,[4] sith[5]
The Eccho of approaching trouble
Upon us now doth daily double.
    My Muse grows solid,[6] and retires   15
From those chill-painted Fancy-Fires

[1] The heavens never grew so bright in vain.
[2] spirit.
[3] in Roman myth, the virgin goddess of the hearth; thus, the earth.
[4] illusion brought on by a headache.
[5] since.
[6] sober.

Wherewith sometimes she lov'd to toy,
And therefore crys, *Pardon à moy*.[7]
A nobler Spark of heavenly heat,
Both Head and Heart doth actuate.   20
Heav'ns Sovereign doth unsheath his Sword,
Because Men do despise his Word,
Declar'd by them whom he hath sent
Into the World for that intent.
Heavens spangled Canopy above   25
Is neatly fill'd by th' hand of *Jove*,
With *Hyrogliphicks*, which contain
The certain draughts of Joy and Pain,
Which mortal Men must undergo:
He's wise who can forsee the Wo,   30
And timely shrowd himself from Harms,
Which usher'd are by loud Alarms.

Upon this eighteenth of *November*,
(God grant we all may it remember!)
A dreadful Comet did appear,   35
Enlightning all our Hemisphear.
It first appear'd in *Libra's* Sign,[8]
And thence went South throughout that Trine[9]
Which winds towards the Moderate Zone,
Beyond which there's a frozen one,   40
And thence it swerves, and so returns
To us whom Southern *Sol* ne're burns.
No Exhalation did combine
To fix this Comet which did shine,
Such notions flow from foggy brains,   45
And *Aristotle's* muddy drains:[10]
But *Sol* did shine with strongest flame,
Declaring that he takes his aim
At mortal Men through Burning-glass,
Because our time to dry, *Alass!*   50
    doth now draw near − −
This Prodigy which blaz'd throughout
Earths vast Circumference, no doubt

[7] pardon me.
[8] the seventh constellation of the zodiac.
[9] the aspect of two heavenly bodies which are a third part of the zodiac.
[10] Aristotle believed that comets were formed from "exhalations" of various gases in the atmosphere.

Presages greater Change at hand,
Than hath yet vexed every Land.   55
Such Signals are *Preludium*
Of direful Changes that will come
Upon the Nations: on Men all,
'Cause Vices epidemical
Do now bear sway, are in their full: 60
Shew me the Land which you can cull,
Secur'd from Vice, to Vertue prone
And I'le engage they shall not moan
The dire effects of Wantonness.
But sit and sing, yea and confess   65
Th' eternal Praise of Sovereign *El*,[11]
Who them secur'd, whilst others tell
With Heart-amazing words full true,
The dismal sorrows which they rue.
Jah[12] hides his Counsels in the dark;   70
No Man of Reason finds one spark
Of light, whereby he can divide
What is supposed, and what's try'd.
Yet many Men, if they'd confer
Each Man his little, may aver   75
In general what is design'd
Against ev'ry perverse Mankind.
    This Comet ran through th' Zodiack wide,
Did quickly through twelve Houses[13] glide,
Through many a Constellation   80
This Comet roam'd, which now is gon;
Which is significant: yet oft
Our Hemisphere with Clouds aloft
Was darkened ore, and would not suffer
Us to behold what still did hover   85
Over our heads, caus'd by its motion,
And joining to each Constellation.
Yet those who are remov'd to th' East,
Unto the North, to th' South, and West,

[11] Hebrew name for God.
[12] shortened form of *Yahweh*, Hebrew for *God*, the root of which means "to live."
[13] The heavens are divided into twelve parts, or houses, and each has a zodiacal constellation and its sign. Wiswall must have used this phrase for its poetic effect and disregarded its plausibility, for his later description of the comet's path refutes this statement.

May by their interwoven light, 90
Discover what to us is night.
And when their Observations all
Compared are, one general
System may be delineate thence,
Which will apparent make to sense 95
What is contriv'd and ratifi'd
Against all that have God deni'd,
Who gape and thirst for sinful pleasures,
That quickly fade; not for the Treasures
Which are divine, and will endure; 100
To which good Men themselves inure.
I'le therefore give some gentle hints
Of this Comets foot-steps and prints,
Engraven in Heavens Adamant
Against the Men who still do pant 105
After Earths Vice and Vanity,
Yet leaving room and liberty
For those refined Wits, that spend
Their time and pains to find the end
Design'd by him who Comets, and 110
Heavens Luminaries doth command,
To be for Signs as well as Seasons,
To punish Men not drawn by Reasons.
Seraphick Souls who mount and fly,
To peep beyond the azure Sky, 115
I'th Sign which *Libra* doth possess,
Which takes its name from th' Ballances.
God fixt this Signal in its day,
As if he did intend to weigh
Men in the Ballance curiously, 120
That so he might their Actions try.
It went thence South, and so came back
To Aries Sign, as if the track
Of every Man by double essays[14]
God would discover in their ways. 125
Tremble O Earth! Heav'ns curious Eye
Looks down upon thee from the Sky:
Dread, lest he that the Mountains high,
And Hills so great, doth frequently
At's pleasure poise with greatest ease, 130

[14] tests.

When he hath try'd both Land and Seas;
Writing *MENE TEKEL BOHU*,
Turn thy Glory into *Tohu*.[15]
This Comet touch'd the Eagle's Wing,[16]
Which will make *Austria's* Ears ting.[17]   135
Look to yourselves whose Eagles fly;
This Comet will rain certainly
Showers of Blood, and grievous things
Both upon small and greater Kings.
It touch'd the *Dolphin*,[18] that's the Fish   140
Which swims with greatest pace: I wish
Poor Seamen might a Licence have
Themselves to keep from *Neptune's* Grave.
Stern *Æolus* will Winds send forth,
And turn the smooth-fac'd Sea to froath.   145
The Heav'ns grow black, the Stars withdraw
Their shining Countenance, to th' Aw
Of many a gallant sprightly Lad,
Who fondly fool'd what once he had.
My Mates, my heart doth almost bleed,   150
Because there are so few that heed
How time runs on, danger draws nigh,
Which will oretake you suddenly.
You nimble Lads, who *Neptune* ride,
And dreadless through fierce Ocean slide,   155
Reef it awhile: All hands aloft!
Mind well your Helm; for you'l have oft
Salt breeming Waves, which will not burn,
Yet must become your dismal Urn.
Your Carcasses when you are dead   160
Will try the Depth, like Sounding-Lead;
Your briny Coats, and swollen Bulks,
Must roul on Shores like Shipwrack'd Hulks.
  It scorch'd the *Swan*,[19] and thence will reach

[15] In the Old Testament, the words *Mene, Mene, Tekel, Upharsin* were written by a mysterious hand on the wall of Belshazzar's palace, and interpreted by David as predicting the doom of the King and his dynasty. *Tohu-bohu* are Hebrew words meaning "emptiness and desolation." Wiswall's word sequence is questionable, but the meaning comes through clearly.
[16] the constellation Aquila.
[17] The Eagle was an armorial bearing of the Austrian Empire.
[18] a northern constellation, Delphinius.
[19] the northern constellation *Cygnus*.

The Man that's rais'd on high to teach.[20]   165
You *Livi's* Race,[21] whom God hath chose
Us to direct, and save from Foes;
Infernal Fie[n]ds, who would us swallow:
See that in Fires you God's Name hallow.
This Comet threatens you also;   170
O mind your work before you go
To darkest Shades, to silent Grave;
To work a season now you have;
O whet your Tongues, your Arrows set
Upon the String: do not forget   175
To draw the Bow with fullest strength,
Let Rovers[22] fly at their full length:
Direct your Arrow with good aim
At those whom you know are to blame.
You Leaders are, O do not yeeld,   180
When you are call'd into the Field,
A Field of War, a Field of Blood,
If *Elion*[23] call you, hee'l make good
His Promises. And tho you fall
In outward view, yet then you shall   185
Victorious prove, even in the end,
When Jesus Christ shall prove your Friend.
Your Robes twice dipt in Blood will shine
With Glory lasting and divine;
Look to your Charge, the Serpent's brood   190
Will range abroad in furious mood;
Sleep not at all, watch carefully,
Lest such sow Tares[24] abundantly;
Lest he that's call'd ὁ πονηδὸς,[25]
Instead of Gold, obtrude his Dross.   195
God's Furnace now in *Zion* is,
Jerusalem walk not amiss.
Th' Refiners Fire will soon kindle
On them that in Religion wrangle.

[20] a northern constellation *Cepheus*, named after the Ethiopian king.
[21] In the Old Testament, Levi was the leader of a pious priestly tribe chosen
to guard the sanctuary and the law.
[22] target arrows.
[23] Hebrew God; a variation of *Elohim*, "He with whom one who is afraid
takes refuge."
[24] wild species of injurious weed.
[25] that which hurts; i.e. Satan.

Proud Hypocrites who have misled   200
The World, shall be [b]rought to their Bed;
A Bed of Sorrows, Shame, Disgrace:
For God will now pluck from their Face
That Vizord of feign'd Sanctity,
Under whose Masque they went awry.   205
Vain-glorious Hypocrites, who made
Religions outward shew their Trade;
Who strain at Gnats, did Camels swallow;[26]
Yet inwardly did not God hallow:
Censorious Wretches, and Back-biters,   210
Who with their Tongues were Neighbour-smiters;
Such must be brought upon the Stage,[27]
Because of their Tongues greatest Rage.
God will his Churches purify
From all such Wretches terribly: 215
The Wheat will soon be clens'd from Chaff,
And they shall mourn who now do laugh.
God will a Witness be with speed
Against all such as do not heed:
I see the frowns of Blood in's Face;   220
El-shadi[28] now lays hold on's Mace;
A Mace of Iron of massy weight,
To crush all them that walk not streight.
He that is higher than all Kings,
Lords, Earls, and Barons, with their Rings   225
Of Pomp, of Power, of greatest Might,
Whose Hand directs the Morning-light;
Who guides the gloomy Shades of Death,
And gives or takes from all their Breath,
Is on his Way, he mounts his Throne,   230
And He will be advanc'd alone.
His Eyes, like sparkling Flames, do view
All that are stain'd with Ethiope's hue,
And will not wash their Robes in Blood,
In th' Blood of him who is our God;   235
That sacred Blood which only can
Purge out the stains of sinful Man,

[26] Milton, Church-Governement, vi, 125: "Can we believe that your govern-
ment strains in good earnest at the petty gnats of schisme, when it makes nothing
to swallow the Camel heresie of Rome?"
[27] a scaffold for execution or exhibition in the pillory.
[28] variation of Hebrew El Shaddai, "God Almighty."

And make him shine with Glory far
More bright than doth the Evening-Star,
Or *Phoebus* in his greatest shine,   240
Whose Glory's next to that's divine.
His Hand that grasps the Mountains large,
And spans Earth to its utmost verge;
Olympus high, and *Vesta* low,
And *Sol* ith' Center which doth go,   245
Can take and toss with greatest ease,
And doth therewith what-ere he please.
His Hand grasps hold on Judgment now,
And will force all to break or bow;
His Sword he draws and flourishes,   250
He whets the same and brandishes
Before the Eyes of Nations all;
Because hee'll war with great and small.
    Storms follow this tremendous Blaze,
Which will some Church-men sore amaze.   255
God's House which did not long since shine
With Love and Peace, which did combine
To make our *Bethels*[29] Seats of Praise,
Will ere-long look like troubled Seas,
Like Seas of Glass mingled with Fire;   260
Because some Spirits would be higher
Than God or Nature doth permit,
Such will their Venom shortly spit
Behind the back, if not ith' face
Of them that are blest *Levi's* Race.   265
    This flaming Comet will infuse
Acoustick heat into those Stews;[30]
And also beam its flaming Darts
Into the canker'd froward hearts
Of Hell's black Legion, *Ishmaelites*,[31]   270
Who still traduce God's *Israelites*,
Because they can't with them combine,
To give God's Holy Things to Swine;
Because they stand upon their Guard,
And, *Argus*-like, strive to retard   275
Wild-beasts inroads, and trampling down
That which a Christian counts his Crown;

[29] Hebrew term for a house of God.
[30] brothels.
[31] outcasts.

Proud Pharisees, false-painted Tombs,
Will with Hell's deep and fertile Wombs
Conjunctions seek, to generate   280
A spurious Bastard-Race, to grate
Upon the edge of Saints divine,
Who will not feed among the Swine.
He that's a Knave and Hypocrite,
Would fain accounted be upright,   285
By twisting other Men awry,
And loading Truth ev'n with a Lye;
Such strive to wash their own foul face,
By casting dirt and foul disgrace;
Like th' Pharisee, or Publican,   290
Yet was he not the better Man.
False Villains that do walk awry,
Will judg the best Men themselves by:
Yet dread it not *Nathaniel*,
God will from hence shortly expel: 295
Those Briars and Thorns which scratch thy face,
He'll root them up, and stop their Race.
These flaming Lights which now appear,
Do shew the Judgment-Day draws near.
These sparkling Lights which flame and die,   300
Are Signs (tho small) the Judg draws nigh,
Who will appear with thundring Voice,
With Flames begirt, and hidden noise;
Tempestuous Storms of flaming Fire
Will seize the Earth, and Heavens higher.   305
Hee'l knead the Earth, and havock make
Of all wherein most pleasure take.
His Voice will roar, Nature will tremble
When Judgments shall themselves assemble
Like armed Troops, for to destroy   310
All those who did his Lambs anoy.
Heavens Firmament will melt like Lead,
And falling down, will scald the head
Of Wickedness. The Earth will burn,
And wrap them in its flaming Urn.   315
This Fire will Heavens purify;
Encircling Earth, it will descry
Close[32] Villany, and evil Men;

[32] hidden.

Then all shall be renew'd agen.
Damn'd Wretches here no more shall grow,　　　　　320
Nor over others shall they crow,
As now they list, but shall be cast
Into the Pit that is so vast,
So comprehensive, and so wide,
That Sinners all in it may bide.　　　　　325
Mean while the best of Men shall rise
Unto that place, which few Mens Eyes
Have seen, except by th' Eye of Faith,
And do believe, because so saith
Jehovah true, who cannot lie,　　　　　330
Nor Men deceive with Falacy.
　I'le give an hint, pray mind it well,
This Comet surely doth foretell
Light breaking forth from darkest Cell,
Strange Rays of Light which shall dispel　　　　　335
Traditions fond, and Practice too,
Tho not without a sad ado;
Mysterious Truths dark Riddles hide,
The which at length are clearly spy'd.
Great strugling shall between both be:　　　　　340
At length you'l Truth triumphant see.
I see the Truth begins to spring,
It shoots the blade: but there's a Sting
With fiery heat, which will consume
All such as kick, and do presume　　　　　345
It to reject, and all forsooth
Because it suits not with their truth.
　A Central Line of darksome Shade
This sweeping Tail to out view made:
Which signifies the House of *Mors*[33]　　　　　350
To those who still without remorse
Are glewed unto fond Tradition,
And to the Truth will not them fashion.
　Must I with sorrow and with grief,
In wasting waste, because relief　　　　　355
Most Men do want; because Fire, Hail,
Frost, Snow and Drought do cause to fail
Those satiate Pleasures, we enjoy'd
Before we were with these annoy'd.

[33] death.

444

Must springs of tears in every face   360
Break forth and run in every place?
Must I still see, or must I hear,
That most things grow excessive dear?
Must Blastings, Mildews,[34] constantly
Be followers of this Prodigy?   365
Must Sailors be drown'd in the deep,
And Shepherds come to lose their Sheep?
Must Husbandmen lose greater Cattel,
And Country-men be forc'd to Battel?
Must Merchants lose their great Estates,   370
And Judges be thrust from their Seats?
Must Cities flame, and Churches burn,
And all things haste to their first Urn?
Must Tradesmen languish, Ladies pine,
And gladly feed among the Swine?   375
Must Surgeans and Physicians have
Much Work to keep Men from the Grave?
Must all things hilter skilter run,
As if that we were quite undone?
——Such times draw nigh.——   380

Must Heathen Nations still combine
To ruine what is prov'd divine?
Shall Infidels boldly presume
God's holy People to consume?
Shall Hereticks be bold to vent   385
Such Fallaces as Churches rent?
Shall Truth be trodden to the Ground
By Policy of Hell profound?
Shall Antichrist his Wound now heal,
By trampling down the Common-weal?   390
Shall Kings and Princes now fall down
Themselves and theirs to th' Triple Crown;[35]
Basely prostrate, and willingly
Adore him who's in Villany
Doth cheat the World fallaciously,   395
Imposing on them cuningly?
Shall they their Swords and Spears cast down
At's Feet, and swear to guard his Crown,
Who is their Vassal, and no Prince,

[34] witherings, rottings.
[35] papal tiara.

As will appear when he goes hence? 400
Shall th' Golden Cup of Mountebanks
Cheat all Men, yea, Men of all ranks?
Shall no Man see and shun the Cheat?
Sure when 'tis thus, God's Wrath is great.
If any ask how this can be? 405
Let him anatomize these three:
I mean the *Pope,* the *Turk,* the *Devil,*
Grand Architects of all that's evil.
   My Heart is cold, my Quill grows dry,
And must a while in silence lie. 410

Sic Cecinit.[36] I. W.
March 6. 1680–1

FINIS.

[36] Thus he celebrated in song.

GEORGE ALSOP

(c. 1638–c. 1680)

We know little of George Alsop's life except for the few facts that can be gleaned from his *A Character of the Province of Maryland* (1666) and from the letters Alsop appends to it. He spent four years as an indentured servant in the household of Thomas Stockett in Baltimore County, apparently fell ill, returned to England, and shortly afterward published the only work that can with certainty be attributed to him.

A Character is a lively piece, in both its prose and verse, perhaps reflecting Alsop's estimate of himself in the "Epistle Dedicatory" as "wilde and confused."

*The
Author
to his
Book*[1]

When first *Apollo* got my brain with Childe,
He made large promise never to beguile,
But like an honest Father, he would keep
Whatever Issue from my Brain did creep:
With that I gave consent, and up he threw   5
Me on a Bench, and strangely he did do;
Then every week he daily came to see
How his new Physick still did work with me.
And when he did perceive he'd don the feat,
Like an unworthy man he made retreat,   10
Left me in desolation, and where none
Compassionated when they heard me groan.
What could he judge the Parish then would think,
To see me fair, his Brat as black as Ink?
If they had eyes, they'd swear I were no Nun,   15

[1] *A Character of the Province of Maryland* (London, 1666).

But got with Child by some black *Africk* Son,
And so condemn me for my Fornication,
To beat them Hemp to stifle half the Nation.
Well, since 'tis so, I'le alter this base Fate,
And lay his Bastard at some Noble's Gate;   20
Withdraw my self from Beadles, and from such,
Who would give twelve pence I were in their clutch:
Then, who can tell? this Child which I do hide,
May be in time a Small-beer Col'nel *Pride*.[2]
But while I talk, my business it is dumb,   25
I must lay double-clothes unto thy Bum,
Then lap thee warm, and to the world commit.
The Bastard Off-spring of a New-born wit.
Farewel poor Brat, thou in a monstrous World,
In swadling bands, thus up and down art hurl'd;   30
There to receive what Destiny doth contrive,
Either to perish, or be sav'd alive.
Good Fate protect thee from a Criticks power,
For if he comes, thou'rt gon in half an hour,
Stifl'd and blasted, 'tis their usual way,   35
To make that Night, which is as bright as Day.
For if they once but wring, and skrew their mouth,
Cock up their Hats, and set the point Du-South,
Armes all a kimbo, and with belly strut,
As if they had *Parnassus* in their gut: 40
These are the Symtomes of the murthering fall
Of my poor Infant, and his burial.
Say he should miss thee, and some ign'rant Asse
Should find thee out, as he along doth pass,
It were all one, he'd look into thy Tayle,   45
To see if thou wert Feminine or Male;
When he'd half starv'd thee, for to satisfie
His peeping Ign'rance, he'd then let thee lie;
And vow by's wit he ne're could understand,
The Heathen dresses of another Land: 50
Well, 'tis no matter, wherever such as he
Knows one grain, more then his simplicity.
Now, how the pulses of my Senses beat,

[2] In December 1648, Colonel Thomas Pride forcibly prevented about ninety members of the House of Commons from entering the chamber and arrested forty others who favored the restoration of Charles I as king: thus, "Pride's Purge." Alsop was an ardent Royalist, contemptuous of Cromwell and the Puritans.

To think the rigid Fortune thou wilt meet;
Asses and captious Fools, not six in ten   55
Of thy Spectators will be real men,
To Umpire up the badness of the Cause,
And screen my weakness from the rav'nous Laws,
Of those that will undoubted sit to see
How they might blast this new-born Infancy: 60
If they should burn him, they'd conclude hereafter,
'Twere too good death for him to dye a Martyr:
And if they let him live, they think it will
Be but a means for to encourage ill,
And bring in time some strange *Antipod'ans*,[3]   65
A thousand Leagues beyond *Philippians*,[4]
To storm our Wits; therefore he must not rest,
But shall be hang'd, for all he has been prest:
Thus they conclude.—My Genius comforts give,
In Resurrection he will surely live.   70

[Could'st thou (O Earth) live thus obscure]

Could'st thou (O Earth) live thus obscure, and now
Within an Age, shew forth thy plentious brow
Of rich variety, gilded with fruitful Fame,
That (Trumpet-like) doth Heraldize thy Name,
And tells the World there is a Land now found,
That all Earth's Globe can't parallel its Ground?
Dwell, and be prosperous, and with thy plenty feed
The craving Carkesses of those Souls that need.

['Tis said the Gods lower down that Chain above]

'Tis said the Gods lower down that Chain above,
That tyes both Prince and Subject up in Love;
And if this Fiction of the Gods be true,
Few, Mary-Land, in this can boast but you:
Live ever blest, and let those Clouds that do
Eclipse most States, be alwayes Lights to you;
And dwelling so, you may for ever be
The only Emblem of Tranquility.

[3] dwellers on the opposite side of the earth.
[4] the Philippines.

[Be just (Domestick Monarchs) unto them]

Be just (Domestick Monarchs) unto them
That dwell as Household Subjects to each Realm;
Let not your Power make you be too severe,
Where there's small faults reign in your sharp Career:
So that the Worlds base yelping Crew
May'nt bark what I have wrote is writ untrue,
So use your Servants, if there come no more,
They may serve Eight, instead of serving Four.[1]

[Trafique is Earth's great Atlas]

Trafique is Earth's great Atlas, that supports
The pay of Armies, and the height of Courts,
And makes Mechanicks live, that else would die
Meer starving Martyrs to their penury:
None but the Merchant of this thing can boast,
He, like the Bee, comes loaden from each Coast,
And to all Kingdoms, as within a Hive,
Stows up those Riches that doth make them thrive:
Be thrifty, Mary-Land, keep what thou hast in store,
And each years Trafique to thy self get more.

[Heavens bright Lamp, shine forth some of thy Light]

Heavens bright Lamp, shine forth some of thy Light,
But just so long to paint this dismal Night;
Then draw thy beams, and hide thy glorious face,
From the dark sable Actions of this place;
Leaving these lustful Sodomites groping still,　　　　　　　　5
To satisfie each dark unsatiate will,
Untill at length the crimes that they commit,
May sink them down to Hells Infernal pit.
Base and degenerate Earth, how dost thou lye,

[1] A term of indenture, at first five years (1635) but by the Act of 1638 reduced to four years, was the means by which an emigrant without funds came to America.

That all that pass hiss, at thy Treachery?   10
Thou which couldst boast once of thy King and Crown,
By base Mechanicks now art tumbled down:[1]
Brewers *and* Coblers, *that have scarce an Eye,*
Walk hand in hand in thy Supremacy;
And all those Courts where Majesty did Throne,   15
Are now the Seats for Oliver *and* Joan:[2]
Persons of Honour, which did before inherit
Their glorious Titles from deserved merit,
Are all grown silent, and with wonder gaze,
To view such Slaves drest in their Courtly rayes;   20
To see a Drayman *that knows nought but Yeast,*
Set in a Throne like Babylons *red Beast,*[3]
While heaps of Parasites do idolize
This red-nos'd Bell, *with fawning Sacrifice.*
What can we say? our King they've murthered,   25
And those well born, are basely buried:
Nobles are slain, and Royalists in each street
Are scorn'd, and kick'd by most men that they meet:
Religion's banisht, and Heresie survives,
And none but Conventicks[4] *in this Age thrives.*   30
Oh could those Romans *from their Ashes rise,*
That liv'd in Nero's *time: Oh how their cries*
Would our perfidious Island shake, nay rend,
With clamorous screaks unto the Heaven send:
Oh how they'd blush to see our Crimson crimes,   35
And know the Subjects Authors of these times:
When as the Peasant he shall take his King,
And without cause shall fall a murthering him;
And when that's done, with Pride assume the Chair,
And Nimrod-*like, himself to Heaven rear;*   40
Command the People, make the Land obey
His baser will, and swear to what he'l say.
Sure, sure our God has not these evils sent
To please himself, but for mans punishment:
And when he shall from our dark sable Skies   45
Withdraw these Clouds, and let our Sun arise,
Our dayes will surely then in Glory shine,

[1] In 1649, Charles I was executed, and Cromwell's forces of commoners came
to power.
[2] Cromwell and his wife Elizabeth, often called "Joan."
[3] the Pope.
[4] dissenters.

Both in our Tenporal, and our State divine:
May this come quickly, though I may never see
This glorious day, yet I would sympathie,   50
And feel a joy run through each vain of blood,
Though Vassalled on t'other side the Floud.
Heavens protect his Sacred Majesty,
From secret Plots, and treacherous Villany.
And that those Slaves that now predominate,   55
Hang'd and destroy'd may be their best of Fate;
And though Great Charles be distant from his own,[5]
Heaven I hope will seat him on his Throne.

Vale.[6]

Yours what I may,

G. A.

From the Chimney-corner upon a
low Cricket, where I writ this in
the noise of some six Women,
Aug. 19. *Anno* [1665]

[Poor vaunting Earth, gloss'd with uncertain Pride]

Poor vaunting Earth, gloss'd with uncertain Pride,
That liv'd in Pomp, yet worse then others dy'd:
Who shall blow forth a Trumpet to thy praise?
Or call thy sable Actions shining Rayes?
Such Lights as those blaze forth the vertues dead,
And make them live, though they are buried.
Thou'rt gone, and to thy memory let be said,
There lies that Oliver *which of old betray'd*
His King and Master, and after did assume,
With swelling Pride, to govern in his room.
Here I'le rest satisfied, Scriptures expound to me,·
Tophet[1] *was made for such Supremacy.*

[5] Charles I's son, in exile after his father's beheading.
[6] farewell.
[1] Hell.

To My Cosen Mris. Ellinor Evins

E' *re I forget the Zenith of your Love,*
L *et me be banisht from the Thrones above;*
L *ight let me never see, when I grow rude,*
I *ntomb your Love in base Ingratitude:*
N *or may I prosper, but the state*
O *f gaping* Tantalus[1] *be my fate;*
R *ather then I should thus preposterous grow,*

E *arth would condemn me to her vaults below.*
V *ertuous and Noble, could my Genius raise*
I *mmortal Anthems to your Vestal praise,*
N *one should be more laborious then I,*
S *aint-like to Canonize you to the Sky.*

Lines on a Purple Cap Received as a Present from My Brother

Haile from the dead, or from Eternity,
Thou Velvet Relique of Antiquity;
Thou which appear'st here in thy purple hew,
Tell's how the dead within their Tombs do doe;
How those Ghosts fare within each Marble Cell,   5
Where amongst them for Ages thou didst dwell.
What Brain didst cover there? tell us that we
Upon our knees vayle Hats to honour thee:
And if no honour's due, tell us whose pate
Thou basely coveredst, and we'l joyntly hate: 10
Let's know his name, that we may shew neglect;
If otherwise, we'l kiss thee with respect.
Say, didst thou cover Noll's *old brazen head,*
Which on the top of Westminster *high Lead*
Stands on a Pole, erected to the sky,   15
As a grand Trophy to his memory.[1]

[1] mythical King of Phrygia who was condemned in Hades to stand up to his chin in water, which constantly receded as he tried to drink, and with branches of fruit above him which just escaped his grasp.

[1] reference is to Oliver Cromwell: his body was disinterred on 29 January 1660/61, his remains hung, then decapitated, and buried. His head was displayed, together with Ireton's and Bradshaw's, on top of Westminster Hall.

From his perfidious skull didst thou fall down,
In a disdain to honour such a crown
With three-pile Velvet? tell me, hadst thou thy fall
From the high top of that Cathedral?   20
None of the Heroes *of the* Roman *stem,*
Wore ever such a fashion'd Diadem.
Didst thou speak Turkish *in thy unknown dress,*
Thou'dst cover Great Mogull, *and no man less;*
But in thy make methinks thou'rt too too scant,   25
To be so great a Monarch's Turberant.[2]
The Jews *by* Moses *swear, they never knew*
E're such a Cap drest up in Hebrew:
Nor the strict Order of the Romish See,
Wears any Cap that looks so base as thee;   30
His Holiness hates thy Lowness, and instead,
Wears Peters *spired Steeple on his head:*
The Cardinals descent is much more flat,
For want of name, baptized is A Hat;
Through each strict Order has my fancy ran,   35
Both Ambrose, Austin, *and the* Franciscan,
Where I beheld rich Images of the dead,
Yet scarce had one a Cap upon his head:
Episcopacy *wears Caps, but not like thee,*
Though several shap'd, with much diversity: 40
'Twere best I think I presently should gang
To Edenburghs *strict* Presbyterian;
But Caps they've none, their ears being made so large,
Serves them to turn it like a Garnesey[3] *Barge;*
Those keep their skulls warm against North west gusts,   45
When they in Pulpit do poor Calvin *curse.*
Thou art not Fortunatus,[4] *for I daily see,*
That which I wish is farthest off from me:
Thy low-built state none ever did advance,
To christen thee the Cap of Maintenance;   50
Then till I know from whence thou didst derive,
Thou shalt be call'd, the Cap of Fugitive.

[2] headdress.
[3] Guernsey.
[4] hero of a popular European romance (1509) who, when in difficulty, received from Fortune a purse which could never be emptied. He also stole from a Sultan's treasure house a hat which could transport the wearer wherever he wished.

BENJAMIN HARRIS

(c. 1640–1720)

Benjamin Harris, London printer and bookseller, lived in New England for nine years between 1686 and 1695. During that time he wrote verses varied in subject and form, among them mock-prophetic almanac stanzas, anti-Catholic polemics, and a political eulogy of the Glorious Revolution. Probably the best-known of Harris' verses, however, are the twenty-four couplets in his *New-England Primer*, which continued, with slight variants, to be published through the eighteenth and nineteenth centuries. Harris returned to England in 1695, remaining there until his death in 1720.

[God *save the King*,[1] that *King* that sav'd the Land]

God *save the King*, that *King* that sav'd the Land;
When *James* your *Martyr's* Son,[2] your *Laws* had shamm'd.
That sav'd your *Babes*, your *Lands, Estates,* and *Wives,*
And your own *Throats* too from *dispencing Knives.*
When bloody Priests did expedite your doom,   5
And *Castlemain*[3] in state was sent to *Rome.*
When plotting *Ely*[4] felt *His Master's Hate,*
And *Sawcy Pen*[5] and *Peters*[6] ruld the State.
'Twas then *He* sav'd us from those Beasts of Prey,

[1] William of Orange, champion of Protestantism, became King of England in 1689.

[2] James II, son of Charles I who was beheaded in 1649.

[3] Roger Palmer, Earl of Castlemaine (1634–1705), an English Catholic sent to the Vatican as an envoy of James II, arrived in Rome amid much pomp on January 8, 1687.

[4] Dr. Francis Turner, Bishop of Ely (c. 1638–1700), was anti-Catholic but pro-James II and the succession; he refused to take an oath of allegiance to William and Mary and was deprived of his see in 1690; in 1691 he was accused of plotting to restore the Stuarts and left England.

[5] William Penn (1644–1718), loyal friend of James II.

[6] Edward Petre (1631–99), Jesuit adviser and confessor to James II, encouraged James in his pro-Catholic policies and then escaped England with him.

Then was *The Time, And That* without delay.　　　　　10
He spar'd no *Toil,* no *Danger* did He dread,
He came and saw *His foes with Terrour fled*
That Prince who never ran, can boldly Fight,
Deserves a Crown, he dares defend His right.
Lord! let His Foes be wrapt in slavish Fears,　　　15
And Storms of Terrour rattle in *their* ears;
Confound their Plots, and Projects that they do,
And if need be confound their Persons too.
But let His Days be long, His Fame increase,
Add to His *Conduct* many Victories,　　　　　　　20
Lord, keep Him safe fixt in his Subjects love,
And to his Crown below, add one above.
Heaven bless his *Arms,* preserve Him in his own,
And *God and Angels,* guard his Tent *and Throne.*

[*Of the French Kings Nativity, &c.*]

GO call a careful *Painter,* let him show
The Poor in Pain, the *Tyrant's*[1] Overthrow:
[Dr]aw[2] the *Oppress'd,* their *Suff'rings* and their *Fears;*
[On]e *King*[3] *in sorrow,* while the other *swears.*
[Show] how the *Priests,* in spite of *Sex* and *Age,*　　5
[Fi]r'd up the Fury of most *Christian Rage.*
[Tim]ely Stroaks let his just Pencil tell
[How] the *Reform'd,* by those *Reformers* fell.
[In de]ep-dy'd Red, shew their fresh *bleeding Wounds;*
[*There*]*'s* bloody Mercy by St *Ruth's*[4] *Dragoons.*　　10
[Show] how the *Tyrant* with the *Churches Rod*
[*Marty*]*r'd* the *Protestants* to please his *God.*
[Then] shew the *Plagues* that by *Gods Laws are due,*
[And b]y just Merit *murd'ring Kings pursue:*
[A *Mur*]*dring Court,* a *Tyrant King* undone;　　　　15
[And] *Nuns* and *Priests* in curst Confusion run.
[Now Ki]ng-scorn'd *Slaves* and *Subjects* do their part,

[1] Louis XIV of France (reigned 1643–1715) supported the Stuart family of England.
[2] bracketed material supplied.
[3] James II of England was deposed in 1688.
[4] St. Ruth, a French general who commanded the Jacobite forces in Ireland in 1691, fell at the battle of Aughrim in that year.

[Draw] their own *Swords*, their *own just Rights* assert
[So tha]t thou may'st the Just again restore,
[Oh let] there be one *Abdication* more.   20

An Account of the Cruelty of the Papists acted upon the Bodies of some of the Godly Martyrs

And thus went out this Lamp of Light,
Who 'gainst the Pope fought a good fight.[1]

A Cruelty beyond compare,
And such the Papists mercies are.[2]

Those who in Blood their chiefest pleasure have,
Most commonly in Blood roul to their Grave.

Blood will have Blood, and seldom seen we have
That Murtherers go quiet to their Grave.

Thus some do make a sport of Cruelty,
And with delight do practice Villany.

Those who to such a height of Pride *aspire,*
The Devil and not God must be their Sire.

[1] This couplet follows a passage on John Wycliffe (c. 1320–84), who attacked the papal hierarchy, the temporal power of the church, its heretical rites, etc.; in 1415 the Council of Constance condemned him and ordered his body disinterred, burned, and thrown into the River Swift.

[2] This couplet follows a passage on George Marsh of Lancashire, who was arrested in 1555 for his anti-papal teachings and was burned.

FRANCIS DRAKE

(c. 1650–post 1668)

"When our Mitchel was dying," wrote Cotton Mather in the *Magnalia*, "he let fall such a speech . . . unto a young gentleman that lodg'd in his house . . . who then compos'd the ensuing lines." The speaker was the Reverend Jonathan Mitchell, fellow of Harvard College, pastor at Cambridge, and the subject of Cotton Mather's *Life of the Reverend and Excellent Jonathan Mitchel* (Boston, 1697). The young gentleman was Francis Drake, who was moved to write the elegy printed below.

We know little else about Drake, except that he went to England with one of the Indian students at Harvard sometime after the middle of 1668. But the controlled smoothness of line and effective imagery of his single preserved poem mark him as one of the most competent elegists of early America.

To the Memory of the Learned and Reverend, Mr.
Jonathan Mitchell, *late Minister of* Cambridge *in*
N. E. *Inhumed* July *10, 1668*

Quicquid agimus, quicquid Patimur venit ex Alto[1]

The Countries Tears, be ye my Spring; *my* Hill
A general Grave; let Groans *inspire my* Quill
With an Heart-rending Sense, *drawn from the* Cries
Of Orphan Churches, *and the* Destinies
Of a Bereaved House: *Let* Children *weep*   5
They scarce know why; and let the Mother *steep*
Her lifeless Hopes *in Brine; The* Private Friend
O'rewhelm'd with grief *falter his* Comforts *end.*
By a warm Sympathie *let* Feaverish Heat
Roam through my Verse *unseen; and a* Cold Sweat   10

[1] Whatever we do, whatever we suffer, comes from above.

Limning Despair, *attend me;* Sighs *diffuse*
Convulsions *through my language, such as use*
To type a Gasping Fancy; *Lastly shroud*
Religions Splendor *in a* Mourning Cloud,
Replete with Vengeance *for succeeding Times* 15
Fertile in Woes, *more fertile in their* Crimes.
These are my Muses; *These inspire the* Sails
Of Fancy *with their* Sighs *in stead of* Gales.
Reader, *reade Rev'rend* Mitchel's Life, *and then*
Confess the World a Gordian Knot² *agen.* 20
Reade his Tear-delug'd Grave, *and then decree*
Our present Woe, *and* future Miserie.
Stars falling *speak* a Storm: *when* Samuel *dies,*
Saul *may expect* Philistia's *Cruelties.*
So when Jehovah's brighter Glory *fled* 25
The Temple, Israel *was Captive led.*
Geneva's *Triple Light³ made* one Divine;
But here that vast Triumvirate *combine*
By a blest Metempsycosis, *to take*
One Person *for their larger* Zodiake. 30
In Sacred Censures, Farrels *dreadfull* Scroul
Of Words, *broke from the* Pulpit *to the* Soul.
[*Indulgent* Parents *when they* spare, *they* spoyle;
Old Wounds *need* Vinegar *as well as* Oyle:
Distastful Cates⁴ *with* Miseries *do suit;* 35
The Paschal Lamb *was eat with* bitter fruit.]
In Balmy Comforts, Virets *Genius came*
*From th'*wrinkled Alps *to wooe the* Western Dame;⁵
And Courting Cambridge, *quickly took from thence*
Her last Degrees *of* Rhetorick *and* Sense. 40
Calvin's *Laconicks through his* Doctrine *spred,*
And Children's Children *with their Manna fed.*
His Exposition Genesis *begun,*
And fatall Exodus *Eclips'd his* Sun.
Some say that Souls *oft sad* Presages *give;* 45
Death-breathing Sermons *taught us last to live.*
One sowes another reaps, *may truely be*
Our Grave-Instruction, *and his* Elegie.

² fashioned by Gordius, King of Phrygia, a knot so ingenious that no one could untie it. Hence, a thing of great difficulty or intricacy.
³ Guillaume Farel (1489–1565), Pierre Viret (1511–71), John Calvin (1509–64).
⁴ provisions, foods.
⁵ perhaps Mary I of England.

His System of Religion *half unheard,*
Full double in his Preaching Life *appear'd.* 50
Happy that place where Rulers Deeds *appear*
I'th' Front *o'th'Battel, and their* Words *i'th'* Rear.
He's gone, to whom his Country *owes a love*
Worthy the prudent Serpent, *and the* Dove.
Religion's Panoply, *the Sinners* Terrour, 55
Death summon'd hence sure by a Writ of Errour.
The Quaker *trembling at his* Thunder, *fled;*
And with Caligula *resum'd his Bed.*[6]
He by the Motions of a Nobler Spirit
Clear'd Men, *and made their Notions* Swine inherit. 60
The Munster *Goblin by his holy flood*[7]
Exorcis'd, like a thin Phantasma *stood.*
Brown's *Babel shatter'd by his* Lightning, *fell;*[8]
And with Confused Horrour *pack'd to hell.*
The Scripture *with a* Commentary *bound* 65
(Like a lost Calice)[9] *in his* Heart *was found.*
When he was Sick, *the* Air *a* Feaver *took,*
And thirsty Phoebus *quaft the* Silver Brook:
When Dead, *the* Spheres *in* Thunder, Clouds & Rain
Groan'd his Elegium, *Mourn'd and Wept* our Pain. 70
Let not the Brazen Schismatick *aspire;*
Lot's *leaving* Sodom, *left them to the* Fire.
'Tis true, the Bee's *now dead, but yet his* Sting
Death's to their Dronish Doctrines *yet may bring.*

Epitaphium

Here lyes within this Comprehensive Span,
The Churches, Courts, and Countries Jonathan.
He that speaks Mitchell, *gives the Schools the* Lie;
Friendship in Him gain'd an Ubiquity.

Vivet post Funera Virtus.[10]

F. D.

[6] perhaps a reference to the "incestuous" relationship American Puritans assigned to the Quakers and Jesuits. See John Wilson's "Tis Braul I Cudgel," p. 385.
[7] an allusion to the Anabaptist rule for one year in the town of Münster, Westphalia.
[8] The allusion here is to Robert Browne (c. 1550–1633) and his followers, "Brownists."
[9] from Latin *calix, calicis* "cup," "chalice."
[10] Virtue survives after death.

JOHN NORTON II

(1651–1716)

John Norton, nephew of the renowned biographer of John Cotton, graduated from Harvard in 1671, and upon the death of Anne Bradstreet the following year wrote perhaps the best elegy on that poet that has survived. Classical in form and style, the elegy is also indebted for two of its lines ("Like a most servile flatterer he will show / Though he write truth, and make the subject, You.") to the last three lines of Francis Beaumont's "Ad Comitissam Rutlandiae" (1618).

A FUNERAL ELOGY,
Upon that Pattern and Patron of Virtue, the truely pious,
peerless and matchless Gentlewoman
Mrs. Anne Bradstreet,
right Panaretes,[1]
Mirror of Her Age, Glory of her Sex, whose Heaven-born-Soul
leaving its earthly Shrine, chose its native home, and was
taken to its Rest, upon 16th. Sept. 1672

Ask not why hearts turn Magazines of passions,
And why that grief is clad in sev'ral fashions;
Why She on progress goes, and doth not borrow
The smallest respite from th' extreams of sorrow,
Her misery is got to such an height,   5
As makes the earth groan to support its weight,
Such storms of woe, so strongly have beset her,
She hath no place for worse, nor hope for better;
Her comfort is, if any for her be,
That none can shew more cause of grief then she.   10
Ask not why some in mournfull black are clad;
The Sun is set, there needs must be a shade.

[1] all-virtuous.

Ask not why every face a sadness shrowdes;
The setting Sun ore-cast us hath with Clouds.
Ask not why the great glory of the Skye   15
That gilds the starrs with heavenly Alchamy,
Which all the world doth lighten with his rayes,
The *Perslan* God,[2] the Monarch of the dayes;
Ask not the reason of his extasie,
Paleness of late, in midnoon Majesty,   20
Why that the palefac'd Empress of the night
Disrob'd her brother of his glorious light.
Did not the language of the starrs foretel
A mournfull Scœne when they with tears did swell?
Did not the glorious people of the Skye   25
Seem sensible of future misery?
Did not the lowring heavens seem to express
The worlds great lose, and their unhappiness?
Behold how tears flow from the learned hill,
How the bereaved Nine do daily fill   30
The bosome of the fleeting Air with groans,
And wofull Accents, which witness their moanes.
How doe the Goddesses of verse, the learned quire
Lament their rival Quill, which all admire?
Could *Maro's*[3] Muse but hear her lively strain,   35
He would condemn his works to fire again.
Methinks I hear the Patron of the Spring,
The unshorn Deity abruptly sing.
Some doe for anguish weep, for anger I
That Ignorance should live, and Art should die.   40
Black, fatal, dismal, inauspicious day,
Unblest for ever by *Sol's* precious Ray,
Be it the first of Miseries to all;
Or last of Life, defam'd for Funeral.
When this day yearly comes, let every one,   45
Cast in their urne, the black and dismal stone.
Succeeding years as they their circuit goe,
Leap o're this day, as a sad time of woe.
Farewell my Muse, since thou hast left thy shrine,
I am unblest in one, but blest in nine.   50
Fair *Thespian* Ladyes, light your torches all,
Attend your glory to its Funeral,

[2] possibly Ormazd, Zoroastrian supreme deity.
[3] Publius Vergilius Maro (Virgil).

To court her ashes with a learned tear,
A briny sacrifice, let not a smile appear.
Grave Matron, whoso seeks to blazon thee, 55
Needs not make use of witts false Heraldry;
Whoso should give thee all thy worth would swell
So high, as 'twould turn the world infidel.
Had he great *Maro's* Muse, or *Tully's*[4] tongue,
Or raping numbers like the *Thracian* Song, 60
In crowning of her merits he would be
Sumptuously poor, low in Hyperbole.
To write is easie; but to write on thee,
Truth would be thought to forfeit modesty.
He'l seem a Poet that shall speak but true; 65
Hyperbole's in others, are thy due.
Like a most servile flatterer he will show
Though he write truth, and make the subject, You.
Virtue ne're dies, time will a Poet raise
Born under better Starrs, shall sing thy praise. 70
Praise her who list, yet he shall be a debtor
For Art ne're feign'd, nor Nature fram'd a better.
Her virtues were so great, that they do raise
A work to trouble fame, astonish praise.
When as her Name doth but salute the ear, 75
Men think that they perfections abstract hear.
Her breast was a brave Pallace, a *Broad-street*,
Where all heroick ample thoughts did meet,
Where nature such a Tenement had tane,
That others souls, to hers, dwelt in a lane. 80
Beneath her feet, pale envy bites her chain,
And poison Malice, whetts her sting in vain.
Let every Laurel, every Myrtel bough
Be stript for leaves t' adorn and load her brow.
Victorious wreathes, which 'cause they never fade 85
Wise elder times for Kings and Poets made.
Let not her happy memory e're lack
Its worth in Fames eternal Almanack,
Which none shall read, but straight their loss deplore,
And blame their Fates they were not born before. 90
Do not old men rejoyce their Fates did last,
And infants too, that theirs did make such hast,

[4] Marcus Tullius Cicero.

In such a welcome time to bring them forth,
That they might be a witness to her worth.
Who undertakes this subject to commend 95
Shall nothing find so hard as how to end.

Finis et non.   John Norton.

Omnia Romanae *sileant Miracula Gentis.*[5]

[5] Let all people of Rome be silent before this miracle.

NEHEMIAH WALTER

(1663–1750)

Nehemiah Walter, son-in-law of Increase Mather and one of the overseers of Harvard College in the late seventeenth century, wrote perhaps the earliest preserved example of blank verse composed in New England. The occasion was the death of Elijah Corlet, master of the Cambridge Grammar School and renowned rhetorician and teacher of young Indian boys who wished to prepare for Harvard. Formal, at times pretentious and wordy, the elegy is an attempt in its elaborate use of figures and use of classical allusion to do justice to Corlet's remarkable learning in Greek and Latin.

An Elegiack Verse,
On the Death
Of the Pious *and* Profound *Grammarian*
And Rhetorician, Mr. Elijah Corlet,
School-master *of* Cambridge, *Who* Deceased Anno
Aetatis 77. Feb. 24,
1687

On *Roman* Feet my stumbling *Muse* declines
To walk unto his Grave, lest by her Fall
She trespass, in accosting of his Head
With undeserved breach. In jingling *Rythme*
She thinks it not convenient to Dance   5
Upon his Sacred Herse; but *mournful* Steps
If Metrically order'd, she computes
The most becoming of this Tragick Scene.

Could Heav'ns *ignific Ball* (whose boundless Womb
Millions of flaming *Ætna's* does ingulf)   10
From Candle's dull and oleaginous
Transfused Beams, a glowing *Atom* draw,
Which might a super-added Lustre give
Unto its conick Rayes; then might our Verse

Swell with impregnant *hopes* of bringing forth 15
Some rich Display of *Corlet's* Vertues rare.
But this *Herculean* Labour forc'd we deem
Not second to *Impossibilities*.
This presses hard our tim'rous heart whence flows
A Torrent of amazing Fears, whose *Waves* 20
Bode Universal *Deluge* to that Verse
That dares pretend to equalize his *Fame*.
Creep then, poor *Rythmes,* and like a *timid Hare*
Encircle his rich Vault, then gently *squatt*
Upon his Grave the Center there proclaim 25
Tho' he *subside,* yet his abounding Worth
Does infinitely *supersede* thy *Layes*.

Tell to the World what Dowries Nature showr'd
Into his large capacious Soul; almost
Profuse in large Donations; yet kind Art 30
Still adds unto the store, striving to reach
Perfection's Top, during a *mortal* state.
Sagacious Nature, provident that nought
Of her dispensed bounty frustrate prove,
Boyls up this *Font* of *Learning* to an head, 35
Which over-topping of its Banks she glides
Through Nature's *Conduit-pipes* into the Soil
Of tender *Youth,* which gaping sucks it in,
Like thirsty *Stars* Bright *Phebus's* liquid *light*.
A *Master of his Trade,* whose Art could *square* 40
Pillars of rooted *strength* whose shoulders might
A Common Wealth uphold. *Aholiab*-like[1]
Divinely qualifi'd with curious Skill
To carve out *Temple* work, and cloath the *Priest*
With sacred Robes, adapted for the Use 45
Of Functions so divine.———
Rivers of *Eloquence* like *Nectar* flow'd
From his Vast Ocean, where a *Tully*[2] might
Surfeit with draughts of *Roman* Eloquence.
Immortal *Oakes*[3] (whose *golden mouth* ne're blew 50
A blast defil'd with indisposed Speech)
Suspecting his own parts, rarely pronounc'd

[1] Exod xxxv 36: "Them hath he [Aholiab] filled with wisdom of heart, to work all manner of work, of the engraver, and of the cunning workman. . . ."
[2] Marcus Tullius Cicero (106–43 B.C.), renowned Roman orator.
[3] Urian Oakes (1631–81), president of Harvard (see p. 207).

His *Ciceronean* lines, until they'd touch'd
This *Lydius Lapis*[4] CORLET: then approv'd
They're *Eloquence-proof* esteem'd, and challeng'd   55
The *Roman* Tribe of Orators to spend
Their subtilty, and pierce their *Eagle's* Eyes
Into their very bottom.――――

   Had *Grecian* Dialect and *Roman* Tongue
Surviv'd this Age within their native Soyl,   60
Endless had been their Feud; *Athens* and *Rome*
Had set their *Tully's* and *Demosthenes*[5] to fight
With Swords brandish'd with shining *Eloquence*
For to decide the Controverse, and prove
To whom by right Great CORLET did pertain.   65
This proving unsuccessful, nought can quench
Their flaming zeal, save by (*Colossos* like)
Erecting his large Statue, whose proud feet
Might fix their Station on the Pinacles
Of each of these *Metropolies* of Art.   70
Nor were his Parts exclusive of his *Zeal*
In serving his rich Donor. No Serpent
Bearing a fulgent Jewel in his Crest,
While cursed Poison steeps his venom'd heart.
But *Grace* the Crown of all shone like a Sun   75
Fix't in the Center of that *Microcosm*.
Blown to the full, perfum'd with sacred smell,
This flower *Heaven* pluckt. When *Natures* Tree
Too feeble grown to bear such ponderous fruit
Elijah's Chariot born on *Seraph's* wings,   80
Mounts with this Treasure to the port of *Bliss*.

        Sic maestus cecinit

      NEHEMIAH WALTER.

[4] Lydian stone.
[5] Athenian orator (c. 385–322 B.C.).

RICHARD HENCHMAN

(c. 1655–1725)

Richard and his brother Daniel, both poets, were the eldest sons of Captain Daniel Henchman of Boston, one of the heroes of the bloody King Philip's War. Richard became a schoolmaster in Yarmouth, then returned to Boston to teach at the North Writing School. A close friend of Samuel Sewall, Richard Henchman often exchanged manuscript verses with the Judge, and wrote a fifty-five-line translation of Nehemiah Hobart's Latin poem in praise of Sewall, "Sewall Our Israel's Judge and Singer Sweet." Henchman's "In Consort to Wednesday," printed below, was dedicated to Sewall and called forth by Sewall's "Wednesday January 1. 1701" (see p. 305).

In Consort to Wednesday, Jan. 1st. 1701
Before Break of Day[1]
Cant. 2. 17
E're the Day *break, and The* Shadows *Fly*

> *Est Deus in Nobis, sunt et Commercia Coeli:*
> *Sedibus Athereis Spiritus Ille venit.*
> A God doth dwell in *Men,* from th'
> > Blessed Seats,
> Th' Immortal Spirit, mortal Man
> > repletes.
>
> Suffer, much Worshipful, A *meaner*
> > Flight,   5
> In Eccho to your sacred *Muse's* Hight,
> Of our *New-year,* which usher'd in the
> > Light.

[1] dedicated to Samuel Sewall whose "Wednesday, January 1. 1701" (see p. 305) stimulated this poem.

Divert from th' Holy-*Path*, whom *Nothing*
can,
Nay *Superstitious* Rites, *Thrice Ble'ssd the*
Man!
Who with an *Heart-rene'wd*, A *New-Year's*
Day   10
Observe's, and Takes it with Him, on his
Way:
And certain 'tis, that the Profane-Abuse
Of Observations, fright them out of Use.

E're ye Day Break.

Thrice Happy He   15

Whose more cœlestial *Phospher* doth out-run
Aurora's Gleames, and ante-vert's the *Sun:*
On whom, Before the *Breaking-Morn*
displai'es
The *Healthful* Warmth of *Phoebus'* Golden
Rayes,
The Brighter Son of *Righteousness* expand's   20
His *Healing*-wings, and Saving-*Health*
command's:
Who, Lying down to Rest, had closely fur'ld
His *Spreading*-Thoughts, to Mind a Better
World:
Sleep's The Beloved's Arms encircled in,
And *waking*, ever find's himself with Him: 25
Who, for Those *Graces*, which the Soul
adorn,
Wait's more than *Morning*-Watchers watch
for *Morn:*
Nor can no more *Jerusalem's* Weal forgit,
Than his own *Soul*, or Nearest- *Intrests* quit.

And ye Shadows fly.   30

Thrice Happy He

Who e're the *Shades* to their *Black*-Den
repair
(And th' next Half-Globe feel's the
Nocturnal-Mare)

Hath *rarifyd* his Thoughts with *purer Air*,
And Breathe's by *Contemplation* in that
                                    Clime,   35

Darkest, just
before Break of
Day

Where *Mist* ne're rose, nor Sun surceased[2] to
                                    shine:
Who in Night's *Darkest-Hours* his Heart hath
                                    gott
To Him, from whom *The Darkness darkneth*
                                    not:
Or, if the *Darkness* occupy his Thought,
'Tis to a Nobler Use *calcined* brought;   40
Præsenting to his *sadder*-Eye Those Realms,
Which *Darkness* and Death's *Shadow*
                                    overwhelm's.
And thence lift's up a Prayer that *Truth* and
                                    Light
Sent thither might dispel those *Foggs* of
                                    Night,
And to a *Goshen*[3] turn the *Darksom* House,   45
Where *Daemons* hold their General-
                                    Rendezvous.
    Then for our *Tawnys,*[4] where Convertion
                                    work
Begun so sadly in the Birth is stuck;
That This *Great-Task,* through Heaven's
                                    indulgent Care,
May thrive throughout our Darker-Woods,
                                    that there   50
It may be said, *Born These and Those Men*
                                    were!
    But most, that That *fair-Morning* may arise,
Repleat wherewith are all Those *Prophesies,*
In Faith whereof, so many Saints now *sleep,*
And Thousands yet *alive,* their *Vigils* keep;   55
Which with it's *Brighter-Beamings* shall
                                    transfuse
The *Darkned* Minds o'th' Obstinater *Jewes,*
On whose Obdurate *Hearts,* unto this Day,
Lie's Unbelief's Thick-*Vail* untooke away;

[2] ceased.
[3] i.e. a fruitful land.
[4] Indians.

And Them with *Mourning* and *Rejoiceing*
bring   60
To their Once *pier'cd,* but now *exalted* King.
Who actually *Earth's-Throne* shall, then,
obtain,
And Gloriously before his Ancients reign.
Then's *Faith,* not hood-winkt by th'
Opacous Screen,
Seal's th' *Evidence* of all these things, as
seen;   65
Yea, through those *Sable*-spectacles beholds
Conjoining into One, the seperate-Folds,
One shepherd Paramount: And *Japhets'*[5] stem
Exulting in the Goodlier *Tents* of *Shem:*[6]

Rom. 11: 12, 15   Through whose Rejection first They rais'd
their Head   70
But, Gathering now, are *rais'd as from the*
Dead.
This *Happy Man,* Dear Sr, is *You,* altho'
Tis next to'a Crime, to tell your Worship so;
In whom *Humility* has *nearly* gain'd
The Point, that is, *It's perfect Work obtain'd;*   75
(And, but that *Flesh and Blood* will hold
their Clue,
I fairly had left out that *Nearly* too)
These *Universal*-Holy-Breathings, yet,
Of your more Holy Soul, I might not quitt.
Nor could my shallow Muse, as take the
Round   80
They did, but Take them thus at the
Rebound.
May th' *Rest* with you the *Reckoning* better
sett,
(For all the *Earth* save *Rome* is in your
Debt)
Whose Hands did first to *Heaven* this *Offring*
lift,
Then to the *World,* A Richer *New-Years Gift,*   85
Than Either *Indias* Bosom could unfold,
Or *Sheba's* Incense yield, Or *Ophir's* Gold.

[5] son of Noah, ancestor of Indo-European peoples.
[6] son of Noah, ancestor of Semitic peoples.

Your *Theam's* a Subject *for* the *Richest*
Muse,
But most of all, (I vote) for *His,* in whose
Fair *Name,* (but more *Good-Heart*) wee See
the Wall　　90
Of *Bethel* rise, and cursed *Babel* fall.

With Thy *Scicilian Muses, Virgil,* hence,
The *Golden-Age* doth with *This Muse*
commence.
Here, than from *Sibil's* Leaves' Praedict, wee
read,

Magnas procedere From *surer*-Writ, *How The Great Months*
menses Cœl. *proceed:*　　95
demisus ab alto And know the *Time's* near, when th' *Eternal*
Birth,
De-miss'd from *Heaven,* shall Bless *again* ye
Earth.

Aggredere, ô 　　Enter, o Mighty Monarch Thy Great State!
magnos honores For which our Groaning-Tract doth
Longing wait;
Whose *full-Possession* (to it's utmost Line)　100
By an Eternal *Gift,* is firmly Thine.

To Capt. S. S. Esq　　Januae. 28. 1700/1

Vox Oppressi
To The Lady Phipps[1]

Press often *for,* (nor, than at This Time,
more)
But never *by,* a *Weight* of Cash before:
(A *Weight* to *me,* scarce less than *That*
whereby,
Wee read, How One, did once oppressed,
die)
Fair Lady, suffer *The Oppressed to CRY.*　　5

Oppressed, in my Generous Lady's *Name,*
By th' Interchanges both of *Joy* and *Shame;*
(For *Joy* and *Sorrow* mutually are sped

[1] Mary (Spencer) Hull Phips, wife of Sir William Phips (1651–95), first
royal governor of Massachusetts.

Of their Extreems; This, by Contraction bred
By Bold *Dilation,* That: Each Passion fill's   10
The Sails, And th' *Cross,* no more than
                                        Kindness, kills.)

Oppress'd by *Joy,* whilst of, at *Home,* my
                                        Stock
The *Streights,* (which Those might of
                                Gibralther mock)
Some Exit found, by' a Pilot, SILVER[2] nam'd,
For Skill, more than Old *Palinurus,*[3] fam'd: 15
No *Jacobs-staff,*[4] nor all th' Intreagues, with
                                        which
The Loadstone doth the *Neptunist* enrich,
Can show such *Art* as HIS, which might prevail
About Old *Gunter's* Head, to Break his
                                        Scale.[5]

Oppress'd with *Shame,* which, since I can
                                        requite   20
Your *Kindness* no way, somewhat *cloud's* it's
                                        Light;
Whilst to that sorry *shift,* I must proceed,
By th' *Will,* which only Complement's the
                                        Deed;
For where th' *Receiver* nothing can advance,
Though it the *Donor's* Largess doth enhance,   25
Yet He, mean while, his Fortune cant but
                                        grieve,
Who's *Good for Nothing else, but to Receive.*

Oppressed thus by What doubly doth
                                        express
Your *Bounty,* and my own *Unworthiness,*
I cannot, since *Both,* in Your *Praise,* agree,   30
But *Lifting up my* CRY, your *Herald* be;

[2] The poet had just received a gift of silver from Mrs. Phips.
[3] in Greek myth, the helmsman of Aeneas who fell asleep at the wheel, fell overboard, and was drowned.
[4] a staff carried by pilgrims to the tomb of the Apostle James the Elder; also applied to a dagger or sword concealed in this staff.
[5] Edmund Gunter (1581–1626), English mathematician who invented several measuring devices including "Gunter's Scale," used to solve problems in navigation.

A CRY of [a]Benediction, still which is,
Or ought to be, *in Causa Pauperis.*[6]
A CRY which, were my Muse but lung'd,
                              should roul
Through th' *Earth's* vast Round, and eccho
                          Either *Pole;*   35
But to the *Poles* this News as soon did *dart,*
As *purpos'd* in Your Ladiships Good Heart:
Than by the *Voice of Alms* no Greater *Rents*
Are giv'n to th' Empyrêal Battlements.
Then *Those,* no *Cries of Wrong,* the yielding
                              spheeres,   40
Cut swifter, to *The Lord of Sabaoth's Ears,*
Whose *Hosts* stand rang'd, as well with
                    [b]*Grace* to 'enlarge
The *Bounteous,* as the *Gripeing* Wretch to
                          [c]Charge.

But What then shall I CRY?
Why, could a *Claudipede*[7] aspire so High
As *Gerizim's*[8] fair Top, He Thus would *Cry.*

MAY Those Rich Graces (which by
                      Nature's Toil,
Were never yet the *Product* of her Soil)   45
Sprung in your Heart, by HIM, and made to
                          Grow,
WHOSE Gifts and Callings no Repentance
                          know,
Still Thrive, still *Efflorescent,* there, persist,
Blown by Those *Gales,* which *Breath where
                      e're They List:*
Nor may *Ripe*-Years, (which *may* your Life
                          attain)   50

Psal. 92: 13, 19   In Their fresh *Verdure,* ever sense a *Wain,*
Until Transplanted to th' Cœlestial-seat,
Those *Graces* shall in *Glory* be compleat.

[a] Well-wishing.
[6] for the sake of the poor.
[b] Favours.
[c] Adoriri.
[7] limping walker.
[8] mountain in Jordan on which the tribes of Israel assembled to hear curses
and blessings connected with the violation and observance of the law (Deuter-
onomy XI).

474

MAY, in Each Good and Charitable *Deed,*
Your *Native* Generosity proceed,   55
Incited from the Memory and the Thought
Of Your Great Phipps, with greater Care, who
                                                    sought
(through Numerous Evil Treats, and's
                                    Neighbour's strife,
Ev'n at th' Expence of's Time, Estate and
                                                    Life)
How He, his Countrey might *Advantage*
                                        most,   60
Than, once, the *Treasure,* on th' *Iberian-*
                                            Coast.

MAY your Dear Son and Heir, (Your
                                    Goodly Choice)
The Heart of Your Good Ladiship rejoice:
May That fair *Branch,* as well in *Deed* as
                                            Name,
Confess That Noble *Line,* whereof he came,   65
The *Spencer's Line,* A *Name* of much
                                        Renown,
Though sometimes suffering under Fortune's
                                        ᵈ*Frown.*
And *may,* when Years have writ Him *Man,*
                                    The *Fame*
Of *HIM,* from whom is his *Adopted*-Name,
And *Acts* of That Great Heroe, make his
                                        Mind   70
To Every *Great* and *Virtuous* Thing inclin'd,
That (celebrated in our Hearts and Lipps)
He may present, A *Redivived PHIPPS.*

But let me Reassume, e're I give o're,
The Threed, I'd partly toucht upon before.   75
MAY Heaven, with Many Daies, our Lady
                                        Grace,
An Honour, to *Religion* and her *Place:*
May she be'amongst us Long and *Nobly-*
                                        Liv'd,
By whose Good Pattern *Piety* hath Thriv'd:
May she, maintain'd, who, in her *station,*
                                        hath,   80

ᵈ Life of Sr. W[illiam] P[hipps]. page 5.

Unto The Saints the Once Delivered ^e*FAITH,*
Receive, when *Death* her Passage hence
shall Tole

Jud. 3

The END of *her's, The Saving of her Soul.*
That when, her *Labours,* here, being
Laid-aside,
She *Resteth* with That LORD, in Whom she
dy'd,   85
By her Good WORKS, she yet may *Speak,*
whilst *Dead,*
And in Each WORLD, by *Them* be followed,
Both This she 'th Left, and That to which
she's fled.

But shall my Muse, e're she her *Wishes*
stay,
No Honours to the *Female-Beauty* pay?   90
A Province, which I never did decline,
Wish, Muse, then, to our Lady Thus, in fine:

MAY Her *Bright* FORM, where yet no
Mote appear's
Of Envious *Age,* but mock's ev'en *Blooming*
Years,
Still hector *Time's* rough *Teeth,* which
mostly plow   95
The Earliest *Furrows,* in the Smoothest-
Brow:
May, in her Cheeks, the *striving* Red and
White
Still hold their own, and Neither gain by
Fight:
May Those Fresh *Roses,* ever in their Bloom,
Unto her *latest* Breath, retain their *June;*   100
And Typify, when *Death* hath clos'd her Eyes,
What she shall, at the *Resurrection,* rise.

^e *Faith and Order of ye Gospel.* . . .

GRINDALL RAWSON

(1659–1715)

A native-born Bostonian, Grindall Rawson graduated from Harvard in 1678, after which he accepted the ministry at Mendon, Massachusetts, where he remained until his death in 1715. Active in community efforts to disseminate the Gospel, Rawson served for a time as ship's chaplain, and also worked for Indian conversion, preaching to the natives in their own language.

Among Rawson's classmates at Harvard had been John Saffin, Jr., and Cotton Mather, both of whom are subjects of Rawson's only two extant verses. The elegy on the young Saffin was occasioned by the boy's untimely death from smallpox, while Rawson's other poem commends Cotton Mather for having written the compendious *Magnalia*. The elegy, by far the more engaging of the two, is more valuable for vivid imagery than for sustained tone. But each poem, one of many of its kind in seventeenth-century America, stands substantially above the majority in quality.

Upon the Death of his much Esteemed friend
Mr Jno Saffin Junr. who Expired on
the Nineth of December 1678

Awake Sound Sleeper! hark, what Dismal knells,
Arrests thy drowsie sences, and compells,
Unbiden Tears to flow, from such a Source
As doth deny Nature her freer Course.
Ah me! to[o] well I know, my Dearest friend,   5
In whom my Joyes did terminate and End,
Hath payd to Death her Dues; Thus God Decrees,
To some their minutes to other some Degrees.
So Irriversible is this our Doome,
That in our Loftiest hopes we find our Tombe!   10
Death rangeth here and there and Nips those Buds

Who might have prov'd worthy, Thrice worthy Studs,
In this our Zion, but what shall we say?
Sculls of all Sizes lye in Golgotha.
Ascend Mount Calvery, and ther you'l see   15
To young and Old Deaths Equall Destinye.
The Rich as well as poor, the low and high,
At last their Nebo[1] must ascend to Dye.
To all God grants their Tallents; some w[i]th ill
Ful fraught doe live whilest they their measures fill.   20
Others (to whom the Largess of Gods grace
Makes sedulous) Employ their time apace,
Rightly improve their towne; Denizon'd then,
Cittizens of the New Jerusalem.
Even such an One we mourne; for many years   25
This justly claimes the Tribute of our Tears.
Call me some Curious Painter whose rare art
In due proportion can Limne Every part,
Exactly well, then (Sirs) where will you find,
Another like Endow'd* with such a Mind,   30
Bigge with Endowments, fraught with Learning so
As did the Bancks of Nature overflow,
Nature to few so kind, yet here we see
Nature Intended Partiall to bee
And must such thriveing in plants thus hurled be   35
Into the Caverns of Oblivitye;
Yes, yes they must we see the Sacred vanne,
By laws more sure than Mede or Persian,
Doth part the Soul and Body and Commands
Them listed Souldiers to Deaths Numerous Bands;   40
And thus Deprives us by a just Decree
Of great Supporters in our Miserie.
Unto the Potter then shall viler clay
Aske reasons of it's Former, shall man gainesay
Or yet Demand a reason of his God   45
For takeing in his hand his Scourging Rod,
Rather be silent seing God so Commands,
Better then in our own, when in God's hands
Had I Witts Monopoly; would some kind Muse

[1] Mount Nebo, from which Moses looked into the Promised Land before his
death.
* Adorn'd [as amended by Saffin and copied into his notebook].

Into my Cloudy Fancy skill infuse 50
By lofty Straines I'd raise his fame so high
As is his Heaven-born Soul's filicity.
But ah! my Simple muse, what flattering smile
Drawn from Apollo's face could so beguile,
Thy feeble hopes to think thou couldst acquitt 55
What's Due unto his Learning, vertue Witt;
Rather Adjourn thy grief Supress this payne
And labour Earnestly for to Constraine
Those that Esteem him to sitt down with thee
And strive to weep him forth an Elegie 60
And softly whisper those that yet Survive
Though John and Marth're[2] Dead yet God's alive.

Ah te mea si partem anime rapit, Horat.
Maturior vis, quid moror alterna. ad Meunatem
Sicflevit[3] 65

To the Learned and Reverend Mr. COTTON MATHER,
On his Excellent Magnalia

SIR,
    My Muse will now by Chymistry draw forth
    The Spirit of your Names Immortal worth.

COTTONIUS MATHERUS.
Anagr.
Tuos Tecum ornasti.
While thus the Dead in thy rare Pages Rise,
Thine, with thy self, thou dost Immortalize.
To view the Odds, thy Learned *Lives* invite,
'Twixt *Eleutherian*[1] and *Edomite.*[2]

[2] Martha, John Saffin's first wife, died December 11, 1678.

[3] slightly incorrect quotation from Horace's *Odes* II. xvii, 4–5. Correctly, the lines read: "A, te meae si partem animae rapit, maturior vis, quid moror altera" (Ah, if a premature death snatches you away, the half of my own being, why do I, the other half, prolong my life?). The remaining three words may be translated "Thus wept Grindall Rawson at Mendon."

[1] Zeus' title as protector of political freedom.

[2] descendants of Esau who later became the hereditary enemies of Israel, were conquered by Saul, rebelled, and became rulers of the Jews.

But all succeding Ages shall despair,
A Fitting Monument for *thee* to Rear.
Thy own Rich Pen (Peace, silly *Momus*,[3] Peace!)
Hath given them a Lasting *Writ of Ease*.

Grindal Rawson, Pastor of *Mendon*

[3] Greek god of ridicule.

JOHN WILLIAMS

(1664–1729)

Born in Roxbury, and a Harvard graduate in 1683, John Williams became pastor of the church at Deerfield, Massachusetts, and with his wife and children was taken prisoner by a band of French and Indians who raided the settlement in 1704. Redeemed in 1706, he wrote the account of his capture, his wife's murder, and his daughter's conversion to Catholicism and marriage to an Indian, that was to become a colonial best-seller, *The Redeemed Captive Returning to Zion* (Boston, 1707). It contains his best verse.

Williams' other lines, printed in Cotton Mather's *Good Fetch'd out of Evil* (Boston, 1706), are memorable only for their title: "Some Instructions, Written by Mr. John Williams, for his Little Son, when the Child was in danger of taking in the Popish Poisons."

Some Contemplations of the poor, and desolate State of the Church at Deerfield

The Sorrows of my Heart enlarged are,
Whilst I my present State, with past compare.
I frequently unto God's House did go,
With Christian Friends, his Praises forth to show.
But now, I solitary sit, both sigh and cry,   5
Whilst my Flock's Misery think on do I.
    Many, both Old and Young were slain out-right;
Some in a bitter Season take their Flight;
Some burnt to Death; and others stifled were;
The Enemy,[1] no Age or Sex would spare.   10
The tender Children, with their Parents sad,
Are carry'd forth as Captives. Some unclad,
Some Murdered in the Way, unburied left;
And some thro' Famine, were of Life bereft.
After a tedious Journey, some are sold,   15

[1] Indians and Canadian French.

Some left in *Heathen* Hands, all from Christ's Fold
By *Popish Rage*, and *Heath'nish* Crueltie,
Are banished. Yea some compell'd to be
Present at *Mass*. Young Children parted are
From Parents, and such as Instructors were.   20
Crafty Designs are us'd by *Papists* all,
In Ignorance of Truth, them to inthrall:
Some threatned are, unless they will comply;
In *Heathens* Hands again be made to lye.
To some, large Promises are made, if they,   25
Will Truths renounce, and chuse their *Popish* Way.
  Oh Lord! mine Eyes on Thee shall waiting be,
Till Thou again turn our Captivitie.
Their *Romish* Plots, Thou canst confound, and save
This little Flock, this Mercy I do crave.   30
Save us from all our Sins, and yet again,
Deliver us from them who Truth disdain.
  Lord! For thy Mercy sake, thy Cov'nant mind;
And in thy House again, Rest let us find.
  So we thy Praises forth will shew, and speak,   35
Of all thy wondrous Works; yea we will seek
Th' Advancement of thy great and glorious Name,
Thy Rich, and Sovereign Grace, we will proclaim.

SARAH KEMBLE KNIGHT

(1666–1727)

Sarah Kemble Knight was the daughter of a well-to-do merchant whose family lived during her girlhood in a fashionable section of Boston near the church where Increase and Cotton Mather officiated. Later married to a shipmaster whose business took him frequently to London, Sarah Knight was often left alone to manage household and family affairs. A sprightly lady of quick intelligence, curiosity, and energetic will, she engaged in land speculation, merchandising, farming, and schoolteaching. Quite possibly it was she who taught Benjamin Franklin to write.

In 1704, at age thirty-eight, Madame Knight traveled south from Boston to Connecticut and New York on a matter of family estate settlement. It was during her travels that she compiled her *Journal,* an account of her observations and experiences in an era when poor transportation, primitive roads, and indifferent innkeepers made even the shortest trip an arduous business. Interspersed throughout her travel narrative are Madame Knight's verses, written on whatever topic engaged her fancy at the moment: the moon, an imagined city, the effects of rum.

[*Thoughts on the Sight of the Moon*]

Fair Cynthia, all the Homage that I may
Unto a Creature, unto thee I pay;
In Lonesome woods to meet so kind a guide,
To Mee's more worth than all the world beside.
Some Joy I felt just now, when safe got or'e   5
Yon Surly River to this Rugged shore,
Deeming Rough welcomes from these clownish Trees,
Better than Lodgings with Nereidees.
Yet swelling fears surprise; all dark appears—
Nothing but Light can disipate those fears.   10
My fainting vitals can't lend strength to say,

But softly whisper, O I wish 'twere day.
The murmer hardly warm'd the Ambient air,
E're thy Bright Aspect rescues from dispair:
Makes the old Hagg[1] her sable mantle loose,   15
And a Bright Joy do's through my Soul diffuse.
The Boistero's[2] Trees now Lend a Passage Free,
And pleasent prospects thou giv'st light to see.

[Resentments Composed because of the Clamor of Town Topers Outside My Apartment]

I ask thy Aid, O Potent Rum!
To charm these wrangling Topers Dum.
Thou hast their Giddy Brains possest—
The man confounded with the Beast—
And I, poor I, can get no rest.
Intoxicate them with thy fumes:
O still their Tongues till morning comes!

[Warning to Travailers Seeking Accomodations at Mr. Devills Inn]

May all that dread the cruel feind of night
Keep on, and not at this curs't Mansion light.
'Tis Hell; 'tis Hell! and Devills here do dwell:
Here dwells the Devill—surely this's Hell.
Nothing but Wants: a drop to cool yo'r Tongue
Cant be procur'd these cruel Feinds among.
Plenty of horrid Grins and looks sevear,
Hunger and thirst, But pitty's bannish'd here—
The Right hand keep, if Hell on Earth you fear!

[1] night.
[2] boisterous.

[*Thoughts on Pausing at a Cottage near the Paukataug River*]

Tho' Ill at ease, A stranger and alone,
All my fatigu's shall not extort a grone.
These Indigents have hunger with their ease:
Their best is wors behalfe then my disease.
Their Misirable hutt wich Heat and Cold
Alternately without Repulse do hold;
Their Lodgings thyn and hard, their Indian fare,
The mean Apparel which the wretches wear,
And their ten thousand ills wich can't be told,
Makes nature er'e 'tis midle age'd look old.
When I reflect, my late fatigues do seem
Only a notion or forgotten Dreem.

[*Pleasent Delusion of a Sumpteous Citty*]

Here stood a Lofty church—there is a steeple,
And there the Grand Parade—O see the people!
That Famouse Castle there, were I but nigh,
To see the mote and Bridg and walls so high—
They'r very fine! sais my deluded eye.

SAMUEL DANFORTH II

(1666-1727)

Born in Roxbury, Massachusetts, Samuel Danforth II graduated from Harvard in 1683, and like his father and brother before him, entered the ministry. He was called to the church at Taunton, Massachusetts, in 1688, where he was lawyer, medical practitioner, and teacher as well as minister in his community. He seems to have been somewhat more a man of affairs in his town than his brother John; he taught Indian boys, instituted an "Indian Lecture Day" at Taunton, bought and operated a grist mill, and wrote an Indian Dictionary.

Only two of Samuel Danforth's poems have come down to us: an elegy on Major Thomas Leonard (1713), and "Ad Librum."

Ad Librum[1]

Goe Little Book,[2] and once a week shake hands
With thy *Good Reader,* whome (by High Commands)
The *Stars* are made to wayt on *dayly,* Shew
Futurityes unto *him;* Bid *Him* view
Seasons of th' *Year,* and *Tides* orderly set   5
As Higher *Influences* them beget.
Shew *Him* how swift his *Time* is and how *He*
Should swiftly pace it with the *Hierarchy*
I' th' *Firmament*[3] above Hasting each *Day*
New ponderous Talents to the world to weigh   10
Of proffitable Opportunity.
Also foreshew *Him* seasonably (by

[1] in the *New-England Almanack . . . 1686.*
[2] Echoes Chaucer, *Troilus and Criseyde,* v, 1786, and Spenser, in the prefatory poem to *The Shepheards Calendar;* the latter, at least, was known to Harvard men and often quoted by them.
[3] in old astrology, the sphere of the fixed stars; the eighth heaven of the Ptolemaic cosmology.

Letters Dominicall)[4] the Holy Day;
That Hee the great Commandment may obey.
This *Doe* yet look to be [For 'tis thy Fate]   15
An *Almanack* the next year out of date.
       Reader!
  Lend me thy Favour, to initiate
My tender Genius, whilst I *calculate*
Heavens Motions say not, that each poring Jack   20
Is (only) fit to make an *Almanack:*
Gods wond'rous works they are of men below
That in them pleasure have sought out. O know
The *Moons Eclipses* thay are not too mean
For the Amozian *Tables;*[5] Nor the scene   25
Of *bright Arcturus course,* Nor yet (to these)
The *Influences* of the *Pleiades*
Accounted are too low for the Divine:
They therfore well deserve the Harvardine.
  Forgive me yet, *Good Reader,* If that I   30
The *Names* impos'd by old Idolatry
On *Months* and *Planets* still reteyn; Because
I'm forc't thereto by cruel Customs Laws.
Forbear thy Censure too, though thou mayst find:
Some *Aspects Epithets* against *thy* mind.   35
Theyr *dayly Influences* to define
Infallibly is far beyond the Line
Of finite Skill; so likewise to deny
Theyr great Dominion, is to defie
The sacred Oracle[6] itself, besides   40
Each Days Experience in *Winds* and *Tydes:*[7]
Theyr Maker made them *signs* and why I grow[8]
Except to *signify;* Then men may *know*
By Observation and Experience:
What 'tis they signify, (In my poor sense)   45

---

[4] Any of the first seven letters of the alphabet as used in church calendars to indicate Sundays are dominical letters.

[5] The reference here may be biblical, alluding to Amoz, father of Isaiah (Isaiah i 1), or to Amos, the prophet who speaks of God who "maketh the morning darkness" (Amos iv 13), "who maketh the day dark with night" (Amos v 8), and who says, "I will darken the earth in the clear day" (Amos viii 9).

[6] the Bible.

[7] i.e. scientific observation and experience confirm what the Scriptures argue.

[8] see Gen i 14 on heavenly lights as signs. Note Danforth's wordplay on "sign" in succeeding lines.

If None can see what 'tis that these signs shew us
They'l be but insignificant unto us.
Yet think not that I'le give my Affidavit
Each Star shall prove as Ptolemy would have it:[9]
I know the contrary: yet let them stand   50
Modestly Ephitheted to thy hand
By former Ages-Sages, Visiting
A Clime unknown, where if they do not bring
The same *Effects* that theyr Experience gave,
Through Mounts, Lakes, Seas that do the passage pave   55
For *Winds* excited by them; They may be
Exact in other climates, while that wee,
Humbly adoring the Divine Decree
To Nature given, Do observe how far[10]
These *Epithets* will hold and where they jar.   60
Observe, or not observe, yet me (pray) damn not
Judicial Astrologer I am not:[11]
That *Art* falsly so call'd I loath, I hate
Both *Name* and *Thing* I much abominate.
Harmless Astronomy yet (I confess)   65
(Wherin my Skill is small, my practise less)
I please my selfe withall, in vacant Houres
Veiwing the Gloryes of th' *Aethereal Powrs*
On which th' Eternall Powr and Godhead are
To Observation Super-Ocular   70
Clearly apparent, Here I find the clew
Of Heavenly Manufacture which doth shew
The way unto the Labarynth Divine
Where the Eternall Glory's brightly shine.
In the Aethereall bodyes Mirrours be   75
Whereat, *Good Reader,* Wonder still with me.
In Joshuah's *Solstice* at the Voyce of man[12]

[9] Danforth's name is inscribed in a copy of Vincent Wing, *Astronomia Britan-nica* (London, 1669), according to Arthur O. Norton, "Harvard Text-Books and Reference Books of the Seventeenth Century," *PCSM*, XXVIII (1933), 397. In this work Danforth was exposed to the hypotheses of Copernicus and to the observations of Tycho Brahe, and in the poem he forsakes the Ptolemaic theory and system.

[10] Natural astrology was concerned with actual influences, usually baneful, of planets upon natural phenomena—hurricane, flood, and all pestilences. See *Dictionary of the Bible*, ed. James Hastings (New York, 1906), XII, 53.

[11] Judicial astrology dealt from the earliest times with the aspects of planets and their supposed influence on men and nations. (Ibid.) Danforth uses the term pejoratively.

[12] At Joshua's command (Josh x 12–13) the sun stood still and thus became

The *Rapid sun* became *Copernican.*
Afterward th' Heavenly hand directly made
Sol's *Excellency* to turn *Retrograde.*   80
The Heavenly Soveraign Powr *the Charioteer*
Made drive apace when Heaven aloft did hear
The Siserean Iron Chariotts rattle[13]
(No fewer then Nine hundred) in the battle
The *Stars* then also in theyr courses fought[14]   85
And the Jabinian Army's put to rout.
   But to Conclude, *Light* was before the *Sun;*
Most Radiant Light shall be when *Sol* hath done.
But first His *Brightness* th' shakings sore shall feel,
And the Off-Takings of his Chariot wheel: 90
Veiwing *his Beauteous Queen,* all turn'd to Blood
And all *his Host* drown'd in a fiery flood;
Of th' *day Divine* the Dawnings hence we date
And hence they that survive may *calculate*
The Blessed *Epicyclar Perigee*   95
Of much Expected long Eternity.
Oh Eighty Six; Thou'rt quickly come about!
This Sheet that brought thee in shall lay thee out.

An *ELEGY in Memory of the Worshipful*
Major Thomas Leonard Esq.
Of Taunton *in* New-England; *Who departed this Life*
on the 24th. Day of November, Anno Domini *1713.*
In the 73d. Year of his Age

We do assemble that a Funeral
With grief and sorrow we may solemnize,
Whereat 'tis proper, that to mind we call
  The Greatness of our Loss; the qualities
    And Usefulness of our deceased Friend,   5
    Whose Pilgrimage on Earth is at an end.

Copernican in the sense that it did not revolve about the earth. Solstice means literally "to cause the sun to stand still."

[13] Sisera, captain of the army of Jabin, King of Hazor, was killed by Jael, Heber's wife, who drove a nail through Sisera's temples while he slept. See Judges iv 2, 21.

[14] This figure is from Deborah's Song in Judges v 20: "They fought from heaven; the stars in their courses fought against Sisera."

Envy and Malice must be reigning Vices
  In those who will not bear to hear his Praise;
To Speak well of the Dead, true Grace advises;
  'Tis Baseness that Reproach on such doth raise.   10
    Such justly may expect Retaliation,
    Who do begrutch to others Commendation.

Tho' I pretend no skill in Poetry,
  Yet will adventure once to Mourn in Verse
Rather than such a Worthy, dead should ly   15
  Without a due Encomium on his Herse:
    Grief will find Vent, and Fulness of affection
    How to express our selves will give direction.

Let's first remark, That GOD should him incline
  In's early days to try with all his might   20
For skill to Write and Cypher, in a time
  When other *Youths* such *Learning* did but slight;
    Yet he redeem'd his Time most carefully
    And made in's Learning, good proficiency.

GOD bless'd his Care and Pains, that he attain'd   25
  With little help from others, useful skill
Wherein he out-shone others, that he gain'd
  Preferment in the Town, Esteem, good Will;
    From meaner Posts made gradual Ascent
    To Offices of Trust, Care and Moment.[1]   30

In Medicine he practised his skill
  Expending Time and Money in the Cure
Of Sick and Wounded, with compassion still.
  This did the Love of all to him procure;
    Many Confess, his kindness did abound   35
    By helpfulness unto his Neighbours round.

For many Years, the chief Affairs in Town
  Prudential, he manag'd carefully
With good Acceptance, unto his Renown
  Perform'd his Trust in all things faithfully;   40
    So that the Governour did him prefer
    In Military Trusts a part to bear;

And in the Civil Government he stood
  Commissioned, to Punish Vice and Sin,

[1] Leonard held the offices of Justice of the Peace and Judge of the Court.

For many Years; His Care and Prudence good 45
    And Faithfulness were well display'd therein.
      He always shew'd Pacifick disposition,
      Trying to end all jarr's by Composition.

He gave himself to GOD in's Youthful days
    Profess'd Religion; and his Family 50
Were well Instructed, Pray'd with all always
    His good Example was before their Eye.
His Pray'rs were heard, his House (the Lord be Prais'd)
    With hopeful numerous Offspring GOD hath rais'd.

GOD grant that all of his Posterity 55
    May imitate his Virtues, and may say
His GOD shall be our GOD, Him faithfully,
    We'l Serve until our Last and Dying day:
      And never will our Fathers GOD forsake;
      But for our GOD sincerely will Him take. 60

His famous crowning work was His great Care
    That Gospel-Worship, Gospel-Ministry
In *Norton*,[2] *Dighton*, Other Places near
    On good Foundations might Setled be:
      He joy'd in Hope, that now were laid Foundations 65
      Of Piety for many Generations.
            Maestus Composuit;[3]

SAMUEL DANFORTH.

[2] Norton developed into a community centered around the iron enterprise of the Leonard brothers who came from Wales in 1643 and in a decade set up a bloomery at Taunton and a forge at Raynham.
[3] Sorrowfully composed.

BENJAMIN LYNDE

(1666–1745)

Born in Boston, graduate of Harvard in 1686, Benjamin Lynde became a Bencher of the Middle Temple in London, returned to New England in 1697, and took up residence in Salem where he became judge of the Superior Court. Like Richard Henchman and Nehemiah Hobart, Lynde exchanged manuscript verse with Samuel Sewall, and it is only through Sewall's letters that we know of the existence of some of Lynde's verse.

One poem, descriptive of Thomson's Island, was preserved in Lynde's *Diary*, published together with his son's *Diary* in 1880. An evocation of the landscape surrounding Boston Harbor, it resembles in style and tone some of Samuel Sewall's verses.

[*Lines Descriptive of Thomson's Island*]

Hor. Epist. 16 AD Quinctium

"Ne percuncteris fundus meus, optime Quincti
Arvo pascat herum, an baccis opulentet olivæ
Pomisne et pratis an amicta vitibus ulmo
Scribetur tibi forma loquaciter et situs agri."

Dear Paulus it's a busy trade of late
T' enquire the value of each man's estate;
What our next neighbour's farm or Isle brings in,
If warm without, it keep him, and within;
What cattle for the plow may be his stock,   5
How large and multiplyed his fleecy flock;
How many milch kine his rich pastures feed,
What stately wanton mares to mend his breed;
How much he mowes, what tillage he may tend,
What gard'n, and how his laden fruit trees bend.   10
To save these queries then about our Isle,

Kind Heaven which placed it well does on it smile;
In form triangular, its gradual sides
Rise from the arms of Neptune's gentle tides,
South West of Royal William's Citadel   15
On Castle Isle, by Romer[1] finish'd well,
Heart of the Province, and its piercing eye,
With bulwarks strong, and bright artillery,
Guarding all parts that near adjacent lye.
Two rural neighbouring townes ly west of it,   20
Two sacred Domes, and Stoughton, Tailer's seat,
With grovy cottages of distant Vills,
That ly beneath the huge Cœrulian Hills.
Close, on the South, a Cliff lifts up its brow,
High, prominent o'er the parting stream below;   25
From whence the Native's fate-predicting squaw
Their Ruine, and the Briton's Rise foresaw;
That Heaven's swift plagues should quickly sweep away
The Indians 'round the Massachusetts Bay.
But she (while they her rage prophetic mock)   30
Flings headlong down from the steep craggy rock;
Mu-Squantum! from her dying murmurs fell,
And thence call'd Squantum Neck, (as antients tell).
A narrow gut, deep swift, and curling tide,
This spacious neck from Thomson's Isle divide;   35
Ebbing or flowing, still its purles displayes,
And branches into two delicious Bayes;
In which, when calm, the verdant hill above
Beholds itself below, a lovely grove;
For grotesque rocks and real sylvan scenes   40
Grace its high top with Pines and Evergreens,
Offering a pleasing prospect to our eyes,
And sheltering us when Eastern storms arise.
Thence in still Summer eves when labour's o'er,
With Pan's sweet pipe, soft echoes fill each shoar   45
With Country songs of Nymphs and Swain's amour.
Then, free from strifes of Law or State affaires,
The dins of war or merchants' pressing feares,
Our chief concern is that we Heaven attain,
Next that we buy and sell for moderate gain.   50

[1] The fortifications of this castle were very irregular till King William's reign, when Colonel Romer, a famous engineer, was sent thither to repair them: the Colonel demolished all the old works, and raised an entirely new fortification, now called Fort William.

The hamlet side affords us this with ease,
To heare the newes and chat it as we please;
A priviledge to other isles deny'd
That ly far distant on the swelling tide,
East and North East of us in curious ranks,   55
And from the raging sea secure our banks;
Yet, Nature kind leaves us an interspace
To view the ships bound o'er the ocean's face.
A league Nor'west, behold Bostonia shrouds
Her lofty hills and fabricks in the clouds;   60
Newe prospects sailing nearer round it showes,
A charming Isthmus all her bayes disclose!
Enrang'd street under street, she forms below
A beauteous crescent, or Heaven's painted Bow
Of various hewes; at either end a fort   65
Defends her boosome and adorns her port.
From her rich centre structures, saches bright
Reflect the blushes of Aurora's light,
And golden spires by turnes waved high in air
Seem planets, Venus, or the Morning Star.   70
A wondrous Pier, with building proud and strong,
From King Street strait protended wide and long,
Stored with rich merchandise, invades the place
Where used to sport sculls of the watery race;
Woods of tall pines float at silver feet,   75
And in her Roads may ride the Royal Fleet.
No Towne so situate, civil, healthy, gay
Throughout the British Vast America.
Thrice happy be, thrice blest thy fertile earth
And ever dear the place that gave me birth;   80
Heaven's goodness ever influence thine aire
And temper all the seasons of the year;
May rich abundance flow from ambient seas,
Thy wealth and forein merchandise increase,
All sad events kind Providence prevent   85
By floods and fires or either element;
May peace and plenty spread the Land and Towne,
And pure religion all these blessings crown!
Thus having given of Thomson's Isle the site,
Which to review is anybody's right,   90
Nay, if thro' Fancy strong one claim the soil
At sight, without possession right or toil,
I'll not mind such whimseys of ye brain,

But next my title clearly shall derein,
From antient seisin, ere New Plymouth's claim,   95
With Livery in Senior Thompson's name;
Who seven years after over came and built,
Improved the land and in his mansion dwelt;
From him, Descents and by mean Purchase Deeds
My father's seisin and just right succeeds;   100
By him to me then was this Island given
Before his soul's ascent to Heaven.
"Of special love," said he "this gift receive,
And here at pleasure may you happy live."
With grateful heart his Blessing I received   105
But with more pleasure, had he longer lived,
For here with joy and dutiful regard
In all my rural comforts he had shared.

JOHN COTTON OF 'QUEEN'S CREEK'

(fl. 1676)

The dramatic struggle we know as Bacon's Rebellion, which ran its course during 1675–76 in Virginia, arose when Nathaniel Bacon (1647–76), a planter, led other Virginians in a "rebellion," ostensibly against Indian brutalities. Governor William Berkeley withheld sufficient support, and the revolt became one against state authority. Bacon died after a brief but ravaging illness, and his epitaph was "drawne by the Man that waited on his person, as it is said." J. B. Hubbell argues persuasively that John Cotton of 'Queen's Creek' was the author of both the epitaph and "Upon the Death of G: B."

Bacons Epitaph, made by his Man[1]

Death why soe crewill! what, no other way
To manifest thy splleene, but thus to slay
Our hopes of safety; liberty, our all
Which, through thy tyrany, with him must fall
To its late Caoss? Had thy riged force   5
Bin delt by retale, and not thus in gross
Griefe had bin silent: Now wee must complaine
Since thou, in him, hast more then thousand slane
Whose lives and safetys did so much depend
On him there lif, with him there lives must end.   10
   If't be a sin to thinke Death brib'd can bee
Wee must be guilty; say twas bribery
Guided the fatall shaft. Verginias foes,
To whom for secrit crimes just vengance owes
Disarved plagues, dreding their just disart   15
Corrupted Death by Parasscellcian art[2]

---

[1] from *The Burwell Papers* [written 1676].
[2] alchemical or medical. Paracelsus (1493–1541) was a renowned Swiss physician and alchemist.

Him to destroy; whose well tride curage such,
There heartless harts, nor arms, nor strength could touch.
 Who now must heale those wounds, or stop that blood
The Heathen made, and drew into a flood?   20
Who i'st must please our Cause? nor Trump nor Drum
Nor Deputations; these alass are dumb,
And Cannot speake. Our Arms (though nere so strong)
Will want the aide of his Commanding tongue,
Which Conquer'd more than Ceaser: He orethrew   25
Onely the outward frame; this Could subdue
The ruged workes of nature. Soules repleate
With dull Child could,[3] he'd annemate with heate
Drawne forth of reasons Lymbick.[4] In a word
Marss and Minerva both in him Concurd   30
For arts, for arms, whose pen and sword alike,
As Catos did, may admireation strike
In to his foes; while they confess withall
It was there guilt stil'd him a Criminall.
Onely this difference doth from truth proceed: 35
They in the guilt, he in the name must bleed,
While none shall dare his Obseques to sing
In disarv'd measures, untill time shall bring
Truth Crown'd with freedom, and from danger free,
To sound his praises to posterity.   40
 Here let him rest; while wee this truth report,
Hee's gon from hence unto a higher Court
To pleade his Cause: where he by this doth know
Whether to Ceaser hee was friend, or foe.

Upon the Death of G: B[1]

 Whether to Ceaser he was Friend or Foe?
Pox take such Ignorance, do you not know?
Can he be Friend to Ceaser, that shall bring
The Arms of Hell, to fight againt the King?
(Treason, Rebellion) then what reason have   5
Wee for to waite upon him to his Grave,
There to express our passions? Wilt not bee
Worss then his Crimes, to sing his Ellegie

[3] chilled cold.
[4] alembic (i.e. "distilled" reasons).
[1] from *The Burwell Papers* [written 1676].

In well tun'd numbers; where each Ella beares
(To his Flagitious name) a flood of teares?   10
A name that hath more soules with sorrow fed,
Then reched Niobe single teares ere shed;
A name that fil'd all hearts, all eares, with paine,
Untill blest fate proclaimed, Death had him slane.
Then how can it be counted for a sin   15
Though Death (nay though my selfe) had bribed bin,
To guide the fatall shaft? we honour all
That lends a hand unto a T[r]ators fall.
What though the well paide Rochit[2] soundly ply
And box the Pulpitt in to flatterey;   20
Urging his Rethorick, and straind elloquence,
T' adorne incoffin'd filth and excrements;
Though the Defunct (like ours) nere tride
A well intended deed untill he dide?
'Twill be nor sin, nor shame, for us, to say   25
A two fould Passion checker-workes this day
Of Joy and Sorrow; yet the last doth move
On feete impotent, wanting strength to prove
(Nor can the art of Logick yeild releife)
How Joy should be surmounted, by our greife.   30
Yet that wee Grieve it cannot be denide,
But 'tis because he was, not cause he dide.
So wep the poore destressed Ilyum Dames[3]
Hereing those nam'd, there Citty put in flames,
And Country ruing'd; If wee thus lament   35
It is against our present Joyes consent.
For if the rule, in Phisick, trew doth prove,
Remove the cause, th' effects will after move,
We have outliv'd our sorows, since we see
The Causes shifting, of our miserey.   40
   Nor is't a single cause, that's slipt away,
That made us warble out a well-a-day.
The Braines to plot, the hands to execute
Projected ills, Death Joyntly did nonsute
At his black Bar. And what no Baile could save   45
He hath commited Prissoner to the Grave;
From whence there's no reprieve. Death keep him close
We have too many Divells still goe loose.

[2] rochet; a close-fitting vestment worn especially by bishops and abbots.
[3] women of Troy.

ROGER WOLCOTT

(1679–1767)

Roger Wolcott, like his contemporary, Edward Taylor of West-field, was not precisely representative of his age. By the time the man who was to become Governor of Connecticut published his *Poetical Meditations* in New London in 1725, most American writers of verse had begun to turn to the poetry of the Augustan age. Yet Wolcott's "The Heart is Deep" and elaboration of a verse from Matthew reflect affinities to the poetry of the seventeenth rather than to that of the eighteenth century, not only in subject matter but also in style, tone, and viewpoint.

Psalm LXIV. 6.
The Heart is Deep

He that can trace a Ship making her way,
Amidst the threatening Surges on the Sea;
Or track a Towering Eagle in the Air,
Or on a Rock find the Impressions there
Made by a Serpents Footsteps. Who Surveys
The Subtile Intreagues that a Young Man lays,
In his Sly Courtship of an harmless Maid,
Whereby his Wanton Amours are Convey'd
Into her Breast; Tis he alone that can
Find out Cursed Policies of Man.

Matthew X. 28

And fear not them that can kill the body, but are not
able to kill the Soul; But rather fear Him, which is
able to destroy both Soul and Body in Hell

And is our Life, a life wherein we borrow
No not the smallest respite from our Sorrow?
Our Profits are they but some Yellow Dust;

Subject to Loss, to Canker-eat and Rust:
Whose very Image breedeth ceaseless Cares   5
In every Mind where it Dominion bears.
And are our Pleasures mainly in Excess?
Which genders Guilt, and ends in Bitterness.
Are Honours fickle and dependent Stuff?
Oft-times blown furthest from us by a Puff.   10
Doth pale-fac'd Envy wait at every Stage,
To bite and wound us in our Pilgrimage?
Is all we have, or hope for, but Adventure?
Then here's nought worth our stay, let us encounter
The King of Terrors bravely, un-dismay'd,   15
As gallant *Aria* to her *Paetus* said.[1]

And so might be my Choice, but that I see
Hells flashes folding through Eternitie;
And hear damn'd Company, that there remain
For very Anguish gnaw their Tongues in twain.   20

Then him for Happy I will never Praise,
That's fill'd with Honour, Wealth, or length of Days:
But Happy be, though in a Dying Hour,
O're whom the Second Death obtains no power.

[1] Arria, wife of Caecina Paetus, who, when her husband was condemned
by the Emperor Claudius, "taught her husband how to die," stabbing herself and
handing him the dagger, saying, "Paetus, non dolet" (Paetus, suffer not).

A Selection of Anonymous Verse

A SELECTION OF
ANONYMOUS VERSE

A good quantity of anonymous verse has come down to us from the seventeenth century. Much of it, of course, is doggerel, worth preserving only for whatever historical interest it may have. Some of it is obviously exercise work, scribbled in commonplace books or on foolscap sheets as unknown aspiring poets strove to learn their craft. Some is just as obviously "filler," composed *pro forma*, to order, or to complete an otherwise empty page in an almanac or early magazine. But some is verse of genuine interest to modern students of the period. The selection of anonymous verse which follows attempts to represent only this latter category.

An Old Song, wrote by one of our first New-England Planters, on their Management in those good Old Times. To the Tune of A Cobbler there was, &c *

New England's annoyances you that would know them,
Pray ponder these verses which briefly do show them.
The place where we live is a wilderness wood,
Where grass is much wanting that's fruitful and good.

From the end of November till three months are gone,
The ground is all frozen as hard as a stone.
Our mountains and hills and our valleys below
Being commonly covered with ice and with snow.

* "An Old Song, wrote by one of our first New-England Planters" is probably the earliest ballad composed in America. Internal evidence suggests a date of composition before 1640, perhaps even as early as 1630. Until now the poem has been known only in incomplete and faulty versions, most of which can be traced back to the printing of "Our Forefathers' Song" in the *Massachusetts Magazine* in 1791.

The version used here has been reconstructed by Professor Harold Jantz from three incomplete versions (1758, 1791, 1829) and is printed here with his permission.

And when the northwest wind with violence blows,
Then every man pulls his cap over his nose:
But if any's so hardy and will it withstand,
He forfeits a finger, a foot, or a hand.

But when the spring opens, we then take the hoe
And make the ground ready to plant and to sow;
Our corn being planted and seed being sown,
The worms destroy much before it is grown.

And while it is growing some spoil there is made
By birds and by squirrels that pluck up the blade.
And when it is come to full corn in the ear,
It is often destroyed by racoon and by deer.

And now our apparel begins to grow thin,
And wool is much wanted to card and to spin.
If we get a garment to cover without,
Our other ingarments are clout upon clout.

Our clothes we brought with us are apt to be torn,
They need to be clouted before they are worn.
But clouting our garments doth injure us nothing:
Clouts double are warmer than single whole clothing.

If fresh meat be wanting to fill up our dish,
We have carrots and pumpkins and turnips and fish;
And if there's a mind for a delicate dish,
We haste to the clam banks and take what we wish.

Stead of pottage and puddings and custards and pies,
Our turnips and parsnips are common supplies.
We have pumpkins at morning and pumpkins at noon,
If it was not for pumpkins, we should be undone.

[If barley be wanting to make into malt,
We must be contented and think it no fault;
For we can make liquor to sweeten our lips
Of pumpkins and parsnips and walnut tree chips.][1]

And of our green cornstalks we make our best beer,
We put it in barrels to drink all the year.
Yet I am as healthy, I verily think,
Who make the spring water my commonest drink.

[1] The four lines in brackets are supplied by Alonzo Lewis, "The Lynn Bard,"
in his *History of Lynn, Including Nahant,* 2d ed. (Boston, 1844), pp. 71–72.

Our money's soon counted, for we have just none,
All that we brought with us is wasted and gone.
We buy and sell nothing but upon exchange,
Which makes all our dealings uncertain and strange.

And we have a cov'nant one with another
Which makes a division 'twixt brother and brother:
For some are rejected and others made saints,
Of those that are equal in virtues and wants.

For such like annoyances we've many mad fellows
Find fault with our apples before they are mellow,
And they are for England, they will not stay here,
But meet with a lion in shunning a bear.

Now while such are going, let others be coming,
Whilst liquor is boiling, it must have a scumming.
And I will not blame them, for birds of a feather
Are choosing their fellows by flocking together.

But you whom the Lord intends hither to bring
Forsake not the honey for fear of a sting:
But bring both a quiet and contented mind,
And all needful blessings you surely shall find.

Thomas Dudley[1]
Ah! old must dye

A death's head on your hand you neede not weare,
A dying head you on your shoulders beare.
You neede not one to mind you, you must dye,
You in your name may spell mortalitye.
Younge men may dye, but old men, these dye must,
'Twill not be long before you turne to dust.
Before you turne to dust! ah! must! old! dye!
What shall younge doe, when old in dust doe lye?
When old in dust lye, what N. England doe?
When old in dust doe lye, it's best dye too.

---

[1] "1645. aboute the 16th of 5th moneth was this anagram sent to mr. Dudley then govnor by some namelesse author." Text from Timothy Alden, Jr., *Collection of American Epitaphs* (New York, 1814), III, 49–50.

[Resplendent studs of heaven's frame]
(c. 1651)

Resplendent studs of heaven's frame,
First borne and bread of Muses nine;[1]
That lately from Parnassus came,
From drinking drams of sacred wine.

No decent aged complement,   5
Nor newfledgd brave invented straine,
In nature's compasse have I pen't,
Or hatched in my madid[2] Braine,

Therewith your vertues to comprise;
They doe by farr transcend my Sphære.   10
Your honors shall ascend the skies,
And sit with glistring Pallas there.

But whilst your stately Countenance
Doth stay below (Earth's ornament):
Pray graunt my mind, may straite advance,   15
And touch some part of firmament.

Where Phœbus with his sounding whip,
(Sitting in glittring Charri't dight)[3]
Doth force his mounting Naggs to skip,
To Amble, Trot, and Gallop right.   20

There was of old a Judgement brew'd;[4]
I deeme by some cold winter Pol.[5]
That is of Late afresh renew'd
By those with little minded Sol.

These say there is no fiery place,   25
Where Lucid Starr's doe take their ease,
No fervent, scorching, burning space,
Where (I durst say) are scalding seas,

[1] Urania, muse of astronomy.
[2] humid, moist.
[3] adorned, decked out.
[4] the ancient belief that the sun did not supply heat to the earth, that there is no celestial realm of fire and heat. See lines 25 ff.
[5] short for Pollux. When Castor, Pollux' mortal brother, died, Pollux petitioned Zeus that he too might die. In answer Zeus decreed that the brothers should live in upper and lower worlds on alternate days.

Where is a red and parching hoast
Of waves above the brinke   30
Of bleuish clouds. It scalds (almost)
My tender head, and heart to thinke

How singing Mitra[6] puft with rage,
Amidst the boiling Breakers flings,
With blackchap't Mulciber[7] his page,   35
That all the crystall heaven rings.

He first begins in March to stray. [he: the sun][8]
Hee flyes apace, (as prick't with thornes)
Hee back's the Ram, and trips away.
The freeze coat Wheather[9] wag's his horns.   40

In Aprille faire the Lowing Bull
Begins to sigh and harbour greife;
He must goe take his yearly pull;
Which pull will make him meager beafe.

In May sun gets on Brethren twaine;   45
Their galled leggs make them to groane,
Who night and day worke might and maine,
In seething or in temp'rate zone.

The crabfish climbs and posts[10] along,
The red cheek't Virgin (quite forlorne),   50
The roaring rampant Lyon strong,
The sturdy welset[11] Capricorne.

The bowman's swift, the serpent creeps,
And Libra rumbles in the skie,
The waterman in Vulcan leaps,   55
And Pisces spouts the flames on high.

What Element but fire can bee,
Where stars doe take their sudden flight,
Whose bodye's full of Levity,[12]
Most active, splendid cleare and bright?   60

[6] Mithra, ancient Persian deity identified with the sun.
[7] black-jawed Vulcan.
[8] bracketed emendation appears in the manuscript.
[9] Wether—a ram; hence Aries in the zodiacal table. In succeeding lines appear
Taurus, Gemini, Cancer, et al. as the year proceeds.
[10] hastes.
[11] well-set: properly or firmly set, symmetrical.
[12] lightness, buoyancy.

The Earth is dull, the water damps,
The aire is weake, and cannot hold
Such princelike, twinckling, swagg'ring lamp's
By highest Primus Mover rowl'd.[13]

Besides which of those el'ment three
(Whose spirits life to mortals brings)
Can yeild such Lustre as wee see
Aloft: or breed such fulgent things:

65

As those same candles alwayes light,
Those Torches, blazing flaming brands;
That peirce Apoll'es house with might,
And glow the golden mellow lands.

70

Whence come those beams that warme the crowne,
Those Rayes as hot as melted brasse:
Are not they cast all headlong downe,
And gather'd by condensing glasse?[14]

75

Whence came those wasting streams of fire;
When Phæton Let loose the raine?
Whence came those tosting showrs most dire
When Neptune star'd, and Jove was faighne[15]

80

To kneele upon his silver knee
And pray the master guide againe
His nimble horse: least[16] I (quoth hee)
Bee burn't alive with all my traine!

When Vulcan flow contrary way
(In danger of a mighty cracke)
Hee fell from skie (as Poets say)
With smoaking bellows at his backe.

85

Thence wise Prometheus stole
And cunningly the gods did gull;
He went unto their glowing coale,
And snatch't a firepan heaped full.

90

[13] ruled.
[14] magnifying glass; here, probably the effect of the earth's atmosphere on the sun's rays.
[15] fain: wont, apt.
[16] lest.

Now Let me ask, what fellow can,
What crafty, slye, deepnoddled one,
That's born on earth of Lethall man,   95
Take coales away if there were none.

Drown'd Icarus had woefull proofe
Of fierce Olympus ardency,
When he did view his wings alooft,
How did he weepe, lament and crye!   100

It is apparent hence there's heat,
Where starrs move cap[17] skip and dance,
Where bearded goats doe ever bleate,
Where skarlet, gastly dragons prance,

Wher' th' shaggy, blacke, and surly beare,   105
[That] gurning,[18] rough, deformed welpe
(With horrid noise) doe snort, and tare,
They snuftle,[19] grumble, bawle, and yelpe.

[Wh]ere sitteth all the parliament
[With] purest robes, and Jewell Carrs,   110
[The] whole supernal regiment,
[The] Sun, and Moon, and gadding[20] starrs.

[Where] angry Mars with bloudy speare
[Where] prying Atlas wishly[21] looks,
[Like] fortune breeding Joy, and feare,   115
[Where] Chiron[22] skild in Physicke books.

[Where] Venus with her plumpgut boy,
[With] graces clad in sparkling shoane [shoes]
[For] moments, dayes, and howers toie,[23]
[They] sing their sad, and merry toane,[24]   120

[17] caper.
[18] snarling.
[19] snuffle.
[20] moving about giddily.
[21] longingly.
[22] Centaur skilled in medicine who was placed among the stars after his death; here, therefore, Sagittarius.
[23] toy.
[24] tune.

Minerva learn'd and Mercury
[Of] arts divine that have no need,
[Of] Nymphs, and all the company,
[Who] on Olympick parks doe tread.

[Where] these in midst of tosting[25] lakes,   125
[And] Furnaces of frying flames,
[Midst] mossy weeds, and ruddy brakes,
[Doe] keepe aeternall lasting names.

There Let them live, with merriment,
[With] tort'ring fire their pleasures take,   130
[Lau]gh, sport, and heare with ears attent,
[The] grating musick orbs doe make.

[I] must forsake that pallace quite,
[Those] gentlemen, and Rustick swaine,
[Those] shining rooms and Chambers bright   135
[And] all that monstrous, frighting traine.

[My] wandering thoughts must now come in,
[From] melting ovens sent to pore;
[The] rugged muse that farr hath bine
[Fir]st to your Worships Topsailes lore.   140

     Fine Lapis tandem cœlo descendis ab alto
     et fundum rursus, cum gravitate petid.[26]

[The Whore That Rides in Us Abides]

    The following rural Lines were written upon a discourse had with one (about the year 1661) about the whore that rides on many waters and that the antichrist was only at roome and amongst the roman Catholicks

The whore that rides in us abides,
A strong beast is within;
Able to beare her finest ware,
There Lives the man of sin
Which if destroyd, be not afraid   5

    [25] tossing, billowing.
    [26] Through the boundary a stone came speeding down from the high heavens, and fell to the earth.

Of rooms great papal power.
Alas wee may, most of us say,
Weer stones of Babels towre,
And if shee fall may suffer all
And sorrow for her Loss—   10
Though some her ruine fix
To that great year which many feard
Of (1) Sixty six and six—

    If antichrist be dead within
    Wee need not feare the man of sin.   15

That Church whose Building on the rock doth stand
Needs not to feare that engineer
Whose bottoms on the sand.

[Time Tryeth Truth]¹

Time tryeth Truth Convicting all that strive
Fain² Systems, dead Chymeraes³ to revive,
And he hath brought to light by good success
The Law which nature never doth transgress.
Sol keeps his throne, and round about him shines
Upon six worlds which walk in single lines,
And eight less Globes,⁴ again encompassing
One Th' *Earth*, four *Jove*, Three *Saturn* with his Ring:
All sing their Maker's Praise, and show his power
In due proportion moving every hour.
Thrice happy they that leaving mandring⁵ wayes
Sloe duely walk to their Creator's praise.
                        T. S.⁶

¹ from John Foster's *Almanack* (Boston, 1681).
² feign: to conjure up (a delusive representation).
³ unfounded conceptions.
⁴ satellites (e.g. "One Th' Earth" is the moon).
⁵ maundering.
⁶ Expanded to "T. Street" in a subsequent edition of the *Almanack*, these initials are thus far unidentified.

On How the Cobler[1]

What How? How now? hath How such hearing found.
To throw Arts curious Image to the ground.
Cambridge and Oxford may their Glory now
Vaile to a Cobler did they know but How;
Though big with Art, they Cannot Overtopp
The Spirits teaching in a Coblers Shopp.

[Almanac Verse[1]]

Thus Reader, by our Astrologick Art,
Future Events we unto thee impart;
But yet 'tis with this Reservation, tho'
If they not come to pass, we'd have them do.
For all Predictions do to this belong,
That Either they are right, or they are wrong.

January's Observations

The best defence against the Cold
Which our Fore-fathers good did hold,
Was early a full Pot of Ale,
Neither too mild nor yet too stale,
Well drenched for the more behoof
With Toast cut round about the Loaf.

The Weather is very cold; but where Jealousie is hot,
that house is Hell, and the Woman the Master Devil thereof.

[1] written in a contemporary hand on the binder's leaf of Samuel Willard's *Ne Sutor ultra Crepidam: or Brief Animadversions upon the New-England Anabaptists Late Fallacious Narrative* (Boston, 1681), with an introduction by Increase Mather. Willard's tract replied to John Russel's *A Brief Narrative of Some Considerable Passages,* published the previous year, and in effect said to Russel and other Anabaptists, "Cobbler, stick to your Last." Hence the theme of the manuscript verses.

[1] from John Tulley, *An Almanack . . . 1688* (Boston, 1687).

February's Observations

You lads and Lasses would repine,
Should we forget St. Valentine:
When Young men do present their Loves
With Scarfs, with Ribons, and with Gloves,
And to shew manners not forgot-all
Give them a lick under the Snot-gall;
Then one a Cur[t]sie drops anon,
And smiling says, I thank thee, John.

March

Now if thy Body be not well
This month for Physick doth excel;
But choose a Doctor skill'd in Art,
Not Quacks growing rich by others smart.

April

This being the time of Spring,
Young Folks do love like any thing.
But Love is made of different mettle,
Of Joy, and Pain; in Dock out Nettle.
A painful pleasure pleasing pain,
A gainful Loss, a loosing Gain,
And therefore Freinds take my advice,
Love none but vertuous, rich, and wise.

May

This is Love's month, else Poets lie, what then?
Why then, young maids are apt to kiss young men:
But for old maids unmarried, 'tis a sign,
They either do want beauty, or else Coyn.

Many Weddings this Month: but the people coup[l]ed very unequally, a sneaking Woodcock joyned to a wanton Wagtail, a Henpeckt Buzzard to a chattering Magpie.

Mars in a Trine aspect with Jupiter, denotes, that a Dung-Cart full of nail pareings will be better to dung Land than a Bushel full of live Buggs or Musquitoes.

June

The Sun is entred now into the Crab,
And days are hot, therefore beware a Drab;
With French diseases, they'l thy body fill,
Being such as bring Grist to the Surgeons Mill.

July

Now wanton Lads and Lasses do make Hay,
Which unto lewd temptation makes great way,
With tumbling on the cocks, which acted duly,
Doth cause much mischief in this month of July.

I assure you upon the word of an Ass-trologer, we shall have no
hard Frosts, nor deep Snows this month, but much blustering Weather
with those women whose Husbands have been at the Ordinaries all
day, and at night come home drunk.

August

Now doth the Dog-Star rule, therefore you must
For your health's sake astain from fleshly Lust.
Better it is your business hard to ply,
For to get in your Barley, Wheat, and Rye.

September

Now Landlords they prick up their ears,
Because St. Michael's day appears.

October

Who takes a Giglet to his wife,
Must look to lead with her this life,
Each morning she will have brought up
A Candle in a silver Cup,
Then lie abed and take her ease,
And goe abroad when ere she please.

November

Cold shivering Winter now makes his addresses,
Adorned with his silver'd colour tresses.
Then get both wood and Rum if thou art able,
For now you'll find they'l both be comfortable.

December

This month the Cooks do very early rise,
To roast their meat, and make their Christmas pies.
Poor men at rich men's tables their gutts forrage
With roast beef, mince-pies, pudding and plum porrige.

TEXT SOURCES

Major Writers

Texts of Anne Bradstreet's poems have been drawn from *The Works of Anne Bradstreet,* ed. John Harvard Ellis (Charlestown, 1867), after collation with *The Tenth Muse* (London, 1650) and *Several Poems Compiled with great variety of Wit and Learning* (Boston, 1678). Michael Wigglesworth's "God's Controversy" text is from the manuscript autograph in the Massachusetts Historical Society; other Wigglesworth texts are from the London editions of 1666 and 1673 of *The Day of Doom* in the British Museum. Texts for Edward Taylor's Meditations 1, 8, 29 (first series); 3, 56 (second series); The Preface to *Gods Determinations,* "The Frowardness of the Elect," "The Joy of Church Fellowship," "Upon a Spider Catching a Fly," "Huswifery," and "The Ebb and Flow" are from *The Poetical Works of Edward Taylor,* ed. Thomas H. Johnson (New York: Rockland Editions, 1939). Taylor's Meditations 32, 39 (first series) and 4 (second series) are from *Yale University Library Gazette,* XXVIII (1954); 1, 2, and 150 (second series) are from *The Poems of Edward Taylor,* ed. Donald E. Stanford (New Haven, 1960).

Minor Writers

Edward Johnson: Poems on Higginson, Eliot, Hooker, Harlackenden, Shepheard, and Buckley, and "Oh King of Saints" are from *A History of New-England* (London, 1654). The verse from *Good News* is from the London, 1648, edition of *Good News from New-England: An Exact Relation. . . .*

Roger Williams: All texts are drawn from *A Key into the Language of America* (London, 1643).

John Fiske: Texts are from the autograph manuscript in the Fiske Commonplace Book, Harris Collection of American Poetry and Plays, Brown University Library, as printed in Harold S. Jantz, *The First Century of New England Verse* (Worcester: American Antiquarian Society, 1943–44).

John Saffin: All texts are from the autograph manuscript commonplace book of John Saffin, Rhode Island Historical Society, corrected from *John Saffin His Book,* ed. Caroline Hazard (New York, 1928).

Urian Oakes: Text is from *An Elegie*. . . . (Cambridge, 1677) in Evans Microcards (E 240).

Benjamin Tompson: Texts for "Edmund Davie" and "To My Honoured Patron Humphery Davie" are from Samuel Sewall's commonplace book, New York Historical Society, as printed in Jantz, *First Century*. Poems from *New-Englands Crisis* are from the Boston, 1676 edition in Evans Microcards (E 225), corrected from *Benjamin Tompson . . . His Poems*, ed. H. J. Hall (Boston, 1924).

Richard Steere: Texts are from *A Monumental Memorial*. . . . (Boston, 1684; Evans 377) repr. in facsim. in George E. Littlefield, *The Early Massachusetts Press*, 2 vols. (Boston, 1907), and from *The Daniel Catcher* (Boston, 1713), in Evans (E 1651).

Nicholas Noyes: "A Praefatory Poem to . . . *Christianus per Ignem*" is from Cotton Mather, *Christianus* (Boston, 1702) in Evans (E 1067). "The Rev. Nicholas Noyes to the Rev. Cotton Mather" is from 1 *Proceedings of the Massachusetts Historical Society*, IX (1866–67), 484–485. "A Prefatory Poem to . . . *Magnalia*" is from Cotton Mather, *Magnalia Christi Americana* (London, 1702), in the Pennsylvania State University Library. "To . . . James Bailey" is from the broadside of 1707, in the Boston Public Library (repr. in facsim. in Ola E. Winslow, *American Broadside Verse* [New Haven, 1930], p. 21). "A Consolatory Poem" is from Cotton Mather, *Meat Out of the Eater* (Boston, 1703), in Evans (E 1127).

Philip Pain: Texts are from *Daily Meditations* (Cambridge, 1668) in Evans (E 128).

Francis Daniel Pastorius: Texts are from the autograph manuscript of *The Bee Hive* in the University of Pennsylvania Library.

Samuel Sewall: Texts of "Wednesday . . . 1701," "The Humble Springs," "Upon the Springs," "Tom Child," and "To John Sparhawk" are from the Sewall Papers in the Massachusetts Historical Society, printed in Sewall's *Diary;* "To be Engraven on a Dial" is from Sewall's commonplace book, New York Historical Society.

John Danforth: "On my Lord Bacon" is from Danforth's signed copy of Lord Verulam's *Sylva Sylvarum* (London, 1626) in the collection of Professor Harold Jantz; "Two Vast Enjoyments. . . ." is from Danforth's *A Sermon Occasioned by the Late Great Earthquake* (Boston, 1728) in Evans (E 1316); "The Mercies of the Year. . . ." from the broadside (1720) in the John Carter Brown Library, repr. in facsim. in *Two New England Poems* (Boston, 1910); "Profit and Loss" from the broadside (1710) in the Boston Public Library; "A Few Lines" from Danforth's *The Right Christian Temper* (Boston, 1702) in Evans (E 1046); "A Poem . . . upon Mrs. Anne Eliot" from Danforth's *Kneeling to God* (Boston, 1697) in Evans (E 780).

Cotton Mather: The Vigilantius elegy is from Mather's *Vigilantius* (Boston, 1706) in Evans (E 1265); the epitaph on Shubael Dummer from Mather's *Fair Weather* (Boston, 1692) in Evans (E 560–561); "Go then, My Dove" from Mather's *Meat Out of the Eater* (Boston, 1703) in Evans (E 1127); "O Glorious Christ of God" from the autograph manuscript in the Massachusetts Historical Society, printed in Mather's *Diary*, II, 786.

Benjamin Colman: "A Quarrel with Fortune," "To Philomela," "To Urania," and "Another to Urania" are from Ebenezer Turell, *The Life . . . of . . . Colman* (Boston, 1749) in Evans (E 6434); *A Poem on Elijah's Translation* is from the Boston, 1707 edition in Evans (E 1295); "A Hymn of Praise" is from the autograph manuscript in the Colman papers, Massachusetts Historical Society.

Texts for selection in the *Bay Psalm Book* are taken from *The Whole Booke of Psalms* (Cambridge, 1640) in Evans (E 4, 20).

Other Representative Writers

Thomas Dudley: "Verses" from Nathaniel Morton, *New Englands Memoriall* (Cambridge, 1669) in Evans (E 144).

Nathaniel Ward: "Mercury Shew'd Apollo" from Anne Bradstreet, *The Tenth Muse* (London, 1650) as repr. in Ellis' edition of Bradstreet; "The World's a Well Strung Fidle," and "Poetry's a Gift" from Ward's *The Simple Cobler of Aggawam* (London, 1647); "Mr. Ward of Anagrams Thus" from the commonplace book of Thomas Welde III in the Massachusetts Historical Society, repr. in Jantz, *First Century.*

Thomas Morton: Texts are from Morton's *New English Canaan* (Amsterdam, 1637) in the British Museum.

Captain John Smith: "The Sea Marke" is from Smith's *Advertisements for the Unexperienced Planters of New England. . . .* (London, 1631), as repr. in the Arber edition (Edinburgh, 1910); "John Smith of . . . John Taylor" is from John Taylor, *An Armado. . . .* (London, 1627), and "In Due Honour . . ." is from Robert Norton, *The Gunner. . . .* (London, 1628), both in the British Museum, as ed. and repr. by Philip Barbour, in *Virginia Magazine of History and Biography*, lxxv (1967), 157–58, and reprinted here with his kind permission.

John Cotton: "To . . . Samuel Stone" is prefixed to Stone's *A Congregational Church. . . .* (London, 1652), in the British Museum; "In Saram" is from Cotton Mather, *Magnalia* (London, 1702); "A Thankful Acknowledgment . . ." is from John Norton, *Abel Being Dead Yet Speaketh* (London, 1658), in the Library of Congress.

John Wilson: "A Copy of Verses . . ." is from the broadside (1657/8) in the Massachusetts Historical Society, as repr. in facsim. in Samuel

A. Green, *Ten Fac-simile Reproductions*. . . . (Boston, 1902); "Claudius Gilbert" is from the autograph manuscript in Gilbert, *The Libertine School'd* (London, 1657) in the American Antiquarian Society, as repr. in Jantz, *First Century*.

William Bradford: Texts from 3 *Collections of the Massachusetts Historical Society*, VII (1838), 27–28, 59–60.

Samuel Gorton: Text from Gorton's *Simplicities Defence against Seven-Headed Policy* (London, 1647), in the British Museum.

Thomas Tillam: Text from autograph manuscript, Massachusetts Historical Society, Davis Papers, I, 15, as repr. in Jantz, *First Century*.

William Wood: Texts from *New Englands Prospect* (London, 1634) in the British Museum.

John Josselyn: "The Poem" from *New England's Rarities Discovered* (London, 1672); "And the Bitter Storm" and "Description of a New England Spring" from Josselyn's *An Account of Two Voyages*. . . . (London, 1674), in the British Museum.

Thomas Thatcher: Text from autograph manuscript, Bentley papers, American Antiquarian Society.

Benjamin Woodbridge: "Upon the Author . . ." from Anne Bradstreet, *The Tenth Muse* (London, 1650), as repr. in Ellis' edition; "Upon . . . John Cotton" from Nathaniel Morton, *New Englands Memoriall* (Cambridge, 1669) in Evans (E 144).

Jonathan Mitchell: Text from Wigglesworth, *The Day of Doom* (London, 1666) in the British Museum.

Samuel Danforth I: Text for almanac verse from Danforth's *An Almanack for . . . 1647* (Cambridge, 1647) in Evans (E 21); for "Awake ye Westerne Nymphs" from Danforth's *An Almanack for . . . 1649* (Cambridge, 1649) in Evans (E 27).

John Rogers: Text from Anne Bradstreet, *Several Poems* (Boston, 1678), in Evans (E 244) as repr. in Ellis' edition.

Richard Chamberlain: Text prefixed to Chamberlain's *Lithobolia* (London, 1698) in the British Museum.

John James: Text of "Of John Bunyans Life" from autograph manuscript in the Harris Collection of American Poetry and Plays, Brown University Library, as repr. in Jantz, *First Century;* "On . . . John Haynes" from the *Annual Report,* Connecticut Historical Society (1908), pp. 20–21.

Samuel Bradstreet: Text from Bradstreet's *Almanack* for 1657, as repr. in Perry Miller and Thomas H. Johnson, *The Puritans* (New York, 1938), p. 632.

Henricus Selyns: Texts from Henry E. Murphy, *An Anthology of New Netherland* (New York, 1865).

Ichabod Wiswall: Text from Wiswall's *A Judicious Observation of that Dreadful Comet*. . . . (London, 1683) in the British Museum.

George Alsop: Texts from Alsop's *A Character of the Province of Maryland* (London, 1666) in the British Museum.

Benjamin Harris: "God Save the King" from John Partridge, *Monthly Observations* (Boston, 1692) in Evans (E 627); "Of the French King's Nativity" from John Tulley, *Almanack* for 1694 (Boston, 1694) in Evans (E 710); "An Account . . ." from John Tulley, *Almanack* for 1695 (Boston, 1695) in Evans (E 740).

Francis Drake: Text from Nathaniel Morton, *New Englands Memoriall* (Cambridge, 1669) in Evans (E 144).

John Norton II: Text from Anne Bradstreet, *Several Poems* (Boston, 1678) in Evans (E 244).

Nehemiah Walter: Text from broadside, courtesy of the Harvard College Library.

Richard Henchman: "In Consort . . ." and "Vox Oppressi . . ." from autograph manuscripts, Boston Public Library.

Grindall Rawson: "Upon . . . John Saffin Junior" from the manuscript commonplace book of John Saffin, Rhode Island Historical Society, corrected from *John Saffin His Book,* ed. Caroline Hazard (New York, 1928); "To . . . Cotton Mather" from Mather, *Magnalia Christi Americana* (London, 1702) in the Pennsylvania State University Library.

John Williams: Text from Williams' *The Redeemed Captive . . .* (Boston, 1707) in Evans (E 1340).

Sarah Kemble Knight: Texts from *The Private Journal Kept by Madame Knight. . . .* (New York, 1825).

Samuel Danforth II: "Ad Librum" from Danforth's *The New England Almanack for . . . 1686* (Cambridge, 1686) in Evans (E 403); "An Elegy . . ." from broadside, Boston Athenaeum.

Benjamin Lynde: Text from *The Diaries of Benjamin Lynde and Benjamin Lynde, Jr.* (Boston, 1880) in the New York Public Library.

John Cotton of "Queen's Creek": Texts from *Proceedings of the Massachusetts Historical Society 1866–67,* ix (1867), 298–342.

Roger Wolcott: Texts from Wolcott's *Poetical Meditations* (New London, Conn., 1725) in the editor's possession.

Anonymous Verse

"An Old Song" from text reconstruction by Harold S. Jantz, printed here with his permission.

"Thomas Dudley Ah! Old Must Die" from Timothy Alden, Jr., *Collection of American Epitaphs* (New York, 1814), III, 49–50.

"Resplendent Studs of Heaven's Frame" from manuscript, Mellen Chamberlain Collection, Boston Public Library.

"The Whore That Rides in Us" from autograph manuscript in the collection of Harold S. Jantz, Johns Hopkins University, and printed here with his permission.

"Time Tryeth Truth" from John Foster, *Almanack* (Boston, 1681).

"On How the Cobler" from manuscript text in Samuel Willard, *Ne Sutor Ultra Crepidam* (Boston, 1681).

"Almanack Verse . . . 1688" from John Tulley, *An Almanack . . . 1688* (Boston, 1688).

INDEX

Author's names, and names of persons referred to in the poems and notes, are printed in small capitals; titles of poems and books in italics; and first lines of poems in Roman.

526

528

535